SHAKESPEARE
CRITICISM

1935–1960

SHAKESPEARE
CRITICISM

1935-1960

SELECTED
WITH AN INTRODUCTION BY
ANNE RIDLER

OXFORD UNIVERSITY PRESS
LONDON   OXFORD   NEW YORK
1970

Oxford University Press

LONDON OXFORD NEW YORK
GLASGOW TORONTO MELBOURNE WELLINGTON
CAPE TOWN SALISBURY IBADAN NAIROBI DAR ES SALAAM LUSAKA ADDIS ABABA
BOMBAY CALCUTTA MADRAS KARACHI LAHORE DACCA
KUALA LUMPUR SINGAPORE HONG KONG TOKYO

First published in The World's Classics 1963
First issued as an Oxford University Press paperback by
Oxford University Press, London, 1970

PRINTED IN GREAT BRITAIN

SHAKESPEARE
CRITICISM

1935–1960

SELECTED
WITH AN INTRODUCTION BY
ANNE RIDLER

OXFORD UNIVERSITY PRESS
LONDON   OXFORD   NEW YORK
1970

Oxford University Press

LONDON OXFORD NEW YORK

GLASGOW TORONTO MELBOURNE WELLINGTON

CAPE TOWN SALISBURY IBADAN NAIROBI DAR ES SALAAM LUSAKA ADDIS ABABA

BOMBAY CALCUTTA MADRAS KARACHI LAHORE DACCA

KUALA LUMPUR SINGAPORE HONG KONG TOKYO

First published in The World's Classics 1963
First issued as an Oxford University Press paperback by
Oxford University Press, London, 1970

PRINTED IN GREAT BRITAIN

CONTENTS

INTRODUCTION

IN 1935, when an earlier selection of modern Shakespearian criticism[1] was made, it appeared that one of the chief novelties in the contemporary approach was to be found in the treatment of dramatic character. The aesthetic of that great critic A. C. Bradley was discredited, and some writers went to an opposite extreme and denied that Shakespeare made any attempt at psychological consistency. No longer was it permissible to speculate what Macbeth would have done in Hamlet's place, and the majority of critics were less interested in Shakespeare's characters than in his imagery and his theatrical craftsmanship.

Twenty-five years later, critics are still faithful to the ideal of treating the plays as wholes—of seeing the characters only in relation to the context in which Shakespeare placed them—but it has again become respectable to direct attention to the psychological truth of his creations, and indeed the work during this period of J. S. Palmer shows how much profit is still to be derived from a direct study of character. But Mr. J. I. M. Stewart speaks for the majority in saying, in the essay here reprinted: 'When our imagination is kindled we do not think to interpret the characters. We know that the characters are interpreting us.' That is, they make known to us aspects of our own nature of which we might otherwise have been unaware; and one may add that they also interpret the critic to his readers, for he betrays his own preoccupations by his comments on them. But to this I shall return later.

To study Shakespeare in his context, then, is still the critic's aim, but if one tries to follow the special interests of the quarter-century, it seems that the focus has shifted somewhat from Shakespeare the craftsman

[1] *Shakespeare Criticism 1919–1935* (1936)

ERRATA

On page viii, line 1 has been dropped. It should read: (and especially the craftsman of the theatre) to Shake-

On page 131, the footnote should have been deleted.

speare the symbolist. The special study of his imagery had already begun, by 1935, with the work of Caroline Spurgeon here and that of Wolfgang Clemen in Germany, and many studies followed: critics were concerned, not only to trace the use of certain images (or groups of images) from play to play, but to find symbolical meanings in whole plays. The study of imagery helped them to show how much Shakespeare's style differs in different works, giving a distinctive and individual stamp even to plays which are not far separated from each other in time.

Every age thinks itself to be in a particularly favourable position for understanding Shakespeare, and it is easy to see the subjectivity of earlier criticism. Our critics are alive to the dangers: 'Even in the case of a single word, or an isolated image, there is a constant need of discipline if we are not to read our own interests into Shakespeare's. . . .'[1] Yet to judge by results in general, the 'dispassionate attention to verbal quality', which this critic mentions as the ideal, is impossible to attain. Future generations will surely consider some of our symbolical interpretations as far-fetched, and perhaps they will question some of our ingenuities—even that of such a distinguished critic as Professor Tillyard, when he tries to account for the fact that Shakespeare's history plays were composed in the wrong chronological order, by suggesting that there was an earlier series now lost.[2] For why must Shakespeare have known from the beginning what form his work was to take?

The modern 'linguistic' (not textual) criticism is sometimes very claustrophobic in its effect on the reader, so that instead of inhabiting the varied world of the plays, with their multipotent characters and outward-raying life, we seem to be shut in a symmetrical com-

---

[1] D. A. Traversi, *An Approach to Shakespeare* (1938, enlarged 1958).
[2] *Shakespeare's History Plays*, the chapter here reprinted.

partment constructed by a scrupulous moralist—a
moralist of aesthetics if there can be such a man—
whose chief concern is for proportion and consonance,
and who allows his characters licence in one direction
only because he intends to check them by a recoil before
the end of the play: 'setting them on' only to 'take
them off', as the Porter in *Macbeth* might put it. But
the great value of this criticism at its best can easily be
judged from the essays by L. C. Knights and Cleanth
Brooks which are here reprinted.

To return to Mr. Stewart's aphorism about the
characters and their interpretation of ourselves. It is a
commonplace that the character of Hamlet holds up
the mirror to his critics, but the character of Henry V
more often seems to provide an anti-mask or alien self.
None the less, it is generally possible to guess the
decade in which a critic is writing, from his attitude to
Hal as King. As to Hamlet—Professor Peter Alexander,
in his delightfully written study of the play,[1] has
described a character who is as sympathetic to our
time as the Hamlet of Coleridge and of Bradley was to
theirs. This Prince feigns madness because it is the only
chivalrous way of warning the King of his intentions,
and spares Claudius at his prayers because it would be
caddish to stab a defenceless man. The play is said to
dramatize 'the perpetual struggle' of civilization 'to be
humane without loss of toughness', and Professor Alexander reminds us of the problem of the democracies in
fighting totalitarianism, of a generation who, as he says
of Hamlet, 'must still carry the sword' knowing that 'it
may well be a sword that will not save'. When T. S. Eliot,
many years ago, spoke of Hamlet as in the grip of an
emotion to which he cannot assign adequate cause, he
was painting another contemporary portrait which has
since been embodied on the stage—for surely Mr.

[1] *Hamlet, Father and Son* (1953).

Osborne's Jimmy Porter is a character who suffers from the causelessness of his discontent.

Some recent critics have attempted to see this play as a whole, rather than as a psychological study of a single character. Professor C. S. Lewis would read it as a poem; Professor Tillyard sees it as conveying above all 'a rich sense of varied humanity and human activity', and he classes it, not among the tragedies but among the 'problem plays', while Professor Kitto (part of whose essay I print here) sees it as a religious drama rather than a tragedy of character, and rejects the thesis of the 'tragic flaw' just as Professor Alexander does, though for rather different reasons.

This collection makes no claim to be comprehensive—nor, indeed, even if an editor were to be found who had read everything that he ought to have read, could a book of this length be fully representative of its period. For there is now a book or article on Shakespeare published for every day of the year,[1] and the painstaking student, wading through oceans of utterance, sometimes feels inclined to echo the cry of one recent reviewer: 'Shakespeare has condemned the world to the everlasting torment of explaining his masterpieces.' And yet, to read and think about Shakespeare is to draw life from an inexhaustible store, and each man has his report to make on what he has found there. This book is intended as a useful companion to the general reader in his own excursions, and I have kept this test in mind—that each essay chosen should send its reader to the original with his power of understanding strengthened. There has been no attempt to include essays, however brilliant, which are substitutes for reading the plays, or those which require a complex technique of understanding, as does the work of Professor William Empson. Apart from this, I have tried to give some idea of the principal

[1] See M. C. Bradbrook, in *Shakespeare Survey 6*.

trends in Shakespeare criticism, and to include essays both textual and imaginative. I have tried to balance the general essay with the particular, and to give some of the best modern work on the tragedies, on the comedies both early and late, and on the histories, about which so much has been written since 1935. One of the chief difficulties has been to select from American criticism, which really needs a couple of volumes to itself: the choice of the two essays included was governed not only by their excellence but by their relation to the others chosen. Among the English omissions, I regret that of S. L. Bethell's *Shakespeare and the Popular Dramatic Tradition,* a book of fruitful ideas.

Only one author represented in the earlier collection has been included here. Professor Wilson Knight has published such important work since 1935 that it would have been absurd not to include him, but where it seemed to me that an author's thought was still adequately represented by the earlier essay, I have not included work published since. Hence there is nothing from Middleton Murry's *Shakespeare,* published in 1936, though if space had allowed I should have liked to include his fine study of the *Merchant of Venice.* The earlier book contained some of the pioneer work of Caroline Spurgeon in the field of imagery, but as a rule these studies need to be read in their whole context rather than in an anthology extract, and this is certainly true of Mr. E. A. Armstrong's *Shakespeare's Imagination,* which provides interesting evidence about the workings of Shakespeare's unconscious mind. The use which can be made of such studies, for the purpose of more general criticism, is shown in Professor Kenneth Muir's book *Shakespeare as Collaborator,* from which I have taken his chapter on *Pericles.* For those who wish to explore the subject farther, the annual *Shakespeare Survey* for 1952 gives a useful book list.

Much has been said about *Measure for Measure* since R. W. Chambers wrote the essay here included, but as a piece of wise and enlivening appreciation it has a permanent place in English criticism. The definitive study of the play is Miss Mary Lascelles's book, published in 1953.[1]

Critics and readers alike need to bear in mind that poetry is a kind of incantation, which is broken if we consider it in paraphrase or summary. As Professor Kitto has said: 'It remains true that drama, like music, is an art; that its real "meaning" is the total impact which it makes on the senses and the spirit and the mind of the audience; and that when we reduce it to the logical formulae of prose, as the critic must, we are gravely attenuating it, we are making a kind of translation; and translations can be poor ones.' But the 'translations' in this book are not poor ones: so long as the reader is aware of their nature, they can do him nothing but good.

ANNE RIDLER

1963

[1] Athlone Press.

ACKNOWLEDGEMENTS

ACKNOWLEDGEMENTS for permission to include copyright material are due to Messrs. Jonathan Cape and the executors of R. W. Chambers's estate for 'Measure for Measure', from *Man's Unconquerable Mind*; to the Cambridge University Press and the authors for essays from *Shakespeare Survey* ('Motivation in Shakespeare's Choice of Materials' by Hardin Craig; 'Restoring Shakespeare' by Peter Alexander; 'The Unity of *2 Henry IV*' by Clifford Leech); to the estate of the late Professor J. Dover Wilson and the Cambridge University Press for 'Riot and the Prodigal Prince' from *The Fortunes of Falstaff*; to Stephen Tillyard, Messrs. Chatto & Windus, and The Macmillan Company, New York, for 'The First Tetralogy' from *Shakespeare's History Plays* by E. M. W. Tillyard; to the President of the British Academy and the estate of F. P. Wilson for 'Shakespeare and the Diction of Common Life' by F. P. Wilson; to the President of the British Academy and the author for 'The Noble Moor' by Helen Gardner; to Dr. F. R. Leavis and Messrs. Chatto & Windus for 'Shakespeare's Late Plays' from *The Common Pursuit*; to Professor H. D. F. Kitto and Messrs. Methuen for 'Hamlet' from *Form and Meaning in Drama*; to Professor G. Wilson Knight and Messrs. Methuen for part of 'The Shakespearian Integrity' from *The Sovereign Flower*; to Professor Nevill Coghill and Messrs. John Murray for 'The Basis of Shakespearian Comedy', shortened and rewritten from the version which appeared in *Essays and Studies*; to Professor Cleanth Brooks, Messrs. Dennis Dobson, and Harcourt, Brace & World Inc. for 'The Naked Babe and the Cloak of Manliness' from *The Well-Wrought Urn*; to Professor L. C. Knights, Messrs. Chatto & Windus, and Stanford University Press for 'King Lear' from *Some*

Shakespearian Themes; to Mr. J. I. M. Stewart and Messrs. Longmans for 'Shakespeare's Men and their Morals' from *More Talking of Shakespeare*; to Mr. W. H. Auden, Messrs. Faber and Faber, and Random House Inc. for 'Music in Shakespeare' from *The Dyer's Hand and Other Essays*; to Professor Kenneth Muir and Messrs. Methuen for 'Pericles' from *Shakespeare as Collaborator*; to Professor M. C. Bradbrook and Messrs. Chatto & Windus for 'The Fashioning of a Courtier', part of a chapter from *Shakespeare and Elizabethan Poetry*.

R. W. CHAMBERS

(1874–1942)

Measure for Measure[1]

IN *Measure for Measure* Shakespeare took as his source
an old play, *Promos and Cassandra*, written by George
Whetstone a quarter of a century before. Now, just as
certainly as *Hamlet* was a play of revenge, so was *Promos
and Cassandra* a play of forgiveness. In this play Cassandra (like Isabel) pleads for her brother, who (like
Claudio) has been condemned to death for unchastity.
The judge, Promos (like Angelo), will grant pardon
only if Cassandra yield to his passion. Cassandra at last
does so. That is the essential difference between the old
plot, and Shakespeare's play. Nevertheless, Promos
orders Cassandra's brother to be beheaded, and the
head to be presented to her. Cassandra complains to
the King: the King gives judgement that Promos first
marry Cassandra, then lose *his* head. But, this marriage
solemnized, Cassandra, now tied in the greatest bonds
of affection to her husband, suddenly becomes an
earnest suitor for his life. In the end it appears that the
kindly jailer has in fact released the brother, and presented Cassandra with a felon's head instead. So, to
renown the virtues of Cassandra, the King pardons
both brother and judge, and all ends well.[2]

The story shows the violence of much Elizabethan
drama. John Addington Symonds says, in *Shakespeare's*

[1] *The Jacobean Shakespeare and Measure for Measure*, British Academy
Shakespeare Lecture, 1937, 2nd part, omitting the final paragraphs. Reprinted in *Man's Unconquerable Mind*, 1939.

[2] Whetstone retold the tale in prose (*Heptameron of Civill Discourses*,
1582). It is derived from the *Hecatommithi* of Cinthio (1565), who also wrote
a play on the subject (*Epitia*). Shakespeare knew some of these, possibly all.

Predecessors, that the sympathies of a London audience were like 'the chords of a warrior's harp, strung with twisted iron and bull's sinews, vibrating mightily, but needing a stout stroke to make them thrill'. The playwrights 'glutted their audience with horrors, cudgelled their horny fibres into sensitiveness'.

Now mark how Shakespeare treats this barbarous story. According to Professor Dover Wilson, at the time when he wrote *Measure for Measure*, Shakespeare 'quite obviously believed in nothing; he was as cynical as Iago, as disillusioned as Macbeth, though he still retained, unlike the first, his sensitiveness, and, unlike the second, his hatred of cruelty, hypocrisy, and ingratitude'. According to Sir Edmund Chambers, in *Measure for Measure* his 'remorseless analysis' 'probes the inmost being of man, and strips him naked'. 'It is the temper of the inquisitor': 'you can but shudder.'

Prepare then to shudder, as you observe William Iago Torquemada Shakespeare at work. Shakespeare, for all the 'self-laceration', 'disgust', and 'general morbidity'[1] which is supposed to have obsessed him and his Jacobean contemporaries, removes from the play the really morbid scene of the heroine kissing the severed head of her supposed brother. Then, he divides the sorrows of the heroine between two characters, Isabel and Mariana. And the object of this duplication is, that, whatever their spiritual anguish, neither of them shall be placed in the 'really intolerable situation'[2] of poor Cassandra. Mariana has been contracted to Angelo formally by oath. It is vital to remember that, according to Elizabethan ideas, Angelo and Mariana are therefore man and wife. But Angelo has deserted Mariana. Now I grant that, according to our modern ideas, it is undignified for the deserted Mariana still to desire union

[1] J. Dover Wilson, *The Essential Shakespeare*, pp. 117, 118.
[2] *Works of Shakespeare*, ed. G. L. Kittredge, p. 97.

with the husband who has scorned her. *We* may resent the elegiac and spaniel-like fidelity of Mariana of the Moated Grange. *But is that the sixteenth-century attitude?* The tale of the deserted bride seeking her husband in disguise is old, approved, beloved. It is a mere anachronism to assume that Shakespeare, a practical dramatist, told this tale with some deep cynical and self-lacerating intention unintelligible to his audience, but now at last revealed to modern criticism. Shakespeare made Mariana gentle and dignified. She, in all shadow and silence, visits her husband in place of Isabel, to save Claudio's life.

And our twentieth-century critics are scandalized over the tale. This surprises me, a Late Victorian, brought up on the Bible and Arthurian story. I did not know that our modern age was so proper. A Professor today cannot deliver a series of lectures on 'The Application of Thought to Textual Criticism' without its being reported as 'The Application of Thought to Sexual Criticism'. Yet this sex-obsessed age of ours is too modest to endure the old story of the substituted bride. I learnt at my Early Victorian mother's knee, how Jacob served seven years for Rachel: 'And it came to pass, that in the morning, behold, it was Leah',[1] and Jacob had to serve another seven years for his beloved. I did not exclaim: 'Oh my mother, you are lacerating my feelings with this remorseless revelation of patriarchal polygamy.' A child could grasp the story of Jacob's service for Rachel, which 'seemed unto him but a few days, for the love he had to her'.

Sir Edmund Chambers is entitled to say that the story of the substituted bride 'does not commend itself to the modern conscience'. Jaques was entitled to say that he did not like the name of Rosalind. And Orlando was entitled to say, 'There was no thought of pleasing

[1] Gen. xxix. 25.

you when she was christened'. In the sixteenth century the story was a commonplace of romance, and Shakespeare used it in order to make more gentle one of the quite horrible situations of the pre-Shakespearian drama. There was a time when Shakespeare had not shrunk from staging the grossest horrors. It is to avoid them, that he now brings in the substitution which offends 'the modern conscience'.

It may be objected that Shakespeare is 'not for an age, but for all time', and that therefore he ought not to have condescended to use stories which, although current in his day, and although he made them less horrible, nevertheless would not appeal to future ages. But the great poets, Homer, Aeschylus, Sophocles, Dante, Shakespeare, speak to all time only through the language, conventions, and beliefs of their own age. How else?

A second fault of the old play is the crudity of the change from Cassandra's thirst for vengeance to her prayer for forgiveness. Shakespeare had permitted himself similar crudities in the past. Now he sets to work to make the plot consistent: he does this by making it turn, from first to last, on the problem of punishment and forgiveness. It is Shakespeare's addition to the story that the Duke is distressed by this problem. Fearing lest his rule has been too lax, he deputes his office to Angelo, whilst remaining, disguised as a friar, to 'visit both prince and people'. And here many critics, among them Sir Walter Raleigh[1] and Sir Arthur Quiller-Couch,[2] object. It is not seemly for a Duke to 'shirk his proper responsibility, and steal back incognito to play busybody and spy on his deputy'.

I am reminded of one of the first essays ever shown up to me, by a Japanese student, some thirty-five years

---

[1] *Shakespeare*, p. 167.
[2] New Cambridge Shakespeare, *Measure for Measure*, p. xxxiv.

ago. He objected to *The Merchant of Venice*. 'Bassanio', he said, 'did not bring honourable surgeon, to bind up wounds of honourable friend. He did not recognize honourable wife, when disguised as a man.'

Why do critics today bring against *Measure for Measure* this kind of objection, which they would be ashamed to bring against Shakespeare's earlier comedies, or later romances?

Disguise and impersonation and misunderstanding are the very life of romantic comedy. The disguised monarch, who can learn the private affairs of his humblest subject, becomes a sort of earthly Providence, combining omniscience and omnipotence. That story has always had its appeal. 'Thus hath the wise magistrate done in all ages';[1] although obviously to introduce into our daily life this ancient habit of the benevolent monarch would be to incur deserved satire. There is no doubt how Shakespeare meant us to regard the Duke. 'One that, above all other strifes, contended especially to know himself: a gentleman of all temperance', says Escalus. Isabel, in her moment of dire distress, remembers him as 'the good Duke'. Angelo, in his moment of deepest humiliation, addresses him with profound reverence and awe. Lucio (like our moderns) regards the Duke cynically; but he ends by admitting that he deserves a whipping for so doing.

The deputy, Angelo, is not so called for nothing. He *is* 'angel on the outward side'—an ascetic saint in the judgement of his fellow citizens, and despite the meanness of his spirit, nay, because of it, a saint in his own esteem. His soliloquies prove this, and Isabel at the end gives him some credit for sincerity.

Now Claudio and Juliet have lived together as man and wife, although their contract has been secret: it has 'lacked the denunciation of outward order'. (The con-

[1] Jonson, *Bartholomew Fair*, II. i.

tract between Angelo and Mariana, on the other hand, had been public, and so had undoubtedly given them the rights of man and wife.) Angelo's puritanical revival of an ancient law, fourteen years out of date, renders Claudio's life forfeit. This Viennese law seems strange, but the Duke says the law is such. If we allow Portia to expound the even stranger law of Venice to the Duke and Magnificoes, we may surely allow the Duke of Vienna to understand the law of his own state. It is a postulate of the story.

Critics speak as if Shakespeare had imagined Claudio a self-indulgent boy, a 'poor weak soul'.[1] Yet it is only Angelo's retrospective revival which makes Claudio's offence capital. 'He hath but as offended in a dream', says the kindly Provost. He 'was worth five thousand of you all', says Mistress Overdone to Lucio and his friends. Claudio is first introduced, bearing himself with great dignity and right feeling, under his sudden arrest. He sends his friend Lucio to his sister in her cloister, to beg her to intercede for him, because, he says,

> in her youth
> There is a prone and speechless dialect,
> Such as move men; beside, she hath prosperous art
> When she will play with reason and discourse,
> And well she can persuade.

Such descriptions of characters before they appear— perhaps before Shakespeare had written a word for them to speak—have surely a great weight. They show how Shakespeare wished the audience to see them. Isabel's characteristic when she does appear is exactly this mixture of winning silence with persuasive speech.

But before she can reach Angelo, his colleague Escalus has already interceded for Claudio, urging that, had

---

[1] E. K. Chambers, *Shakespeare: A Survey*, p. 209.

time cohered with place, and place with wishing, Angelo
might himself have fallen. Angelo replies:

> When I, that censure him, do so offend,
> Let mine own judgement pattern out my death,
> And nothing come in partial. Sir, he must die.

Isabel begins her pleading slowly and with characteristic silences: then she grows eloquent, and to Angelo's
stern refusal she at last replies:

> I would to Heaven I had your potency,
> And you were Isabel! Should it then be thus?
> No; I would tell what 'twere to be a judge.
> And what a prisoner.

Isabel has no notion as yet of the depth of sin which may
have to be pardoned in Angelo. But there is 'irony'
behind these two speeches, and we can forecast that
in the end the places will be reversed: the fate of the
convicted Angelo depending upon Isabel.[1]

Will she then be true to the pleas which she now
pours forth? 'Well she can persuade.' Her marvellous
and impassioned pleadings, unsurpassed anywhere in
Shakespeare, are based on her Christian faith, and upon
the Sermon on the Mount: all men are pardoned sinners, and *must* forgive:

> Why, all the souls that were, were forfeit once;
> And he that might the vantage best have took
> Found out the remedy.

'Judge not, that ye be not judged. For, with what
measure ye mete, it shall be measured to you again.'

---

[1] The phrase 'dramatic irony' may be misunderstood. Shakespeare, like
Sophocles, puts into the mouths of his characters words which they speak
in all sincerity, but which, as the play proceeds, will be found to have a
deeper meaning than the speaker knew. Dramatic irony does *not* mean that,
at every turn, we are justified in suspecting that Shakespeare may have
meant the reverse of what he makes his characters say. When he does that
('honest Iago') he leaves us in no doubt. As a great American critic has put
it: 'However much the *dramatis personae* mystify each other, the audience
is never to be perplexed.' (G. I. Kittredge, *Shakespeare*, 1916, p. 20.)

Measure for Measure. But how is the Sermon on the
Mount to be reconciled with the practical necessities
of government? That is the problem which puzzles
people—and particularly perhaps young people—so
much today. In the Tudor Age men met it by exalting
Government. The King is 'the image of God's majesty':
to him, and to his Government, the divine office of
rule and punishment is committed. The private man
must submit and forgive. Accordingly, Angelo appeals
to his 'function': and there is real force in his answers
to Isabel—remembering, as we always must, that, for
the purposes of the play, Claudio is supposed guilty of
a capital offence.

Never does Shakespeare seem more passionately to
identify himself with any of his characters than he does
with Isabel, as she pleads for mercy against strict
justice:

> O, it is excellent
> To have a giant's strength; but it is tyrannous
> To use it like a giant. . . .
> man, proud man,
> Drest in a little brief authority . . .
> Plays such fantastic tricks before high heaven
> As make the angels weep . . .

Angelo does not fall without a sincere struggle. But
more than one of Isabel's pleadings find a mark which
she never meant:

> Go to your bosom;
> Knock there, and ask your heart what it doth know
> That's like my brother's fault . . .
> Hark how I'll bribe you . . .

Angelo has thought himself superior to human weakness, because he is free from the vulgar vices of a Lucio.
And the 'beauty of mind' of a distressed, noble woman
throws him off his balance.[1] If we fail to see the nobility

[1] Cf. Masefield, *William Shakespeare*, p. 179.

of Isabel, we cannot see the story as we should. The plot is rather like that of Calderon's *Magician*, where the scholarly, austere Cipriano is overthrown by speaking with the saintly Justina. Cipriano sells himself literally to the Devil to gain his end by magic. Angelo tempts Isabel in a second dialogue, as wonderful as the first. In her innocence Isabel is slow to see Angelo's drift, and it is only her confession of her own frailty that gives him a chance of making himself clear. 'Nay,' Isabel says,

> call us ten times frail;
> For we are soft as our complexions are,
> And credulous to false prints.

If Shakespeare is depicting in Isabel the self-righteous prude which some critics would make of her, he goes strangely to work.

But when she perceives Angelo's drift, Isabel decides without hesitation. Now whatever we think of that instant decision, it is certainly not un-Christian. Christianity could never have lived through its first three hundred years of persecution, if its ranks had not been stiffened by men and women who never hesitated in the choice between righteousness and the ties to their kinsfolk. We may call this fanaticism: but it was well understood in Shakespeare's day. Foxe's *Martyrs* was read by all; old people could still remember seeing the Smithfield fires; year after year saw the martyrdoms of Catholic men (and sometimes of Catholic women like the Ven. Margaret Clitherow). It was a stern age—an age such as the founder of Christianity had foreseen when he uttered his stern warnings. 'He that loveth father or mother more than me . . .' 'If any man come to me, and hate not his father, and mother, and brethren and sisters, he cannot be my disciple.'[1]

[1] Matt. x. 37; Luke xiv. 26.

It is recorded of Linacre, the father of English medicine, that, albeit a priest, he opened his Greek New Testament for the first time late in life, and came on some of these hard sayings. 'Either this is not the Gospel', he said, 'or we are not Christians', and refusing to contemplate the second alternative, he flung the Book from him and returned to the study of medicine. Now it is open to us to say that we are not Christians: it is not open to us to say that Isabel's instant decision is un-Christian. So she goes to her brother, not because she hesitates, but that he may share with her the burden of her irrevocable decision. Claudio's first reply is, 'O heavens! it cannot be'; 'Thou shalt not do't.' But the very bravest of men have quailed, within the four walls of a prison cell, waiting for the axe next day. I am amazed at the way critics condemn Claudio, when he breaks down, and utters his second thoughts, 'Sweet sister, let me live'. Isabel overwhelms him in the furious speech which we all know. And I am even more amazed at the dislike which the critics feel for the tortured Isabel. But when they assure us that their feeling towards both his creatures was shared by the gentle Shakespeare, I am then most amazed of all.

It is admitted that no greater or more moving scenes had appeared on any stage, since the masterpieces of Attic drama ceased to be acted. Yet our critics tell us that Shakespeare wrote them in a mood of 'disillusionment and cynicism', 'self-laceration' and, strangest of all, 'weariness'.[1] 'A corroding atmosphere of moral suspicion'[2] hangs about this debate between 'the sainted Isabella, wrapt in her selfish chastity', and 'the wretched boy who in terror of death is ready to sacrifice his sister's honour'.[3] Isabel's chastity, they say, is 'rancid', and

---

[1] J. Dover Wilson, op. cit., pp. 116, 117.
[2] E. K. Chambers, op. cit., p. 214.
[3] J. Dover Wilson, op. cit., p. 116.

she is 'not by any means such a saint as she looks';[1]
her inhumanity is pitiless, her virtue is self-indulgent,
unimaginative, and self-absorbed.[2]

And yet, think of Rose Macaulay's war-poem, 'Many
sisters to many brothers', and let us believe that a sister
may suffer more in agony of mind than the brother can
suffer in physical wounds or death. Shakespeare has
made Isabel say to Claudio

> O, were it but my life,
> I'ld throw it down for your deliverance
> As frankly as a pin.

It is standing the play on its head,[3] to say that Shakespeare wrote those words in irony and cynicism. How
did he convey that to his audience? If such assumptions
are allowed, we can prove anything we like, 'eight years
together, dinners and suppers and sleeping-hours excepted'.

Isabel then, as Shakespeare sees her and asks us to
see her, would frankly, joyously, give her life to save
Claudio: and, let there be no mistake about it, *'greater
love hath no man than this'*. And now Claudio is asking
for what she cannot give, and she bursts out in agony.
Have the critics never seen a human soul or a human
body in the extremity of torment? Physical torture
Isabel thinks she could have stood without flinching.
She has said so to Angelo:

> The impression of keen whips I'ld wear as rubies,
> And strip myself to death, as to a bed
> That longing have been sick for, ere I'ld yield
> My body up to shame.

[1] New Cambridge Shakespeare, *Measure for Measure*, p. xxx.

[2] U. M. Ellis-Fermor, *The Jacobean Drama*, pp. 261, 262.

[3] I borrow this very excellent phrase from W. W. Lawrence (p. 70).
The brevity of a lecture compels me to pass over many points that a critic
may think should have been more fully argued, but I do this the more cheerfully, because they have been already so fully discussed by Lawrence in his
Shakespeare's Problem Comedies, 1931, and their moral emphasized in an
excellent leading article in *The Times Literary Supplement* of 16 July 1931.

To suppose that Shakespeare gave these burning words to Isabel so that we should perceive her to be selfish and cold, is to suppose that he did not know his job. The honour of her family and her religion are more to her than mere life, her own or Claudio's.

Sir George Greenwood prefers Cassandra's character. The New Cambridge Shakespeare quotes this dictum of Sir George with more approval than it would give to his other dicta.[1] Still, though Cassandra may yield, Isabel can't. And most of those who have criticized her, from Hazlitt downwards, agree that she can't. And she has got to make that clear to Claudio. It is just here that her critics quarrel with her. Sir Arthur Quiller-Couch digs out Mrs. Charlotte Lennox from the obscurity of the mid-eighteenth century to tell us how the scene should have been written. Isabel, Charlotte says,

should have made use of her superior understanding to reason down Claudio's fears, recall nobler ideas to his mind, teach him what was due to her honour and his own, and reconcile him to his approaching death by arguments drawn from that religion and virtue of which she made so high a profession.

'To reason down Claudio's fears!' 'By arguments drawn from religion and virtue!' Why, the Duke had just preached to Claudio the most eloquent Sermon Against the Fear of Death that has ever been written since Lucretius completed his Third Book. Claudio had expressed himself convinced; and then the Duke's discourse had shrivelled like a thread in the flame of Claudio's longing for life.

How will pi-jaw help Claudio? Shakespeare imagined Claudio as a good lad, but not, like his sister, devout; he doesn't keep devout company, exactly. Isabel 'well can persuade'. She is one of a few women in Shakespeare who can persuade. (Not Portia: 'The quality of

[1] p. xxxi.

mercy is not strain'd' produces no persuasion in the
soul of Shylock.) Volumnia is a special case. The other
great persuaders are: Isabel, Beatrice, and Lady Macbeth. And they all use the same arguments—the arguments which, I expect, the first Cave-woman, when in
dire straits, used to her Cave-man: You are a coward;
You have no love or respect for me; I have no longer
any love for you.

Isabel is the most vehement of the three. Sisterly
technique has its own rules; there is a peculiar freedom
about the talk of those who have known each other from
babyhood. And Isabel can use arguments outside the
range of Beatrice or Lady Macbeth. Don't forget that
Escalus, when he first pleaded for Claudio, remembered
his 'most noble father'. Isabel had exclaimed, when she
first found Claudio firm,

> there my father's grave
> Did utter forth a voice.

And now she cries,

> Heaven shield my mother play'd my father fair.

Isabel appeals to the passion which, in an Elizabethan
gentleman, may be presumed to be stronger than the
fear of death—pride in his gentle birth and in the
courage which should mark it. Don't people see that
there are things about which we cannot argue calmly?
The fierceness of Isabel's words is the measure of the
agony of her soul. 'The fortress which parleys, the
woman who parleys, is lost.' I grant that, at the end of a
lifetime's training, a saint like Thomas More could
smile on his daughter when she tempted him, 'What,
Mistress Eve?' But the young martyrs are apt to be
more stern, whether it be Cordelia or Antigone, the
spitfire St. Eulalia, or St. Juliana putting the fear of
death upon the Devil. And it is our fault if we don't see

that Isabel is suffering martyrdom none the less because her torment is mental, not physical.

One of the most significant of Shakespeare's alterations of his original is to make the heroine a 'votarist of St. Clare'. At the root of the movement of St. Francis and St. Clare was the intense remembrance of the sufferings of Christ, in atonement for the sins of the whole world—the 'remedy' of which Isabel in vain reminds Angelo. Isabel, as a novice, is testing herself to see whether she is called to that utter renunciation which is the life of the 'poor Clare'. Whether she remains in the Convent or no, one who is contemplating such a life can no more be expected to sell herself into mortal sin, than a good soldier can be expected to sell a stronghold entrusted to him.

Imagine an officer and his subaltern commanded to hold to the uttermost a fortified post against rebels. In a sortie the rebels capture the subaltern, and threaten to shoot him unless the fort surrenders. The subaltern breaks down, and implores his commandant to save his life. I can imagine that the commandant would reply, firmly but gently, that surrender is impossible. But suppose the subaltern were his beloved younger brother, or his only son. I can imagine that then the commandant would reply to his son's appeal by passionate denunciation, telling him that he is a disgrace to his family. To discuss the matter calmly would lead to the surrender which he knows he must not make: his instinct would tell him that. So, at least, it seems to me in my ignorance. And when I find Shakespeare in his wisdom depicting the matter so, I don't see anything cynical about it.

Those who dislike the vehemence of Isabel would do well, in Ben Jonson's phrase, to 'call forth Sophocles to us', and to ponder on the *Philoctetes*. In that play Neoptolemus is asked to sell his honour and betray his father's friend by a base lie, for the good of his country, and for the ultimate good of the friend who is to be deceived. Neoptolemus refuses indignantly, but he lets himself be drawn into discussion, and so sells his honour and his friend. But the anticipated good does not follow, and Neoptolemus has to make amends to his friend, though this means treason to the Greek army. The play is ending, with Neoptolemus deserting the army, and even contemplating war with his own countrymen, when the god appears from the machine to solve the knot. All this follows because Neoptolemus listens and debates when he hears the voice of the tempter: 'Now give thyself to me for one short, shameless day, and then, for the rest of thy time, be called of all mortals the most righteous.' We cannot argue with the tempter, when our own desires are already so much enlisted on his side. We can only refuse, instinctively, vehemently.

It is precisely the alternation of vehemence with silence which gives Isabel her individuality. Remember that when she first understands the real drift of Angelo's temptation, the poor child flies at him with a pathetic attempt at blackmail: 'Sign me a present pardon for my brother, or . . . I'll tell the world . . .' Remember also that when she is told that Angelo has slain Claudio, she exclaims:

O, I will to him and pluck out his eyes!

Shakespeare sometimes puts his heroines in pairs, coupling the fierce, vehement girl, with the gentle, swooning girl: Hermia with Helena, Beatrice with Hero, Isabel with Mariana. For all her silence and modesty, Isabel has the ferocity of the martyr. Yet I don't think Shakespeare disliked his vixens. Hermia has nails which can reach her enemy's eyes. Benedick foresaw a predestinate scratched face for the husband of Beatrice. Yet would you, Mr. Chairman, take Hero in to dinner, if you could get Beatrice? Would you, Mr.

Secretary, go hiking through the Athenian forest with Helena, if you could get Hermia?

Critics ask, as does Sir Edmund Chambers, whether Isabel too 'has not had her ordeal, and in her turn failed', whether she was 'wholly justified in the eyes of her creator'. They are entitled to ask the question. But they ought to wait for the answer. The Duke enters, takes Claudio aside, and tells him there is no hope for him. And we find that Claudio, who before Isabel's outburst had been gripped by the mortal fear of death, is now again master of his soul:

> Let me ask my sister pardon. I am so out of love with life, that I will sue to be rid of it.

'Hold you there', says the Duke. Claudio does. Later, we see him quiet and self-possessed when the Provost shows him his death-warrant. To the Provost he is 'the most gentle Claudio': and to Shakespeare, the word 'gentle' is a word of very high praise, not consistent with any want of spirit.[1] 'Gentle' and 'most gentle' is how his worthy friends and fellows—Ben Jonson, Heminge, Condell—described Shakespeare. Claudio, 'most gentle' in his cell, has passed his ordeal well, showing quiet courage equally removed from the hilarity of a Posthumus and the insensibility of a Barnardine.

Mrs. Lennox says that Isabel ought to have taught Claudio what is due to her honour and his own. She has.

Now, if Isabel's speech had been intended to depict a 'cold' and 'remorseless' woman, 'all for saving her own soul', acting cruelly to her brother in the 'fiery ordeal' which (we are told) 'his frail soul proves ill-fitted to endure', why does Shakespeare show Claudio, far from resenting his sister's reproaches, only wishing to ask her pardon, and henceforth courageous and resolute?

---

[1] 'He's gentle, and not fearful,' says Miranda to Prospero, warning him not to presume too much on Ferdinand's patience.

Why, above all, does Shakespeare make the Duke, when he overhears Isabel's whole speech, comment on the beauty of her goodness? This is intelligible only if Shakespeare means Isabel's speech as an agonized outcry, working on her brother as no calm reasoning could have done. If Shakespeare's critics think they could have written the scene better, they are welcome to try; but it does not follow that Shakespeare was a disillusioned cynic because he did not write Isabel's speech as Charlotte Lennox would have done.

When the Duke suggests that Isabel may yet be able to save her brother, she replies, 'I have spirit to do any thing that appears not foul in the truth of my spirit'. And now Isabel's critics disapprove of her because of the 'business-like' way in which she sets about saving her brother and assisting the Duke's plot. If Shakespeare's Jacobean audiences were as perverse as his modern critics, I can well understand how 'gloom and dejection' may have driven the poor man 'to the verge of madness', as critics assert that it did. That Shakespeare imagined Isabel as business-like, should be clear to any one who studies with care her words in the earlier scenes. She is a sensible Elizabethan girl, with no nonsense about her, and she knows that it is no sin to bring husband and wife together.

So Mariana takes Isabel's place, to save Claudio's life.

Again, if Shakespeare meant us to regard Isabel cynically, why did he picture her not only as touching by her goodness both Angelo and the Duke, though to different issues, but even as aweing the frivolous Lucio into sobriety and sympathy? To Lucio she is 'a thing ensky'd and sainted',

> an immortal spirit;
> And to be talk'd with in sincerity,
> As with a saint.

Sir Arthur disqualifies Lucio's evidence because Lucio is a sensualist, and sensualists, he says, habitually divide women into angels and those who are 'their animal prey'.[1] Even if that be true, could Shakespeare seriously expect his audience to grasp such a subtlety? Critics see Isabel 'hard as an icicle'.[2] If Shakespeare meant that, why did he make Lucio see her differently: 'O pretty Isabella, I am pale at mine heart to see thine eyes so red.'[3] Even a sensualist can tell when people's eyes are red.

Angelo's own words make it clear that it is his conviction of the innocence and goodness of Isabel which overthrows him.

As for Claudio—the critics may despise him, but Angelo knows better. He knows that Claudio is a plucky lad who, 'receiving a dishonour'd life with ransom of such shame', might take his revenge in time to come. So he commands Claudio's execution. The Duke, of course, prevents it, and continues to weave his toils round Angelo, till the moment when he will fall on him, and grind him to powder.

And, immediately, Angelo's remorse begins. He realizes what he really is: 'This deed unshapes me quite.' Yet his state is more gracious now, when he believes himself to be a perjured adulterer, than it was a few days before, when he believed himself to be a saint.

I pass over the agonies of Angelo's repentance. 'Dull to all proceedings', he fights to maintain all that is left him, the 'credent bulk' of a public esteem which has become a mockery to him. When Lucio brings the struggle to an end, by tearing the Friar's hood off the Duke, Angelo realizes that his master is one from whom no secrets are hid:

---

[1] New Cambridge Shakespeare, p. xxvii.
[2] U. M. Ellis-Fermor, op. cit., p. 262.   [3] IV. iii. 158.

Duke. Hast thou or word, or wit, or impudence,
   That yet can do thee office? . . .
Angelo.   O my dread lord,
   I should be guiltier than my guiltiness,
   To think I can be undiscernible,
   When I perceive your Grace, like power divine,
   Hath looked upon my passes.

A cold-hearted, self-righteous prig is brought to a sense of what he is, in the sight of his Master. A few hours before, Angelo had turned a deaf ear to the plea 'Why, all the souls that were, were forfeit once'. But now he can conceive no depth of guilt so deep as his own. 'Guiltier than my guiltiness.' It is like the repentance of Enobarbus, 'I am alone the villain of the earth', or of Posthumus,

               it is I
  That all the abhorred things o' the earth amend
  By being worse than they.

For Angelo, as for Enobarbus and for Posthumus, nothing remains save a passionate prayer to be put out of his misery:

             Then, good prince,
  No longer session hold upon my shame,
  But let my trial be mine own confession:
  Immediate sentence then, and sequent death,
  Is all the grace I beg.

Surely it is concerning repentance like this that it is written, 'There is joy in the presence of the angels of God'.

The ninety and nine just persons which need no repentance naturally think otherwise. Coleridge began the outcry against *Measure for Measure*, which he found most painful because, he said, cruelty, lust, and damnable baseness cannot be conceived as repented of or forgiven.[1] Swinburne endorsed this judgement at great

---

[1] *Notes on Shakespeare.*

length. Justice, he said, 'is buffeted, outraged, insulted, struck in the face'. 'We are tricked out of our dole, defeated of our due, lured and led on to look for some equitable and satisfying upshot, defrauded and derided and sent empty away.'[1] Hazlitt could not allow Mariana to love Angelo 'whom we hate'.[2] To enumerate the ninety-six other just persons would be to write a bibliography of *Measure for Measure*, which is no part of my intention. Rather I turn to Mariana as she implores pardon for her husband—a scene which Coleridge thought degrading to the character of woman. Yet repentance, intercession, and forgiveness are the stuff of Christianity and of the old stories of Christendom. In the story which Calderon used, Cipriano, after selling himself to the Devil in order to win Justina to his will, repents and dies a martyr at her side, comforted by her words: 'So many stars has not the Heaven, so many grains of sand the sea, not so many sparks the fire, not so many motes the sunlight, as the sins which He forgives.'

But the Duke again and again rejects Mariana's plea for mercy. She turns at last to Isabel:

> Sweet Isabel, take my part;
> Lend me your knees and all my life to come
> I'll lend you all my life to do you service.

Isabel stands silent.

It is many years ago that I saw acted, within this building where we are now met, Calderon's *Life is a Dream*, in the version of Edward Fitzgerald. In that play Basilio, King of Poland, has learnt from his study of the stars that his new-born son will end by trampling on his father's head. So Prince Segismund is kept, from his birth, in a cruel prison, not knowing who he is. But

---

[1] *Study of Shakespeare.*   [2] *Characters of Shakespeare's Plays.*

his father, relenting, determines to test whether he has read the stars aright: so he brings Segismund drugged to the palace. There Segismund awakes to find himself heir to the throne of Poland; but he abuses his one day of power, and is carried back in sleep again to his prison, to be told that all that he has seen and done that day has been a dream. Yet later the mutinous army releases him. Segismund marches at the head of the army, not knowing whether he dreams or no, and his victories end with the King Basilio kneeling humbled at the feet of his wronged son.

What will Segismund now do? Has he learnt the lesson of forgiveness, the greatest lesson that can be learnt from the Dream which is called Life?

It is not often that one can see a classical masterpiece acted without knowing how it will end. Whether it was the acting of Miss Margaret Halston, who took the part of the boy-prince, or the stage production of Mr. Poel, I have never since felt the suspense of a great scene as I felt that. I like to think that those who first saw Shakespeare's play acted at the Christmas revels of 1604 may perhaps have felt such a suspense. The title, *Measure for Measure*, gave them no clue as to the ending.

A second time Mariana appeals:

> Isabel,
> Sweet Isabel, do yet but kneel by me;
> Hold up your hands, say nothing, I'll speak all.

Still Isabel stands silent, whilst Mariana pleads on pitifully:

> They say, best men are moulded out of faults;
> And, for the most, become much more the better
> For being a little bad: so may my husband.

At her third appeal,

> O Isabel, will you not lend a knee?

Isabel kneels at the feet of the Duke.

While Isabel is pleading for his life, Angelo is longing for death. Escalus turns to him, regretting his fall. Angelo only says:

> I am sorry that such sorrow I procure:
> And so deep sticks it in my penitent heart,
> That I crave death more willingly than mercy;
> 'Tis my deserving, and I do entreat it.

The wheel is come full circle.

Only two days before, Angelo had rejected the plea of mercy for Claudio with the words

> When I, that censure him, do so offend,
> Let mine own judgement pattern out my death.

And Isabel had longed for the potency of Angelo that she might 'tell what 'twere to be a judge, and what a prisoner'. Later we have seen Angelo 'unshaped' by his remorse, though still confident that he will escape undetected, whilst Isabel longs to 'pluck out his eyes', and is promised revenges to her heart on 'this wretch' who has murdered her brother. And now Angelo, publicly shamed, longing for death, faces an Isabel who can bring herself to say, after an agony of silent struggle, 'let him not die'. It was not in a spirit of 'weariness, cynicism, and disgust' that the Master Craftsman made the whirligig of time bring in revenges like these.

Isabel's sufferings are over. The muffled Claudio is brought in. Sister meets brother with that 'prone and speechless dialect' which moves, or should move, men.

Sir Edmund Chambers asks, Why does the Duke conceal from Isabel in her grief the knowledge that her brother yet lives? Sir Walter Raleigh asked the same question thirty years ago. His answer was that the reason is dramatic; the crisis must be kept for the end. And, as a piece of stage-craft, the ending justifies itself; it is magnificent. But Sir Edmund Chambers is surely right when he says that a play dealing seriously with the problems of life must be taken seriously; the Duke, he thinks, symbolizes the workings of Providence. Is not such treatment of Providence, then, he asks, ironical?

The Duke certainly reminds us of the ways of Providence. And we feel so in the great final scene, where Mariana is imploring the silent Isabel to intercede for Angelo. Why, then, does the Duke gather up all his authority, as former Friar and present Monarch, and crash it, with a lie, in the path Isabel must tread?

> Should she kneel down in mercy of this fact,
> Her brother's ghost his paved bed would break,
> And take her hence in horror.

Yet all this time the Duke is keeping her brother in reserve, to produce him when Isabel shall have fulfilled her destiny, by making intercession for the man she most hates.

I can only reply that life undoubtedly *is* sometimes like that. There are some souls (Isabel is one) for whom it is decreed that no trial, however agonizing, no pain, however atrocious, is to be spared them. Nevertheless, it is also true that there is no trial so agonizing, no pain so atrocious, but that some souls can rise above it, as Isabel does when, despite the Duke's stern warning, she kneels at his feet to intercede for Angelo.

Is it then true, as Sir Arthur Quiller-Couch says, that Isabel writes no lesson on the dark walls, and that they teach none to her soul? Or is it true when Sir Edmund Chambers echoes the complaint of Coleridge, and says that *Measure for Measure* 'just perplexes and offends', because there is no poetic justice? Is it true that 'to no profit of righteousness has Isabella's white soul been dragged through the mire'?

I know that many readers find a stumbling-block in this culminating scene, in Isabel's pleading for Angelo. Why should she plead, they ask, for her brother's murderer?

We must be prepared to accept the postulates of Shakespeare's plays, as we do, for example, of Sophocles' *Oedipus Tyrannus*. And, generally, we are so prepared: we accept the caskets and the pound of flesh, King Lear's love-test and Prospero's art. It is a postulate of our story that Claudio has committed a capital offence. Angelo has not committed a crime in letting the law take its course upon Claudio; he has not committed a crime in his union with Mariana, to whom he has been publicly betrothed; those are assumptions on which the play is based. Angelo would be despicable if he put forward any such plea for himself, and he does not. But the fact remains that Angelo's sin has been, not in act, but in thought, and human law cannot take cognizance of thought: 'thoughts are no subjects.' Besides, Isabel is conscious that, however innocently, she herself has been the cause of Angelo's fall:

> I partly think
> A due sincerity govern'd his deeds,
> Till he did look on me; since it is so,
> Let him not die.

And Angelo is penitent. There can be no doubt what the words of the Sermon on the Mount demand: 'Judge not, and ye shall not be judged.' That had been Isabel's plea for Claudio. It is a test of her sincerity, if she can put forward a plea for mercy for her dearest foe, as well as for him whom she dearly loves.

Criticism of *Measure for Measure*, from Coleridge downwards, has amounted to this: 'There is a limit to human charity.' 'There is,' says Chesterton's Father Brown, 'and that is the real difference between human charity and Christian charity.' Isabel had said the same:

> O, think on that;
> And mercy then will breathe within your lips
> Like man new made.

Shakespeare has so manipulated the story as to make it end in Isabel showing more than human charity to Angelo, whilst at the same time he has avoided, by the introduction of Mariana, the error, which he found in his crude original, of wedding Isabel to Angelo.

Is it then true that in *Measure for Measure* 'the evidence of Shakespeare's profound disillusionment and discouragement of spirit is plain enough', that 'the searchlight of irony is thrown upon the paths of Providence itself'?[1]

The way in which the Duke, an earthly Providence, tortures Isabel till he wrings her agonized forgiveness out of her, reminds us of the way in which, in Shakespeare's contemporary tragedies, Providence seems to ordain that no suffering is spared to Lear or Cordelia, to Othello or Desdemona. It is very terrible. But it cannot be called, as it often is called, un-Christian, when we observe how Lear and Othello, Cordelia and Desdemona rise 'superior to the world in which they appear'.[2] The last word on this has been said by that wise critic, A. C. Bradley:

The extremity of the disproportion between prosperity and goodness first shocks us, and then flashes on us the conviction that our whole attitude in asking or expecting that goodness should be prosperous is wrong; that, if only we could see things as they are, we should see that the outward is nothing and the inward is all.[3]

This rather grim thought was, perhaps, better understood by the Englishmen of Shakespeare's day than it is now. Mr. Bettenham, Reader of Gray's Inn, was wont to say 'that virtuous men were like some herbs and spices, that give not their sweet smell, till they be broken and crushed'. And Francis Bacon, of the same

[1] E. K. Chambers, in the *Encyclopaedia Britannica* (1911), xxiv. 785.
[2] A. C. Bradley, *Shakespearean Tragedy*, p. 324.
[3] Ibid., p. 326.

Inn, put this doctrine into his Essay *Of Adversity*, to show that 'Prosperity is the blessing of the Old Testament; adversity is the blessing of the New, which carrieth the greater benediction, and the clearer revelation of God's favour'.

And I heard A. E. Housman, who, of all men I have known, was sternest in refusing to break his proud reserve, say in his first lecture:

> Fortitude and continence and honesty are not commended to us on the ground that they conduce, as on the whole they do conduce, to material success, nor yet on the ground that they will be rewarded hereafter: those whose office it is to exhort mankind to virtue are ashamed to degrade the cause they plead by proffering such lures as these.

Forty-one years later, in his last great public utterance, in which he bade us 'Farewell for ever', he quoted: 'Whosoever will save his life shall lose it, and whosoever will lose his life shall find it.' 'That', he said, 'is the most important truth which has ever been uttered, and the greatest discovery ever made in the moral world; but I do not find in it anything which I should call poetical.'

Now it would take me altogether out of my depth, to discuss whether there is anything poetical in those words. But it can surely be contended that Shakespearian tragedy is an expression *in poetry* of that 'most important truth which has ever been uttered'. And so, equally, is *Measure for Measure* an expression of 'the greatest discovery ever made in the moral world': the highly unpleasant discovery that there are things more important, for oneself and for others, than avoiding death and pain.

That, of course, is not a Christian discovery. One of the founders of modern Japan uttered it in two lines of Chinese verse, as he was led to execution, speaking with a loud voice, so that he might take farewell of his friend without implicating him by turning his head:

> It is better to be a crystal and be broken
> Than to remain perfect like a tile upon the housetop.

It is not Christian: but it is a foundation upon which Christianity, in common with every other religion worth the name, is built.

Measure for Measure is a play of forgiveness, more distinctly even than *The Tempest*. Isabel forgives in her moment of direst loss: Prospero only when he has recovered his Dukedom. Isabel urges forgiveness because a Christian must forgive: Prospero forgives because he does not condescend to torment his enemies further. And the contrast applies also to those forgiven. Angelo longs for death, because the Duke, *'like power divine'*, has seen his sinfulness. Sebastian and Antonio learn from Prospero, when he forgives them, that besides their crimes against him, he knows also how they have plotted to kill their king; to the pardoned Sebastian, just as to Angelo, there naturally seems to be something superhuman in such knowledge; but Sebastian expresses his conviction differently from Angelo:

> The devil speaks in him.

'No!' says Prospero; and then he turns to his brother Antonio:

> For you, most wicked Sir, whom to call brother
> Would even infect my mouth, I do forgive
> Thy rankest fault . . .

Antonio makes no answer to this forgiveness. But he and Sebastian, unabashed, continue their joyless jests to the end.

Now, when we mark how evil, and its forgiveness, is depicted in *Measure for Measure* in 1604, can we agree that Shakespeare's philosophy about 1604 was 'obviously not a Christian philosophy'? On the contrary, it seems to me more definitely Christian than that of *The Tempest*, though I don't deny that the philosophy of the Romances can also be called Christian. I would not deny that, on the whole, Shakespeare's last plays *are* 'happy dreams', 'symbols of an optimistic faith in the beneficent dispositions of an ordering Providence'.[1] But I see no ground to believe that there is any 'complete breach' between the mood of 1604 and that of 1611, or that we must assume a 'conversion', caused by 'a serious illness which may have been a nervous breakdown, and on the other hand may have been merely the plague'.[2]

We are told that the low-comedy characters of *Measure for Measure* are 'unwholesome company': that whereas Shakespeare, in Falstaff and his associates, had represented sin as 'human', he now represents it as 'devilish'.[3] But is this really so? Surely the answer was given by Sir Walter Raleigh years ago. These characters 'are live men, pleasant to Shakespeare'. Pompey is 'one of those humble, cheerful beings, willing to help in anything that is going forward, who are the mainstay of human affairs. . . . Froth is an amiable, feather-headed young gentleman—to dislike him would argue an ill-nature, and a small one. . . . This world of Vienna, as Shakespeare paints it, is not a black world; it is a weak world, full of little vanities and stupidities, regardful of custom, fond of pleasure, idle, and abundantly human.'[4]

As to Barnardine, his creator came to love him so much that he had not the heart to decapitate him, although Barnardine was only created to be decapitated.

In *Measure for Measure* sin is not represented as 'devilish': it is represented as sinful, and that is necessitated by the serious and earnest character of the whole

---

[1] E. K. Chambers, in the *Encyclopaedia Britannica* (1911), xxiv. 785.

[2] E. K. Chambers, *William Shakespeare*, 1930, i. 86, 274.

[3] E. K. Chambers, *Shakespeare: A Survey*, 1935, p. 211.

[4] *Shakespeare*, p. 166.

play. Yet there are few things funnier in all Shakespeare than Lucio pouring his scandal about the Duke into the hooded ears of the Duke himself; the poor Duke trying to keep his end up by giving himself a handsome testimonial as 'a scholar, a statesman, and a soldier'; asking the name of his libeller, and being told, 'Lucio; well known to the Duke'; and at last frustrated when he tries to escape from his tormentor by Lucio's, 'Nay, friar, I am a kind of burr; I shall stick'. And when the unmasked Duke finally taxes Lucio with his slanders, he is not unequal to the occasion:

Faith, my lord, I spoke it but according to the trick. If you will hang me for it, you may; but I had rather it would please you I might be whipt.

One of my women students once told me that her greatest regret over not being born a man was that she could not act Lucio. I admit that the lady was a greater ornament of the College Dramatic Society than of my lecture room, and that she ultimately left the University without taking a degree. When I last heard of her, she had entered the nursing profession, where I hope she will find scope for her generous and truly Shakespearian sympathy.

This, then, is how Shakespeare treats the barbarous old story of *Promos and Cassandra*, removing its morbid details, harmonizing its crudities, giving humanity and humour to its low characters, turning it into a consistent tale of intercession for sin, repentance from and forgiveness of crime. Yet *Measure for Measure* is adduced as the supreme proof that, about 1603, Shakespeare was in a mood of 'self-laceration, weariness, discord, cynicism, and disgust'.[1] He has been in that mood for the two years since the execution of Essex,

[1] J. Dover Wilson, op. cit., p. 117.

and will remain in it for another four or five. This dominant mood of gloom and dejection will bring him on one occasion to the verge of madness, and lead him to write dramas greater than any other man ever wrote save Aeschylus and Sophocles alone. Then in 1608 Sir Edmund Chambers will cure him of his seven years of 'profound disillusionment and discouragement of spirit' by giving him either the plague, or (alternatively) a nervous breakdown.

I hear a gentle voice from Stratford murmur

> Good frend, for Jesus sake forbeare.

Yet the critics have one final kick at *Measure for Measure*. More Papistical than the Pope, they feel outraged that Isabel should 'throw her novitiate headdress over the mill'[1] and marry the Duke. Even the sober A. C. Bradley thought that here Shakespeare lent himself to 'a scandalous proceeding'.[2] Yet Isabel is a novice, and her business as a novice is to learn her Creator's intentions for her future. Whether she ought to return to the cloister from which she has been so urgently summoned rests with her creator—William Shakespeare. And he leaves her silent, and us guessing. For myself, I am satisfied that Isabel will do her duty in that state of life unto which it shall please William Shakespeare to call her, whether as abbess or duchess.

Yet in Shakespeare's greatest plays, his greatest characters, for all their individuality, have also an imaginative, a symbolic suggestion. It is so in *The Tempest*, it is so in *Hamlet*. Thus also in the person of Lear, not only a helpless old man, but Paternity and Royalty are outraged; and 'Glamis hath murder'd Sleep'. No woman in Shakespeare is more individual than Isabel: silent yet eloquent, sternly righteous yet capable of infinite

---

[1] New Cambridge Shakespeare, p. xxxi.
[2] *Shakespearean Tragedy*, p. 78.

forgiveness, a very saint and a very vixen. But, first and last, she 'stands for' mercy.[1] The Duke is shown to us as a governor perplexed about justice, puzzled in his search for righteousness, seeking above all things to know himself. Is it altogether fanciful to remember once again that *Measure for Measure* was acted before the court at Christmas, 1604: that when Isabel at the beginning urges her plea for mercy (which she also makes good at the end) it is on the ground that

> He that might the vantage best have took
> Found out the remedy.

The day before *Measure for Measure* was acted, the finding out of that remedy was being commemorated. All sober criticism must remember the part which the accepted theology played in the thought of Shakespeare's day; that the Feast of the Nativity was—is—the union of Divine Mercy and of Divine Righteousness, and was—is—celebrated in the Christmas psalm:

Mercy and truth are met together: righteousness and peace have kissed each other.

Shakespeare's audience expected a marriage at the end: and, though it may be an accident, the marriage of Isabel and the Duke makes a good ending to a Christmas play.

[1] This does not make her allegorical, any more than Beowulf is an allegory because, as W. P. Ker says, he 'stands for' valour.

HARDIN CRAIG

(b. 1875)

Motivation in Shakespeare's Choice of Materials[1]

THE field of study which I propose for consideration
has to do with Shakespeare's plots in two aspects, the
general and the detailed. When he utters the familiar
lines in *A Midsummer Night's Dream*,

> And as imagination bodies forth
> The forms of things unknown, the poet's pen
> Turns them to shapes and gives to airy nothing
> A local habitation and a name,

he gives a perfect description of the most fundamental
operation of the human mind. As the possessor of one
of the greatest minds on record, he is at the same time
describing his own transcendent skill.

There is usually to be discovered in Shakespeare's
plays a form or pattern, sometimes easily identified,
sometimes not; sometimes apparently consciously developed, sometimes seemingly almost accidental. These
are 'the forms of things unknown'. The power of deter-
mining forms, that is, of regarding as irrelevant all
attending circumstances except a certain conceptual
form that controls the complex of events, is the most
characteristic mental trait of mankind, and in the recognition of significant form in any configuration presented
to experience Shakespeare excelled. This operation is
psychologically equivalent to the formation of concepts,
and we may go farther and say that, as soon as the concept is formed, the imagination takes it up, completes it,

[1] *Shakespeare Survey 4* (1951).

often amplifies it, gives it its environment, and makes of it a conception special to the mind of the thinker; let us say gives it 'a local habitation and a name'. There are thus two processes involved in the building up of a fully formed conception, namely, the abstractive ability which sees and grasps a central form and a later mental operation in which imagination adds to this concept the subsidiary details which complete the picture or the play.

There is no reason to think that these two operations were successive with Shakespeare or consciously discriminated. Indeed, the genesis of his plays no doubt presents a wide series of special circumstances. It may be that his interest in any particular subject was first aroused by some relatively minor feature of the plot, and there is, of course, no way of telling how it was; but, on the other hand, there is no doubt that the greatness of the greatest literature resides very largely in the treatment in detail of a central thought or concept. Let it be remembered that the artist does not invent the forms of things but discovers them as the scientist discovers facts and laws.

Let me illustrate this by a conjectural account, not without some plausibility, of Shakespeare's experience in the writing of *Measure for Measure*. He had read Whetstone's *Promos and Cassandra*, or, more probably, the tale on which it is based, and learned that Cassandra, who is represented as a faithful and virtuous woman, yielded to the base demands of Promos and sacrificed her honour in order to save her brother's life. Shakespeare, celebrated for his faith in the integrity of women, fresh from the depiction of Desdemona in *Othello*, and perhaps even then engaged in the delineation of Cordelia in *King Lear*, said to himself, 'Cassandra would never have sacrificed her honour'. So enraptured was he with his idea that he proceeded to represent what would actually happen if his heroine was a faithful and virtuous woman. With this concept in mind he proceeded to write for two acts and a part of one scene on the very highest level of his ability. At this point he found himself involved as a dramatist in serious difficulties and one can see evidence of his perplexity. Having to his own satisfaction rescued his heroine, how was he to save her brother's life, punish her would-be seducer, and, since this was to be a comedy, provide everybody with a matrimonial union at the end? Shakespeare in comedy never lets an eligible bachelor or a lonely maid escape. He bethought himself of the device of the bed trick he had used in *All's Well That Ends Well* and shamelessly used it over again. It served the purpose very well, but how did the Duke know about Mariana? His knowledge of Angelo's past behaviour and therefore of his base character is certainly a surprising thing for him now to know and does not agree at all with the high opinion which the Duke seems to have entertained about Angelo in the first act. Perhaps Shakespeare's major interest in the subject was exhausted. At any rate, he never wrote so well in the play again. He engages himself with a lot of not very original or successful satirical low comedy, and at the end, as a sort of confession of weakness, he resorts to theatrical intrigue, and ends the play with the usual pairing off of lovers, even marrying off Isabella to the Duke without, so to speak, asking her consent, since she is at least unexpectedly silent.

Shakespeare inherited from his sources many stories whose significance lies in their unity. They had already been selected and told because of their embodiment of some striking concept. The story of Antony and Cleopatra, for example, had rested for ages on the concept of an empire lost through the sin of lust. The story of Romeo and Juliet came to Shakespeare complete in its members; the pattern is the tragic conflict between age with its prudence and prejudice and youth with its impetuosity, so that it was and had been impossible to tell that story badly from Xenophon of Ephesus to Shakespeare. The story of Marlowe's *Dr. Faustus* is also of this naturally unified sort. Plutarch was a master in the production of significant unity, and the English chronicles by the time they reached Holinshed had been, so to speak, well abstracted. They had been re-worked along the lines of classical historiography, and most of the stories of English kings, at the hands of Polydore Vergil, Sir Thomas More, the authors of *The Mirror for Magistrates*, and others, had come to present certain moral abstractions. A good many of Shakespeare's subjects were, so to speak, pre-digested, but it is hardly necessary to add that he was not dependent, as *Othello* shows, on such pre-workings of his plots.

The Renaissance inherited a belief that human behaviour is characterized by universality and that a particular line of conduct repeats itself in pattern. Historical records were thus looked upon as mirrors in which men might see reflections of themselves as individuals and of the states and societies around them. Such books as John Barclay's *The Mirrour of Mindes*, Thomas Wright's *The Passions of the Minde in Generall*, and Pierre de la Primaudaye's *The French Academie* differentiated the people of various nations, classified the passions, the described types of conduct. The doctrine of elements and humours, fundamental to the physiology and psychology of the time, provided a 'scientific' basis for these stereotyped treatises, and similitudes, such as those found in the explanations of the microcosm and the macrocosm, perpetuated modes of expression and modes of thought.[1] The learning of

[1] See Ruth Anderson Maxwell, 'The Mirror Concept and its relation to the Drama of the Renaissance', *N.W. Missouri State Teachers College Studies*, iii (1939), no. 1, and an as yet unpublished paper 'Ideation in Renaissance Plays depicting Ambition and Tyranny'.

the past, acquired in grammar school, was put to use in writing without thought of plagiarism. Indeed, the whole theory and practice of composition was based on the teaching of the art of copiousness or amplification of already existent themes with already existent matter. Repetition of thought and imagery is inseparable from the concept of the universality of man, and the idea is not false. Men are still similar organisms that mirror, by and large, pretty much the same environment, and the similarities of men are still far greater than their differences. Shakespeare did not reject this fundamental idea of his age, and his greatness consists largely in the perfection with which he expresses the concept of the universality of man. As to the literary method which his indoctrination in school and the custom of his age forced upon him, that too is not out of line with the creation of great literature and great art. It is interesting to note that Poe acknowledges the virtue of Shakespeare's practice[1] when he says 'to originate is carefully, patiently, and understandingly to combine'.

This method of operation seems to have been taken for granted by Sidney and by Shakespeare himself, and neither has any suggestion that stories may be invented by poets, although they both have something to say about the improvement or betterment of nature at the poet's hands. They both proceed on the basis of an established body of material. In Sidney's *The Defence of Poesie*, the poet and the historian are, as regards their subject-matter, on exactly the same basis. What distinguishes them are certain liberties allowed to the poet. He says:

So, then, the best of the historian is subject to the poet; for, whatsoever action or faction, whatsoever counsel, policy, or war stratagem the historian is bound to recite, that may the poet, if he list, with his imitation make his own, beautifying it

---

[1] 'Peter Snook', *Complete Works*, ed. James A. Harrison (1902), xiv. 73.

both for further teaching and more delighting, as it please him; having all, from Dante his heaven to his hell, under the authority of his pen.

To the Poet in *Timon of Athens* the poet's material is nature, and nature is plastic:

> My free drift
> Halts not particularly, but moves itself
> In a wide sea of wax; no levell'd malice
> Infects one comma in the course I hold,
> But flies an eagle-flight, bold, and forth on,
> Leaving no tract behind.   (I. i. 45–50)

Certainly, in any case, there is little outright invention of plots and incidents in Elizabethan literature, whether drama or fiction. This is borne out by the notorious ransacking of the writings of the past and present by Elizabethan authors and confirmed by the long-continued practice of source-hunting by generations of scholars. As subjects for their plays Elizabethan dramatists hunted all over the world of literature. Nothing was safe from them. They found events and situations in the Bible, in folk-lore, in popular literature, and in local happenings. A favourite hunting ground was the Italian and French short story, itself an aggregate of historical or local event and of popular and traditional matters of all sorts. English dramatists used Plutarch, Livy, Virgil, Ovid, and casual history, story and mythology from other sources; particularly, they used the history and traditions of their own country as embodied in the chronicles.

Source-hunting practised industriously in the eighteenth, nineteenth, and twentieth centuries was and is a sound instinct and a natural and fruitful approach to the study of Elizabethan literature. The trouble has been that those engaged in *Quellenuntersuchungen* have not known why they did it or have not known what to do with sources after they are found. Accounts of sources have been tucked away in the pages of learned journals and special studies, whence they have been available for mention, and for very little else, by editors of the works of Elizabethan authors. But the instinct was sound, because sources tend to furnish basal concepts. The age was *one* to a degree we can scarcely comprehend. To read one author is in some sense to read them all. Sources have an added importance in the age, because Elizabethan authors seem to have been unaware that incident could be invented, manufactured out of whole cloth or even the raw materials of whole cloth. This dependence on sources is true, even if it is only roughly true, and one can at least say that Elizabethan dramatists had no habit of inventing plots and apparently very slight tendency to invent incidents. Instead of inventing what they needed, they sought for it widely, and it may be said without derogation that from the point of view of plot-construction an Elizabethan play is built like a mosaic with varying skill and ingenuity in putting the parts together. In some instances the parts are collected from wide areas. In others, as in Shakespeare's history plays and in his plays derived from Plutarch, the immediate source itself was so well filled out that most of the necessary parts were close at hand. We shall have to do with the methods and principles apparently employed by Shakespeare in filling in his plots and fitting together various constituent elements. It is to be presumed that in most instances these filling-in operations were controlled by patterns.

When the necessary parts had been found, Elizabethan dramatists were set free. They were then in the region of amplification or copy, to the practice of which they had been trained in school. Amplification was their challenge, the test of their literary ability, and they met the challenge so well that there are few limits to their ingenuity. It is a remarkable fact that there are almost no plot elements in Shakespeare's plays for which some source, analogue or suggestion has not been found. The same is true of Greene, Lyly, Marlowe, Dekker, Heywood, Webster, Middleton, Jonson himself, and, so far as I know, of most of the rest. So true is this that when some incident or character for which no source has been found exists, one bears it in mind for years in the belief that somewhere a source or originating suggestion will be unearthed. There may yet be found an original for Malvolio in *Twelfth Night*, and I myself have at last found at least a suggestion for the sinful liaison between Edmund and the wicked daughters of Lear in *King Lear*.

A good deal of erroneous criticism of Elizabethan drama has come from the fact that this same invention of plots is in our time considered a primary characteristic of originality. Modern writers of fiction and drama are not, however, so wholly new as perhaps they think they are, since a limited body of themes and situations are in common currency in contemporary as well as in Elizabethan fiction and drama. Perhaps the Elizabethans, who supported their originality by means of a wide search, were the more varied of the two. It is, at any rate, an error to belittle Shakespeare's genius on the ground that he did not supply from some vague reservoir of general human experience such incidents as he might need to complete his patterns, but actually sought out and borrowed from definite places such incidents as he might need. In *Cymbeline*, for example, Shakespeare needed to get in princely fashion Guiderius and Arviragus, the lost sons of the King, back into the main action of the play, and he found the perfect means of doing this as far afield as Holinshed's *Chronicle of Scotland*, in which it is related of a Scottish husbandman named Haie how he and his sons, observing the

dangerous approach of the Danish army, placed themselves in a sunken roadway and stayed the advance of
the enemy; as Shakespeare puts it (v. iii. 52):

> A narrow lane, an old man, and two boys.

Shakespeare's originality seems to have consisted in the
selection of great significant patterns, in the discovery
of incidents, in unequalled ingenuity in fitting parts
together so that they reinforced one another, and in
masterly skill in realistic amplification. It did not con-
sist for some reason in the exercise of the facile modern
ability to invent incidents.

Perhaps this apparent limitation of operation may be
accounted for, in part at least, on the ground that to the
Renaissance a basis of truth was always to be preferred
to a basis of fiction. Authors liked to think that they
were recording actual truth, and true stories were commended as such on title-pages. All authors seemed to
feel secure when they were dealing with something that
had actually happened. Truth was sufficiently strange
and carried with it a greater weight of importance than
fiction. Perhaps, indeed very probably, the very idea of
outright invention had not occurred to them, had not
been discovered.

This attitude of the acceptance only of that which
already existed was in line with the philosophy of the
age, which was pre-Baconian and pre-Cartesian. The
mind of the age went backward toward a lost perfection
and not forward toward unknown and unexploited
novelty. The age believed in exploration in the hope of
the discovery of the already existent. Everything that
had been still existed for the guidance of humanity, and
man must exert himself to find it; there was strictly
nothing new under the sun. One would not apply this
principle too strictly, for people were much as they are
now, but one might use it safely to describe a tendency.

It merely says that literary methods were governed by the same system of thought as were scientific methods.

Out of this discussion comes the idea that the significance of the pattern is a first consideration in the study of Shakespeare's work as a dramatist. One might say for this occasion that a pattern or design is something simpler and of wider general significance than is a plot. For example, the pattern of a morality play of the full-scope kind presents a central figure, symbolic of humanity, called Mankind or Humanum Genus, born with an ultimately irresistible compulsion to sin. This figure is tempted by error in the person of Satan (operating as Mundus, Caro et Diabolus, the Seven Deadly Sins, or a variety of Vitia) to leave the path of righteousness and follow a course or career of wickedness at the end of which he is convicted of sin and becomes a manifest candidate for damnation. He is, however, saved in the only possible way by the intercession of Christ, the Blessed Virgin Mary, or some kindly saint and is taken without merit of his own into the bosom of God. This simple pattern cannot disappear. It is seen in its pure form in *Dr. Faustus* and *Macbeth*, except that in neither play does the element of intercession appear. The former has, however, so many morality features that it may certainly be regarded as a transitional document. All great literature subsists in some measure because of its bearing on man's salvation, and universality of scope with the appearance or absence of special application and situations serves as a sort of criterion. There are many such generalized works from *Pilgrim's Progress* to *The Egoist*. There is no attempt here to connect such works in a chain of conscious imitation, but only to claim that such works are recurrent. To this form of literature so conceived that a hero stands in some sense for all mankind, since his adventures and reactions are of the most general sort,

Macbeth belongs. *Odyssey, Aeneid, Prometheus, Oedipus, Job,* and many of the greatest works of literature, modern as well as ancient, are also here. To do evil is to wander from the true way, to enter into a career of error and sin, to encounter some sort of retribution or punishment, and to end unhappily. Such seems to be the common judgement of humanity, and it matters not whether the force inciting to evil and ending in calamity is thought of as fate, the displeasure of the gods, or voluntary action under delusion or rebellion.

The oldest and as yet the best explanation of why men do this is that they are deluded, so that they mistake evil for good. There is a mystery about temptation and sin, as there is about love and other powerful human motives, and the oldest symbolization of that mystery is Satan and his angels—the devil, the evil one, imps, witches, and malign spirits—and it is to that conception that morality plays belong. The central figure, which represented mankind in the broadest possible way, passed, consciously or unconsciously, into romantic tragedy. *Macbeth* is such a case, and in such tragedies we necessarily find the two forms of thought described above, a concept and a conception or, we might say, a primary pattern and a completed drama. The story of Macbeth supplies what might be called the morality pattern. Shakespeare got it from the chronicles of Duncan and Macbeth in Holinshed's *Chronicle of Scotland.* There he got the figure of a great warrior, a loyal subject, and a man of normal human kindness. He is deluded by the emissaries of Satan, as truly as was Everyman, and entered upon and pursued a career of crime until he was overtaken and destroyed by the righteous judgement he had provoked.

But the Macbeth of the chronicles kills his king as an open rebel, and this was insufficient for Shakespeare's enlarged conception. In his dramatic treatment he demanded more particular motivations. Banquo belonged to the story of Macbeth and there were other parts supplied from it, but mainly Shakespeare resorted for amplification to the chronicle of King Duff. In that he found the story of Donwald, a man whom King Duff never suspected, who murdered King Duff in the castle of Forres. This deepens Macbeth's guilt, since in his own story he had been an open rebel against King Duncan, but the story of Donwald amplified the plot in another way. Having, with the aid of his wife, drugged the two chamberlains who lay with the King, Donwald, although he greatly abhorred the deed and did it only at the instigation of his wife, induced four of his servants to cut the King's throat. When morning came, he slew the chamberlains and cleared himself of the crime by his power and authority, though not without being suspected by certain noblemen because of his over-diligence. Thus from the chronicle of King Duff came Lady Macbeth and all that pertains to her. Shakespeare also laid many parts of his brilliant and spirited source under contribution. The voice of sleeplessness comes from the chronicle of King Kenneth, and it was only last year that a pupil of mine, A. L. Crabb, found in Holinshed a source for the pageant of the kings which was needed to form a connexion between the descendants of Banquo and King James I.

In the morality pattern of *Macbeth*, which has been amplified but not changed, we see the aberration of a hero, under delusion of the powers of evil, pursue a career of crime and wickedness, violent to the last degree and continued until such time as his course of evil was arrested. It is still the faith of men that such careers will eventually be arrested, and this faith was ardently held by Shakespeare and his age. Macbeth stands at the end the same man he was at the beginning, but weakened by his sins and confronted by outraged

man acting as the punitive agent of God. It will be
recalled that he had always feared this recoil of human
justice, but he is none the less a sinner in the hands of an
angry God. His situation is not different from that of
Mankind, or Everyman, or Humanum Genus. He is
overthrown by an enemy his sins have created. Another
way of saying this is that he is in the clutches of a tragic
fate. Macduff, laden with wrongs and burning with the
fire of righteous revenge, is the hand of fate, or God, or
immutable justice. There is even in Macbeth a peripeteia not always recognized by critics. I said that
Macbeth stands at the end the same man he was at the
beginning. His state is weakened, but he sees what has
happened to him and utters the perfect definition of
evil, which is delusion:

> And be these juggling fiends no more believed,
> That palter with us in a double sense;
> That keep the word of promise to our ear,
> And break it to our hope.   (v. viii. 19–22)

Macbeth's last act is to resort to his sword, and he dies
as a man.

I have advanced a theory of Shakespeare's use of bits
of truth which, under the guidance of significant concepts, he fitted together into significant and convincing
wholes. Perhaps the clearest illustration I can give of
this is to be drawn from *King Lear*. The old play which
Shakespeare used as a source, *The True Chronicle
History of King Leir, and his three Daughters, Gonorill,
Ragan and Cordella*, is not a tragedy. It never threatens
to be, and it is not tragic in tone or outcome. It contains villainy, and two wicked daughters plot the murder
of their father, but they are easily thwarted. There are
no deaths in the play. It has been customary to say that
the very logic of Lear's errors, sufferings, and disasters
caused Shakespeare to give the drama of *King Lear*

a tragic ending. I do not pretend to know how Shakespeare felt about it, and I do not deny the perfection of his tragic genius in writing and concluding the play as he did, and yet I have another and a different account of the matter to offer. There are certain circumstances which reveal in my judgement a more original movement of his thought and provide naturalistic reasons for his handling the story of Lear as he did.

The old *King Leir* was apparently a Queen's Company play which for some unexplained reason Shakespeare seems to have known very well indeed. One would like to think that Shakespeare had acted in it, since not only the Second Murderer in *Richard III*, but other bits in other plays seem to echo the old *King Leir*. It seems doubtful, however, whether he had the play actually at hand when he wrote *King Lear*. From the point of view of the old play the story is imperfectly retold by Shakespeare, and new invention takes the place of good and naturalistic devices in the old play. For one thing, Shakespeare, without apparent cause, inverts the roles of Cornwall and Albany (called Cambria in *King Leir*); likewise he gives to Goneril some acts and qualities which belong to Ragan in the old play and to Regan certain features which belong to Gonorill. These circumstances and some others seem to indicate that, although he knew the old play well, he worked on it from memory.

The True Chronicle History of King Leir is a rather bright and cheerful play. It furnished events for Shakespeare's *King Lear*, but it did not furnish tone, atmosphere, the deeper significances and the tragic concept. These came from the story of the 'Paphlagonian unkinde King, and his kinde sonne' as narrated in the tenth chapter of the second book of Sidney's *Arcadia*. The story of the Paphlagonian king is tragic, that of the old King Leir is not. The concept or pattern of Sidney's story is the tragic consequences of filial ingratitude. That concept is taken over from the *Arcadia* and applied to the Lear story. It is natural to conclude that the genesis of the tragedy of *King Lear* is to be found in the story of the blind king of Paphlagonia; that is, that the tragic possibilities of filial ingratitude came from the reading of *Arcadia* and not from familiarity with the old *King Leir*. Sidney furnishes active cruelty, filial ingratitude in a dreadful form, base deceit and dark intrigue. He furnishes the theme of hunted fugitives, exposure to storm, a cave of refuge (which may be the hovel), blindness, danger, destitution, and, more than all, the deepest possible reflection on tragic folly and the worthlessness of miserable life. To be sure, there is in the old play the attempted murder of Leir and Perillus by the Messenger, but it is a poor thing compared even with Oswald's attempt on the life of Gloucester. Finally, in Sidney the prototype of Gloucester dies. In the case of *King Lear*, Shakespeare through the influence of *Arcadia* becomes bound by the conventions of tragedy just as in the writing of *Measure for Measure* he had been bound by the conventions of comedy.

Perhaps the greatest contribution of *Arcadia* to *King Lear* is the element of sinful and dangerous intrigue. From the fifteenth chapter of the second book of *Arcadia*, which treats of the story of Plangus, come by plain suggestion the machinations by which Edmund undermines and uproots Edgar.[1] It is by means similar to those used by Edmund against Edgar that the corrupt stepmother achieves the downfall and banishment of Plangus. From that story also comes the suggestion for the disagreeably appropriate liaison between Edmund and the wicked daughters of King Lear.

[1] See D. M. McKeithan, '*King Lear* and Sidney's *Arcadia*', *Studies in English*, Austin, Texas, no. 14 (1934), pp. 45–49.

It was natural and yet a stroke of genius that made Shakespeare combine two stories so different in their tone and yet so closely parallel in their course as that of King Leir and the blind king of Paphlagonia. He knitted these stories together with a naturalness which will always be amazing, but his general task may be described as that of permeating the Lear story with the tragic tone and temper of the Gloucester story. The tragedy as tragedy is to be found in the tale from *Arcadia*. Shakespeare retains from the old play the sweetness of Cordelia and the faithfulness of Kent (Perillus). The stoutness in the character of the aged Lear is yet to be accounted for, since the Leir of the old play is merely pathetic. Again, few parts of *King Lear* seem to be invented outright. There is the figure of the Fool, a traditional part provided no doubt for Robert Armin, the trial by combat, no very difficult thing to invent, and the patriotic change from British defeat to British victory. When, however, one talks about this glibly as an indication of Shakespeare's own patriotic feeling, one should remember that Shakespeare needed it as a means of entangling Lear and Cordelia in the mesh of tragedy. In other words, the British victory serves Shakespeare as a device for the carrying out of his tragic purpose.

I have endeavoured to apply to Shakespeare's choice of materials a fundamental principle of the psychology of art and have illustrated Shakespeare's practice from some of his plays. Behind what I have said lies a consideration of still greater importance. Shakespeare's sources are worth studying because they have significance, value, meaning; Shakespeare chose them for that reason. This statement finds its place in the most promising philosophy of art in our age. To the definitions of the logic of Aristotle and of modern science this philosophy has added the idea of value. Symbolic logic is not content with denotation and connotation only, but insists on a third definitive element which is significance or value. This philosophy promises to change our attitude toward art by uniting it to life, and it offers a broad and adequate epistemology for the acceptance of symbolic truth. It carries with it an extension of our conception of man; as, for example, that man is known by his actions and not by any analytical formulae; in other words, that man is an organism whose function is living. It thus comes about that Shakespeare's sources are usually formulations of function. The fact that these sources have been neglected or disdained is not a matter of any importance whatever, since much of the work so far done in the interpretation of Shakespeare needs to be rendered more comprehensive and more adequate.

J. DOVER WILSON

(1881–1969)

Riot and the Prodigal Prince[1]

FALSTAFF may be the most conspicuous, he is certainly the most fascinating, character in *Henry IV*, but all critics are agreed, I believe, that the technical centre of the play is not the fat knight but the lean prince. Hal links the low life with the high life, the scenes at Eastcheap with those at Westminster, the tavern with the battlefield; his doings provide most of the material for both Parts, and with him too lies the future, since he is to become Henry V, the ideal king, in the play that bears his name; finally, the mainspring of the dramatic action is the choice I have already spoken of, the choice he is called upon to make between Vanity and Government, taking the latter in its accepted Tudor meaning, which includes Chivalry or prowess in the field, the theme of Part I, and Justice, which is the theme of Part II. Shakespeare, moreover, breathes life into these abstractions by embodying them, or aspects of them, in prominent characters, who stand, as it were, about the Prince, like attendant spirits: Falstaff typifying Vanity in every sense of the word, Hotspur Chivalry, of the old anarchic kind, and the Lord Chief Justice the Rule of Law or the new ideal of service to the state.

Thus considered, Shakespeare's *Henry IV* is a Tudor version of a time-honoured theme, already familiar for decades, if not centuries, upon the English stage. Before its final secularization in the first half of the sixteenth

[1] *The Fortunes of Falstaff* (1943). The footnotes have been much abbreviated by the editor.

century, our drama was concerned with one topic, and one only: human salvation. It was a topic that could be represented in either of two ways: (i) historically, by means of miracle plays, which in the Corpus Christi cycles unrolled before spectators' eyes the whole scheme of salvation from the Creation to the Last Judgement; or (ii) allegorically, by means of morality plays, which exhibited the process of salvation in the individual soul on its road between birth and death, beset with the snares of the World or the wiles of the Evil One. In both kinds the forces of iniquity were allowed full play upon the stage, including a good deal of horse-play, provided they were brought to nought, or safely locked up in Hell, at the end. Salvation remains the supreme interest, however many capers the Devil and his Vice may cut on Everyman's way thither, and always the powers of darkness are withstood, and finally overcome, by the agents of light. But as time went on the religious drama tended to grow longer and more elaborate, after the encyclopaedic fashion of the Middle Ages, and such development invited its inevitable reaction. With the advent of humanism and the early Tudor court, morality plays became tedious and gave place to lighter and much shorter moral interludes dealing, not with human life as a whole, but with youth and its besetting sins.

An early specimen, entitled *Youth*[1] and composed about 1520, may be taken as typical of the rest. The plot, if plot it can be called, is simplicity itself. The little play opens with a dialogue between Youth and Charity. The young man, heir to his father's land, gives insolent expression to his self-confidence, lustihood, and contempt for spiritual things. Whereupon Charity leaves him, and he is joined by Riot, that is to say wantonness, who presently introduces him to Pride and

[1] *The enterlude of youth*, ed. by W. Bang and R. B. McKerrow, Louvain (1905).

Lechery. The dialogue then becomes boisterous, and continues in that vein for some time, much no doubt to the enjoyment of the audience. Yet, in the end, Charity reappears with Humility; Youth repents; and the interlude terminates in the most seemly fashion imaginable.

No one, I think, reading this lively playlet, no one certainly who has seen it performed, as I have seen it at the Malvern Festival, can have missed the resemblance between Riot and Falstaff. The words he utters, as he bounces on to the stage at his first entry, give us the very note of Falstaff's gaiety:

> Huffa! huffá! who calleth after me?
> I am Riot full of jollity.
> My heart is as light as the wind,
> And all on riot is my mind,
> Wheresoever I go.

And the parallel is even more striking in other respects. Riot, like Falstaff, escapes from tight corners with a quick dexterity; like Falstaff, commits robbery on the highway; like Falstaff, jests immediately afterwards with his young friend on the subject of hanging; and like Falstaff, invites him to spend the stolen money at a tavern, where, he promises, 'We will drink diuers wine' and 'Thou shalt haue a wench to kysse Whansoeuer thou wilte'; allurements which prefigure the Boar's Head and Mistress Doll Tearsheet.

But Youth at the door of opportunity, with Age or Experience, Charity or Good Counsel, offering him the yoke of responsibility, while the World, the Flesh, and the Devil beckon him to follow them on the primrose way to the everlasting bonfire, is older than even the medieval religious play. It is a theme to which every generation gives fresh form, while retaining its eternal substance. Young men are the heroes of the Plautine and Terentian comedy which delighted the Roman world; and these young men, generally under the direction of a clever slave or parasite, disport themselves, and often hoodwink their old fathers, for most of the play, until they too settle down in the end. The same theme appears in a very different story, the parable of the Prodigal Son. And the similarity of the two struck humanist teachers of the early sixteenth century with such force that, finding Terence insufficiently edifying for their pupils to act, they developed a 'Christian Terence' by turning the parable into Latin plays, of which many examples by different authors have come down to us. In these plot and structure are much the same. The opening scene shows us Acolastus, the prodigal, demanding his portion, receiving good counsel from his father, and going off into a far country. Then follow three or four acts of entertainment almost purely Terentian in atmosphere, in which he wastes his substance in riotous living and falls at length to feeding with the pigs. Finally, in the last act he returns home, penniless and repentant, to receive his pardon. This ingenious blend of classical comedy and humanistic morality preserves, it will be noted, the traditional ratio between edification and amusement, and distributes them in the traditional manner. So long as the serious note is duly emphasized at the beginning and end of the play, almost any quantity of fun, often of the most unseemly nature, was allowed and expected during the intervening scenes.

All this, and much more of a like character, gave the pattern for Shakespeare's *Henry IV*. Hal associates Falstaff in turn with the Devil of the miracle play, the Vice of the morality, and the Riot of the interlude, when he calls him 'that villainous abominable misleader of Youth, that old white-bearded Satan', 'that reverend Vice, that grey Iniquity, that father Ruffian, that Vanity

in years', and 'the tutor and the feeder of my riots'.
'Riot', again, is the word that comes most readily to
King Henry's lips when speaking of his prodigal son's
misconduct. And, as heir to the Vice, Falstaff inherits
by reversion the functions and attributes of the Lord of
Misrule, the Fool, the Buffoon, and the Jester, antic
figures the origins of which are lost in the dark backward
and abysm of folk-custom. We shall find that Falstaff
possesses a strain, and more than a strain, of the classical
miles gloriosus as well. In short, the Falstaff–Hal plot
embodies a composite myth which had been centuries
amaking, and was for the Elizabethans full of meaning
that has largely disappeared since then: which is one
reason why we have come so seriously to misunderstand
the play.

Nor was Shakespeare the first to see Hal as the
prodigal. The legend of Harry of Monmouth began to
grow soon after his death in 1422; and practically all
the chroniclers, even those writing in the fifteenth century, agree on his wildness in youth and on the sudden
change that came upon him at his accession to the
throne. The essence of Shakespeare's plot is, indeed,
already to be found in the following passage about King
Henry V taken from Fabyan's *Chronicle* of 1516:

This man, before the death of his fader, applyed him unto
all vyce and insolency, and drewe unto hym all ryottours and
wylde disposed persones; but after he was admytted to the
rule of the lande, anone and suddenly he became a newe man,
and tourned al that rage into sobernesse and wyse sadnesse,
and the vyce into constant vertue. And for he wolde contynewe
the vertue, and not to be reduced thereunto by the familiarytie
of his olde nyse company, he therefore, after rewardes to them
gyuen, charged theym upon payne of theyr lyues, that none
of theym were so hardy to come within x. myle of such place
as he were lodgyd, after a day by him assigned.

There appears to be no historical basis for any of this,

and Kingsford has plausibly suggested that its origin may be 'contemporary scandal which attached to Henry through his youthful association with the unpopular Lollard leader' Sir John Oldcastle. 'It is noteworthy', he points out, 'that Henry's political opponents were Oldcastle's religious persecutors; and also that those writers who charge Henry with wildness as Prince find his peculiar merit as King in the maintaining of Holy Church and destroying of heretics. A supposed change in his attitude on questions of religion may possibly furnish a partial solution for his alleged "change suddenly into a new man".'[1] The theory is the more attractive that it would account not only for Hal's conversion but also for Oldcastle's degradation from a protestant martyr and distinguished soldier to what Ainger calls 'a broken-down Lollard, a fat old sensualist, retaining just sufficient recollection of the studies of his more serious days to be able to point his jokes with them'.

Yet when all is said, the main truth seems to be that the fifteenth and early sixteenth centuries, the age of allegory in poetry and morality in drama, needed a Prodigal Prince, whose miraculous conversion might be held up as an example by those concerned (as what contemporary political writer was not?) with the education of young noblemen and princes. And could any more alluring fruits of repentance be offered such pupils than the prowess and statesmanship of Henry V, the hero of Agincourt, the mirror of English kingship for a hundred years? In his miracle play, *Richard II*, Shakespeare had celebrated the traditional royal martyr; in his morality play, *Henry IV*, he does the like with the traditional royal prodigal.

He made the myth his own, much as musicians adopt and absorb a folk-tune as the theme for a symphony.

[1] C. L. Kingsford, *The First English Life of King Henry the Fifth* (1911), pp. xlii, xliii.

He glorified it, elaborated it, translated it into what were for the Elizabethans modern terms, and exalted it into a heaven of delirious fun and frolic; yet never, for a moment, did he twist it from its original purpose, which was serious, moral, didactic. Shakespeare plays no tricks with his public. He did not, like Euripides, dramatize the stories of his race and religion in order to subvert the traditional ideals those stories were first framed to set forth. Prince Hal is the prodigal, and his repentance is not only to be taken seriously, it is to be admired and commended. Moreover, the story of the prodigal, secularized and modernized as it might be, ran the same course as ever and contained the same three principal characters: the tempter, the younker, and the father with property to bequeath and counsel to give. It followed also the fashion set by miracle, morality and the Christian Terence by devoting much attention to the doings of the first-named. Shakespeare's audience enjoyed the fascination of Prince Hal's 'white-bearded Satan' for two whole plays, as perhaps no character on the world's stage had ever been enjoyed before. But they knew, from the beginning, that the reign of this marvellous Lord of Misrule must have an end, that Falstaff must be rejected by the Prodigal Prince, when the time for reformation came. And they no more thought of questioning or disapproving of that finale, than their ancestors would have thought of protesting against the Vice being carried off to Hell at the end of the interlude.

The main theme, therefore, of Shakespeare's morality play is the growing-up of a madcap prince into the ideal king, who was Henry V; and the play was made primarily—already made by some dramatist before Shakespeare took it over—in order to exhibit his conversion and to reveal his character unfolding towards that end, as he finds himself faced more and more directly by his responsibilities. It is that which determines its very shape. Even the 'fearful symmetry' of Falstaff's own person was welded upon the anvil of that purpose. It is probably because the historical Harry of Monmouth 'exceded the meane stature of men', as his earliest chronicler tells us; 'his necke . . . longe, his body slender and leane, his boanes smale',[1]—because in Falstaff's words he actually was a starveling, an eel-skin, a tailor's yard, and all the rest of it—that the idea of Falstaff himself as 'a huge hill of flesh' first came to Shakespeare. It was certainly, at any rate in part, in order to explain and palliate the Prince's love of rioting and wantonness that he set out to make Falstaff as enchanting as he could. And he succeeded so well that the young man now lies under the stigma, not of having yielded to the tempter, but of disentangling himself, in the end, from his toils. After all, Falstaff *is* 'a devil . . . in the likeness of an old fat man', and the Devil has generally been supposed to exercise limitless attraction in his dealings with the sons of men. A very different kind of poet, who imagined a very different kind of Satan, has been equally and similarly misunderstood by modern critics, who no longer believing in the Prince of Darkness have ceased to understand him. For, as Professor R. W. Chambers reminded us in his last public utterance,[2] when Blake declared that Milton was 'of the Devil's party without knowing it', he overlooked the fact, and his many successors have likewise overlooked the fact, that, if the fight in Heaven, the struggle in Eden, the defeat of Adam and Eve, and the victory of the Second Adam in *Paradise Regained*, are to appear in their true proportions, we must be made to realize how immeasurable, how indomitable, is the spirit of the Great Enemy. It may also be noted that Milton's

[1] Kingsford, op. cit., p. 16.
[2] *Poets and their Critics* (British Academy Warton Lecture), 1941.

Son of God has in modern times been charged with priggishness no less freely than Shakespeare's son of Bolingbroke.

Shakespeare, I say, translated his myth into a language and endued it with an atmosphere that his contemporaries would best appreciate. First, Hal is not only youth or the prodigal, he is the young prodigal *prince*, the youthful heir to the throne. The translation, then, already made by the chroniclers, if Kingsford be right, from sectarian terms into those more broadly religious or moral, now takes us out of the theological into the political sphere. This is seen most clearly in the discussion of the young king's remarkable conversion by the two bishops at the beginning of *Henry V*. King Henry, as Bradley notes, 'is much more obviously religious than most of Shakespeare's heroes',[1] so that one would expect the bishops to interpret his change of life as a religious conversion. Yet they say nothing about religion except that he is 'a true lover of the holy church' and can 'reason in divinity'; the rest of their talk, some seventy lines, is concerned with learning and statecraft. In fact, the conversation of these worldly prelates demonstrates that the conversion is not the old repentance for sin and amendment of life, which is the burden, as we have seen, of Fabyan and other chroniclers, but a repentance of the renaissance type, which transforms an idle and wayward prince into an excellent soldier and governor. Even King Henry IV, at the bitterest moments of the scenes with his son, never taxes him with sin, and his only use of the word refers to sins that would multiply in the country, when

> the fifth Harry from curbed licence plucks
> The muzzle of restraint.

If Hal had sinned, it was not against God, but against

[1] *Oxford Lectures*, p. 256.

Chivalry, against Justice, against his father, against the
interests of the crown, which was the keystone of
England's political and social stability. Instead of edu-
cating himself for the burden of kingship, he had been
frittering away his time, and making himself cheap,
with low companions

> that daff the world aside
> And bid it pass.

In a word, a word that Shakespeare applies no less than
six times to his conduct, he is guilty of Vanity. And
Vanity, though not in the theological category of the
Seven Deadly Sins, was a cardinal iniquity in a young
prince or nobleman of the sixteenth and seventeenth
centuries; almost as heinous, in fact, as Idleness in an
apprentice.

I am not suggesting that this represents Shakespeare's
own view. Of Shakespeare's views upon the problems
of conduct, whether in prince or commoner, we are
in general ignorant, though he seems to hint in both
Henry IV and *Henry V* that the Prince of Wales learnt
some lessons at least from Falstaff and his crew, Francis
and his fellow-drawers, which stood him in good stead
when he came to rule the country and command troops
in the field. But it is the view that his father and his own
conscience take of his mistreadings; and, as the spectators would take it as well, we must regard it as the
thesis to which Shakespeare addressed himself.

When, however, he took audiences by storm in 1597
and 1598 with his double *Henry IV* he gave them something much more than a couple of semi-mythical figures
from the early fifteenth century, brought up to date
politically. He presented persons and situations at once
fresh and actual. Both Hal and Falstaff are denizens of
Elizabethan London. Hal thinks, acts, comports himself as an heir to the Queen might have done, had she

delighted her people by taking a consort and giving them a Prince of Wales; while Falstaff symbolizes, on the one hand, all the feasting and good cheer for which Eastcheap stood, and reflects, on the other, the shifts, subterfuges, and shady tricks that decayed gentlemen and soldiers were put to if they wished to keep afloat and gratify their appetites in the London underworld of the late sixteenth century. It is the former aspects of the old scoundrel that probably gave most pleasure to those who first saw him on the stage; and, as they are also those that we moderns are most likely to miss, I make no apology for devoting most of the rest of this chapter to an exposition of them.

SWEET BEEF

Riot invites Youth, it will be remembered, to drink wine at a tavern, and tavern scenes are common in other interludes, especially those of the Prodigal Son variety. But Shakespeare's tavern is more than a drink-shop, while his Riot is not only a 'huge bombard of sack' but also a 'roasted Manningtree ox with the pudding in his belly'.

The site of the Boar's Head tavern in Eastcheap is now as deep-sunk in the ooze of human forgetfulness as that of the palace of Haroun. But it was once a real hostelry, and must have meant much to Londoners of the reigns of Elizabeth and James. Records are scanty, but the very fact that Shakespeare makes it Falstaff's headquarters suggests that it was the best tavern in the city. And the further fact that he avoids mentioning it directly, though quibbling upon the name more than once, suggests, on the one hand, that he kept the name off the stage in order to escape complications with the proprietors of the day, and on the other that he could trust his audience to jump to so obvious an identification without prompting. In any event, no other tavern in

Eastcheap is at all likely to have been intended, and as Eastcheap is referred to six times in various scenes, there can be little real doubt that what Falstaff once calls 'the king's tavern' is the famous Boar's Head, the earliest known reference to which occurs in a will dating from the reign of Richard II.[1] Whether there is anything or not in Skeat's conjecture that the Glutton in *Piers Plowman* made it the scene of his exploits like Falstaff, it was a well-known house of entertainment more than two hundred years before Shakespeare introduced it into his play, and had come therefore by his day to be regarded as a historic hostelry, for which reason it was probably already associated in popular imagination with the floating legends of the wild young prince. What, however, seems to have escaped the attention of modern writers is that the house, with a name that symbolized good living and good fellowship above that of any other London tavern, was almost certainly even better known for good food than for good drink.

Eastcheap, there is plenty of evidence to show, was then, and had long been, the London centre at once of butchers and cook-shops. Lydgate, writing in the reign of Henry V, puts the following words in the mouth of his *London Lyckpenny*:

> Then I hyed me into Estchepe;
>   One cryes 'rybbes of befe and many a pye';
> Pewter pots they clattered on a heap;
>   There was a harp, pype, and minstrelsy.

The street was famed, in short, not only for meat and drink, but also for the 'noise' of musicians, which belonged to 'the old Tauerne in Eastcheap' in *The Famous Victories*, and which 'Mistress Tearsheet would fain hear' in Part II of *Henry IV*. As for 'rybbes of

---

[1] See 'East Cheap' in Sugden's *Topographical Dictionary to the Works of Shakespeare*.

befe', though we never see or hear of Falstaff eating, or desiring to eat, anything except Goodwife Keech's dish of prawns and the capon, anchovies, and halfpenny worth of bread recorded with 'an intolerable deal of sack' in the bill found upon him while asleep, Shakespeare none the less contrives to associate him perpetually with appetizing food by means of the imagery that plays about his person. For the epithets and comparisons which Hal and Poins apply to him, or he himself makes use of, though at times connected with his consumption of sack, are far more often intended to recall the chief stock-in-trade of the victuallers and butchers of Eastcheap, namely meat of all kinds, and meat both raw and roast.

Falstaff is once likened to a 'huge bombard', once to a 'hogshead', once to a 'tun', and twice to a 'hulk', that is, to a cargo-boat; the nature of the cargo being specified by Doll, who protests to Mistress Quickly, 'There's a whole merchant's venture of Bourdeaux stuff in him, you have not seen a hulk better stuffed in the hold'. But beyond these there is little or nothing about him in the vintner's line. When, on the other hand, Shakespeare promises the audience, through the mouth of his Epilogue in Part II, to continue the story, with Sir John in it, 'if you be not too much cloyed with fat meat', the phrase sums up the prevailing image, constant in reference though . ever-varying in form, which the physical characteristics of Falstaff presented to his mind's eye, and which he in turn was at pains to keep before the mind's eye of his public. Changes in London, and even more, changes in the language, have obliterated all this for the modern reader, so that what was intended, from the first, as little more than a kind of shimmering half-apprehended jest playing upon the surface of the dialogue, must now be recovered as a piece of archaeology, that is, as something long dead.

The laughter has gone out of it; yet I shall be disappointed if the reader does not catch himself smiling now and again at what follows.

'Call in Ribs, call in Tallow' is Hal's cue for Falstaff's entry in the first great Boar's Head scene; and what summons to the choicest feast in comedy could be more apt? For there is the noblest of English dishes straightaway: Sir John as roast Sir Loin-of-Beef, gravy and all. 'Tallow', a word often applied to him, generally in opprobrium, is not rightly understood, unless two facts be recalled: first, that it meant to the Elizabethans liquid fat, as well as dripping or suet or animal fat rendered down; second, that human sweat, partly owing perhaps to the similarity of the word to 'suet', was likewise thought of as fat, melted by the heat of the body. The most vivid presentation of Falstaff served up hot, so to say, is the picture we get of him sweating with fright in Mistress Page's dirty linen basket, as it was emptied by her servants into the Thames; and though *The Merry Wives* does not strictly belong to the Falstaff canon, the passage may be quoted here, as giving the clue to passages in *Henry IV* itself. For however different in character the Windsor Falstaff may be from his namesake of Eastcheap, he possesses the same body, the body that on Gad's Hill 'sweats to death, and *lards* the lean earth, as he walks along'.

'And then', he relates to the disguised Ford,

to be stopped in, like a strong distillation, with stinking clothes that fretted in their own grease! Think of that, a man of my kidney! think of that—that am as subject to heat, as butter; a man of continual dissolution and thaw; it was a miracle to 'scape suffocation. And in the height of this bath, when I was more than half stewed in grease, like a Dutch dish, to be thrown into the Thames, and cooled, glowing-hot, in that surge, like a horse-shoe. Think of that—hissing hot: think of that, Master Brook!

The 'greasy tallow-catch', again, to which the Prince compares him, much to the bewilderment of commentators, betokens, I believe, nothing more mysterious than a dripping-pan to catch the fat as the roasting joint turned upon the spit before the fire. Or take the following scrap of dialogue:

> *L. Chief Justice.* What, you are as a candle, the better part burnt out.
>
> *Falstaff.* A wassail candle, my lord, all tallow—if I did say of wax, my growth would approve the truth.
>
> *L. Chief Justice.* There is not a white hair on your face, but should have his effect of gravity.
>
> *Falstaff.* His effect of gravy, gravy, gravy.

Falstaff's repeated 'gravy' is a quibble, of course. But it is not just a feeble jest upon his table manners, as seems to be usually assumed: it follows upon the mention of 'tallow' and refers to the drops of sweat that never cease to stand upon his face. In fact, to use a seventeenth-century expression, applicable to one bathed in perspiration, he may be said perpetually to 'stew in his own gravy'.

Indeed, he glories in the fact. Was it not, according to the physiological notions of the time, the very warrant of his enormous vitality? Never is he more angered to the heart than when the Prince likens him one day to a dry withered old apple-john. His complexion is merely sanguine; heat and moisture mingle to form the element he moves in; except in moods of mock-repentance he leaves to baser earth the cold and dry of melancholy.

Once we have the trick of it, all sorts of other allusions and playful terms of abuse are seen to belong to the same category, while the analogy between that vast carcass, as a whole or in its parts, and roasts of various kinds is capable of almost infinite elaboration. 'Chops', for instance, as he is twice called, carries the double significance of 'fat cheeks' and 'cutlets'; 'guts', the

Elizabethan word for 'tripe', is an epithet that occurs no less than five times; and 'sweet beef' as a term of endearment requires no explaining. Nor is he only served up as beef; pork, still more appropriate to the Boar's Head, though brought in less often, provides some magnificent examples. The term 'brawn', which means a large pig fattened for the slaughter, is applied to him on two occasions; on his return from Wales the Prince, inquiring of Bardolph, 'Is your master here in London? . . . Where sups he? doth the old boar feed in the old frank?' refers to the familiar inn-sign; Falstaff himself declares that he walks the streets followed by the diminutive page 'like a sow that hath overwhelmed all her litter but one'; last, and best of all, when Doll salutes him between her 'flattering busses' as her 'whoreson little tidy Bartholomew boar-pig', she is alluding to the tender sweet-fleshed little sucking-pigs which formed the chief delicacy at Bartholomew Fair.

The mention of Bartholomew Fair, the most popular annual festivity of Elizabethan and Jacobean London, may be linked with two other comparisons, which take us beyond the confines of Eastcheap and help to bestow on Falstaff that 'touch of infinity' which Bradley discovers in him, associating him, as they do, with feasting on a vast and communal scale. The first, already quoted above, is the Prince's description of him as a 'Manningtree ox with the pudding in his belly', in other words, as an ox roasted whole and stuffed with sausages, after the fashion of the annual fairs at Manningtree, an Essex town famed for the exceeding fatness of its beasts. But the extremest inch of possibility is reached by Poins when he asks Bardolph 'How doth the Martlemas, your master?' Martlemas, or the feast of St. Martin, on 11 November, was in those days of scarce fodder the season at which most of the beasts had to be killed off

and salted for the winter, and therefore the season for
great banquets of fresh meat. Thus it had been for
centuries, long before the coming of Christianity, and
thus it remained down to the introduction of the crop-
ping of turnips in the eighteenth century. In calling
him a 'Martlemas' Poins is at once likening Falstaff's
enormous proportions to the prodigality of fresh-killed
meat which the feast brought, and acclaiming his
identity with Riot and Festivity in general.[1] But perhaps the best comment upon Falstaff as Martlemas
comes from Spenser's procession of the seasons in the
Book of Mutabilitie. His November might almost be
Falstaff himself, though the dates prove that the two
figures must be independent:

> Next was Nouember, he full grosse and fat,
> As fed with lard, and that right well might seeme;
> For, he had been a fatting hogs of late,
> That yet his browes with sweat did reek and steem,
> And yet the season was full sharp and breem.

One might go to the other end of the scale and point
out that the objects Falstaff chooses as a contrast to his
person, objects excessively thin, wizened, or meagre,
are likewise often taken from the food-shops. There is,
for instance, the shotten herring, the soused gurnet,
the bunch of radish, the rabbit-sucker or poulter's hare,
and wittiest of all perhaps, the carbonado—the rasher
of bacon, we should say—which he will only allow
Hotspur to make of him, if he is foolish enough to come
in his way. But enough to have shown that by plying
his audience with suggestions of the choicest food that
London and Eastcheap had to offer, whenever the person of Falstaff is mentioned, Shakespeare lays as it were
the physical foundations of his Falstaff myth.

The prodigiously incarnate Riot, who fills the Boar's

[1] I owe this point to the late Lord Ernle: *Shakespeare's England*, i. 356.

Head with his jollity, typifies much more, of course, than the pleasures of the table. He stands for a whole globe of happy continents, and his laughter is 'broad as ten thousand beeves at pasture'.[1] But he is Feasting first, and his creator never allows us to forget it. For in this way he not only perpetually associates him in our minds with appetizing images, but contrives that as we laugh at his wit our souls shall be satisfied as with marrow and fatness. No one has given finer expression to this satisfaction than Hazlitt, and I may fitly round off the topic with words of his:

Falstaff's wit is an emanation of a fine constitution; an exuberance of good-humour and good-nature; an overflowing of his love of laughter and good-fellowship; a giving vent to his heart's ease, and over-contentment with himself and others. He would not be in character, if he were not so fat as he is; for there is the greatest keeping in the boundless luxury of his imagination and the pampered self-indulgence of his physical appetites. He manures and nourishes his mind with jests, as he does his body with sack and sugar. He carves out his jokes, as he would a capon or a haunch of venison, where there is *cut and come again*; and pours out upon them the oil of gladness. His tongue drops fatness, and in the chambers of his brain 'it snows of meat and drink'. He keeps perpetually holiday and open house, and we live with him in a round of invitations to a rump and dozen. . . . He never fails to enrich his discourse with allusions to eating and drinking, but we never see him at table. He carries his own larder about with him, and is himself 'a tun of man'.

MONSIEUR REMORSE

Like all great Shakespearian characters Falstaff is a bundle of contradictions. He is not only Riot but also Repentance. He can turn an eye of melancholy upon us, assume the role of puritan sanctimony, and when it pleases him, even threaten amendment of life. It is,

[1] George Meredith, *The Spirit of Shakespeare.*

of course, *mock*-repentance, carried through as part of the untiring 'play extempore' with which he keeps the Prince, and us, and himself, entertained from beginning to end of the drama. And yet it is not mere game; Shakespeare makes it more interesting by persuading us that there is a strain of sincerity in it; and it almost completely disappears in Part II, when the rogue finds himself swimming on the tide of success. There is a good deal of it in Part I, especially in the earliest Falstaff scenes.

But, Hal, I prithee, trouble me no more with vanity. I would to God thou and I knew where a commodity of good names were to be bought.

Thou hast done much harm upon me, Hal—God forgive thee for it: before I knew thee, Hal, I knew nothing, and now am I, if a man should speak truly, little better than one of the wicked: I must give over this life, and I will give it over: by the Lord, an I do not, I am a villain. I'll be damned for never a king's son in Christendom.

One of his favourite poses is that of the innocent, beguiled by a wicked young heir apparent; he even makes it the burden of his apologia to the Lord Chief Justice at their first encounter. It serves too when things go wrong, when resolute men who have taken £1,000 on Gad's Hill are left in the lurch by cowardly friends, or when there's lime in a cup of sack:

There is nothing but roguery to be found in villainous man, yet a coward is worse than a cup of sack with lime in it. A villainous coward! Go thy ways, old Jack, die when thou wilt, if manhood, good manhood, be not forgot upon the face of the earth, then am I a shotten herring. . . . There lives not three good men unhanged in England, and one of them is fat, and grows old. God help the while! a bad world, I say. I would I were a weaver—I could sing psalms or anything.

But beside this talk of escaping from a wicked world and the toils of a naughty young prince, there is also the pose of personal repentance. At his first entry Poins hails him as Monsieur Remorse, an indication that this is one of his recognized roles among Corinthians and lads of mettle. And we may see him playing it at the opening of Act III, Scene 3, when there is no Hal present to require entertaining.

Well, I'll repent, and that suddenly, while I am in some liking. I shall be out of heart shortly, and then I shall have no strength to repent. An I have not forgotten what the inside of a church is made of, I am a peppercorn, a brewer's horse. The inside of a church! Company, villainous company, hath been the spoil of me.

Such passages, together with the habit of citing Scripture, may have their origin, I have said, in the puritan, psalm-singing, temper of Falstaff's prototype—that comic Lollard, Sir John Oldcastle in the old *Henry IV*. But, if so, the motif, adapted and developed in Shakespeare's hands, has come to serve a different end. In this play of the Prodigal Prince it is Hal who should rightly exhibit moods of repentance; and on the face of it, it seems quite illogical to transfer them to Falstaff, the tempter. Yet there are reasons why Hal could not be thus represented. In the first place, as already noted, repentance in the theological sense, repentance for sin, is not relevant to his case at all, which is rather one of a falling away from political virtues, from the duties laid upon him by his royal vocation. And in the second place, since Henry V is the ideal king of English history, Shakespeare must take great care, even in the days of his 'wildness', to guard him from the breath of scandal. As has been well observed by a recent editor: 'His riots are mere frolics. He does not get drunk and is never involved in any scandal with a woman.'[1] And there is a third reason, this time one of dramatic tech-

---

[1] See p. xi of *1 Henry IV*, ed. by G. L. Kittredge.

nique not of morals, why the repentance of the Prince must be kept in the background as much as possible, viz. that as the only satisfactory means of rounding off the two parts, it belongs especially to the last act of the play.

Yet Monsieur Remorse is a good puppet in the property-box of the old morality, and may be given excellent motions in the fingers of a skilful showman, who is laying himself out, in this play especially, to make fun of the old types. Why not shape a comic part out of it, and hand it over to Falstaff, who as the heir of traditional medieval 'antics' like the Devil, the Vice, the Fool, Riot and Lord of Misrule, may very well manage one more? Whether or not Shakespeare argued it out thus, he certainly added the ingredient of melancholy, and by so doing gave a piquancy to the sauce which immensely enhances the relish of the whole dish. If only modern actors who attempt to impersonate Falstaff would realize it!

Falstaff, then, came to stand for the repentance, as well as the riotous living, of the Prodigal Son. And striking references to the parable, four of them, seem to show that his creator was fully aware of what he was doing. 'What, will you make a younker of me? shall I not take mine ease in mine inn but I shall have my pocket picked?' Sir John indignantly demands of Mistress Quickly, on discovering, or pretending to discover, the loss of his grandfather's seal-ring. The word 'younker' calls up a scene from some well-known representation of the parable, in picture or on the stage, a scene to which Shakespeare had already alluded in the following lines from *The Merchant of Venice*:

> How like a younker or a prodigal
> The scarféd bark puts from her native bay,
> Hugged and embracéd by the strumpet wind!
> How like a prodigal doth she return,

With over-weathered ribs and ragged sails,
Lean, rent, and beggared by the strumpet wind!

Equally vivid is Falstaff's description of the charge
of foot he led into battle at Shrewsbury as so 'dishonourable ragged' that 'you would think that I had a
hundred and fifty tattered prodigals, lately come from
swine-keeping, from eating draff and husks'. And seeing
that he calls them in the same speech 'slaves as ragged
as Lazarus in the painted cloth, where the Glutton's
dogs licked his sores', we may suppose that, here too,
he is speaking right painted cloth, from whence he had
studied his Bible;[1] an inference which seems borne out
by his third reference, this time from Part II. Having,
you will remember, already honoured Mistress Quickly
by becoming indebted to her for a hundred marks, that
is for over £65, he graciously condescends to borrow
£10 more from her. And when she protests that to raise
the sum she must be fain to pawn both her plate and
the tapestry of her dining-chambers, he replies: 'Glasses,
glasses, is the only drinking—and for thy walls, a pretty
drollery or the story of the Prodigal or the German
hunting in waterwork is worth a thousand of these bed-
hangers and these fly-bitten tapestries.' This is not just
the patter of the confidence-trickster; Falstaff, we must
believe, had a real liking for the Prodigal Son story, or
why should that tactful person, mine Host of the Garter
Inn, have gone to the trouble of having it painted, 'fresh
and new', about the walls of the chamber that he let to
the greasy philanderer who assumed the part of Sir
John, in Windsor? Not being a modern critic, the good
man could not know that his guest was an impostor.

But jollification and mock-repentance do not exhaust
Falstaff's roles. For most of *Henry IV* he plays the
soldier, taking a hand in a couple of campaigns, the

---

[1] Cf. *As You Like It*, III. ii. 271: 'I answer you right painted cloth, from
whence you have studied your questions.'

first culminating in the death of Hotspur at Shrewsbury, and the other in the encounter between Prince John and the Archbishop of York at Gaultree Forest, where the rebels are finally overthrown. In both of these he performs the useful dramatic function of supplying the light relief, and in so doing he exhibits himself as at once the supreme comic soldier of English literature and a variation of a time-worn theme, the *miles gloriosus* of Plautus.

E. M. W. TILLYARD

(1889–1962)

The First Tetralogy[1]

TEN plays of the First Folio have English history as their theme. They are distributed in a curious regularity. First there is a sequence of four closely linked plays: the three parts of *Henry VI* and *Richard III*. There follows an isolated play, *King John*. Then comes a second sequence of four: *Richard II*, the two parts of *Henry IV*, and *Henry V*. And there is a second isolated play, *Henry VIII*. Disregarding the two isolated plays, we can say further that the two tetralogies make a single unit. Throughout the *Henry VI's* and *Richard III* Shakespeare links the present happenings with the past. We are never allowed to forget that, as Hall said in his preface, 'King Henry the Fourth was the beginning and root of the great discord and division'. For instance, in *1 Henry VI* the dying Mortimer says to his nephew, the future Duke of York:

> Henry the Fourth, grandfather to this king,
> Depos'd his nephew Richard, Edward's son,
> The first-begotten and the lawful heir
> Of Edward King, the third of that descent;
> During whose reign the Percies of the north,
> Finding his usurpation most unjust,
> Endeavour'd my advancement to the throne.

In *2 Henry VI* York, explaining his titles to Salisbury and Warwick, goes back to Edward III and his sons to the lucky number of seven, whom he solemnly enumerates, and fixes the mainspring of subsequent English history in the murder of Richard II:

[1] *Shakespeare's History Plays* (1944).

Edward the Black Prince died before his father
And left behind him Richard, his only son:
Who after Edward the Third's death reign'd as king,
Till Henry Bolingbroke, Duke of Lancaster,
The eldest son and heir of John of Gaunt,
Crown'd by the name of Henry the Fourth,
Seiz'd on the realm, depos'd the rightful king,
Sent his poor queen to France, from whence she came,
And him to Pomfret; where, as all you know,
Harmless Richard was murder'd traiterously.

In *Richard III* Earl Rivers, awaiting execution in Pomfret Castle, links present with past by recalling the murder of Richard II:

O Pomfret, Pomfret, O thou bloody prison,
Fatal and ominous to noble peers!
Within the guilty closure of thy walls
Richard the Second here was hack'd to death.
And for more slander of thy dismal seat
We give thee up our guiltless blood to drink.

These are precisely the themes which Shakespeare repeated when he makes Henry V before Agincourt pray to God,

Not to-day, O Lord,
O not to-day, think not upon the fault
My father made in compassing the crown.
I Richard's body have interred new,
And on it have bestow'd more contrite tears
Than from it issued forced drops of blood.

Further, Shakespeare seems himself to declare the continuity of the two tetralogies when the Chorus at the end of *Henry V* makes a link with the next reign and refers back to the earlier written sequence.

Henry the Sixth, in infant bands crown'd king
Of France and England, did this king succeed;
Whose state so many had the managing,
That they lost France and made his England bleed:

> Which oft our stage hath shown; and for their sake
> In your fair minds let this acceptance take.

The last line and a half mean: let the good success of my plays about *Henry VI* influence you in favour of the play you have just witnessed, *Henry V*. Shakespeare not only implies the continuity of the two tetralogies but expresses satisfaction with the one he had written in his youth. That he should, as it were, accept responsibility for all eight plays at the end of the last written one is important because it helps to confirm what even without this confirmation should be evident: that Shakespeare had in his early years disposed what for the Elizabethans was the most exciting and significant stretch of English history into a pattern; a pattern of such magnitude that it needed the space of eight plays and about ten years in the execution. The outlines of the pattern he derived from Hall, but the sustained energy of mind needed to develop them he got from his own ambitions and the example of other works, particularly of the *Mirror for Magistrates*.

There is no need to give details of Shakespeare's debt to Hall, as these can be found in articles by Edleen Begg and W. Gordon Zeeveld. But it is likely that Shakespeare got the hint of organizing Hall's material into two tetralogies by taking for his culminating points the two reigns to which Hall had stuck specifically dramatic labels (the *Victorious acts of Henry V* and the *Tragical doings of Richard III*) and which he had treated in a heightened way exceptional to the rest of his chronicle. Shakespeare can end with the reign of Richard III because Richard's death both resolves the plot and fulfils the title of Hall's history: *The Union of the two noble and illustre Families of Lancaster and York.*

Why Shakespeare wrote the second half first we can only guess. Perhaps, like others, he thought that vice was easier to picture than virtue, hell than paradise, and that it would be safer to spend his present energies on pictures of chaos and a great villain, leaving the more difficult picture of princely perfection to his maturity. But there is a very different explanation of what is after all a curious procedure. That it is hazardous and revolutionary should not preclude its being seriously considered. In the nature of things so fluent an author as Shakespeare probably wrote in his youth much that has perished. He may well have written early versions of the plays of the second tetralogy, *Richard II*, *Henry IV*, and *Henry V*, now lost but recast in the plays we have. Further, the *Famous Victories of Henry V* may well be an abridgement—a kind of dramatic Lamb's Tale—of Shakespeare's early plays on the reigns of Henry IV and Henry V. With the first version of the plays dealing with history from Henry VI onwards Shakespeare would have been sufficiently content to forbear revision. And he is not ashamed to refer to them in his epilogue to *Henry V*.

Shakespeare's first debt then in his earlier tetralogy is to Hall; but this must not cause us to overlook the many different strains Shakespeare here unites. It is indeed this masterly inclusiveness that raises to greatness a series of plays which in the execution are sometimes immature and ineffective. I will recapitulate these strains and illustrate them from the actual plays.

First, this tetralogy to an equal extent with the later tetralogy and more powerfully than the most civilized of the Chronicle Plays shows Shakespeare aware of order or degree. Behind all the confusion of civil war, and the more precious and emphatic because of the confusion, is the belief that the world is a part of the eternal law and that earthly mutability, as in Spenser's last cantos, is itself a part of a greater and permanent pattern. Further, human events as well as being subject to the eternal law are part of an elaborate system of

correspondences and hence the more firmly woven into
the total web of things. The very first words of the first
of the four plays will illustrate. They are spoken by the
Duke of Bedford at the funeral procession of his brother
Henry V.

> Hung be the heavens with black, yield day to night,
> Comets, importing change of times and states,
> Brandish your crystal tresses in the sky
> And with them scourge the bad revolting stars
> That have consented unto Henry's death!

Here the stars that have 'consented unto', which means
'conspired to procure', the death of Henry are intended
to be the counterpart in the heavens of the English
nobility who have already fallen into discord. The universe, in fact, was so much of a unity that the skies had
to re-enact the things that happened in the human
polity. It is the same correspondence that occurs in the
speech on 'degree' in *Troilus and Cressida*.

> But when the planets
> In evil mixture to disorder wander,
> What plagues and what portents, what mutiny,
> What raging of the sea, shaking of earth,
> Commotion in the winds, frights changes horrors,
> Divert and crack, rend and deracinate
> The unity and married calm of states
> Quite from their fixure!

In *Troilus and Cressida* Ulysses is maintaining the need
for degree, and in *Henry VI* Bedford assumes as the
righteous norm his brother Henry V, the strong up-
holder of order in his own kingdom.

The same play, though like the rest mainly occupied
with revolt and disorder and misfortune, finds place
for a positive example of the virtue of degree. It is
where Henry VI, now in Paris for his coronation,
accepts the homage of Talbot and rewards him with an
earldom.

Tal. My gracious prince and honourable peers,
  Hearing of your arrival in this realm,
  I have awhile given truce unto my wars,
  To do my duty to my sovereign:
  In sign whereof this arm, that hath reclaim'd
  To your obedience fifty fortresses,
  Twelve cities and seven wall'd towns of strength,
  Besides five hundred prisoners of esteem,
  Lets fall his sword before your highness' feet,
  And with submissive loyalty of heart
  Ascribes the glory of his conquest got
  First to my God and then unto your grace.
Hen. Welcome, brave captain and victorious lord!
  When I was young, as yet I am not old,
  I do remember how my father said
  A stouter champion never handled sword.
  Long since we were resolved of your truth,
  Your faithful service and your toil in war;
  Yet never have you tasted our reward
  Or been reguerdon'd with so much as thanks,
  Because till now we never saw your face.
  Therefore, stand up, and for these good deserts
  We here create you Earl of Shrewsbury;
  And in our coronation take your place.

Any Elizabethan would have perceived that the scene
was a deliberate setting up of an ideal norm. Every
detail suggests an exact and orderly disposition. God,
the king, the peers, the captives are ranged in their
degrees. Talbot, the last created earl, will take his
proper place in the coronation. The very numbers of
the things or persons captured suggest precise significances. Henry, in contrast to his usual practice, does
exactly the right thing; and, in violent contrast to the
facts of history (for he was only nine months old when
Henry V died), is momentarily animated by the judgements of the perfect king, his father.

But the most effective statement of the principle of
order occurs in the passage which largely by accident

is the most famous of all three Henry VI plays, Henry's pathetic soliloquy where he regrets that he was born a king and not a shepherd.

> O God! methinks it were a happy life
> To be no better than a homely swain;
> To sit upon a hill, as I do now,
> To carve out dials quaintly, point by point,
> Thereby to see the minutes how they run,
> How many make the hour full complete;
> How many hours bring about the day;
> How many days will finish up the year;
> How many years a mortal man may live.
> When this is known, then to divide the times:
> So many hours must I tend my flock;
> So many hours must I take my rest;
> So many hours must I contemplate;
> So many hours must I sport myself;
> So many days my ewes have been with young;
> So many weeks ere the poor fools will ean;
> So many years ere I shall shear the fleece:
> So minutes hours days months and years,
> Pass'd over to the end they were created,
> Would bring white hairs unto a quiet grave.
> Ah, what a life were this, how sweet, how lovely!

It is a beautiful passage, justly famous. But it is famous partly because it is so easily anthologized and partly because it is almost omitted from the *True Tragedy of Richard Duke of York*, once thought to be the play on which Shakespeare founded the third part of *Henry VI* and now proved to be a pirated version of it. The passage thus appeared to be a clear addition to the old play, hence genuine Shakespeare, hence to be read without embarrassment. Actually its full meaning, its full pathos and irony, are quite hidden when it is taken as a mere Shakespearian afterthought, fit for a volume of beauties. The context is the Battle of Towton, where the Lancastrians suffered their bloodiest defeat and which

Shakespeare selects from all the battles as most emphatically illustrating the full horrors of civil war. Henry has been 'chidden from the field' by his terrible queen and the fierce Clifford, because he brings bad luck; but immediately after his soliloquy he witnesses two spectacles of the utmost horror, first a son discovering that he has killed his father and then a father discovering that he has killed his son. Henry's speech must be judged before this background of chaos. It signifies not, as naturally thought of out of its context, a little bit of lyrical escapism but Henry's yearning for an ordered life. This ordered life of the shepherd is a pitifully small thing compared with the majestic order he as a king should have been able to impose. Yet it stands for the great principle of degree, while bringing out Henry's personal tragedy: his admirable intentions and his utter inability to carry them out.

Another most explicit version of the same thing is the contrast between the lawlessness of Jack Cade and the impeccable moderation and discipline of the Kentish squire Iden, in 2 *Henry VI*. Cade openly boasts, 'But then we are in order when we are most out of order.' All degree is to be levelled away:

> There shall be in England seven halfpenny loaves sold for a penny; the three-hooped pot shall have ten hoops; and I will make it a felony to drink small beer: all the realm shall be in common; and in Cheapside shall my palfry go to grass . . . there shall be no money; all shall eat and drink on my score; and I will apparel them all in one livery that they may agree like brothers and worship me their lord.

Iden, who catches the fugitive Jack Cade in his garden and kills him, is a flat symbolic character, beautifully contrasted with the realism of the rebels. He is entirely content with his own station in the social hierarchy, as smug as any eighteenth-century moralist over the virtues of the middle station of life. He introduces himself to us by this soliloquy in his garden:

> Lord, who would live turmoiled in the court,
> Who may enjoy such quiet walks as these?
> This small inheritance my father left me
> Contenteth me, and worth a monarchy.
> I seek not to wax great by others' waning;
> Or gather wealth I care not, with what envy:
> Sufficeth that I have maintains my state
> And sends the poor well pleased from my gate.

This speech for all its smugness is perfectly serious in giving the norm of order, upset by Cade.

As powerful as the theme of order in the tetralogy is the continual insistence on cause and effect in the unfolding of history. Shakespeare adopts the whole teaching of Hall and of the *Mirror for Magistrates*. The passages about the death of Richard II quoted above serve to illustrate this just as well as to illustrate the conceptual continuity of the two tetralogies. But again and again, at any great happening, Shakespeare seeks to bring out the concatenation of events. Thus in *2 Henry VI* Gloucester, about to be murdered, sees his death the cause of great misery to the land and of ruin to his king. He says to Henry:

> I know their complot is to have my life,
> And if my death might make this island happy
> And prove the period of their tyranny,
> I would expend it with all willingness.
> But mine is made the prologue to their play;
> For thousands more, that yet suspect no peril,
> Will not conclude their plotted tragedy.

And, referring to his own services as Protector of the realm in Henry's minority, he adds:

> Ah, thus King Henry throws away his crutch
> Before his legs be firm to bear his body.

Thus is the shepherd beaten from thy side
And wolves are gnarling who shall gnaw thee first.
Ah, that my fear were false, ah, that it were!
For, good King Henry, thy decay I fear.

Again Margaret of Anjou is not merely a strong-minded and troublesome woman who prolongs the civil wars by her tenacity and fulfils the dramatic part of avenging fury; she has her precise place in the chain of events. Her marriage with Henry VI was from the first a disaster and brought to a head the troubles between Lancaster and York which otherwise would have lain quiet. Edward IV, in front of York, addresses these words to her about Henry's marriage:

And had he match'd according to his state,
He might have kept that glory to this day;
But when he took a beggar to his bed
And grac'd thy poor sire with his bridal day,
Even then that sunshine brew'd a shower for him,
That wash'd his father's fortunes forth of France
And heap'd sedition on his crown at home.
For what has broach'd this tumult but thy pride?
Hadst thou been meek, our title still had slept;
And we, in pity for the gentle king,
Had slipp'd our claim until another age.

Many examples, and there are a great many, would be tedious. It is enough to mention the most elaborate of all. The ghosts that terrify and comfort the sleeps of Richard and Richmond on the night before Bosworth are not just enemies or friends but a convergence of causes leading to the defeat of Richard and to the issue of England's fortunes into prosperity through the union of the red rose and the white.

Shakespeare is more interested in the chain of cause and effect than in the ideas that history repeats itself and hence that we may apply to the present the exemplary lessons of the past. But these motives are not absent. For instance when in *Richard III* Queen Margaret breaks in on Richard making trouble with Queen Elizabeth's kindred she calls down curses on her enemies to correspond with the troubles she has had herself, as if this repetition of history were a probability. Addressing herself to Elizabeth, wife of Edward IV, she says:

> Edward thy son, which now is Prince of Wales,
> For Edward my son, which was Prince of Wales
> Die in his youth by like untimely violence;
> Thyself a queen, for me that was a queen,
> Outlive thy glory like my wretched self;
> Long mayst thou live to wail thy children's loss,
> And see another, as I see thee now,
> Deck'd in thy rights, as thou art stall'd in mine!

And behind all the unfolding of civil war there is the great lesson (implied always and rarely stated) that the present time must take warning from the past and utterly renounce all civil dissension. Here, for instance, is Sir William Lucy's comment on York's refusal to help Talbot on account of his jealousy of Somerset:

> Thus while the vulture of sedition
> Feeds in the bosom of such great commanders,
> Sleeping neglection doth betray to loss
> The conquest of our scarce cold conqueror,
> That ever living man of memory,
> Henry the Fifth. Whiles they each other cross,
> Lives, honours, lands, and all hurry to loss.

There is a short scene (II. iii) in *Richard III*, the kind of scene that is omitted from modern performance because it does not advance the plot and apparently can be spared, which in a brief space epitomizes a number of Tudor commonplaces on history. It is a choric comment by three citizens on the death of Edward IV. The third citizen is a pessimist, who 'looks to see a troublous world' and quotes the adage,

> Woe to that land that's govern'd by a child!

The other two are more optimistic, and the first citizen hopes that history will repeat itself in making the early years of Edward V prosperous like those of Henry VI when his uncles Bedford and Gloucester 'enrich'd the land with politic grave counsel'. But the third citizen denies the analogy: Edward's uncles are not at all like Henry VI's. He fears the worst, but adds

> All may be well. But if God sort it so,
> 'Tis more than we deserve or I expect.

In other words, the troubles of a country are God's punishment for its sins. His mixed sentiments are prophetic: God both punished the land and caused all to be well through the Earl of Richmond. Shakespeare is perfectly clear in making Richmond the emissary of God.

It is in the last two plays of the tetralogy that the prevalent high theme of the *Mirror for Magistrates*, the fall of an eminent and erring statesman, is most evident. In the first two plays Talbot and Humphrey of Gloucester are too individual and too virtuous to fit into the norm of that poem. But in the third play the tragedy of Richard Duke of York is solemnly enacted, and in *Richard III* the motive of the *Mirror* occurs with great power. Clarence perishes for his false oath, and in the fate of Buckingham Shakespeare may actually allude to the most famous portions of the *Mirror*: the contributions of Sackville. At the beginning of the fourth scene of the fourth act Queen Margaret says:

> So, now prosperity begins to mellow
> And drop into the rotten mouth of death.
> Here in these confines slily have I lurk'd
> To watch the warring of mine adversaries.
> A dire induction am I witness to,
> And will to France, hoping the consequence
> Will prove as bitter, black, and tragical.

The use of the words *induction* and *tragical* may well

contain a hint of Sackville's *Induction* and his *Tragedy of Buckingham*; especially as Buckingham's fall is the theme of the next scene. And Buckingham confesses to his sin of treachery and to a false oath and admits the justice of his fate—

Wrong hath but wrong, and blame the due of blame—

in a spirit entirely in accord with the morality of the *Mirror for Magistrates*.

So much for Shakespeare's use in his tetralogy of the conceptions of world order and the processes of history: the ideas that appear so little in the Chronicle Plays and seem to have been the property of a select and educated class, that ally Shakespeare with Chapman and Daniel and Sir John Hayward. His use of them illustrates the academic side of himself that was so prominent in his early years. It is to his History Plays what the Plautine form is to the *Comedy of Errors* and the Senecan and Ovidian elements and conventions to *Titus Andronicus*.

But Shakespeare was not only academic in his first historical tetralogy: he was a popular dramatist too. Not that the populace would have objected to his superior opinions on history; they would have been willing to be impressed if they also got the things they expected: which they most certainly did. And first, for this popular material, there is what I have called sometimes Higden and sometimes Holinshed: the mediation of sheer fact. For though Shakespeare did see history in an intelligible pattern he compressed into a popular and lively form an astonishing quantity of sheer historical fact. He can indeed be nearly as informative as the author of the *True Tragedy of Richard III*, from which extracts were quoted above.[1] This, for instance, is how York begins the genealogical statement on which he claims his title to the throne in *2 Henry VI*:

[1 i.e. on p. 100 of *Shakespeare's History Plays*.]

Edward the Third, my lords, had seven sons:
The first, Edward the Black Prince, Prince of Wales;
The second, William of Hatfield, and the third,
Lionel Duke of Clarence; next to whom
Was John of Gaunt, the Duke of Lancaster;
The fifth was Edmund Langley, Duke of York;
The sixth was Thomas of Woodstock, Duke of Gloucester;
William of Windsor was the seventh and last.

There seems to have been a genuine popular demand for this sheer information. And beyond presenting this unmitigated fact Shakespeare succeeded conspicuously in making palatable to his public a greater bulk of chronicle material than other dramatists were able to do.

Shakespeare also satisfied the popular taste in setting forth the great popular political theme, the horror of civil war, and in giving his plays the required chauvinist tone. Joan of Arc is a bad enough woman, Margaret of Anjou an intriguing enough queen; an Englishman is worth a sufficient number of Frenchmen; Frenchmen are sufficiently boastful and fickle, to satisfy every popular requirement.

Finally, Shakespeare occasionally satisfies the taste for the startling but irrelevant anecdote; the pieces of sensation that pleased the people but could be spared from the play. There is for example the scene in *1 Henry VI* (II. iii) where the Countess of Auvergne plots Talbot's death by inviting him to her house and he prevents her by summoning his men by a blast from his horn; and the scene in *2 Henry VI* (I. iv) where Bolingbroke the conjurer calls up spirits at the command of the Duchess of Gloucester.

In sum Shakespeare in his first effort could beat the writers of Chronicle Plays on their own ground.

Among the strains found in Tudor history was that akin to Froissart and shown in the work of More and Cavendish: a dramatic liveliness and a closeness to the event. This strain appears in Shakespeare's first historical tetralogy; but how much he owed to Berners's Froissart and to the lives of Richard III and Wolsey, and how much to his own dramatic inclinations, it is impossible to assess. However, it matters little whence he got the strain, but much more that it should be there. It is, of course, precisely this strain that the disintegrators have been after whenever they have wished to fish out any fragments of true Shakespeare from the general wreckage; and they have found it, for instance, in the first declaration of the feud between red and white rose in *1 Henry VI* and in the Jack Cade scenes in *2 Henry VI*. There is nothing wrong in praising these scenes and calling them typical of Shakespeare. But it is very wrong indeed to emphasize them and to make them the norm by which to judge the whole tetralogy. They enrich the tetralogy but on a balance they are exceptional to it.

To redress this wrong emphasis we must think of yet another strain in this tetralogy: that of formalism and stylization. It is something archaic, inherited from the Morality Play. But it is the very feature through which the essential life of the poetry is expressed. When we encounter an unnatural and stylized balance of incident or an artificial pattern of speech we must not think that here is merely an archaic survival: we must accept them as things having contemporary vitality and must make them the norm of the play. We must in fact be good Aristotelians, for the moment, and believe that the soul of the play is in plot rather than in character. The realism of the Jack Cade scenes is not their main point but a subsidiary enrichment. Their main point is to make half a pattern, the other half being implied by the blameless orderliness of Iden. We are apt to praise the Cade scenes for being realistic and jeer at Iden for being a dummy, when we should merge praise and blame into the appreciation of a piece of stylization which includes the whole. Similarly Henry VI's pathetic piece of nostalgia as he sits on the molehill watching the Battle of Towton has been isolated into a piece of poetic and 'human' writing in a boring and inhuman context. Actually it loses most of its virtue apart from the context; apart from the terrible scene of the father killing his son and the son killing his father. That scene embodies a traditional motive; for these acts had been chosen by the authors of the Homilies, by Hall, and by the authors of the *Mirror for Magistrates* as the clearest symbol of the horrors of civil war. Shakespeare's fathers and sons here are as flat characters as Iden; and they have no business to be anything else. They stand as great traditional types, in whom realism would be impious. They enact a tableau; though they speak they are not far off a dumb-show: and their flatness adds enormous point to the ineffective humanity of the weak king. The most moving of all the scenes in the tetralogy, the ghosts visiting the sleeps of Richard III and Richmond in *Richard III*, is perhaps the most rigidly patterned and most grossly unrealistic of any. What could be remoter from actuality than the juxtaposition of the two tents and the liturgical chantings of each ghost as it passes? But to object to this scene on these grounds is as stupid as to blame the *Eumenides* of Aeschylus for being deficient in the realistic psychology of the *Electra* of Euripides. When this principle has been grasped and accepted the tetralogy comes out a much more assured and solid affair than it is generally thought to be.

But if the Morality Play prompted the formality of Shakespeare's first tetralogy it also supplied a single pervasive theme; one which overrides but in no way interferes with the theme he derived from Hall. In none of the plays is there a hero: and one of the reasons is that there is an unnamed protagonist dominating all

four. It is England, or in Morality terms Respublica.
Just as London, which appears only in the prologue,
is the hero of Wilson's *Three Lords and three Ladies of
London* (itself more a Morality Play than a developed
Elizabethan drama), so England, though she is now
quite excluded as a character, is the true hero of Shakespeare's first tetralogy. She is brought near ruin through
not being true to herself; yielding to French witchcraft
and being divided in mind. But God, though he punishes
her, pities her and in the end through his grace allows
the suppressed good in her to assert itself and restore
her to health. I reserve the details of this scheme till
the sections on the separate plays. How in the first three
plays of his second tetralogy Shakespeare developed
and enriched the Respublica theme will be described
in due course.

Finally, Shakespeare reinforces the structural unity
which the themes of the Morality and of Hall create,
by sowing in one play the seeds that are to germinate
in the next and by constant references back from a later
play to an earlier. In *1 Henry VI* he gives us modestly
but with sufficient emphasis the first clash of York and
Lancaster and the rivalry of Cardinal Beaufort with
the good Protector, Humphrey Duke of Gloucester,
which are to be a prevailing theme of the second play.
In *2 Henry VI* Margaret of Anjou is important, yet she
is kept subordinate to other characters in readiness to
develop into a major character in the third play. Again,
York begins faintly in the first play, gathers force in
the second, and is cut off in the third, while the ruthless-
ness and hypocrisy of Richard Crookback begin faintly
in the second play, grow big in the third, and over-
reach themselves to destruction in the last.

For all the inequality of execution, the vast crowding
in of historical incident (some of it inorganic), Shakespeare planned his first historical tetralogy greatly,

reminding one of Hardy in the *Dynasts*. When we consider how deficient his fellow-dramatists were in the
architectonic power, we can only conclude that this
was one of the things with which he was conspicuously
endowed by nature. Far from being the untidy genius,
Shakespeare was in one respect a born classicist.

F. P. WILSON

(1889–1963)

Shakespeare and the Diction of Common Life[1]

WE have heard much in recent years of the necessity
of making ourselves Shakespeare's contemporaries. We
shall understand him better, it is said, be in less danger
of misunderstanding him, if we know as much as we
can of the stage for which he wrote, of the actors who
performed his plays, of the audience which saw them
acted, of the psychological theories of the age, of its
economic, political, and social life, of its taste in rhetoric,
in language, and in criticism; in short, if we make ourselves good Elizabethans, if possible intelligent Elizabethans. I shall not quarrel with this ideal. It is one to
which every scholar aspires, and most of this paper is
taken up with some of the difficulties. But while it is
impossible to exaggerate the difficulties, it is sometimes
possible to exaggerate the results. It has been said that
nothing but a whole heart and a free mind are needed
to understand Shakespeare, and if we interpret this to
mean a robust heart and an acute and sensitive mind
that is true, and true in an important sense. How little
Keats knew of Shakespearian scholarship may be a
cooling card for the scholar's fancy. He read Shakespeare not in Malone's edition, but in plain texts without
commentary, yet he understood Shakespeare 'to his
depths'. If ever man made Shakespeare a part of his life,
that man was Keats. He is the great Shakespearian
humanist. And if we are ever tempted to forget, his
example is a perpetual reminder that while we strive to

[1] British Academy Shakespeare Lecture (1941).

make ourselves Shakespeare's contemporaries, it is even more important to make Shakespeare our contemporary, to keep him level with life and with our lives.

The title of this lecture was suggested by a man who believed in keeping literature level with life. In the Preface to his *Dictionary* Johnson observes:

From the authors which rose in the time of Elizabeth, a speech might be formed adequate to all the purposes of use and elegance. If the language of theology were extracted from Hooker and the translation of the Bible; the terms of natural knowledge from Bacon; the phrases of policy, war, and navigation from Raleigh; the dialect of poetry and fiction from Spenser and Sidney; and the diction of common life from Shakespeare, few ideas would be lost to mankind, for want of English words, in which they might be expressed.

Johnson does not say that a lexicographer could find in Shakespeare the diction of common life and nothing else. Shakespeare may have had 'small Latin and less Greek', but he had enough Latin to use English words from that language with confidence. 'With cadent tears fret channels in her cheeks', 'My operant powers their functions leave to do', 'The multitudinous seas incarnadine', these and many other lines contain words or senses of words not yet found earlier than Shakespeare. Within fifteen lines of a speech of Agamemnon's there are four such words.[1] But while he realized the value to his cadence and meaning of the learned word beside the familiar, he was never in danger of becoming an inkhornist. He may use the word 'remuneration' comically in *Love's Labour's Lost* and seriously in *Troilus and Cressida*, or 'festinately' comically in *Love's Labour's Lost* and 'festinate' seriously in *King Lear*, but at no time could the creator of Holofernes have admired the sixteenth-century poet who asked his mistress what

[1] *Troilus and Cressida*, I. iii. 7–21: conflux, tortive, protractive, persistive.

thing was 'equipollent to her formosity'.[1] And although he profits from them all, he cannot be attached to any one of the various schemes for enriching the English vocabulary recommended by sixteenth-century grammarians and rhetoricians—whether with inkhorn terms, outlandish terms, archaic words, or dialect. What a Greek writer said of Homer is very true of Spenser but is not in the least true of Shakespeare: 'he did not stop at his own generation, but went back to ancestors; had a word dropped out, he was sure to pick it up, like an old coin out of an unclaimed treasure-house, all for love of words; and again many barbarian terms, sparing no single word which seemed to have in it enjoyment or intensity.'[2] The conditions of Shakespeare's art as a dramatist did not permit him to stray far from popular idiom, but even if they had his mind was of a cast that would still have found the material upon which it worked mainly in the diction of common life. The best of the Sonnets are evidence of that and all the familiar images in his plays which, as his art matures, flow more and more freely from the less conscious levels of his mind. At the same time his instinct for what was permanent in the colloquial language of his day is stronger than that of any contemporary dramatist. No other Jacobean would have displayed 'a Rogue' with so little use of canting or 'pedlar's French' as does Shakespeare in Autolycus. In the words of Coleridge, his language is that which belongs 'to human nature as *human*, independent of associations and habits from any particular rank of life or mode of employment. . . . It is (to play on Dante's words) in truth the NOBILE *volgare eloquenza*.'[3]

His retentive mind received its stores from books,

---

[1] T. C., *A Pleasant and Delightful History of Galesus, Cymon, and Iphigenia* (1560?), sig. A6.

[2] Dion Chrysostom, translated by A. O. Prickard (*Longinus on the Sublime*, 1906, pp. 93–94).

[3] *Coleridge's Shakespearean Criticism*, ed. T. M. Raysor (1930), i. 149–50.

more still from speech and his own penny of observation. 'It is probable', wrote J. M. Synge, 'that when the Elizabethan dramatist took his inkhorn and sat down to his work he used many phrases that he had just heard, as he sat at dinner, from his mother or his children.'[1] Shakespeare may often have cried 'My tables—meet it is I set it down', as Shaw represents him doing in *The Dark Lady of the Sonnets*. When we find in earlier writers that as in *Love's Labour's Lost* a hat or veil comes over a face 'like a pent-house',[2] that as in *Hamlet* this world is 'a sea of troubles',[3] or even that a man's humour is 'tickle of the sear',[4] we may be in doubt whether these are phrases which Shakespeare had read or overheard, but we cannot doubt that in their boldness and concreteness they are characteristic of what he might have read or heard and of the climate in which his own image-making flourished. So, too, when Sir Thomas Egerton, Lord Keeper, urges the Parliament of 1597 to thank God 'upon the knees of our hearts',[5] we are not surprised at the bold extravagance of the metaphor. Egerton is not clipping the Queen's English: this was the current coinage of the realm. He and his contemporaries did not suffer from 'the Danger of thinking without Images'.[6]

We could not know what wealth Shakespeare had to draw upon or how much by his own invention he added to that wealth until the completion of the great *Oxford Dictionary*, and we shall know more fully if the University of Michigan publishes its Early Modern English Dictionary. Perhaps it is not much of an exaggeration to

[1] *Works* (1910), ii. 3–4.
[2] *Love's Labour's Lost*, III. i. 15, and L. Wager, *Mary Magdalene* (1566), l. 585.
[3] *Hamlet*, III. i. 59, and Sir R. Barckley, *Of the Felicity of Man* (1598), pp. 147, 275.
[4] *Hamlet*, II. ii. 321, and *O.E.D.*, s.v. sear, *sb.*[1] I b.
[5] Hayward Townshend, *Historical Collections* (1680), p. 80.
[6] *Unpublished Letters of S. T. Coleridge*, ed. E. L. Griggs (1932), i. 163.

F. P. WILSON

say that a mere recital of the number of ways in which
the Elizabethans could and did refer to their besetting
vice of drunkenness would take up the greater part of
this hour. Their dictionaries, especially Florio's and
Cotgrave's, give us some indication of the wealth of
synonym and of the delight these lexicographers took in
assembling it. They practised 'copy' (*copia verborum*)
even in their dictionaries. Florio calls his second edition
'A New World of Words': it is his voyage of discovery
into the land of diction. Watch him exploring the possibilities of two Italian words. Under *tinca*: 'a fish called
a Tench. Used also for a fresh-water soldier, or unexpert
Captain that will have thirty men with him be it but to
dig up a Turnip'; and under *squassapennacchio*: 'a tisty-
tosty, a wag-feather, a toss-plume, a swashbuckler'.
Shakespeare does not use one of these four words, yet
every one is rounded to an actor's palate, every one a
moving picture.

Unlike J. M. Synge, Shakespeare needed no 'chink
in the floor' to enable him to overhear what was being
said in the country-kitchen; he was free of it by birth;
but he eavesdropped in the City and at Court and found
there talk as fully flavoured. Landor has said that the
best language in all countries is that which is spoken by
intelligent women, of too high rank for petty affectation,
and of too much request in society for deep study.[1]
That is the language of Rosaline, of Beatrice, of Rosalind. If Shakespeare ever had a weakness for court
affectations, he worked it out of his system in *Love's
Labour's Lost*. We hear much of these affectations of
speech in Elizabethan literature, of 'Arcadian and Eu-
phuized gentlewomen', but as we should expect there
were few affectations in the speech of those who were
closest to the Queen. In *Cynthia's Revels* it is not Crites

[1] *Imaginary Conversations*, 'Samuel Johnson and John Horne Tooke'
(*Works*, ed. T. Earle Welby, 1927, v. 5).

or Arete who drink of the fountain of self-love; and it is not Cynthia. However picked and patterned may be the language of Elizabeth's formal writings, there was no trace of affectation in her private speech or public utterances. Her very oaths identified her with all classes of her people except those who swore by 'yea and nay' or 'indeed la'. In a pious and spirited book which formed half the dowry of Bunyan's wife, Arthur Dent wrote of men who swore less vigorously than his Queen that 'Hell gapeth for them';[1] but fortunately for him his Plain Man's Pathway did not lead him into the Presence. And when she spoke to her people, then, as her great scholar Camden would have wished, she did not follow 'the minion refiners of English'; she spoke not State English, not Court English, not Secretary English, but plain English.[2]

Though God hath raised me high; yet this I count the glory of my Crown, That I have reigned with your loves. This makes me that I do not so much rejoice, That God hath made me to be a Queen, as, To be a Queen over so thankful a People. . . . There will never Queen sit in my seat, with more zeal to my Country, care for my Subjects; and that sooner with willingness will venture her life for your good and safety, than my self. For it is not my desire to live nor reign longer, than my life and reign shall be for your good. And though you have had, and may have, many Princes, more mighty and wise, sitting in this State; yet you never had, or shall have, any that will be more careful and loving.[3]

As we read these strong and straightforward sentences we may flatter ourselves that we can read Elizabeth and Shakespeare as good Elizabethans, yet apart altogether from changes in pronunciation the words cannot mean to us what they meant to contemporaries. The words we most value rise from a well of associations fed by a thousand memories, and we cannot rid

[1] *The Plain Man's Pathway to Heaven* (1601), p. 165.
[2] *Remains* (1605), p. 28.   [3] Townshend, p. 263.

ourselves of these associations. But we can make an approximation, and in making it the greatest difficulty does not come from obsolete expressions and obscure allusions. When we meet with 'miching mallecho' either we look up a commentary or we pass on. There is a possibility of ignorance here, but not of misunderstanding, unless indeed the commentators mislead us. Nor in some contexts is the danger very great from words which have survived into modern English with very different meanings. Only a very stupid reader would misunderstand when it is said that in the Scotland of Macbeth 'violent sorrow seems A modern ecstasy'. The real danger comes with words to which it is possible to attach the modern meaning and make a sense. But the sense is not Shakespeare's. Sometimes the difference is so slight that the modern meaning does little or no harm. It matters little, to take an example of Henry Bradley's,[1] whether we understand Polonius's 'Still harping on my daughter' to mean 'Now as heretofore harping on my daughter' or, as Shakespeare meant, 'Always harping on my daughter'. It matters more if we forget how the dilatoriness of man has deprived of its urgency such a word as 'presently'.[2] How many a word has lost its vigour by continual usage may be illustrated from a famous passage in *Othello*:

> When you shall these unlucky deeds relate,
> Speak of me as I am; nothing extenuate,
> Nor set down aught in malice: then must you speak
> Of one that loved not wisely but too well;
> Of one not easily jealous, but, being wrought,
> Perplex'd in the extreme.

[1] *Shakespeare's England*, ii. 559.

[2] 'By and by' and 'anon' could still mean 'at once', and they sometimes bear their older meaning in the Bible of 1611; but in Shakespeare they can be given the modern meaning of 'soon'. In the 'anon, anon, sir' of the drawer the promise seems to bear the older meaning and the performance the modern.

'These unlucky deeds', 'perplexed in the extreme'. What colourless words, we are tempted to say, and good critics have seen here the irony of understatement. But in Elizabethan English 'unlucky' means or can mean ill-omened, disastrous; and 'perplexed' means or can mean grieved, tortured, the mind on the rack. There is no hyperbole here, but neither is there understatement. In the noble and simple magnificence of Othello's speech, the emotion is fully and exactly stated.

Editors have not given us enough help here—Professor Dover Wilson in the later volumes of the New Cambridge Shakespeare is a notable exception—yet since Dr. Onions's *Shakespeare Glossary* of 1911 and the completion of the *Oxford Dictionary* in 1928 much of the evidence has been available. Even with this expert assistance the difficulty of choosing between the many possible meanings of some of the commonest words is often great. It may be important to remember that in addition to bearing its modern meanings the noun 'will' often signifies lust, the carnal passions in control of the reason. It is the last word in the longest speech in which Hamlet rebukes his mother, and it is a climax to the mood of disgust and revulsion which has almost unseated his reason:

> Rebellious hell,
> If thou canst mutine in a matron's bones,
> To flaming youth let virtue be as wax
> And melt in her own fire: proclaim no shame
> When the compulsive ardour gives the charge,
> Since frost itself as actively doth burn,
> And reason pandars will.

And as we should expect, the word is prominent in the plays in which Shakespeare is above all at grips with the sin of lust. 'Redeem thy brother', cries Angelo, 'By yielding up thy body to my will'; of Antony it is said that he 'would make his will Lord of his reason'; and to Troilus eyes and ears are

> Two traded pilots 'twixt the dangerous shores
> Of will and judgement.

So far I have been considering the words apart as if in a dictionary, but let me no longer 'crumble my text into small parts' but draw my observations 'out of the whole text, as it lies entire and unbroken'[1] in Shakespeare himself. For more than a century critics have observed how his line became animated, and his paragraph interanimated, by the rhythms of speech. They have noticed, too, his growing mastery of dramatic prose, and how while never relinquishing its colloquial base it could become upon the lips of Falstaff and Hamlet as quick and forgetive as poetry. And all the time he was slowly working himself free from the over-elaborate use of schemes and tropes inherited by him from his age and by his age from scholastic rhetoric. 'That wonderful poet, who has so much besides rhetoric, is also the greatest poetical rhetorician since Euripides'— these words of Matthew Arnold's[2] remain true of Shakespeare to the end, but there is as much difference between the rhetoric of *Richard III* and *King Lear* as between the verse. An Elizabethan schoolmaster might have set his boys many a speech in Shakespeare's early plays as an exercise in the identification of schemes and tropes, and to name the figures in (say) the soliloquy of Henry VI which begins 'This battle fares like to the morning's war', with its elaborate examples of anaphora with and without climax, would have been well within the capacity of the meanest scholar in Mulcaster's school,[3] although perhaps he would not have observed

---

[1] Cf. George Herbert, *A Priest to the Temple*, chap. 7.

[2] *Merope* (1858), p. xlv.

[3] The Elizabethan equivalent of 'every schoolboy knows'. Cf. F. Hering, *A Modest Defence* (1604), p. 27: 'a meane scholler of *Mulcasters* schoole will easily tell him that . . .'.

how the speech is redeemed by the lyricism which cuts across the formalism of the rhetoric. But if the boy had been confronted with *Hamlet* or *King Lear* his task would have been more difficult. There is a development in Shakespeare similar to that which Professor Manly noticed in Chaucer: 'a process of general release from the astonishingly artificial and sophisticated art with which he began and the gradual replacement of formal rhetorical devices by methods of composition based upon close observation of life and the exercise of the creative imagination.'[1] Even in Shakespeare's earliest manner, as in Chaucer's, the natural is ever present with the artificial, but by the turn of the century Shakespeare has forged verse, prose, and rhetoric into the subtlest instrument of dramatic speech the world has known. How this dramatic speech is dependent upon language familiar to all his audience, upon the language of common life, may be illustrated by examining his use of three figures, paronomasia, the image, and the proverb. Paronomasia and the proverb were more valued in his age than in later ages, but command of the image, especially metaphor, has seemed since Aristotle the greatest thing by far for a poet to have.

Johnson recognized that every age has its modes of speech and its cast of thought, but Shakespeare's use of agnomination or paronomasia, or more simply quibbling with words, he could not condone. Camden, too, while quoting Giraldus Cambrensis to the effect that the English and the Welsh 'delighted much in licking the letter, and clapping together of Agnominations', felt that 'this merry playing with words' had been 'too much used by some'.[2] There will be few readers of Shakespeare's comic scenes who do not at times agree.

[1] 'Chaucer and the Rhetoricians' (*Proceedings of the British Academy*, 1926, p. 97).
[2] *Remains* (1605), p. 27.

The contrast between Speed's verbal wit and Launce's mother-wit is to be remarked: the one perished almost as soon as it was born, and the other is, in its kind, imperishable. Shakespeare inherited a ripe tradition of clowning—it was Tarleton's legacy to the English stage— and in ripe clowning, in 'merry fooling', there is little to choose between his early work and his late. As his art matures, he may bring everything more and more into a unity—Dogberry and Stephano are essential to the action, while Launce is a music-hall turn—but the humour of Launce's talk with his dog is already ripe, as nothing else in that play is ripe. But if being a good Elizabethan means enjoying word-spinning on the level of Speed, few of us can be good Elizabethans. It is some consolation to have Camden on our side, and Camden's greatest pupil who attacked the 'Stage-practice' of 'mistaking words' in *Bartholomew Fair*. Fortunately Shakespeare grew out of the abuse of the practice, and the fool in *Othello* is the last of his characters of whom it can be said: 'How every fool can play upon the word.'

Ben Jonson was inclined to attack all 'Paranomasie or Agnomination'—it is significant that he puts the words into the mouth of his Poetaster—but like most Elizabethans Shakespeare was never willing to relinquish it altogether. The figure played a chief part in their jests and riddles and in the many word-games of which they were so fond. If we wish to see to what good purpose Shakespeare puts the pun we cannot do better than turn to Beatrice and Falstaff. About the time that Shakespeare was creating them, Jonson's friend John Hoskins was blaming 'the dotage of the time upon this small ornament',[1] but there was no longer any question of Shakespeare doting upon it. While the quibble is Speed's only weapon it is one of many in the crammed arsenal of Beatrice's wit and Falstaff's. Beatrice's 'civil count,

[1] *Directions for Speech and Style*, ed. H. H. Hudson (1935), p. 16.

civil as an orange, and something of that jealous complexion' is gay and stimulating, one of many touches in Shakespeare's greatest exemplar of a love between man and woman that does not abase but sharpens the wits, so that in both sexes the mind and the senses are fully exercised. Falstaff's puns, too, do not merely spin upon themselves. The quibbles in 'thou camest not of the blood royal, if thou darest not stand for ten shillings' are quibbles with sense and are intimately concerned with the action. In this lively lordship over words he shows the agility of his mind. A contemporary proverb said that he who sought for a fine wit in a fat belly lost his labour. That is only one of the many incongruities that are reconciled in this character. A cony-catcher, he hob-nobs with princes of the realm. A coward, he never shows fear or loses presence of mind in the heat of battle. Surrounded by men who would sacrifice their lives for ambition or honour, he believes only in good fellows, sack, and sugar. An old man, he would persuade himself that he is for ever young. Shaken and diseased by his excesses, he is so exuberant with life that he seems to stand for the indestructibility of matter. No wonder he exacted from Dr. Johnson what is perhaps the only apostrophe in his edition of Shakespeare: 'But Falstaff unimitated, unimitable Falstaff, how shall I describe thee?'

To an Elizabethan the play upon words was not merely an elegance of style and a display of wit; it was also a means of emphasis and an instrument of persuasion. An argument might be conducted from step to step—and in the pamphleteers it often is—by a series of puns. The genius of the language encouraged them. 'So significant are our words', writes Richard Carew, 'that amongst them sundry single ones serve to express divers things; as by *Bill* are meant a weapon, a scroll, and a bird's beak; by *Grave*, sober, a tomb, and to

carve.'[1] And we remember Mercutio's dying jest—
which is so much more than a jest—'Ask for me to-
morrow, and you shall find me a grave man.' The rich
ambiguities of the language were used not merely for
fun. Falstaff can jest: 'I would my means were greater,
and my waist slenderer'; while in the additions to *The
Spanish Tragedy* Hieronimo, in great agony of mind,
can implore 'infective night' to 'Gird in my waste of
grief with thy large darkness'. So in the famous lines of
Lady Macbeth

> If he do bleed,
> I'll gild the faces of the grooms withal,
> For it must seem their guilt

the play upon words is no jest put in to enhance the
horror of the scene, nor does it suggest hysteria, for at
this point in the play Lady Macbeth is mistress of herself and of the situation. It underlines her determination,
it is in Coleridge's words an 'effectual intensive of
passion',[2] and it gives to her departure from the stage
something of the emphasis and finality of a rhyming
couplet.

I have said that the Elizabethans sometimes conducted an argument from step to step by a series of
verbal quibbles. In Shakespeare the progression is often
indirect and involuntary. This was noticed by Walter
Whiter, a friend of Porson's, in his *Specimen of a Commentary on Shakspeare Containing I. Notes on As You
Like It. II. An Attempt to Explain and Illustrate Various
Passages, on a New Principle of Criticism derived from
Mr Locke's Doctrine of the Association of Ideas* (1794), a
book which anticipates in a most interesting way much
modern work on Shakespeare's imagery. Whiter showed
among other things how the images in which Shakespeare's train of thought is clothed may be suggested

---

[1] *Elizabethan Critical Essays*, ed. G. Gregory Smith, 1904, ii. 288.
[2] Op. cit. i. 150.

to his unconscious mind sometimes by similarities of sound, sometimes by words with an equivocal meaning, 'though the signification, in which they are really applied, has never any reference and often no similitude to that which caused their association'. Whiter's most elaborate researches, in part still unpublished, were made upon the words and images which came to Shakespeare's mind, often involuntarily, from association with the theatre and with masques and pageantry. What is perhaps his most interesting discovery relates to the nexus of images which in varying combinations recurs in play after play to express disgust at false flattery and fawning obsequiousness, a nexus represented by Antony's

> The hearts
> *That spaniel'd me at heels*, to whom I gave
> Their wishes, do *discandy, melt* their *sweets*
> On blossoming Caesar.

But the passage which started Whiter on his inquiries was from the speech in which Apemantus upbraids Timon 'with the contrast between his past and present condition':

> What, think'st
> That the bleak air, thy boisterous *chamberlain*,
> Will put thy *shirt* on *warm*? Will these *moist* trees,
> That have outlived the eagle, page thy heels,
> And skip when thou point'st out?

Hanmer in 1744 had read 'moss'd trees', remembering perhaps the description of the oak in *As You Like It* 'whose boughs were moss'd with age'; and in this reading he has been followed not indeed by the *Oxford Dictionary*[1] but by most, if not all, editors. To make a participial adjective of the past participle 'moss'd', where the metre did not accommodate itself to 'mossy',

---

[1] See under 'mossed', *ppl. a.*, and 'moist', *adj.* 2.

was not beyond the capacity of any Elizabethan, particularly of Shakespeare, yet there is no evidence that any writer did this before Hanmer did it for the purpose of his emendation. But the seventh canon of criticism for an editor of Shakespeare is, according to Thomas Edwards, that 'he may find out obsolete words, or coin new ones; and put them in the place of such as he does not like or does not understand'. By changing 'moist' to 'moss'd' the editors have given the passage a meaning the very opposite to that which Shakespeare intended. The emphasis in *Timon* is not on aged trees. The bleak air, Apemantus means, the trees whose strength is such that they have withstood the harshness of nature longer than the long-lived eagle, the cold brook, the naked creatures of nature, these will not flatter Timon. Whiter did not see that 'moist' in this passage bears the meaning 'full of sap', 'pithy'; but he did see that by an unconscious association of ideas the image of the chamberlain putting his master's shirt on 'warm' or 'aired' impressed the opposite word 'moist' or 'unaired' upon the imagination of the poet, and that while 'moss'd' may be the more elegant epithet, what Shakespeare wrote and intended was 'moist'.[1]

'In the fictions, the thoughts, and the language of the poet,' Whiter writes, 'you may ever mark the deep and unequivocal traces of the age in which he lived, of the employments in which he was engaged, and of the various objects which excited his passions or arrested his attention.' Later and more systematic inquirers have proved, what the researches of Whiter suggest, that the great bulk of Shakespeare's images is taken from everyday things, from the goings-on of familiar life, images as familiar as the chamberlain putting his master's shirt on warm, or that image of heaven peeping 'through the blanket of the dark' which excited Johnson's risibility

[1] Whiter, pp. 70, 73, 81–82, 138–40.

but does not excite ours.[1] Remoter images there are, for example the simile—to Pope 'an unnatural excursion'—in which Othello likens his determination for revenge to the Pontic sea

> Whose icy current and compulsive course
> Ne'er feels retiring ebb, but keeps due on
> To the Propontic and the Hellespont.

But usually the images are images from sights and sounds and experiences of a kind that came home immediately to the senses of his audience, and even in Othello's simile the emphasis is not on the remote geographical names, as it might have been in Marlowe, but on a natural phenomenon readily grasped by a people that used sea and river as the Elizabethans did. Owing to Shakespeare's instinct for what was permanent and central, his images are perhaps less often obscure than those of some of his contemporaries, but it must sometimes happen that what was obvious to the groundlings of the Globe Theatre because they had seen it with their own eyes or heard it with their own ears becomes apparent to us only after painful research. I take an example from a puzzling passage in *Love's Labour's Lost*. Berowne and the King of Navarre have broken their oaths to renounce love, and when the third perjurer Longaville is unmasked, Berowne observes:

> Thou makest the triumviry, the corner-cap of society,
> The shape of Love's Tyburn that hangs up simplicity.

What image did 'corner-cap' call up in the minds of Shakespeare's audience and by what association of ideas did he proceed from 'corner-cap' to Tyburn? Corner-caps were worn in Shakespeare's time in the universities, in the church, and by the judges of the land, but by an injunction of 1559 these caps were always square,

---

[1] *Macbeth*, I. v. 53; *Rambler*, no. 168. It is a judgement on Johnson that in this essay he should give Lady Macbeth's speech to Macbeth.

nor do I know of one scrap of evidence that Shakespeare could have seen in England the three-cornered cap which his image so clearly demands. But we may be very sure that a Catholic scholar, Dr. John Story, 'a Romish Canonical Doctor', wore 'a three-cornered cap'. Story was martyred at Tyburn on 1 June 1571, and the execution was recorded in the usual way by ballad, broadside, dying confession, and by pamphlets both official and unofficial. What impressed itself upon the memory of the people was the use in this execution of 'a new pair of Gallows made in triangle manner',[1] and for many a year Tyburn or the gallows was known as 'Dr. Story's corner-cap' or his 'triangle', or simply as his 'cap'. It is not likely that Shakespeare was thinking of Story or of his 'simplicity' or folly; it was sufficient that 'corner-cap' could be associated without difficulty with a triumviry and with Tyburn. Longaville, as the third member of the company or 'society', has made up the triumviry and so recalls the shape of the gallows upon which Love hangs these foolish men who have tried to escape from her in their little academe. To an archaeologist 350 years is a short span, but the historian of manners may find all in doubt after the passage of a generation.

I have mentioned paronomasia, and I have mentioned the image. Let me mention another figure in rhetoric much valued by the Elizabethans. It can best be introduced by quoting a speech made in the Parliament of 1601. After the member for Southwark had begun to speak, had shaken for very fear, stood still a while, and at length sat down, the member for Hereford made this speech on a bill to avoid double payments of debts:

It is now my chance to speak something, and that without humming and hawing. I think this law is a good law; even

[1] *A Declaration of the Life and Death of John Story, late a Romish Canonical Doctor by Profession* (1571), sig. C2.

reckoning makes long friends; as far goes the penny, as the penny's master. *Vigilantibus non dormientibus jura subveniunt.* Pay the reckoning over night, and you shall not be troubled in the morning. If ready money be *Mensura Publica*, let every man cut his coat according to his cloth. When his old suit is in the wain, let him stay till that his money bring a new suit in the increase. Therefore, I think the law to be good, and I wish it a good passage.[1]

If this were played upon a stage now—those of us who do not read Hansard will say—we could condemn it as an improbable fiction, and indeed Thomas Jones's speech, with its clusters of homely proverbs, is paralleled by many a speech put by the dramatists into the mouths of downright or simple characters; Downright in *Every Man in his Humour*, Basket Hilts in Jonson's only play of rustic humours, *A Tale of a Tub*, and the goldsmith Touchstone in the citizenly *Eastward Ho* are as full of proverbs as an egg of meat. Shakespeare seldom uses proverbs in this way. He does, however, in two of his earliest plays, use the catch-phrase as a pointer to character or the lack of it, and the Elizabethans made no sharp distinction between catch-phrases and proverbs. Every age has its own catch-phrases, and in every age they are the staple of conversation among those whose wits barely cross the threshold of intelligence. Luce in *The Comedy of Errors* and Jaquenetta in *Love's Labour's Lost* have no conversation outside such pert, ready-made phrases as 'Lord! how wise you are!', 'When? can you tell?', 'With that face?', 'Fair weather after you'. There is a similar dialogue in Lyly's *Mother Bombie* which Shakespeare may be imitating. Lyly calls them 'all the odd blind phrases that help them that know not how to discourse'. Some of them have survived to this day with little change: 'The better for your asking', 'You are such another', 'And therewithal

[1] Townshend, p. 283.

you waked', 'Yea, in my other hose', and 'quoth you'. Some dramatists exploited the elementary humour which comes from the repetition of a catch-phrase, but in the first quarto of *Hamlet*—the doctrine is Shakespeare's if not the words—the clown is condemned who keeps one suit of jests, like 'You owe me a quarter's wages' or 'Your beer is sour'. The laugh it raised was too easy for Shakespeare, the label it attached to character too superficial, the character to which the label could be attached too shallow. Falstaff has no catch-phrases. His sentiments are a perpetual surprise.

There must still be many a proverb in Shakespeare which his audience recognized as proverbial and which we do not. 'The nature of his work', says Johnson, 'required the use of the common colloquial language, and consequently admitted many phrases allusive, elliptical, and proverbial, such as we speak and hear every hour without observing them; and of which, being now familiar, we do not suspect that they can ever grow uncouth, or that, being now obvious, they can ever seem remote.'[1] When Lovell in *Henry VIII* speaks of 'fool and feather', and the Princess in *Love's Labour's Lost* asks 'What plume of feathers is he that indited this letter?', the collocation was already so well established as to have become proverbial, and for many generations 'he has a feather in his cap' was a periphrasis for a fool. Again, when Falstaff says that if Bardolph were any way given to virtue he would swear by his face and his oath would be 'By this fire, that's God angel', it has been supposed that Shakespeare was borrowing from Chapman in whose *Blind Beggar of Alexandria* a similar expression is to be found. But he was drawing upon the proverbial stock of oaths—the saying is at least as old as the *Misogonus* of about 1570[2]—and his audience

---

[1] *Proposals* (1756), p. 5.
[2] III. i. 240: 'By this fier that bournez thats gods aungell.'

received that peculiar delight which comes from the apt application of an old saying to a modern instance, Bardolph's nose.

Sometimes we are left in doubt whether Shakespeare was using a proverb or inventing one. Was Portia's 'a light wife doth make a heavy husband'[1] proverbial or is it Shakespeare's punning variation of 'Light gains make heavy purses'? And when Dekker and Webster use the same sentiment in *Westward Ho*,[2] were they borrowing from Shakespeare or making use of proverbial stock?

Then there are many 'sentences' in Shakespeare which are commonplace of his age yet were never crystallized into a set proverbial form. Hamlet's 'there is nothing either good or bad, but thinking makes it so' is an example. Spenser's 'It is the mind that maketh good or ill' has been cited in evidence, and a closer parallel is found in *Politeuphuia, Wit's Commonwealth*, an anthology of 'sententiae' published in 1597: 'There is nothing grievous if the thought make it not.'[3] Whether Shakespeare kept a commonplace book like Jonson, Bacon, Webster, and most of his contemporaries, is not known. Long before the evidence was discovered by Charles Crawford, J. A. Symonds hinted that Webster kept one.[4] But in Shakespeare there are no ill-fitting joins which betray the borrower. He brings everything into a unity. In the anthology just mentioned we find 'Our good name ought to be more dear unto us than our life',[5] and the sentiment may be as old as civilized man; it is no temporary opinion; but when Iago says to Othello

> Good name in man and woman, dear my lord,
> Is the immediate jewel of their souls

[1] *Merchant of Venice*, V. i. 130.   [2] V. iii.   [3] p. 59b.
[4] 'Vittoria Accoramboni' (*Italian Byways*, 1883, p. 179): 'The sentences, which seem at first sight copied from a commonplace book, are found to be appropriate'; C. Crawford, *Collectanea*, First (1906) and Second (1907) Series.   [5] p. 106b.

the commonplace takes on a new meaning. The maxim is embedded in the evil in the play: it has become an essential part of a great design.

It is a little difficult to adjust ourselves to the seriousness with which the Elizabethans treated the proverb. Soon after Shakespeare's death it began to lose favour. The decline of the native and homely proverb is suggested by the preference of George Herbert for 'outlandish proverbs', which, in comparison, have 'too much feather and too little point',[1] or by Glanvill's attack on preachers who use 'vulgar Proverbs, and homely similitudes';[2] and before Swift made the graveyard of proverbs and catch-phrases which he called *Polite Conversation* proverbs had almost disappeared from polite literature. This change in taste happened long before Lord Chesterfield called them 'the flowers of the rhetoric of a vulgar man' and said that 'a man of fashion never has recourse to proverbs and vulgar aphorisms'.[3] But to an Elizabethan the proverb was not merely or mainly of use for clouting a hob-nailed discourse; it still retained its place as an important figure in rhetorical training, and the many sixteenth-century collectors and writers who acclimatized foreign proverbs to the English soil were hailed as benefactors who enriched the 'copy' of their native tongue. Proverbs were invaluable for amplifying a discourse, or they added grace and variety to wit-combats. Sometimes they are hardly distinguishable in kind or function from the 'sentence' and the 'example': as Richard Carew said, they prescribed 'under the circuit of a few syllables . . . sundry available caveats'.[4] Preachers, orators, wits, dramatists, found them excel-

[1] *Baconiana* (1679), ed. T. Tenison, p. 93: 'the *Jacula Prudentum*, in Mr. *Herbert*; which latter some have been bold to accuse as having too much Feather, and too little Point.' So Fuller may have thought, but not Jeremy Taylor, who adds Italian proverbs to the margins of *Holy Living*.

[2] *An Essay Concerning Preaching* (1678), p. 77.

[3] Letter to his son, 27 Sept. 1749.   [4] Op. cit. ii. 288.

lent persuasion. They could strengthen an argument, for they contained in themselves the authority of experience—'it must needs be true what every one says'; they were vivid and epigrammatic so that they stuck in the mind when abstract precepts were forgotten; and the use of a homely proverb might put preacher and congregation, orator or dramatist and audience, upon a friendly and familiar footing, one with each other.

Of the great English poets only Chaucer makes so good use of proverbs as Shakespeare. The contrast between Shakespeare and Jonson is striking. On the title-page of his best and most popular comedy, *The Alchemist*, Jonson put the words:

> —Neque, me ut miretur turba, laboro:
> Contentus paucis lectoribus.

As he despised the 'green and soggy multitude', so he despised their collective wisdom. Ancient proverbs, he said, might illuminate 'A cooper's wit, or some such busy spark',[1] and they have their place in his comedies, but they could serve no serious function in the work of this robust and independent writer. In *Volpone* one proverb, and only one, stands out by reason of its position and the new turn which Jonson gives it. It is the last line of the scene in which the Fox departs in disguise to gloat over the discomfiture of his victims. 'Sir, you must look for curses', says Mosca, to which Volpone replies in one of Jonson's magnificent exits:

> Till they burst;
> The Fox fares ever best, when he is curst.

If we turn to *Sejanus* and *Catiline* we shall not be surprised to find a dearth of proverbs or even proverbial phrases. Gnomic passages there are in plenty, and in the first quarto of *Sejanus* the reader's attention is directed to the tragedy's 'fullness and frequency of

---

[1] *A Tale of a Tub*, Prologue.

sentence' by inverted commas. But English proverbs he rigorously excluded from the dignity of tragedy. His practice is of a piece with that fundamental contempt for the people which gives to his art so much of its bent and bias. Of all ancient proverbs, he would most strenuously have repudiated that which maintained that the voice of the people was the voice of God. And when in his tragedies his verses 'break out strong and deep in the mouth',[1] as they often do, they owe little or nothing of their strength to colloquial English idiom.

In Shakespeare proverbs are used as rhetorical ornaments, as moral sententiae, and occasionally as a means of building up character. From Richard's dissimulations in *Henry VI, Part 3*, until he achieves his throne in *Richard III*, old saws like 'I hear, yet say not much, but think the more' come pat to his purpose, especially in sardonic aside. He clothes his 'naked villany' with 'odd old ends'. In Faulconbridge, a character that sees the worst, seems to approve of it, and follows the best, bluntness and good humour are strongly marked in the first scene by the proverbs that pour from his mouth, but as his character is tested and proved by events his speech, while remaining direct and vigorous, becomes less proverbial. Richard seeks popularity for his own ends, Faulconbridge has a native disposition to it, while Coriolanus despises it. To him the 'vulgar wisdoms' of the people are contemptible.

> They said they were an-hungry; sigh'd forth proverbs,
> That hunger broke stone walls, that dogs must eat,
> That meat was made for mouths, that the gods sent not
> Corn for the rich men only: with these shreds
> They vented their complainings.

It is a little ironical that when Aufidius prophesies the doom of Coriolanus he does so with a couple of proverbs: 'One fire drives out one fire; one nail, one nail.'

---

[1] *News from the New World* (1640, ii. 42).

What the proverb meant to Shakespeare is best shown not by the number and variety which he uses, although those so far identified are indeed many, but by his use of them in the gravest and greatest passages in his plays. Proverbs are mingled with folk-tale and ballad in the snatches, half sense and half nothing, spoken by the mad Ophelia: 'They say the owl was a baker's daughter. Lord, we know what we are, but know not what we may be.' In *King Lear* Shakespeare puts into the mouth of the Fool the silliest catch-phrase—'Cry you mercy, I took you for a joint-stool'—with poignant effect, and the Fool's last speech is a reference to the homely, ironical proverb: 'You would make me go to bed at noon.' Perhaps the most famous proverb in the whole of Shakespeare is that of the cat who would eat fish but would not wet her feet, to which Lady Macbeth refers in pluming up her husband's faltering will; but there are others in this play as striking and powerful in their operation. Keats has said that 'nothing ever becomes real till it is experienced. Even a proverb is no proverb to you till your life has illustrated it.'[1] Macbeth has indeed tested the truth of the line, 'It will have blood: they say, blood will have blood', and with what potency is the proverb charged. As moving is the 'what's done is done' of Lady Macbeth. It is one of the many thoughts and deeds which recur to her broken mind in the sleep-walking scene—'What's done cannot be undone: to bed, to bed, to bed.' They give to her prose the concentration and associative force of poetry.

I have mentioned Jonson's care to exclude popular proverbs from his tragedies, and the reason lies not only in his conception of tragedy as something 'high and aloof'[2] but also in his strict sense of decorum. Shake-

---

[1] *Letters*, ed. M. Buxton Forman (1935), p. 318.
[2] *The Poetaster*, 'To the Reader', l. 238, and again in the 'Ode to Himself' in *Underwoods*.

speare interprets the Renaissance doctrine of decorum
more liberally. His decorum is dramatic, not historical.
His tact in translating the manners of the ancient world
to the modern stage is superb. He concentrates on what
is permanent in spiritual and human values, and if clocks
strike and doublets go unbraced, there is no offence,
for he never sacrifices the dignity of his theme by
introducing the trivialities of the present or the pedan-
tries of the past. He is as far from the revolting ana-
chronisms of Heywood's *Rape of Lucrece, a true Roman
Tragedy*, in which a Roman senator sings a ditty

> Shall I woe the lovely Molly,
> She's so fair, so fat, so jolly, . . .

as from Jonson's attempts at exact reconstruction of the
manners and sentiments of the old Roman world. As
the translators of the Bible did not hesitate, when necessary, to change the remote for the familiar, the unknown
for the known—the musical instruments of Israel for
the cornets, flutes, harps, and sackbuts of Elizabethan
England, or the vanities of the attire of Israelitish
women for the mufflers, the bonnets, the mantles, the
wimples, the crisping pins of the sixteenth century—
so Shakespeare writes of the entry of Coriolanus into
Rome in words which are also applicable to the tri-
umphal entry of James into the City of London:

> the kitchen malkin pins
> Her richest lockram 'bout her reechy neck,
> Clambering the walls to eye him: stalls, bulks, windows,
> Are smother'd up, leads fill'd and ridges hors'd
> With variable complexions, all agreeing
> In earnestness to see him.

Unlike Jonson, Shakespeare thinks nothing unclean
that can deepen and widen his tragic art. He works not
by exclusion but by bringing all aspects of life into a
sense of order. Other men of his day, Webster or

Middleton, tried to be as all-embracing, but the Shake-spearian unity is incomparably more sensitive and more closely articulated. The poet's power reveals itself, says Coleridge, in the balance or reconciliation of opposite or discordant qualities. Only the disinterested artist who has no cause to serve (for the moment) except his art can bring himself to balance or reconcile such dis-cordant and opposite qualities as are revealed, for example, in *Antony and Cleopatra*. In this many-sided play he seems to balance nobility and self-indulgence, renunciation and vanity, the glory and the corruption of the flesh, the greatness and the pettiness of the world. In the scene on Pompey's galley, where if anywhere in Shakespeare we find the diction and conduct of com-mon life, the famous triumvirate, 'These three world-sharers, these competitors', drown their schemings and enmities in drink until Lepidus, the weak member of the axis, is carried drunk away, and the first and second parts of the world sing the refrain 'Cup us, till the world go round'. Is this a play then about a set of fools and rogues struggling for power in a world which does not signify? It is, and it would be less rich if it were not. But we remember how these baser elements are balanced by others, and as the play ends it is all 'fire and air'.

I have tried to suggest a few of the ways in which Shakespeare's drama is continually irrigated by the diction of common life. But it does not remain the dic-tion of common life. It is transmuted, and with what nobility let us remind ourselves from his greatest play. When the tempests in Lear's mind and in nature have spent themselves, when 'the great rage . . . is kill'd in him', there is a simplicity in his speech which persists to the end. It is no mannered simplicity such as we sometimes find in Webster when he is trying to write like Shakespeare; but it is as if the fire of genius had reduced language to its elements. The monosyllabic

590   E

base which some of his contemporaries thought the misfortune of our language he turns into glory. In these sentences there is no gap between the inspiration and the expression, between the mind and the hand, and without wastage they gather up together all the love, terror, and pity that have gone before:

> Pray, do not mock me:
> I am a very foolish fond old man,
> Fourscore and upward, not an hour more nor less;
> And, to deal plainly,
> I fear I am not in my perfect mind.
> Methinks I should know you and know this man;
> Yet I am doubtful; for I am mainly ignorant
> What place this is, and all the skill I have
> Remembers not these garments, nor I know not
> Where I did lodge last night. Do not laugh at me;
> For, as I am a man, I think this lady
> To be my child Cordelia.

These are among the words and rhythms in which Shakespeare expresses his vision of good and evil. It is no system of morality which remains in the mind. The play provides symbols for the experience which it gives us—a wheel of fire, or incense of the gods upon such sacrifices—but there are no words to express our experience, or only Shakespeare's words.

PETER ALEXANDER

(b. 1893)

Restoring Shakespeare[1]

ABUSE of the commentators and of the editors is a form of recreation with which many readers of Shakespeare have from time to time diverted themselves. Familiar, perhaps from their early years, with his plays in some well-known and standard text, they come in their maturer days upon remarks that disturb their repose in their long-cherished knowledge or on suggestions that offend their sense of propriety. Such reactions may be wise or unwise according to circumstances and the capacity of the reader; they are at least natural, but only some familiarity with the commentator's problem will enable even the judicious reader to pass a fair judgement on new suggestions and to reject them, if necessary, with the charitable allowance that the case usually deserves. For the commentator is doing his best to help in what is both a difficult and a delicate task, and only an arrogant assumption of omniscience on his part should call forth the reader's objurgation.

The offended, and often incensed, reader is of course in good company. The poets themselves have not hesitated to abuse the 'classical' editors whose monuments are now preserved in the particular Pantheon which their successors of today enter with reverence. The remarks which Keats made in his copy of Shakespeare have been preserved and edited for us, and they show how little compunction he felt in discharging on the eighteenth-century editors a fusillade of the most uncomplimentary comment. 'Lo fool again!' after some weighty pronouncement by Dr. Johnson himself is not

[1] *Shakespeare Survey* 5 (1952).

uncharacteristic of the taxation, in the Shakespearian sense of that word, to which the learned editors are subjected. But Keats was a poet to the manner born and native to a domain which even Dr. Johnson entered at his peril. The question whether Keats was always justified in his censure is not for the moment at issue; only those however, it is clear, who feel as free and sure in the element in which Keats soared should venture on the critical flights he naturally allowed himself.

There is, too, the irate reader may plead, the example of the commentators themselves, for they have not spared one another. 'Perhaps', as Dr. Johnson observed, 'the lightness of the matter may conduce to the vehemency of the agency; when the truth to be investigated is so near to inexistence, as to escape attention, its bulk is to be enlarged by rage and exclamation.' The example set by the offenders themselves is not one that can be recommended as a model of general deportment, and their mutual censures often point the moral of the futility of such exasperation. To assess the relative merits of the editors would be an invidious and perhaps odious task; but whatever the judgement given after such a scrutiny, the claims of Theobald would have to be weighed with care. Yet Theobald is the first hero of the *Dunciad*, a poem by the poet who may be considered the outstanding man of genius who has given his time to editing Shakespeare. But in editing Shakespeare the race has not always been to the swift or the battle to the strong. Those who have done most to elucidate Shakespeare are not of the type of which Bentleys, Porsons, and Housmans have been made; and Dr. Johnson could describe Theobald as a man of narrow comprehension and small acquisitions, though there is no modern edition of Shakespeare that does not include many of the happy suggestions first proposed by Theobald.

Before condemning the commentators there is a story of W. G. Grace the reader would do well to remember. To a proud mother who introduced her son to Grace as a prodigy that had never dropped a catch, the Doctor replied: 'He can't have played much cricket, Mam.' The editor or commentator who has never made a bad shot is unlikely to have made any good ones. In the earlier days of editing the commentator was without the numerous aids that are now available in the shape of concordance and dictionary, and he laboured in the belief that the field needed a more thoroughgoing weeding than we now know was required. Those who fancied that Shakespeare's manuscripts had been left to the care of door-keepers and prompters were bolder in the exercise of conjecture than those can be who believe that in many instances the text they examine was printed from Shakespeare's own manuscript. The exuberance of conjecture in the earlier editors now that time has blown aside the froth, or filtered the body of their work from the lees, yields a lasting satisfaction to readers of Shakespeare. Beside the abandon of the early editors the circumspection that is required of their successors may seem unheroic, and modern corrections uninspired.

Most modern corrections are strictly speaking not emendations at all, but merely restorations of what was there already before the editorial process began. Compared with the *lucida tela diei*—the words of Lucretius that Housman so aptly used of those divinations that turn the obscurity of corruption to the sunshine of poetry—modern corrections seem matter-of-fact observations that afford merely a comfortable daylight. The reader confronted with the Folio text at *Timon of Athens*, IV. iii. 12,

> It is the Pastour Lards, the Brothers sides,
> The want that makes him leaue:

may fail to see what relevance such words have in

Timon's fierce denunciation of his fellows and their society. But read

> It is the pasture lards the rother's sides
> The want that makes him lean

(where 'rother' means 'ox') and all is clear in sense and appropriate to the misanthrope's mood. This is a good instance of the contribution editors have made to the reader's ease and enjoyment. Those who are oblivious of their debts, and yet exclaim against their benefactors, should be condemned to read their Shakespeare only in the original texts. The modern editor despairs of achieving so startling a transformation in reading as Rowe and Collier effected in these two lines. He is working on a close glean'd field, and though there is sufficient left to satisfy the ambition of genius, the modern editor has usually to be content with a more modest return.

In the Globe text, prepared for Macmillan and Co. in 1864, the editors Clark and Wright marked with an obelus passages that seemed to them corrupt and to have defied emendation. Two of these passages have recently been corrected by Percy Simpson, with no or with so little change in the text that they may serve as typical instances of the kind of correction that is perhaps most characteristic of recent years. At *The Tempest*, III. i. 14–15, the Folio reads:

But these sweet thoughts, doe euen refresh my labours,
Most busie lest, when I doe it.

Ferdinand, in the midst of his log-carrying, is musing on Miranda. Many suggestions have been proposed to make sense of the second line; but, as Simpson observes, the comma after 'lest', the stumbling-block in the expression, need be regarded not as a modern comma separating 'lest' (= least) from what follows but as a mark of emphasis binding it to the final words. The sense is clear: Ferdinand is busiest when thinking of

Miranda, and the text can stand when the dramatist's punctuation is translated into modern terms.

Simpson's correction illustrates what is now an important question for editors: the interpretation of the punctuation of the early copies. Before the work of the bibliographers—Pollard, McKerrow, and Sir Walter Greg—few regarded that punctuation as of any significance. Simpson, however, converted many to a different view, and before him Alfred Thiselton had used it to advantage. Now that our ideas of the history of the text are so altered, much attention is necessarily given to such detail. Where doctors disagree the laymen may be permitted to suspend judgement, for the critics are not unanimous about the interpretation of the punctuation; but the main point is not in debate: the punctuation demands study and may prove significant. As an illustration of the possibilities in this field two further corrections may be cited. At *Merry Wives of Windsor*, III. iii. 69–70, the Folio reads:

> I see what thou wert if Fortune thy foe, were
> not Nature thy friend.

Clark and Wright do not obelize the passage, but their version:

> I see what thou wert, if Fortune thy foe were not,
> Nature thy friend

is not satisfactory, and various emendations have been proposed. Here again the interpretation turns on the significance of the comma. Falstaff is trying to flatter Mistress Ford by admiring her parts—those that Nature gave her—and insisting how they would adorn a more exalted rank in society and the attire that is associated with such a station. But Fortune is her foe, since, as Rosalind reminds us, 'Fortune reigns in gifts of the world, not in the lineaments of Nature': Mistress Ford is merely a citizen's wife. The comma, therefore, after 'foe' is an emphatic one joining it to 'were' and the passage should read:

> I see what thou wert if Fortune thy foe were
> —not Nature—thy Friend.

For if Fortune were her friend (not Nature, for Nature is that already) she would have the position in the world to match the lineaments that Nature has given her. Again at *All's Well that Ends Well*, IV. iii. 295, the Folio reads:

> A pox upon him for me, he's more and more a Cat.

Editors usually adopt the Folio punctuation, but the passage should stand in a modernized text as,

> A pox upon him! For me he's more and more a Cat.

for the comma is again for emphasis.

These may seem slight and unimportant corrections, and so they are no doubt to the general reader. But they involve very important principles of interpretation that must eventually determine the correct reading at a number of places in the text of some of the best-known plays—places where the general reader, however indifferent to editorial principles, would at once be arrested by changes in the long-familiar wording.

Simpson's second correction requires no change whatever in the text. At *Love's Labour's Lost*, V. ii. 67–68, the Quarto reads:

> So perttaunt like would I ore'sway his state,
> That he should be my foole, and I his fate.

The Folio, which is more or less a reprint of the Quarto, reads similarly, with 'pertaunt' for 'perttaunt'. This word is, of course, the crux of the matter, and many emendations have been proposed and some adopted in texts. But Simpson has shown why it must remain as it is in the early versions. He is able to cite the following passage, in support of his contention, from a treatise on certain terms used in card games: 'A double Paire Royall, or a Paire-Taunt, is four cards of a sort.' 'Pertaunt' is therefore in all probability a winning holding or declaration at the obsolete game of 'Post and Pair'; and it would be in place in *Love's Labour's Lost* where the Queen and her three ladies may be said to be four of a sort about to win the hand from the love-lorn King and his gentlemen in the scene that immediately follows.[1]

Dover Wilson has made another restoration to the text at *Titus Andronicus*, II. iii. 222, that seems as certain as Simpson's in *Love's Labour's Lost*. The readings in the First Quarto and the Folio are given in that order:

> Lord *Bassianus* lies bereaud in blood,
> Lord *Bassianus* lies embrewed heere,

The reading of the First Quarto (1594) was changed in the Second Quarto (1600) to what now stands in the Folio, and the Folio obtained this wording from the Third Quarto (1611), for the Folio is substantially a reprint of the edition of 1611, although there are certain additions from manuscript material. The changes made in the Second Quarto were in part due to the fact that the printer was working from a damaged copy of the First Quarto. The particular alteration now under consideration, however, seems to have been made because the word 'bereaud' did not make sense. But Dover Wilson's suggestion that 'bereaud' is a misprint for 'beray'd' ('bereied') seems as certain as such suggestions can be; for the word is certainly used by the dramatists in the sense required here, e.g. Beaumont and Fletcher's *Knight of the Burning Pestle*, II. iv. 20:

> Unless it were by chance I did beray me—

where 'beray' means 'befoul'.

[1] Professor J. C. Maxwell notes that this defence seems to have been anticipated by F. A. Marshall.

Dover Wilson's correction here illustrates a principle he has been at some pains to emphasize, particularly in his work on the text of *Hamlet*. The words, in the Folio text, 'embrewed heere' do make sense of a sort; the First Quarto reading does not, at least at first sight. But here as in *Hamlet* Dover Wilson insists that where we may suspect the later reading of being itself an attempt to restore the sense to a passage that is obscured in an earlier version, we must address ourselves to the original obscurity for the correct interpretation and not be content with words that may indeed make sense, but not perhaps the precise sense intended by the author.

This correction also illustrates another aspect of emendation to which Dover Wilson has given much attention. It is not an exact restoration of the word of the text; there is a slight alteration, but of nothing more than a letter. This kind of correction in which the editor tries to restore the original by some trifling adjustment of the letters is, if Housman is to be believed, a favourite resource of Scots editors, for these cautious souls seemed to him to trust overmuch to this apparently conservative expedient. Dover Wilson has, however, made a special study of the handwriting used by Shakespeare, and a comparison of certain quarto and folio texts does bear out his contention that certain letters in that script do lend themselves to confusion one with another. Perhaps in his pleasure at finding a new key to certain difficulties he has overstressed its importance, but the next correction shows a very neat and certain use of the *ductus litterarum* by two American scholars.

At *Merchant of Venice*, III. i. 111–12, the Folio reads:

I thanke thee good *Tuball*, good newes, good newes: ha, ha, here in Genowa.

The puzzling word is 'here', for the speakers are in

Venice; and 'where' or some other word disposing of the confusion is usually substituted. But the American editors Neilson and Hill have by the simplest of devices made all clear. The letters most regularly confused by the compositors working from a script such as Shakespeare's are final *e* and *d*. Good instances of such a confusion in the printing of Shakespeare's text are so numerous that illustration is unnecessary, especially as it can be seen so clearly here. If the final *e* in 'here' should be *d*, we have 'herd', a spelling of 'heard', and what Shylock says, as one can see from Tubal's earlier remark ('as I heard in Genowa'), is

ha, ha, heard in Genowa.[1]

This type of correction which not only restores a sense required by the context, but which also provides, as it were, its own justification on transcriptional grounds is naturally felt to be specially satisfactory; but many good corrections do not carry with them an explanation of the confusion that has given rise to them, and we can see from a comparison of versions that may be independent of each other (e.g. the First Quarto and the Folio texts of *Othello*) that confusions or alterations do occur that no tracing or readjustment of the letters could unravel or explain.

It is often possible, however, especially where we have for a particular play two versions that are printed from different manuscripts and we can obtain a more stereoscopic view, as it were, of the text that one version would afford us, to offer some justification based on transcriptional grounds for the proposed correction. At *Troilus and Cressida*, v. vii. 11–12, the readings of the First Quarto and the Folio are in that order as follows:

now my double hen'd spartan, . . . lowe the
bull has the game, ware hornes ho?

[1] As Professor Maxwell has pointed out, this reading of 'heard' should have been attributed to Leon Kellner.

> now my double hen'd sparrow . . . lowe; the
> bull has the game: ware hornes ho?

The 'double hen'd spartan' or 'double hen'd sparrow' has naturally been found perplexing; but Leon Kellner (in his *Restoring Shakespeare*, p. 55) proposes to read 'double horn'd Spartan'. This fits the context admirably. Menelaus the Spartan is fighting with Paris, and, as Paris has seduced Helen, her first husband is given the cuckold's horns by that scurvy commentator Thersites. Here we have to suppose that the Quarto compositor misread 'horned' as 'hen'd' and that the editor or corrector who was preparing a copy of the printed Quarto, to give to the printer for use as his copy in printing the Folio, failed to make the necessary correction. The corrector had before him not only the First Quarto but a manuscript, perhaps in Shakespeare's own hand and not too clear in places, and, puzzled by the Quarto reading and finding his manuscript difficult to decipher, made a shot at the meaning and hit on the wrong word. The strength of Kellner's correction, however, does not depend on any guess we may make as to the origin and history of the corruption but almost solely on its fitness to the immediate context and propriety in the light of the larger context of Shakespeare's style and manner.

Very few of Shakespeare's plays have come down to us in two texts, each printed from a manuscript of a different kind from the other, and where the Quarto text has not been used in some form as copy for the Folio. *Othello* perhaps provides one of these exceptional opportunities for a comparison of two such texts.[1] Neither the Quarto nor the Folio text is free from corruption, but so well do they supplement each other that the evidence we have for *Othello* is unusually good. Two recent corrections in this text may illustrate some

[1] Dr. Alice Walker has since argued very cogently that *Othello* Q1 was used in the setting of the Folio text.

of the considerations arising from a study of this evidence. At v. ii. 68–70 the Quarto and Folio read:

FOLIO	QUARTO
Oth. He hath confest.	He has confest.
Des. What, my Lord?	What, my Lord?
Oth. That he hath us'd thee.	That he hath . . . uds death.

The readings 'us'd thee' and 'uds death' have been regarded as variants; but a consideration of the nature of the texts suggests that they are each a part and a different part of the original, and that only when they are both included do we get what Shakespeare intended Othello to say. In a modernized text the passage should stand:

Des. What, my Lord?
Oth.   That he hath—ud's death!—us'd thee.

The explanation of the difference between the Folio and Quarto texts presents in this instance no difficulty. The Quarto compositor fell into the well-known type of trap set by similar beginnings to adjacent phrases: the likeness of 'uds' to 'usd' leads to the omission of the second limb. The Folio compositor was working from a different manuscript, and this had been purged of the oaths and asseverations such as 'uds death' that are so frequent a feature in the other text: 'uds death' had been marked for omission and the Folio compositor accordingly omitted it; the conclusion that is essential to the thought of the passage was, however, naturally retained. From the context we see that Othello can hardly bring himself to utter the words that he feels of such terrible significance, and the Quarto phrase emphasizes the struggle with which he expresses himself.

In another place in *Othello* the restoration proposed by Richard Flatter seems as warranted. In the quarrel in the guard-room the wounded Montano, according to the Folio, II. iii. 64, exclaims:

> I bleed still, I am hurt to th' death. He dies.

while the Quarto reads:

> Zouns, I bleed still, I am hurt, to the death:

Editors have regarded the termination of the Folio line—'He dies'—as a stage direction, inserted in the Folio text by some confusion of mind on the part of the individual responsible for its preparation for the printer, and included by the printer, confused in his turn by the addition, as part of the dialogue. Montano does not die, nor does it seem probable that he faints, as some editors suggest, for he at once closes with the drunken Cassio, as the exclamations of Othello and Iago indicate. It is hard, therefore, to resist Flatter's conclusion that 'He dies' is really, as the Folio indicates, a part of the dialogue and is the expression of Montano's determination to retaliate on the man who has wounded him so grievously. The Quarto printer may have omitted the phrase for the same reason that modern editors have rejected it. It seemed odd, and could not be a stage direction. The colon after 'death' may suggest that the Quarto printer did at first intend to add something, though such evidence is not indeed conclusive.

One last example of the dovetailing of texts must suffice as illustration of that process. Here the second text is a bad quarto, put together by needy actors, and printed by an unscrupulous stationer. At *2 Henry VI*, IV. i. 68–71 the Folio reads:

> *Lieu.* Conuey him hence, and on our long boats side
>   Strike off his head.   *Suf.* Thou dar'st not for thy owne.
> *Lieu. Poole*, Sir *Poole*? Lord,
>   I kennel, puddle, sinke, whose filth and dirt
>   Troubles the siluer Spring, where England drinkes:

The Bad Quarto, changing the Lieutenant to a Captain, reports this passage as follows:

> *Suf.* Thou darste not for thine owne.
> *Cap.* Yes Poull.
> *Suffolke.* Poull.
> *Cap.* I Poull, puddle, kennell, sinke and durt,

Capell, making use of the Bad Quarto, reconstructed the text as we have it today:

> *Suf.* Thou darest not, for thy own.
> *Cap.* Yes, Pole.
> *Suf.* Pole!
> *Cap.* Pool! Sir Pool! lord!
> Ay, kennel, puddle, sink, &c.

Capell noted that the disrespectful form of address 'Pole' draws from the Duke of Suffolk, whose name was William de la Pole, the outraged exclamation 'Pole!' But the texts fit more neatly than Capell observed and the hardly intelligible 'Pool! Sir Pool! lord!' can be eliminated. If the two versions are superimposed (the Quarto version modified for comparison):

> *Lieu. Poole,* Sir   *Poole?* Lord,
> *Cap.* Poull. *Suffolke.* Poull. *Cap.*

We can see that the Folio printer, confused by his copy, should have read:

> *Lieu.* Poole. *Suf.* Poole! *Lieu.*

—although he would put *Poole* in italic as a proper name. The passage as modernized should therefore stand:

> *Lieutenant.* Poole.
> *Suffolk.* Poole!
> *Lieutenant.* Ay, kennel, puddle, sink, &c.

These illustrations of modern 'corrections' that improve the text by restoring it more or less to the

condition in which it was first transmitted to us may
conclude with two examples of the art of the late
Alfred Thiselton. At times he stoutly defended what is
undoubtedly corrupt and unacceptable but, though he
may have dropped some catches, he did excellent work
in the Shakespearian field. *Measure for Measure*, IV. i.
61–63, where the Duke somewhat suddenly muses on
the slanders that assail the man in authority, reads in
the Folio:

> Volumes of report
> Run with these false, and most contrarious Quest
> Upon thy doings:

Editors usually read:

> Run with these false and most contrarious quests

but there is no need to remove the comma or make
'Quest' a plural noun. As Thiselton observes: ' "Quest"
is, of course, the verb—capitalized because it is a technical term of the chase and used metaphorically—which
signifies the giving tongue of the dog on the scent of
game. "Most contrarious Quest" is best explained by
the phrase "hunt-counter".' Thiselton's explanation is
as neat as it is conclusive. The second example, for
there are others to choose from, may be taken from
Antony and Cleopatra, V. ii. 93–100, where the Folio
reads:

> *Cleo.* Thinke you there was, or might be such a man
>   As this I dreampt of?
> *Dol.* Gentle Madam, no.
> *Cleo.* You Lye up to the hearing of the Gods:
>   But if there be, nor euer were one such
>   It's past the size of dreaming: Nature wants stuffe
>   To vie strange formes with fancie, yet t'imagine
>   An *Anthony* were Natures peece, 'gainst Fancie,
>   Condemning shadowes quite.

The 'nor' in 'if there be, nor euer were' is usually

changed to 'or', but this destroys the sense and continuity of Cleopatra's argument. She first asks:

Think you there was, or might be such a man?

And when the answer is No, she insists that there might
be and was indeed one such by asking, How, if there
neither is nor ever were a man like Antony, could we
possibly imagine him? For his greatness exceeds our
powers of imagination. The 'nor ever' implies the
'neither' in the first alternative, just as the 'nor' in the
line from Sonnet 86—

He nor that affable familiar ghost—

indicates that 'neither' is understood before 'He'.
Though I am aware that there are good judges who
still prefer the 'or ever' of the Third Folio, I am persuaded that Thiselton is right and that the First Folio
reading should stand.

This final 'correction', however doubtful, is submitted to the reader's judgement to suggest to him
that the textual critic even when agonizing over the
choice between 'or' and 'nor' may be making a genuine
effort to interpret Shakespeare and that this critical
task, however humble in comparison with the great
work of the literary masters in exploring the profundities of Shakespeare's mind and art, is a useful contribution to the interpretation, criticism, and enjoyment of
Shakespeare.

Notes to pp. 122 and 125. As Professor J. C. Maxwell has pointed out,
'heard' at *Merchant of Venice*, III. i. 112, should have been attributed to
Leon Kellner, and Percy Simpson's defence of *Love's Labour's Lost*, V. ii. 67,
seems to have been anticipated by F. A. Marshall.

F. R. LEAVIS

(b. 1895)

The Criticism of Shakespeare's Late Plays[1]

A CAVEAT

I HAVE before me two essays on *Cymbeline*. In the later[2] of them Fr. A. A. Stephenson both criticizes the account of the play offered by F. C. Tinkler in the earlier,[3] and offers a positive account of his own. With the criticisms I find myself pretty much in agreement; but I also find myself as unconvinced by the new interpretation as by Tinkler's—or any other that I have read. Fr. Stephenson, judging that Tinkler's attempt to explain the play in terms 'of critical irony' and 'savage farce' doesn't cover the admitted data, himself observes, and argues from, what he takes to be a significant recurrence of 'valuation-imagery'. But while developing his argument he at the same time—and this is the curious fact that seems to me to deserve attention—makes a firm note of another set of characteristics, and draws an explicit conclusion:

the inequalities, the incongruities, the discontinuity, the sense of different planes, the only spasmodic and flickering life in *Cymbeline*. It must, I think, be recognized that *Cymbeline* is not an 'organic whole', that it is not informed and quickened by an idea-emotion in all its parts.

The stress laid on these characteristics of the play seems to me much more indisputably justified than that laid on the valuation-imagery. So much so, in fact, that the

[1] *Scrutiny*, x. 339, reprinted in *The Common Pursuit* (1952).
[2] *Scrutiny*, vol. x, no. 4.   [3] Ibid., vol. vii, no. 1.

question arises: Why didn't both Fr. Stephenson and Tinkler (whose argument also derives from observation of these characteristics) rest in the judgement that the play 'is not an "organic whole", that it is not informed and quickened by an idea-emotion in all its parts'? Why must they set out to show that it is, nevertheless, to be paradoxically explained in terms of a pressure of 'significance'—significance, according to Fr. Stephenson, of a kind that cannot be conveyed?

That two such intelligent critics, bent on conclusions so different, should countenance one another in this kind of proceeding suggests some reflections on the difficulties and temptations of Shakespeare criticism— and especially of criticism of the late plays—at the present time. We have left Bradley fairly behind. We know that poetic drama is something more than drama in verse, and that consideration of the drama cannot be separated from consideration of the poetry. We are aware of subtle varieties of possibility under the head of convention, and we know we must keep a vigilant eye open for the development of theme by imagery and symbolism, and for the bearing of all these on the way we are to take character, action, and plot. Shakespeare's methods are so subtle, flexible, and varied that we must be on our guard against approaching any play with inappropriate preconceptions as to what we have in front of us. By assuming that the organization is of a given kind we may incapacitate ourselves for seeing what it actually is, and so miss, or misread, the significance. What a following-through of F. C. Tinkler's and Fr. Stephenson's account will, I think, bring home to most readers is that we may err by insisting on finding a 'significance' that we assume to be necessarily there.

I have put the portentous word in inverted commas in this last use of it, in order not to suggest a severity of judgement that is not intended. The play contains a

great variety of life and interest, and if we talk of
'inequalities' and 'incongruities' it should not be to
suggest inanity or nullity: out of the interplay of contrasting themes and modes we have an effect as (to fall
back on the usefully corrective analogy) of an odd and
distinctive music. But the organization is not a matter
of a strict and delicate subservience to a commanding
significance, which penetrates the whole, informing and
ordering everything—imagery, rhythm, symbolism,
character, episode, plot—from a deep centre: *Cymbeline*
is not a great work of art of the order of *The Winter's
Tale*.

The Winter's Tale presents itself as the comparison
with which to make the point, in that it belongs with
Cymbeline to the late group of plays—plays that clearly
have important affinities, though my purpose here is to
insist on the differences. In academic tradition *The
Winter's Tale* is one of the 'romantic' plays; the adjective implying, among other things, a certain fairy-
tale licence of spirit, theme, and development—an
indulgence, in relation to reality, of some of the less
responsible promptings of imagination and fancy. Thus
we have the sudden, unheralded storm of jealousy in
Leontes, the part played by the oracle, the casting-out
and preservation of the babe, the sixteen-year gap in
the action, the pastoral scene (regarded as a pretty piece
of poetical by-play) and, finally, the return to life
after sixteen years' latency of Galatea-Hermione, in the
reconciliation-tableau. But all this has in the concrete
fullness of Shakespeare's poetry an utterly different
effect from what is suggested by the enumeration. *The
Winter's Tale*, as D. A. Traversi shows so well in his
Approach to Shakespeare, is a supreme instance of
Shakespeare's poetic complexity—of the impossibility,
if one is to speak with any relevance to the play, of considering character, episode, theme, and plot in abstrac-

tion from the local effects, so inexhaustibly subtle in their inter-play, of the poetry, and from the larger symbolic effects to which these give life.

Properly taken, the play is not romantically licentious, or loose in organization, or indulgent in a fairy-tale way to human fondness. What looked like romantic fairy-tale characteristics turn out to be the conditions of a profundity and generality of theme. If we approach expecting every Shakespearian drama to be of the same kind as *Othello*, we criticize Leontes's frenzy of jealousy as disconcertingly sudden and unprepared. But if our preconceptions don't prevent our being adverted by imagery, rhythm, and the developing hints of symbolism—by the subtle devices of the poetry and the very absence of 'psychology'—we quickly see that what we have in front of us is nothing in the nature of a novel dramatically transcribed. The relations between character, speech, and the main themes of the drama are not such as to invite a psychologizing approach; the treatment of life is too generalizing (we may say, if we hasten to add 'and intensifying'); so large a part of the function of the words spoken by the characters is so plainly something other than to 'create' the speakers, or to advance an action that can profitably be considered in terms of the interacting of individuals. The detail of Shakespeare's processes this is not the place for discussing; anyone who wants hints for the analysis will find all that can be asked in D. A. Traversi's book. It is enough here to remind the reader of the way in which the personal drama is made to move upon a complexity of larger rhythms—birth, maturity, death, birth ('Thou mettest with things dying, I with things new-born'); Spring, Summer, Autumn . . .

> Sir, the year growing ancient,
> Not yet on summer's death, nor on the birth
> Of trembling winter . . .

—so that the pastoral scene is something very much other than a charming superfluity. The power and subtlety of the organization—and this is a striking instance of Shakespeare's ability to transmute for serious ends what might have seemed irremediably romantic effects—are equal to absorbing into the profoundly symbolic significance of the whole even the *coup de théâtre* with which Pauline justifies her sixteen years of double-living and funereal exhortation.

As Fr. Stephenson points out, there is no such organization in *Cymbeline*. The romantic theme remains merely romantic. The reunions, resurrections, and re-conciliations of the close belong to the order of imagination in which 'they all lived happily ever after'.[1] Cloten and the Queen are the wicked characters, stepmother and son, of the fairy-tale: they don't strike us as the expression of an adult intuition of evil. Posthumus's jealousy, on the other hand (if I may supplement Fr. Stephenson's observation: 'the "evil" characters, in particular, do not receive full imaginative realization'), is real enough in its nastiness, but has no significance in relation to any radical theme, or total effect, of the play. And here there is opportunity for a brief aside in illustration of the variety of Shakespeare's dramatic modes. Jealousy is a theme common to *The Winter's Tale*, *Othello*, and *Cymbeline*. In *The Winter's Tale* there is no psychological interest; we don't ask (so long as we are concerning ourselves with Shakespeare): What elements in Leontes's make-up, working in what way, explain

[1] 'A ce moment parut doña Luz, l'air timide. (Dès qu'il l'aperçut, le général la prit par la main.)

"Ma nièce, lui dit-il, le visage joyeux, tu peux aimer sans crainte Cœur-Loyal, il est vraiment mon fils. Dieu a permis que je le retrouve au moment où j'avais renoncé à jamais au bonheur!"

La jeune fille poussa un cri de joie et abandonna sa main à Rafael, qui tomba à ses pieds. En même temps le général s'approcha de sa femme et dans la réunion qui suivit on oublia tous les malheurs du passé en songeant à l'avenir qui promettait tant de joie.' (*Les Trappeurs de l'Arkansas*, Gustave Aimard.)

this storm? The question is irrelevant to the mode of the play. *Othello*, on the other hand, it would not be misleading to describe as a character-study. The explosive elements have been generated between the very specifically characterized Othello and his situation, and Iago merely touches them off. Posthumus's case actually answers to the conventional account of Othello's: the noble hero, by nature far from jealous, is worked on and betrayed by devilish Italian cunning—Iachimo is, quite simply, the efficient cause that Iago, in the sentimentalized misreading of *Othello*, is seen as being. Posthumus suffers remorse for his murderous revulsion, but we are not to consider him degraded by his jealousy, or seriously blamable. Simply, he is a victim. He falls in with a villain who, out of pure malice, deceives him about Imogen, and, after strange vicissitudes, fairy-tale fortune brings the lovers together again to enjoy a life of happiness. Shakespeare, that is, has taken over a romantic convention and has done little to give it anything other than a romantic significance.[1]

Why then should two such intelligent critics as those in question not settle down in the obvious judgement that the play challenges? I have already suggested that the answer should be sought in terms of a reaction against what may be called the Bradley–Archer[2] approach to Shakespeare. In the case of *Cymbeline* the assumption that a profound intended significance must be discovered in explanation of the peculiarities of the play is fostered by the presence of varied and impressive evidence of the Shakespearian genius.

Strength could be adduced in a wealth of illustration. I myself have long carried mental note of a number of

[1] In *Pericles* he took over a romantic play, and the three acts that are clearly his are remarkable for the potency of the transmuting 'significance'.

[2] See *The Old Drama and the New* by William Archer. T. S. Eliot comments interestingly on the book in the essay called 'Four Elizabethan Dramatists' (*Selected Essays*).

passages from *Cymbeline* that seemed to me memorable
instances of Shakespeare's imagery and versification
Two in particular I will mention. One is Posthumus's
description of the battle [v. iii, lines 14 to 51]. It is a
remarkable piece of vigorous dramatic felicity. The
precisely right tone, a blend of breathless excitement,
the professional soldier's dryness, and contempt (towards the Lord addressed), is perfectly got. There are
some fine examples of Shakespearian compression and
ellipsis; and here, surely, is strength in imagery:

> and now our cowards,
> Like fragments in hard voyages, became
> The life of the need: having found the back-door open
> Of the unguarded hearts, heavens, how they wound!

In 'like fragments in hard voyages' and the 'back-door'
we have, in imagery, the business-like and intense
matter-of-factness, at once contemptuous and, in its
ironical dryness, expressive both of professional habit
and of controlled excitement, that gives the speech its
highly specific and dramatically appropriate tone. The
other passage is Posthumus's prison speech in the next
scene [v. iv. 3–29], so different in tone and movement:

> Most welcome, bondage! for thou art a way,
> I think, to liberty: yet am I better
> Than one that's sick of the gout; since he had rather
> Groan so in perpetuity than be cured
> By the sure physician, death, who is the key
> To unbar these locks.

This doesn't belong to 'romantic comedy', nor does
the dialogue with the jailer at the end of the scene.
And here, and in the many vigorously realized passages,
we have the excuse for the attempt, in spite of 'the
inequalities, the incongruities, the discontinuity, the
sense of different planes', to vindicate the play (for that,
paradoxically, is Fr. Stephenson's aim as well as Tinkler's) in terms of a profound significance. But surely

there should be no difficulty in recognizing that, wrestling with a job undertaken in the course of his exigent profession, Shakespeare might, while failing to find in his material a unifying significance such as might organize it into a profound work of art, still show from place to place, when prompted and incited congenially, his characteristic realizing genius?

Cymbeline, then, is not like *The Winter's Tale* a masterpiece. *The Tempest* is by more general agreement a masterpiece than *The Winter's Tale*, but it is a very different kind of thing (to complete briefly the hint of comparison I threw out above). Lytton Strachey, in his essay on 'Shakespeare's Final Period' (see *Books and Characters*), gives us an opening: 'There can be no doubt that the peculiar characteristics which distinguish *Cymbeline* and *The Winter's Tale* from the dramas of Shakespeare's prime are present here in still greater degree. In *The Tempest*, unreality has reached its apotheosis.' Lytton Strachey's 'unreality', strongly derogatory in intention, has to be understood, of course, in relation to the Bradley–Archer assumptions of his approach. Actually, it seems to me that *The Tempest* differs from *The Winter's Tale* in being much closer to the 'reality' we commonly expect of the novelist. The 'unreality', instead of penetrating and transmuting everything as in *The Winter's Tale*, is in *The Tempest* confined to Prospero's imagery and its agents. Prospero himself, the Neapolitan and Milanese nobility and gentry, Stephano and Trinculo, the ship's crew—all these belong as much to the 'reality' of the realistic novelist as the play of *Othello* does. Prospero manages the wreck, lands the parties, and directs their footsteps about the island to the final convergence, but they strike us, in their behaviour and conversation, as people of the ordinary everyday world. The courtiers are Elizabethan quality, and Gonzalo's attempt to distract the king and raise the tone of the conversation with a piece of advanced thought from Montaigne is all in keeping. Even Caliban (though sired by the devil on a witch) leads the modern commentator, quite appropriately, to discuss Shakespeare's interest in the world of new discovery and in the impact of civilization on the native.

The 'unreality' functions in Ariel and in the power (as it were a daydream actualized) that enables Prospero to stage the scene of repentance and restitution. But the nature of this power as a licence of imagination stands proclaimed in the essential symbolism of the play; and not only does Prospero finally renounce magic, break his staff, and drown his book, but the daydream has never been allowed to falsify human and moral realities. That Alonso should, without the assistance of magic, suffer pangs of conscience is not in the least incredible; on the other hand, we note that the sinister pair, Sebastian and Antonio, remain what they were. They may be fairly set over against Ferdinand and Miranda, and they represent a potent element in that world to which the lovers are returning, and in which, unprotected by magic, they are to spend their lives.

> O brave new world,
> That has such people in't!

—that is both unironical and ironical. Shakespeare's power to present acceptably and movingly the unironical vision (for us given in Miranda and Ferdinand) goes with his power to contemplate the irony at the same time.

Rightly, then, is *The Tempest* accounted a masterpiece; but I am not sure that it deserves the relative valuation it commonly enjoys. The judgement that *The Winter's Tale* is a masterpiece would not, I think, in general be as readily concurred in; and it is true that *The Tempest* has nothing in it to trouble in the same way the reader who finds difficulty in arriving at an un-qualified acceptance of the statue business as part of a total unromantic response. But the perfection (or something like it) of *The Tempest* is achieved within limits much narrower than those of *The Winter's Tale*; and the achievement by which, in *The Tempest*, the time-gap of *The Winter's Tale* is eliminated ought not to be allowed to count improperly in the comparative valuation. With the absence of the time-gap goes also an absence of that depth and richness of significance given, in *The Winter's Tale*, by the concrete presence of time in its rhythmic processes, and by the association of human growth, decay, and rebirth with the vital rhythms of nature at large. The range, the depth, the effect that I have described as both generalizing and intensifying, for which *The Winter's Tale* is remarkable, are missing in *The Tempest*. Not that while reading *The Tempest* we are at all inclined to judge that this inspired poetry and this consummate art reveal any falling-off in the poet's creative vigour; yet we may perhaps associate the mood expressed in Prospero's farewell to *his* art and in the 'insubstantial pageant' speech (the mood in which Shakespeare can in the symbolic working of the drama itself so consciously separate his art from the life it arranges and presents—life that is 'such stuff as dreams are made on')—perhaps we may associate this mood with an absence of that effect as of the sap rising from the root which *The Winter's Tale* gives us. No doubt it might as truly be said of Florizel and Perdita as it has been of Ferdinand and Miranda, that they are lovers seen by one who is himself beyond the age of love, but Florizel and Perdita are not merely two individual lovers; they are organic elements in the poetry and symbolism of the pastoral scene, and the pastoral scene is an organic part of the whole play.

H. D. F. KITTO

(b. 1897)

Hamlet[1]

I. THE PROBLEM OF HAMLET

SURELY the real problem of *Hamlet* lies in certain facts briefly reported by Waldock,[2] that up to the year 1736 no critic seems to have found any great difficulty in the play, but since that date one interpretation after another has been proposed and rejected. In 1736 Sir Thomas Hanmer, inquiring why Hamlet does not kill Claudius at once, explained that if he had done, the play would have ended somewhere in Act II; and that Shakespeare, anxious to avoid this disaster, did not manage to make Hamlet's delay dramatically convincing. As we have seen, there is a strong family likeness between this reasoning and what the Scholiast said about the *Ajax*, that Sophocles, wishing to prolong the play, made a mess of it. But let us not laugh too soon at Hanmer: our own day has produced critics willing to make his necessary assumption, namely that *Hamlet* is incompetently constructed. There are critics of the 'historical' school who have persuaded themselves—or at least have sought to persuade others—that the play contains chunks of earlier material which Shakespeare could not or did not assimilate, like some ostrich with tin-cans inside him. Critics of a psychological turn have woven fantasies around the play so tightly that it has become quite unable to move, with the natural result that Mr. Eliot has written it off as a

[1] *Form and Meaning in Drama* (1956).
[2] *Hamlet: A Study in Critical Method*, p. 3.

failure, since 'nothing that Shakespeare can do with the plot can express Hamlet for him'. Hamlet has been professionally psycho-analysed. What the Baker Street Irregulars do for fun certain Stratford Irregulars have tried to do in earnest: to treat Hamlet as a real person, having an existence outside the play. The irreverent outsider is tempted to say that the great triumph of Mr. Michael Innes's *The Mysterious Affair at Elsinore* is that it succeeds in being even funnier than some of the serious books about the play.

In this confusion of criticism there is not much that is entirely unfamiliar to the student of Greek Tragedy. What is new to him is the *mystique* which has grown up about *Hamlet*: the suggestion that there is in it something unique and ineffable which sets it apart not only from other plays but also from all other works of art, except perhaps the Mona Lisa. Perhaps this is well founded, but it is a little bewildering—and, if Waldock is right, it did not begin until a century after Shakespeare's death. A thing is commonly said about the role of Hamlet which would scarcely be said of any other role; it is accepted and expanded by Professor Dover Wilson as follows:

> There are as many Hamlets as there are actors who play him; and Bernhardt has proved that even a woman can score a success. Of a role so indeterminate almost any version is possible; with a character so fascinating and so tremendous in outline hardly any impersonator can fail.[1]

As for Bernhardt's exploit, and what it proves, we may reflect that in 441 B.C., or thereabouts, a man played the role of Antigone. Whether or not he scored a success in it is not recorded; if he did, it is certainly not because the role is indeterminate in composition. Since a play, like a piece of music, must be interpreted, something must necessarily be left to the interpreter; but so

[1] *What Happens in Hamlet*, p. 238.

elementary a point as this is not in question if we say 'There are as many Hamlets as there are actors capable of playing the part.' What is implied, to put it bluntly, is that in creating this part, as in creating no other, Shakespeare signed a blank cheque, and left it to the actor to draw what sum he can. Did he? About Goethe's idea of Hamlet, Dover Wilson says that its 'condescending sentimentalism' almost makes one angry. He has not much more patience—nor have I—with the paralysed intellectual that Coleridge imagined, nor with the ruthless Renaissance Prince that Dr. de Madariaga has recently devised. Here then, for a start, are three Hamlets whom Dover Wilson is willing not only to boo off the stage but also to argue out of existence. And rightly, for they have no existence; to give them existence we should have to remake the play.

The cheque, then, is not a blank one. It may be that in creating this role Shakespeare left more than usual to the player of it, but this is far from saying that 'almost any version is possible'. Perhaps almost any version can be made effective on the stage—but only to an audience which does not very much mind whether the play as a whole makes sense or not. We ought not to quarrel with the producer or actor whose first concern is to 'put the play across'—which he will do, naturally, by rendering the play according to the intellectual and emotional idiom of his own time; if he does not to some extent do this, he is not likely to act or produce Shakespeare very often. But as the scholar and critic does not live by selling theatre seats, his duty is a different one: it is to disregard contemporary habits of thought entirely, so far as he can, in order to understand Shakespeare's, so that he may see the play without distortion. Today the amateur critic of *Hamlet* can profit greatly by the information which modern scholarship has made available about Elizabethan and Jacobean thought. We should, however, reflect that no such study can do more than tell us what Shakespeare *might* have thought; if we would know what he did think, there is nothing to do but to study the play, and to be very careful neither to bring anything into it which its creator did not put there, nor to leave out anything that he did.

It seems that criticism of the play has been concerned, in the main, with the character of Hamlet; the play is something draped around him, something designed to present his character. For example, the recent film version carried as a sub-title: 'The tragedy of a man who could not make up his mind.' Since this film was as far as possible from being a travesty made by barbarians for illiterates, but was a distinguished piece of work, we may assume that this is a representative modern view; but how far it is from the truth, how little it explains the form of the play, becomes apparent as soon as we begin to consider that form constructively. What if *Hamlet* is a play which it would be reasonable to call 'religious drama', as we are using the term here? What if the ingrained individualism of the last two centuries—to say nothing of romanticism—has blinded us to one aspect of the play without which it cannot possibly appear as a firm and coherent structure? To put it provocatively: suppose that *Hamlet* is just as much a play about Hamlet as the *Ajax* is a play about Ajax, and no more?

That a modern audience can be baffled by a classical English play, precisely because it is now unfamiliar with the wide perspective of 'religious' drama, I happened to have demonstrated to me while struggling with this chapter. It befell me to see, four times within a week, an admirable production, on an Elizabethan stage, of *The Duchess of Malfi*. The interesting point was the behaviour of the audiences. They laughed consumedly in the right places, but they also laughed in wrong places, notably in the last scene, where corpse is piled on corpse; but in these places the laughter would begin—and then fall stone-dead; the audiences were obviously puzzled.

In comparison with Shakespeare, Webster is perhaps not more than a poster-artist of genius. Still, the play has a perfectly clear moral structure: the French Court has been purged, and is at peace with itself; the Italian Courts have not, and the play works out the 'inevitable or probable' ruin caused by the various forms of wickedness rampant in Ferdinand's Court. There is room perhaps for civilized amusement at Webster's violence, but the puzzled laughter indicated an audience confronted—and who can wonder?—by something which was outside its experience, but quite intelligible, and familiar, to another layman who happened to be familiar with Greek religious drama. Talk about 'the Elizabethan taste for horrors' should not blind us to the fact that all those who die in this last act have caused their own death, directly or indirectly, by their own sins. To Webster, sin was horrible; to us it is merely out of fashion.

In *Hamlet*, eight people are killed, not counting Hamlet's father; of the two families concerned in the play, those of King Hamlet and Polonius, both are wiped out. Eight deaths are enough to attract attention, and to make us wonder if the essential thing has been said when the play is called 'the tragedy of a man who could not make up his mind'. And the manner of these deaths is no less significant than their number. Claudius murders King Hamlet by poison; thereafter, a metaphorical poison seeps through the play: rottenness, cankers, 'things rank and gross in nature' meet us at every turn. Then at the end it once more becomes literal poison: Gertrude, Claudius, Laertes, Hamlet are all poisoned; and on Claudius, already dead or dying from the poisoned rapier, Hamlet forces the poisoned cup. The Ghost had said:

> Nor let thy soul contrive
> Against thy mother aught; leave her to Heaven.

So too Horatio observed:

> Heaven will direct it.

And what does Heaven do with Gertrude? Of her own accord, and in spite of a warning, she drinks poison. These are plain and striking dramatic facts; how far does 'Hamlet's fatal indecision' explain them? Are they an organic part of a tragedy of character? Or did Shakespeare kill so many people merely from force of habit?

Before examining the structure in detail we may orientate ourselves a little more exactly by examining another dramatic fact: the way in which Shakespeare presents the death of Polonius. Polonius seems often to be interpreted as something of a Dickens character. Thus Granville Barker, writing about the Reynaldo scene, and its 'verbiage', speaks of 'a tedious old wise-acre meddling his way to his doom'; and explains that in this scene Shakespeare, having changed his mind about Polonius, is making a transition from 'the not un-impressive figure' of the earlier scenes 'who has talked sound sense to Laertes and Ophelia' to the more comic figure that he later becomes.[1] The facts of the play, as it seems to me, directly contradict such an estimate. Polonius, like everything else in Denmark, is rotten. The proof of this may wait; we are concerned at present with the manner of his death.

In Act III, scene i—a magnificent scene, provided we do not try to be clever with it—Claudius and Polonius arrange to spy on Ophelia and Hamlet. There will be occasion later to consider the scene in detail; for the moment we will consider only this, that Shakespeare is concerned to emphasize the indecency of it.

---

[1] *Introduction to Hamlet*, p. 61.

Hamlet is—or was—in love with Ophelia and she with him. (The other view, that she is a hussy and he a trifler, brings to mind an unamiable phrase of Housman's: 'This suggestion does dishonour to the human intellect.') It will do us no harm to remember what Love so often is in Shakespeare: not merely a romantic emotion, but a symbol of goodness, even a redemptive power. We have been told often enough in the play what Claudius and Gertrude have made of Love; we ought to have noticed how Polonius thinks of it. In this scene the pure love of Ophelia is being used by two evil men who besmirch everything they touch. This would need argument—and plenty is available— except that in this very scene Shakespeare makes further argument unnecessary: Polonius gives Ophelia a book, evidently a holy book. Lying, spying, double-dealing, are second nature to this wise old counsellor; even so, the formal indecency of what he is doing now makes him uneasy:

> Read on this book,
> That show of such an exercise may colour
> Your loneliness.—We are oft to blame in this,
> 'Tis too much proved, that with devotion's visage
> And pious action we do sugar o'er
> The Devil himself.

So, Polonius, there you are—and there too is Claudius, who also confesses at this moment the rottenness of his soul.

These two, then, for their own purposes exploit a young love and the exercise of devotion, sugaring o'er the Devil himself. At the end of the scene Polonius proposes to do the same thing again. He hides behind a second arras, and finds that to be too busy is some danger.

Evidently, the character of Hamlet and the death of Polonius are not unconnected, but it is not the case that

Shakespeare contrived the latter merely to illustrate the former. The perspective is wider than this. If we will not see the 'divine background', whatever that may prove to be in this play, what shall we make of what Hamlet now says?—

> For this same lord
> I do repent: but Heaven hath pleased it so,
> To punish me with this, and this with me,
> That I must be their scourge and minister.

A shuffling-off responsibility? No; this has the authentic ring of Greek, that is to say of 'religious', tragedy. The deed is Hamlet's, and Hamlet must answer for it. But at the same time it is the work of Heaven; it is, so to speak, what *would* happen, what ought to happen, to a man who has been sugaring o'er the Devil himself. Denmark is rotten, Polonius is rotten; his death, and the death of seven others, are the natural outcome.

The case is similar with Rosencrantz and Guildenstern. What kind of a man, we may ask, was this Hamlet, that without turning a hair he should so alter the commission that

> He should the bearers put to sudden death,
> Not shriving-time allowed?

It is a legitimate question, but not the first one to ask. The first question is: what is the significance of the whole incident in the total design of the play? Where does Shakespeare himself lay the emphasis? For after all, it is his play. When Hamlet tells the story to Horatio, Shakespeare might have made Horatio say:

> Why, man, this was a rash and bloody deed!

What Horatio does say is very different:

> So Guildenstern and Rosencrantz go to 't.

Before we tell Shakespeare what we think of Hamlet's

behaviour we should listen to what Shakespeare tells
us. These two young men are friends to Hamlet:

> Good gentlemen, he hath much talked of you;
> And sure I am two men there are not living
> To whom he more adheres.

Hamlet himself corroborates:

> My excellent good friends! How dost thou, Guildenstern?
> Ah, Rosencrantz! Good lads, how do you both?

The casual, undergraduate-like obscenity that follows
establishes the unaffected ease that subsists between
them at this moment. Hamlet has no closer friends,
unless perhaps it is Laertes, whom also he kills and by
whom he is killed, or Horatio, whom he just prevents
from killing himself.

But something has just happened to these two young
men: they have been suborned by Claudius and Gertrude:

> *Guildenstern.*   But we both obey,
> And here give up ourselves in the full bent
> To lay our service freely at your feet
> To be commanded.

'We here give up ourselves'—to a murderer and to his
guilty wife. Nor is this all that Shakespeare has to tell
us about them:

> The cease of majesty
> Dies not alone, but like a gulf doth draw
> What's near it with it; it's a massy wheel
> Fixed on the summit of the highest mount,
> To whose huge spokes ten thousand lesser things
> Are mortis'd and adjoined; which when it falls,
> Each small annexment, petty consequence,
> Attends the boisterous ruin. Never alone
> Did the king sigh, but with a general groan.

Sophocles was not the only tragic poet to understand
tragic irony. For these words, spoken of King Claudius,

have a much more vigorous reference to the death of King Hamlet; he is the 'massy wheel' which in its fall brings down sundry small annexments—one of whom is the wise speaker of these verses; for they are spoken by Rosencrantz. If then our first question is, What kind of man is Hamlet, that he sends these two to their death? the fault is not Shakespeare's but our own, for lowering our sights contrary to his instructions.

Much of what has just been said needs further justification. We have also many other dramatic facts to note and to use. Perhaps we can kill two birds with one stone by surveying the first six scenes of the play, in which are laid down the foundations of the whole structure, and by prefixing to this a consideration of a matter which has not indeed escaped notice, that there is a resemblance between *Hamlet* and the *Oedipus*.

2. HAMLET AND THE OEDIPUS

The *Oedipus Tyrannus* begins by describing twice, once in dialogue and once in lyrics, the plague which is afflicting Thebes. The cause of the plague is the presence in the city of a man who has done two things foul and unnatural above all others: he has killed his own father, and he is living incestuously with his own mother. The details of the plague are so described that we can see how its nature is strictly proportioned to its cause: to death is added sterility; the soil of Thebes, the animals, and the human kind are all barren. The meaning is obvious—unless we make it invisible by reducing the play to the stature of Tragedy of Character: what Oedipus has done is an affront to what we should call Nature, to what Sophocles calls Dikê; and since it is the first law of Nature, or Dikê, that she cannot indefinitely tolerate what is ἄδικον, or contrary to Nature, she rises at last against these unpurged affronts. The plague of sterility is the outcome of the unnatural things which Oedipus has done to his parents.

Hamlet begins in the same way. The two soldiers, Marcellus and Bernardo, and Horatio, who is both a soldier and a scholar, are almost terrified out of their wits by something so clean contrary to the natural order that

> I might not this believe
> Without the sensible and true avouch
> Of mine own eyes.

Professor Dover Wilson, learned in sixteenth-century demonology, has explained that the eschatology of Horatio and Hamlet is Protestant, that the Ghost is a Catholic ghost, and that Bernardo and Marcellus are plain untheological Elizabethans. On this it would be impertinent for an ignoramus to express an opinion, but it does seem that if the 'statists' in Shakespeare's audience, and scholars from the Inns of Court, saw and savoured theological *expertise* in this scene, they would be in danger of missing the main point: that the repeated appearances of the Ghost are something quite outside ordinary experience. Horatio the scholar has heard of something similar, in ancient history, 'a little ere the mightiest Julius fell'. So perhaps this present unnatural terror 'bodes some strange eruption to our state'; or —a less disturbing thought—perhaps the Ghost is concerned for some uphoarded treasure hidden in the womb of the Earth.

But at this point Shakespeare decides to write some poetry—and he is never so dangerous as when he is writing poetry:

> It faded on the crowing of the cock.
> Some say that ever 'gainst that season comes
> Wherein our Saviour's birth is celebrated,
> The bird of dawning singeth all night long:

And then, they say, no spirit dare stir abroad,
The nights are wholesome; then no planets strike,
No fairy takes, nor witch hath power to charm,
So hallowed and so gracious is the time.

Pretty good, for a simple soldier. The intense and solemn beauty of these verses lifts us, and was designed to lift us, high above the level of Horatio's conjectures. The night 'wherein our Saviour's birth is celebrated' is holy and pure beyond all others; therefore these nights which the Ghost makes hideous by rising so incredibly from the grave, are impure beyond most. Unless Greek Tragedy has bemused me, this passage does more than 'give a religious background to the supernatural happenings' of the scene;[1] they give the 'background', that is, the logical and dynamic centre, of the whole play. We are in the presence of evil. Hamlet's own prophetic soul recognizes this as soon as he hears of the Ghost:

Foul deeds will rise,
Though all the earth o'erwhelm them, to men's eyes.

If we may assume that Shakespeare had not read Sophocles—and that Hamlet had not read him, at Wittenberg, behind Shakespeare's back—the parallel with the *Oedipus* becomes the more interesting; for when Oedipus has at last discovered the truth the Chorus observes:

ἐφηῦρέ σ' ἄκονθ' ὁ πάνθ' ὁρῶν χρόνος,
δικάζει τὸν ἄγαμον γάμον πάλαι
τεκνοῦντα καὶ τεκνούμενον.

Time sees all, and it has found you out, in your own despite. It exacts Dikê from you for that unnatural marriage that united mother with son. (1213–15)

'Foul deeds will rise': there are evils so great that Nature

---

[1] Dover Wilson, *What Happens in Hamlet*, p. 67.

will not allow them to lie unpurged. So, returning to
the battlements with Hamlet, and inquiring with him

> Why thy canonized bones, hearsed in death,
> Have burst their cerements; why the sepulchre
> Wherein we saw thee quietly inurned
> Hath op'd his ponderous and marble jaws
> To cast thee up again—

we learn the cause: fratricide, incest, 'Murder most
foul, strange and unnatural'.

Here, most emphatically stated, are the very foundations and framework of the tragedy. We can, of course,
neglect these, and erect a framework of our own which
we find more interesting or more congenial to us. We
can say, with Dr. Greg, that the Ghost is all my eye;
or, with Professor Dover Wilson, that the first act, 'a
little play of itself', is 'an epitome of the ghost-lore
of the age'—in which case it becomes something of a
learned Prologue to the real play;[1] or, like Dr. de
Madariaga, we can neglect this encircling presence of
evil, and substitute what we know of sixteenth-century
Court manners; or, again without constant reference to
the background which Shakespeare himself erected, we
can subtly anatomize the soul and mind of Hamlet, on
the assumption that Hamlet is the whole play. But if
we do these things, let us not then complain that Shakespeare attempted a task too difficult for him, or conclude that the play is an ineffable mystery. Turning it
into 'secular' tragedy we shall be using the wrong focus.
The correct focus is one which will set the whole action
against a background of Nature and Heaven; for this is
the background which the dramatist himself has provided.

[1] Or, if it is not this, let it be shown what its organic function is. Shakespeare, having a capacious mind, may well have been keenly interested in
contemporary ghost-lore, but our first question is: what has he done with it
as a creative artist? Or has he done nothing with it?

[Professor Kitto proceeds to discuss the play in detail: *Form and Meaning in Drama*, pp. 256–328. His 'Conclusion' follows.]

This examination of *Hamlet* has been based on the same assumptions as our examination of certain Greek plays: that the dramatist said exactly what he meant, through the medium of his art, and means therefore exactly what he has said. We have tried, therefore, to observe what in fact he has said, considering every scene and every considerable passage (as one would in analysing a picture, for example, or a piece of music), not passing over this or that because it did not happen to interest us, or illustrate our point; nor being too ready to disregard a passage on the grounds that it was put there for some extraneous reason; remembering too that a dramatist can 'say' things by means other than words. I do not so flatter myself as to suppose that anything new has been brought to light. Nevertheless, if this general account of the play is acceptable, if its structure has been made to appear purposeful, in details big and small, such that the interpretation (blunders excepted) carries some measure of authority, then the critical method and the assumptions on which it is based may be held to be sound. It seems to me that this may be true.

As we said at the outset, the first thing that strikes us, or should strike us, when we contemplate the play is that it ends in the complete destruction of the two houses that are concerned. The character of Hamlet and the inner experience that he undergoes are indeed drawn at length and with great subtlety, and we must not overlook the fact; nevertheless, the architectonic pattern just indicated is so vast as to suggest at once that what we are dealing with is no individual tragedy of character, however profound, but something more like religious drama; and this means that unless we are ready, at every step, to relate the dramatic situation to its religious or philosophical background—in other words, to look at the play from a point of view to which more recent drama has not accustomed us—then we may not see either the structure or the meaning of the play as Shakespeare thought them.

Why do Rosencrantz and Guildenstern die, and Ophelia, and Laertes? Are these disasters casual by-products of 'the tragedy of a man who could not make up his mind'? Or are they necessary parts of a firm structure? Each of these disasters we can refer to something that Hamlet has done or failed to do, and we can say that each reveals something more of Hamlet's character; but if we see no more than this we are short-sighted, and are neglecting Shakespeare's plain directions in favour of our own. We are told much more than this when we hear Horatio, and then Laertes, cry 'Why, what a King is this!', 'The King, the King's to blame'; also when Guildenstern says, with a deep and un-conscious irony 'We here give up ourselves . . .', and when Laertes talks of 'contagious blastments'. Shake-speare puts before us a group of young people, friends or lovers, none of them wicked, one of them at least entirely virtuous, all surrounded by the poisonous air of Denmark (which also Shakespeare brings frequently and vividly before our minds), all of them brought to death because of its evil influences. Time after time, either in some significant patterning or with some phrase pregnant with irony, he makes us see that these people are partners in disaster, all of them borne down on the 'massy wheel' to 'boisterous ruin'.

In this, the natural working-out of sin, there is noth-ing mechanical. That is the philosophic reason why character and situation must be drawn vividly. Neither here nor in Greek drama have we anything to do with characters who are puppets in the hands of Fate. In both, we see something of the power of the gods, or the designs of Providence; but these no more override or reduce to unimportance the natural working of individual character than the existence, in the physical world, of universal laws overrides the natural behaviour of natural bodies. It is indeed precisely in the natural behaviour of men, and its natural results, in given circumstances, that the operation of the divine laws can be discerned. In *Hamlet*, Shakespeare draws a complete character, not for the comparatively barren purpose of 'creating' a Hamlet for our admiration, but in order to show how he, like the others, is inevitably engulfed by the evil that has been set in motion, and how he himself becomes the cause of further ruin. The conception which unites these eight persons in one coherent catastrophe may be said to be this: evil, once started on its course, will so work as to attack and overthrow impartially the good and the bad; and if the dramatist makes us feel, as he does, that a Providence is ordinant in all this, that, as with the Greeks, is his way of universalizing the particular event.

Claudius, the arch-villain, driven by crime into further crime, meets at last what is manifestly divine justice. 'If his fitness speaks . . .' says Hamlet; the 'fitness' of Claudius has been speaking for a long time. At the opposite pole stands Ophelia, exposed to corruption though uncorrupted, but pitifully destroyed as the chain of evil uncoils itself. Then Gertrude, one of Shakespeare's most tragic characters: she is the first, as Laertes is the last, to be tainted by Claudius; but while he dies in forgiveness and reconciliation, no such gentle influence alleviates her end. In the bedchamber scene Hamlet had pointed out to her the hard road to amendment; has she tried to follow it? On this, Shakespeare is silent; but her last grim experience of life is to find that 'O my dear Hamlet, the drink, the drink! I am poisoned'—poisoned, as she must realize, by the cup that her new husband had prepared for the son whom she loved so tenderly. After her own sin, and as a direct consequence of it, everything that she holds dear is blasted. Her part in this tragedy is indeed a frightening one. She is no Claudius, recklessly given to crime, devoid of any pure or disinterested motive. Her love for her son shines through every line she speaks; this, and her affection for Ophelia, show us the Gertrude that might have been, if a mad passion had not swept her into the arms of Claudius. By this one sin she condemned herself to endure, and, still worse, to understand, all its devastating consequences: her son driven 'mad', killing Polonius, denouncing herself and her crime in cruel terms that she cannot rebut, Ophelia driven out of her senses and into her grave—nearly a criminal's grave; all her hopes irretrievably ruined. One tragic little detail, just before the end, shows how deeply Shakespeare must have pondered on his Gertrude. We know that she has seen the wild struggle in the grave-yard between Laertes and Hamlet. When the Lord enters, to invite Hamlet to the fencing-match, he says: 'The Queen desires you to use some gentle entertainment to Laertes before you fall to play.' 'She well instructs me', says Hamlet. What can this mean, except that she has vague fears of Laertes's anger, and a pathetic hope that Hamlet might appease it, by talk more courteous than he had used in the graveyard? It recalls her equally pathetic wish that Ophelia's beauty and virtue might 'bring him to his wonted ways again'. The mischief is always much greater than her worst fears. We soon see how Hamlet's gentle entertainment is received by Laertes; and she, in the blinding flash in which she dies, learns how great a treachery had been prepared against her Hamlet.

We cannot think of Gertrude's death, and the manner of it, without recalling what the Ghost had said: Leave her to Heaven. But if we are to see the hand of Providence—whatever that may signify—in her death, can we do other with the death of Polonius? A 'casual slaughter'? A 'rash and bloody deed'? Certainly; and let us by all means blame Hamlet for it, as also for the callousness with which he sends Rosencrantz and Guildenstern to their doom; but if we suppose that Shakespeare contrived these things only to show us what Hamlet was like, we shall be treating as secular drama what Shakespeare designed as something bigger. In fact, Hamlet was *not* like this, any more than he was, by nature, hesitant or dilatory; any more than Ophelia was habitually mad. This is what he has become. The dramatist does indeed direct us to regard the killing of Polonius in two aspects at once: it is a sudden, unpremeditated attack made by Hamlet, 'mad', on one who he hopes will prove to be Claudius; and at the same time it is the will of Heaven:

> For this same lord
> I do repent; but Heaven hath pleased it so
> To punish me with this and this with me,
> That I must be their scourge and minister.

Surely this is exactly the same dramaturgy that we meet in Sophocles' *Electra*. When Orestes comes out from killing his mother, Electra asks him how things are. 'In the *palace*',[1] he says, 'all is well—if Apollo's oracle was well.' Perhaps it was a 'rash and bloody deed'; it seems to bring Orestes little joy. We may think of it what we like; Sophocles does not invite us to approve, and if we suppose that he does, we have not understood his play, or his gods. Apollo approves, and Orestes, though he

[1] I italicize this word in order to represent Sophocles' untranslatable μέν, which suggests a coming antithesis that in fact is not expressed.

acts for his own reasons, is the gods' 'scourge and minister'. Polonius, no unworthy Counsellor of this King, a mean and crafty man whose soul is mirrored in his language no less than in his acts, meets a violent death while spying; and that such a man should so be killed is, in a large sense, right. Hamlet may 'repent'; Orestes may feel remorse at a dreadful act, but in each case Heaven was ordinant.

The death of Laertes, too, is a coherent part of this same pattern. To this friend of Hamlet's we can attribute one fault; nor are we taken by surprise when we meet it, for Shakespeare has made his preparations. Laertes is a noble and generous youth, but his sense of honour has no very secure foundations—and Polonius' farewell speech to him makes the fact easy to understand. His natural and unguarded virtue, assailed at once by his anger, his incomplete understanding of the facts, and the evil suggestions of Claudius, gives way; he falls into treachery, and through it, as he comes to see, he is 'most justly killed'.

Of Rosencrantz and Guildenstern, two agreeable though undistinguished young men, flattered and suborned and cruelly destroyed, there is no more to be said; but there remains Hamlet, last and greatest of the eight. Why must he be destroyed? It would be true to say that he is destroyed simply because he has failed to destroy Claudius first; but this is 'truth' as it is understood between police-inspectors, on duty. The dramatic truth must be something which, taking this in its stride, goes much deeper; and we are justified in saying 'must be' since this catastrophe too is presented as being directed by Providence, and therefore inevitable and 'right'. If 'there is a special providence in the fall of a sparrow', there surely is in the fall of a Hamlet.

Of the eight victims, we have placed Claudius at one

pole and Ophelia at the other; Hamlet, plainly, stands near Ophelia. In both Hamlet and Ophelia we can no doubt detect faults: she ought to have been able to see through Polonius, and he should not have hesitated. But to think like this is to behave like a judge, one who must stand outside the drama and sum up from a neutral point of view; the critic who tries to do this would be better employed in a police-court than in criticism. We must remain within the play, not try to peer at the characters through a window of our own constructing. If we do remain within the play, we observe that what Shakespeare puts before us, all the time, is not faults that we can attribute to Ophelia and Hamlet, but their virtues; and when he does make Hamlet do things deserving of blame, he also makes it evident on whom the blame should be laid. The impression with which he leaves us is not the tragedy that one so fine as Hamlet should be ruined by one fault; it is the tragedy that one so fine should be drawn down into the gulf; and, beyond this, that the poison let loose in Denmark should destroy indiscriminately the good, the bad, and the indifferent. Good and bad, Hamlet and Claudius, are coupled in the one sentence 'If his fitness speaks, mine is ready'. That Claudius is 'fit and seasoned for his passage' is plain enough; is it not just as plain that Hamlet is equally 'ready'? What has he been telling us, throughout the play, but that life can henceforth have no meaning or value to him? Confronted by what he sees in Denmark, he, the man of action, has been reduced to impotence; the man of reason has gone 'mad'; the man of religion has been dragged down to 'knavery', and has felt the contagions of Hell. There is room, though not very much, for subtle and judicious appraisal of his character and conduct; the core of his tragedy is not here, but in the fact that such surpassing excellence is, like the beauty and virtue of Ophelia, brought to nothing by evil. Through all the members of these two doomed houses the evil goes on working, in a concatenation

> Of carnal, bloody and unnatural acts,
> Of accidental judgments, casual slaughters,
> Of deaths put on by cunning and forced cause,

until none are left, and the slate is wiped clean.

The structure of *Hamlet*, then, suggests that we should treat it as religious drama, and when we do, it certainly does not lose either in significance or in artistic integrity. As we have seen more than once, it has fundamental things in common with Greek religious drama— yet in other respects it is very different, being so complex in form and texture. It may be worth while to inquire, briefly, why this should be so.

One naturally compares it with the two Greek revenge-tragedies, the *Choephori* and Sophocles' *Electra*, but whether we do this, or extend the comparison to other Greek religious tragedies like the *Agamemnon* or *Oedipus Tyrannus* or *Antigone*, we find one difference which is obviously pertinent to our inquiry: in the Greek plays the sin, crime, or error which is the mainspring of the action is specific, while in Hamlet it is something more general, a quality rather than a single act. Thus, although there are crimes enough in the *Oresteia*, what we are really concerned with, throughout the trilogy, is the problem of avenging or punishing crime. The *Agamemnon* is full of hybris, blind folly, blood-lust, adultery, treachery; but what humanity is suffering from, in the play, is not these sins in themselves, but a primitive conception of Justice, one which uses, and can be made to justify, these crimes, and leads to chaos; and the trilogy ends not in any form of reconciliation or forgiveness among those who have injured each other, nor in any purging of sin, or acceptance of punishment, but in the resolution of the dilemma.

Hamlet resembles the *Choephori* in this, that the murder of a King, and adultery, or something like it, are the crimes which have to be avenged; also that these can be avenged only through another crime, though perhaps a sinless one; but the differences are deep and far-reaching. They are not merely that Orestes kills, and Hamlet shrinks from killing. We may say that both in the Greek trilogy and in Shakespeare's play the Tragic Hero, ultimately, is humanity itself; and what humanity is suffering from in *Hamlet* is not a specific evil, but Evil itself. The murder is only the chief of many manifestations of it, the particular case which is the mainspring of the tragic action.

This seems to be typical. In the *Antigone* a whole house is brought down in ruin, and, again, the cause is quite a specific one. It is nothing like the comprehensive wickedness of Iago, or the devouring ambition of Macbeth, or the consuming and all-excluding love of Antony and Cleopatra. It is, quite precisely, that Creon makes, and repeats, a certain error of judgement, ἁμαρτία; and I use the phrase 'error of judgement' meaning not that it is venial, nor that it is purely intellectual, but that it is specific. It is not a trivial nor a purely intellectual mistake if a man, in certain circumstances, rejects the promptings of humanity, and thinks that the gods will approve; but this is what Creon does, and the tragedy springs from this and from nothing else. He is not a wicked man—not lecherous or envious or ambitious or vindictive. All this is irrelevant. He is simply the man to make and maintain this one specific and disastrous error.

This contrast between the specific and the general obviously has a close connexion with the contrast between the singleness of the normal Greek tragic structure and the complexity of *Hamlet*. In the first place, since Shakespeare's real theme is not the moral or theological or social problem of crime and vengeance, still less its effect on a single mind and soul, but the corroding power of sin, he will present it not as a single 'error of judgement' but as a hydra with many heads. We have shown, let us hope, how this explains, or helps to explain, such features of the play as, so to speak, the simultaneous presentation of three Creons: Claudius, Gertrude, and Polonius, each of them, in his own degree, an embodiment of the general evil. Hence too the richer character-drawing. Claudius is a drunkard, and the fact makes its own contribution to the complete structure; if Sophocles had made Creon a drunkard, it would have been an excrescence on the play. Hence too the frequent changes of scene in the first part of the play; also the style of speech invented for Polonius and Osric. The general enemy is the rottenness that pervades Denmark; therefore it is shown in many persons and many guises.

Then, not only are the sources of the corruption diverse, but so are its ramifications too. We are to see how it spreads, whether from Claudius or from Gertrude or from Polonius, and how it involves one after another, destroying as it goes. To be sure, Greek tragedy shows us something similar—but it is not the same. For example, the condemnation of Antigone leads to the death of Haemon, and that to the death of Eurydice; in the *Oresteia* too there is a long succession of crime. In fact, we remarked above that Claudius recalls the *Agamemnon* and its $\pi\rho\acute{\omega}\tau\alpha\rho\chi o\varsigma$ $\mathring{\alpha}\tau\eta$, the crime that sets crime in motion. So he does; but there is a big difference. Both in *Hamlet* and in the Greek plays crime leads to crime, or disaster to disaster, in this linear fashion, but in *Hamlet* it spreads in another way too, one which is not Greek: it spreads from soul to soul, as a contagion, as when Laertes is tempted by Claudius, or, most notably, when, by his mother's example and Polonius' basely inspired interference, Hamlet's love is corrupted into lewdness, or when he turns against his two compromised friends and pitilessly sends them to death.

Extension of evil in this fashion is, I think, foreign to Greek tragedy. Clearly, it involves a dramatic form which is complexive, not linear and single, like the Greek. Of his successive victims, Sophocles does not even mention Haemon until the middle of the play, and Eurydice not until the end; and the effect is most dramatic. In *Hamlet* there are eight victims, all of whom we have to watch, from time to time, as they become more and more deeply involved.

Further, not only are more people involved at the same time in this more generalized Tragic Flaw, but they are involved more intimately, which again makes for a richer dramatic texture. We may compare Hamlet with Orestes. Externally, they are in a similar position. But when Aeschylus has shown us that Orestes is an avenger pure in heart, and that his dilemma is from every point of view an intolerable one, it is not far wrong to say that his interest in Orestes, as a character, is exhausted; anything more would be unnecessary. Hamlet exists in a different kind of tragedy, one which requires that we should see how the contagion gradually spreads over his whole spirit and all his conduct.

The same contrast exists between Hamlet and Sophocles' Orestes and Electra. She, one might say, is drawn much more intimately than the Orestes of Aeschylus. True; but still she is drawn, so to speak, all at once: There is the situation, here is Electra, and this is the way in which it makes her act. It is not Sophocles' conception to show how her mother's continuing crime gradually warps her mind, by a stealthy growth of evil. If she is warped, it has all happened already. His dramatic interest in the characters of the avengers is focused on this, that they, being what they are, and being affected by Clytemnestra's crime in this way, will naturally act as they do.

It is, in short, a general statement which I think will bear examination, that Greek tragedy presents sudden and complete disaster, or one disaster linked to another in linear fashion, while Shakespearian tragedy presents the complexive, menacing spread of ruin; and that at least one explanation of this is that the Greek poets thought of the tragic error as the breaking of a divine law (or sometimes, in Aeschylus, as the breaking down of a temporary divine law), while Shakespeare saw it as an evil quality which, once it has broken loose, will feed on itself and on anything else that it can find until it reaches its natural end. So, for example, in *Macbeth*: in 'noble Macbeth', ambition is stimulated, and is not controlled by reason or religion; it meets with a stronger response from Lady Macbeth, and grows insanely into a monstrous passion that threatens a whole kingdom. It is a tragic conception which is essentially dynamic, and demands the very unhellenic fluidity and expansiveness of expression which the Elizabethan theatre afforded. Whether this is a reflection of some profound difference between Greek and Christian thought is a question which I am not competent to discuss.

G. WILSON KNIGHT

(b. 1897)

The Shakespearian Integrity[1]

I

THOUGH in period stretching well into the reign of King James, Shakespeare's work is pre-eminently Elizabethan, rooting from the soil of *The Shepherds' Calendar* and *Endimion*. But *The Spanish Tragedy* is behind him too: that is, if he did not write parts of it himself. Its strong action, its pathos, its family sympathy, its use of dark personal symbols, such as Revenge and Andrea's Ghost, its melodramatic yet strangely human horrors, its nature-imagery, the surge and fall of its blank-verse modulations, are closely Shakespearian. Shakespeare includes both the graces and the horrors of his age, working to transmute by a significant action the murder and revenge motifs of *The Spanish Tragedy* into the actualized divinity of *Endimion*.

Alexander and Caesar stride colossal across the Elizabethan imagination, imperial prototypes prefiguring Elizabeth. Ancient Rome was as much a stately ideal as Hellenic mythology a lover's paradise. Both coalesce in the perfect sovereign of Lyly's *Endimion*, Cynthia, whose court searches truth 'not in colours but life' and claims virtues 'not in imagination but execution'; the ideal being, to quote a pregnant phrase of Alexander's in *Campaspe*, the 'joining' of 'letters with lances' (*Endimion*, IV. iii. 48–50; *Campaspe*, I. i. 82).[2] Shakespeare's drama gives us blood and murder: tales of pagan revenge—how else, indeed, can the widest problems of

---

[1] *The Burning Oracle* (1939); revised and reprinted in *The Sovereign Flower* (1958); shortened for this collection.

[2] The importance of John Lyly is discussed in my article on his work in the *Review of English Studies*, April 1939.

action in face of evil be better dramatized?—and political anarchy. A bloody theme may arrest our attention to a number of profound truths, as in Christianity itself, but the Shakespearian poetry aims also to reintegrate its world into some person of royal strength or some lady of sunshine love. Neither may be, in themselves, Christian symbols; but the process to which I refer has vital Christian analogies. Each movement aims to organize itself into a living stillness; the conflict builds a peace; from the temporal is created the eternal. This is how the interplay of tempests and music becomes the axis of Shakespeare's world.

In all this pre-eminent among his contemporaries, Shakespeare becomes the consummate dramatist. But what is drama? First, it must rivet and hold attention, and at once. The economic pressure exerted on a poet-entertainer by this necessity is, within limits, good, since he is thereby forced to do the very things which are most helpful. And, second, it must convince with a truth: startling alone is of no use. The balance of significance and action has been struck by Shakespeare as by no other playwright. *Tamburlaine* has a levelled activity without true progress, and little meaning: what would it be, stripped of rhetoric? *Othello*, without its rhetoric, would still have a gripping plot. *Doctor Faustus* has spiritual significance, but the true conflict is ideological and static. *The Duchess of Malfi* holds deepest significances, but they are transmitted almost wholly by impressionistic language or events subdued to, or moulded by, the impressionistic plan: the story is weighted, clogged, stifled. Impossible as it may be to abstract finally plot from poetry, there remains meaning in the statement that Shakespeare gives us a good story. This is true of the parts as well as the whole, since each full-length scene has in isolation a significant dramatic value. Just think of what happens in *Richard III, Romeo and Juliet, A Midsummer Night's Dream,* in all the plays. Things move from the start and are kept going. Action rises on action, event scrambles over the shoulders of event; it is an attack. On what? On the audience's attention, for one thing; but, deeper, an onslaught on all fundamental negations in terms of human energy. In battering down inattention it also batters down a certain blindness. The action is not superficial: it is rather sacramental. Infinite subtleties are involved: irony, suspense, surprise, tempo-variation, climax, anti-climax; resolution in pathos or humour; channelling of subjective feelings of fear, hatred, horror, pride, and love; all are struts to build into us a lively sense of action shaped by some high-reaching intellectual and spiritual significance. At intensest moments we *are* the action. Shakespeare is the voice of an age which was in love with the various purposes and fortunes of men. He therefore helps to restore mankind's faith in its existence.

Action which is truly significant must be, however, or at least seem, natural. And the Shakespearian vitality is organic through and through: you get little feeling of artifice or mechanical schemes. His work is rooted in nature.

The country of Shakespeare's birth is continually recalled in his writing. His poetry is soil-rooted, nature-rooted. Flowers, weeds, trees, and woodland glades; birds of all sorts, animals kind and cruel; rivers and seas and sea-cliffs; winds and weather in all moods; moon, sun, stars, shadowed or shining—they are on page after page, image after image. The elements of earth, water, air, and fire are dramatic persons on his stage of impressions, sometimes with an explicit, sometimes an unobtrusive and embedded, schematic interrelation among themselves or reference to plot and action; but always significant. Impressions of sunrise are peculiarly beautiful, suiting the upward and energic tendency of Shakespeare's work. The process of the seasons plays its part. Rivers and the sea, especially the latter, are symbols of strength and urgency. The only natural image under-emphasized is, perhaps, the mountain.

This vast mesh of naturalistic impressionism is enwoven throughout with human emotions and actions; as when at the close of *King Lear* the impressions become more spring-like to tone with Cordelia's re-entry. These emotions and actions in their turn are felt as sprouting from a natural context, so that man is known to be no stranger in his world. The synthesis Wordsworth pined for is related to all the complexities of human life, the inward and the outward worlds being felt as subtly interaffective. Where images from daily affairs are found, they are more likely to be drawn from the country than from the town; and natural images in general tend to show first-hand experience and observation. Even when the associations are of communal and traditional immediacy they strike us, nevertheless, as fresh rather than ready made. The traditional is, as it were, newly discovered at every moment. Appeal is to all the senses in turn. At any moment you may all but touch and smell, not so much by definite sensory provisions as by direct metaphoric contact with that whole situation of which the tactile or olfactory image is really our own, literary, abstraction. Shakespeare may often assume a comparison not explicit, though felt, his imagery involving an action or animal not directly named, the ladder he rose by knocked away; and one such, when his more complex manner is at work, may blend into another, the real change taking place behind the words, to give us the sense of vitality without its sight. Analysis of separate impressions only the more clearly silhouettes their nature: they are, like everything else, always parts of an organic whole, impelled by a central unseen, but felt, force. So Shakespeare's language, even when no naturalistic impression is involved, is charged with a vital non-bookish energy; the speech coheres, in one organic rhythmic indissolubility, without either the assertive intellectual agilities of Donne—since the transferences, however swift, never outpace the already gathered momentum of their context—or the studied mosaic of Milton. Even the best beauties of Shakespearian verse are, as it were, carried on the rising and subsiding swell of the main flood, and you are conscious primarily of that psychic whole behind, calling them into being and calling them back at will. They relate not to each other so much as to this whole, on which their life and meaning depend. A Shakespearian speech is a microcosm of both his own poetic universe and creation in general, where all these qualities inhere.

Shakespeare's human drama is organically related to widening circles of society and nature. A central person or persons will normally, in the greater plays, be shown involved in some subjective conflict widening out to a family interest; filial in *Hamlet* and *Coriolanus,* paternal in *King Lear,* matrimonial in *Othello* and *Macbeth,* romantic in *Romeo and Juliet* and *Antony and Cleopatra.* The family psychology is penetrating. Next, there is the community; most strongly felt in *Romeo and Juliet, Julius Caesar, Troilus and Cressida, Macbeth, Coriolanus,* and the Histories, where citizens may be used as choric and communal voices. The tragic hero being normally a king or some equivalent the social implications of his fortunes properly go deeper than we, today, at first suspect; and his faith in kings clearly gives Shakespeare an advantage in dramatic condensation which succeeding generations have lacked. In each greater play you get a tight social unit of hero, family, and community in reciprocal action, with body-metaphors applied to the state and continual thought of social disorder as a disease, the well-known dialogue in *Coriolanus* (I. i. 92–169) being the most elaborate example of a normal tendency. You cannot here uproot the protagonist's psychology from his communal soil: disorder-effects in *Macbeth* apply equally to both. The implied metaphysic corresponds to the Pauline doctrine of the 'body' of Christ. The individual is, in a sense, the community, and therein lies the dramatic advantage of a king-hero, since in him most clearly personal and general significances coincide.

The Shakespearian art-form reflects both the queen-centred nationalism of its birth and that organic stability claimed by the British constitution today. All the swarming resources of this most holistic period are at Shakespeare's call. No aspect is quite neglected—quotations could be adduced against any one of my statements—but the stresses are his own. He is always in masterly fashion recognizing the significant, winnowing it from the chaff: not only his kings, but those most important symbols, his sea-tempests and music, are beautiful dominant abstractions from the Elizabethan world. His recognition of the significant, the apparently romantic, directions, is one with his nature-quality, since he uses mainly, and with an unswerving insight, only what has positive strength and survival-value. That is, he is prophetic. To recognize, explore, and express what was most significant in England during the medieval-Renaissance transition was necessarily to be prophetic, since we still, as a nation, as men, move by the momentum then generated.

II

The central thrust is thus positive and creative; indeed, a love. This love is both an outward sensuousness and an inward sympathy. The sensuousness is not Marlowe's. Marlowe's descriptions in *Hero and Leander* are sensuous to danger-point, and the danger will be found to lie in his abstracting tendency. His sensuousness is mental and therefore limited. In *Venus and Adonis* we have an even stronger sensuousness, and yet it appears, because not so limited, healthy in the sense that D. H. Lawrence is, or tried to be, healthy. Marlowe's poem concentrates externally on Leander's beautiful body, the erotic ornamentation of Venus' temple and the lascivious approaches of Neptune. Pictorial art[1] may be by itself a too facile way to sensuous description; and, for the rest, the poem's territory is both mentalized and narrow; and there are touches bordering on the lascivious, charged with poetic approval but with ever so faint a sense of sin to increase the delight. Shakespeare's physical descriptions work outside the sin-consciousness altogether: they apply equally to flowers, animals, and man, and do not expand the superficially desirable any more than he elsewhere descends to the superficially ugly. In *Venus and Adonis* the beauty of Adonis, seen through Venus's mind, is indeed most lusciously felt; but so also is the horse, restless with hot instincts, his stallion magnificence, buttock and all, finely described; there is an inclusive purity together with a fine and sympathetic realization of animal vitality, as in descriptions of the horse and 'poor Wat', the hunted hare; the hound's baying 'to the welkin', the snail's withdrawn antlers, the 'angry-chafing' boar (259–318, 679–708, 921, 1033–8, 662).

Everything is inwardly conceived: the poet even imagines the darkness closing over the frightened snail in his tiny shell-house. Adonis's blood-life is felt through his physique; he is, as it were, a body lighted from within, and you get more of a real physical existence than in Marlowe's description of Leander's nakedness.

[1] Cf. C. S. Lewis's discussion of artificial metal-work in Spenser's 'Bower of Bliss' (*The Allegory of Love*, pp. 324–33).

Shakespeare is inside one object after another and this is, paradoxically, the one condition of being properly outside it and able to show it in convincing action, the famous description of 'poor Wat' being only a peculiarly obvious example of a general sympathy. In *Venus and Adonis* and *The Rape of Lucrece* Shakespeare gets his main poles of reference clear, his later intensities of love and evil being already implicit. The subjectively conceived agony of Venus predicts the later tragedies, and a study of *Venus and Adonis* alone reveals the psychological centre of Shakespeare's work: a love which, though powerfully physical, is not merely a lust; a vital identification rather than a confined sense-suggestion of eye or touch, as in Marlowe's Leander; and this not limited to the beautiful, and thence by a rebound to the ugly, as in the plays of Marlowe, but dispassionately universal. Exact differentiation is hard, since every one of the opposite qualities is contained: lust, sense-perception, beauty. The difference is one of inclusion. All is so trusted, as Marlowe seldom trusts, that each object expands, dissolves, into a universal particularity where inward and outward are not distinct; and this is perhaps what the Gospels mean by being 'pure in heart'. Thence everything becomes sacramental. The difference is analogous to that between marriage-love and flirtation, between a dynamic adventure and a static enjoyment. Shakespeare is continually *married* to whatever he is treating, accepting it as itself and as a whole. His animals and people are thus neither ideal nor realistic, but real; the vital principle of each is apprehended and their actions therefore powerful.

The originating source of such creation should be already, in its general nature, clear. If one were to press for a personal and less valuable deduction there is some evidence. The Sonnets express a tortured heterosexual desire and idealize a homosexual love. *Venus and Adonis,* more likely to be in this sense revealing than any play, is written from the woman's view and the sensuous attractiveness is all male. *The Two Gentlemen of Verona* celebrates the victory of a masculine friendship over sexual love; and the Antonio-Sebastian drama in *Twelfth Night* is a miniature *Othello*. Antonio in *The Merchant of Venice* loves Bassanio as warmly as does Portia, and indeed their loves are once finely compared by Antonio, with perhaps a touch of jealousy (IV. i. 277–8); and we feel that everyone would be most uncomfortable were a wife, instead of ships, found for him at the end. It has been suggested that Mercutio was in love with Romeo, which might explain much, including both his love-ridicule and flare-up at the word 'consort' (*Romeo and Juliet*, III. i. 49). Cassius is a fervent lover: of Brutus, of Titinius. *Timon of Athens*, a play whose artistic cumbersomeness joined to titanic power might well present an imperfectly objectified experience, displays a universal love of man to men with, outside the dance, no feminine persons except, significantly, two prostitutes. The one play which seems to need a key which we have not got, *All's Well that Ends Well*, dramatizes a woman's terrifically sincere tracking down of a young man; and an obscure speech of Helena (I. i. 181–92) goes nearer than anything in Shakespeare to characterize the sweet, almost feminine, abandon, the seeing into persons and forces generally, which is the essence of Shakespeare's art.[1] The admiration of masculine action and the heavy stress on loyalty throughout, as in Enobarbus, might derive from some especially fiery centre of a man-to-man love or admiration. Such a tendency would be for the most part expressed dramatically in heterosexual terms, whereas a normal nature would scarcely have left these hints. The boys who turn out to be girls

[1] The thought here provides the needed 'key', which was subsequently used to make my essay on *All's Well that Ends Well* in *The Sovereign Flower*.

in many of the plots may be in this regard deeply significant. Of course, 'lover' to an Elizabethan can denote a relationship at once less than sexual and more than friendly, and the Sonnets probably reflect a complex of love and social worship similar to that of love and allegiance in *Endimion* which we, in a less aristocratic and royalistic age, cannot quite understand. I have no desire to stress a point which some might find disconcerting. There is, however, further evidence of what might be called a 'bisexual' temperament, as I shall shortly indicate. But whatever the personal facts there is no unhealthiness; by which I do not mean no perversions. Rather the reverse: a nature not afraid of, and serenely able to create from, whatever so-called perversions it possesses.[1] Sadism, such as you get in Flecker's *Hassan*, is quite absent, since cruelty is not presented with pleasing associations. The whipping incident in *Antony and Cleopatra* is precisely used to meet a correct demand, nor do the horrors of *Titus Andronicus* or eye-gouging in *King Lear* come under the meaning of the term.

The first half of Shakespeare's work concentrates on two primary emotional positives: (i) the normal romance interest of human love, and (ii) royalty, with especial reference to martial action. Both are approached with a profundity too easily missed. The two are related imagistically as eros-charged symbols: love may be compared to a kingly presence, and both love and kings are associated with the sun, repeating age-old religious associations.

Shakespeare's love-understanding goes deeper than Lyly's, with emotions more rounded and convincing. The Comedies have deep tragedy-contacts and smiles play through tears. *A Midsummer Night's Dream* has

[1] For a more comprehensive treatment of the substance of this paragraph, see my book *The Mutual Flame*.

nightmare fears, and *Twelfth Night* a melodic pathos. In *As You Like It* melancholy and bitter satire, as in Jaques's speech on the Seven Ages of Man (II. vii. 139–66), are interspaced with happiness, all toning into the shadowed glades of the forest to make a dappled world. Feste is a wistful figure, so is Touchstone, and both are deep, sometimes trenchant, thinkers. But most depends on the heroines. They are sunshine, laughing women enjoying a wisdom and happy mockery beyond the heroes. They are conceived as superior beings, with Christian sympathies, able to teach their men like children, as at the conclusion of *Love's Labour's Lost*; or to right the plot gone wrong through masculine error as in *The Merchant of Venice*. Both Rosalind and Viola show a maturity of love, almost maternal in wisdom yet paradoxically half on the brink of tears, sunshine and rain together as in Cordelia (*King Lear*, IV. iii. 20), which contrasts with the more gaudy passions and petulant jealousies of the men. Of Venus and Helena we have already spoken. Shakespeare shows a less inward sympathy for masculine love. Orlando, Orsino, Bassanio, and Romeo are, as lovers, weak, often rhetorical, figures compared with their ladies. What actor of Romeo has not felt instinctively that something, not all his own fault, has gone wrong during the Balcony Scene? Yet again, when tragedy thickens, what Romeo can fail to gain a new lease of life? Shakespeare's men become grandly and purposively tragic as his women do not. Then at once he is within them. They endure conflicts unknown to the singly purposeful heroines, and the specifically tragic resolution is theirs. Compare Romeo's death with Juliet's, Othello's with Desdemona's. The women may be allowed to show fear, but not the men, except in face of the supernatural, and then only temporarily. The greatest of his women miss *tragic* stature at their end: Lady Macbeth dwindles off somnambulistically, and

Cleopatra inverts death to life. Even Queen Katharine's end is rather weak in self-pity. Compare Romeo's set purpose in the tomb; the grandeur of Lear and Timon; the almost heroic self-pitying, because less than self-condemnation, of Othello and Macbeth; the noble reserve of Buckingham and Wolsey. Shakespeare is most within his men when tragedy overcomes them, lending them strength to overcome tragedy.

Yet he is not really then so much inside his heroes as inside the whole ritualistically conceived tragic sacrifice of which normally men are the protagonists. This sacrifice, in its reversal of material action, might again be called feminine. Those heroes Shakespeare seems most 'within' for a long period, such as Richard II and Hamlet, tend to the philosophic and the feminine, the death-shadowed. And yet the word 'within' begs the question, since it is really we who feel ourselves 'within' certain sorts of writing, and not others: finally, love and death are bound to hold a subjective appeal over fine action. In making women strongest in love and men in action, Shakespeare is the voice for a deep truth. But in tragedy you get a union, and so we have the eternal marriage and archetypal sacrifice of Cleopatra's self-immolation for Antony, a woman at once becoming and conquering that whole destiny whose maternal presence encloses earlier heroes. We can hazard at least this: a certain feminine or masculine-subjective strain, in Shakespeare, or in us, or, still better, in creation, is to be associated with love and death; a certain masculinity with action of a more superficial sort. These wrestle for mastery. Full of action as Shakespeare's stage is, it yet continually works to transmute action to a peace. That peace is in his heroines from the beginning: notice how the women in *Richard III*, *King John*, *Richard II*, *Henry IV*, and *Julius Caesar* suffer from man's political conflicts, sometimes pathetic, sometimes denouncing, as from a deeper wisdom, man's schoolboy quarrels; and how the heroines of the later plays, Ophelia, Desdemona, Cordelia, Hermione, Imogen, Queen Katharine, suffer instead from man's psychological conflicts. Moreover, ultimate forces of evil and love, negative and positive, flow most directly from two women, Lady Macbeth and Cleopatra. These tap, without conflict, the universal energy, good or evil, as the men do not. The sunshine fun and deep unrhetorical love of his ladies suggest, as does also the humour of Falstaff, some universal force beyond man's philosophy or ethic. Shakespeare's three most rounded and complex figures are Falstaff, Hamlet, and Cleopatra: the non-ethical mountain of fleshly enjoyment and keen satire on all manly ideals and action; the figure of man and all his problems shadowed by the mothering nearness of death; and woman in her unmoral, cosmic fascination, over-arching empires and transmuting death to life. Within the dramas feminine love is, like that of Shakespeare himself in the Sonnets, the 'star to every wandering bark', unshaken by tempests (Sonnet 116). It is a deep, unlustful, marriage-consciousness: witness Katharina the Shrew's final speech on marriage; or Portia's equally lovely surrender to Bassanio. I emphasize the deep conception of marriage here: it is implicit in Shakespeare's drawing of the snail; a perception of the self-hood's integrity, its inward music. There is a metaphysical depth, a totally non-moralizing yet Christian profundity about it. I point again to Helena's 'Not my virginity yet . . .' (*All's Well that Ends Well*, I. i. 181–92).

It is the same with Shakespeare's more masculine themes. There is any amount of nobility, but not tinsel glitter, in his perception of soldiership or kings. Kingship is presented as a burden. Kings may be saintly as Henry VI, villainous as Richard III, weak as Richard II, practical as Henry V: all are human individuals as well as sacred symbols. The dualism of sacred office and human character is, especially in *Richard II*, pregnant, the balance struck dramatically forecasting the balance of constitution and monarchy which England enjoys today. From the poetic rhapsodies on divine authority in *Richard II* we pass to problems of political order in *Henry IV*, and so on to the all-but-perfect king *Henry V*, where kingship functions in direct alignment with both religion and comradeship. Outwardly Shakespeare's world is often intensely selective, if you like romantic, as in his sublimation of soldierly valour and honour, but his inward realism is unmatched. There is no superficial sense of glory such as we find in *Tamburlaine*. Shakespeare's mind is married to, while Marlowe has an affair with, valour, honour, kingship; he takes each and all for better or worse with their rooted tentacular relationships, sins, and responsibilities. So kings are conceived tragically. The three burdened soliloquies of Henry VI, Henry IV, and Henry V might be said to reflect the spiritual royalty of Shakespeare's mind; since he too aims to hold vast conflicting forces in a peaceful balance. Himself a king of one sort, he sees and feels into kingship of another. Indeed, kingship is always a dramatic intensification of personality, raising to the highest power the wider significances inhering in all men. The king is the objectified super-self of each subject, from ancient ritual to modern times holding an especially dramatic office. So Shakespeare's kings have an inward dignity and the sequence of their stories an epic, if tragic, power which we find nowhere else in our literature. In them there beats, as a heart in a body, a deep romantic yet spiritual perception, reaching to the inward music of man and community alike.

Having so felt into the essence, Shakespeare re-creates the externals with full yet never assertive splendour; having recognized the suffering passivity in all things, he can infuse into them the energies of action. The rough English type of a Faulconbridge is as typical as Richard II. Shakespeare's martial splendours and kingly sceptres, his deeds of turmoil and battle, never appear materialistic, since they are fed from deeper levels. Any one person or event, as we saw with any one image, is a provisional expression only, pointing to a greater whole. As before, we are drawn to think of a rather feminine nature, yet only in the sense that Christ might be called 'feminine', because cosmic, in comparison with Alexander or Caesar: in other words, creative. Whatever it be, this love gives us an exposition of princely action and communal insight which levels all other English poets but Byron on the plain beneath, their differences unnoticed, and charges the Shakespearian stage with ever new creative significance, working not from the outside, but from the inner springs. Again, the inwardness is one with the objectivity; the feminine strain in man's nature being the condition, paradoxically, of any masculine achievement that shall last. So passive and active blend. Henry V, the hero-king, must be apprenticed, not to arms, but to the satiric humour of a Falstaff. Shakespeare is the poet of national action not deceived by its surface glory; the prophet of kingship never forgetting the pygmy stature of kings; the poet of active life, remembering death. The working out of this sequence leading to the accomplishment of Tudor supremacy was a task far greater than is usually supposed, dependent on a unique insight into social forces, in order and disorder alike, and a central honesty of love, human and thence national, intrinsically outside the range of any other poet of his, or our, day. Shakespeare writes, as it were, the Old Testament of the Elizabethan age; and, alone joining perfectly 'letters with lances', shows the slow resolution of discordances towards that high, if temporary, harmony of which his own art is the sovereign flower.

If Shakespeare's kings are men, so all his men are, in their way, kings. All are conceived with native force, direction, and wholeness. Each, whatever his faults, asserts himself in his own right. Hotspur is typical. Bottom has his own royalty, and the humour which he radiates is one with our recognition of it, as when we enjoy his boldness before Theseus. When Shakespeare comes near ridicule, as with Malvolio—and we may observe that excessive puritanism is here in question—the man's dignity is handed back at the end, with a fine exit. Shakespeare's humour is eminently sympathetic. Parolles, his braggadocio ludicrously exposed, remarks to himself that, if his heart were great, it would crack; but it is not, so 'simply the thing I am shall make me live' (*All's Well that Ends Well*, IV. iii. 373). Each, however dishonourable, is himself, and neither man nor God can take that from him. Autolycus needs no advertisement: the humour is one with our admiration. So, too, with the protagonist villains: Aaron and Iago, the worst, do not repent, and they at least have the virtue of consistency. The villainy of Richard III is subtly motivated in terms of inferiority, and his integrity, though weakened during the Ghost scene, is magnificently recaptured; while Shylock is in danger not of despisal but of excessive sentiment. At the extreme Caliban has *spiritual* dignity. The poet sees each, not perhaps precisely as he sees himself, since rationally one may be seriously deluded about oneself, but with an objective conception taking into full account all subjective and emotional profundities. He knows all men with that sympathy which each feels for himself. To complain of Shakespeare's aristocratic sympathies and lack of interest in other social strata would be superficial; whenever he is dealing with an individual from another class—and he has little interest in men in the mass except through symbolisms of order or kings— he crowns him before our eyes; as, for example, with the gravedigger who outwits Shakespeare's most profound hero, Hamlet, with a profundity; or the Messenger's 'I have done my duty' (II. v. 88) in contrast to the childish petulance of his most showily regal figure, in *Antony and Cleopatra*.

His fondness for kings and dukes is one with his fondness for lovers. The equating of kingship with successful love occurs throughout the Sonnets; and it is clearly a universal association. Aristocratic themes are used partly as the cinema today shows the heroine in a fine dress; and what hard worker, having paid for a seat, would wish it otherwise? Shakespeare exploits dramatically the kingship in every man, as does the kingly office itself, being a communal possession. Therefore his greater heroes are not 'characters' known as we know acquaintances, but aspects of our own, kingly, selves; just as his love-themes are our own fine love-affairs, not the rather silly business of our neighbours. Such identification is the quintessence of the properly dramatic. A significant moment occurs between Falstaff and Doll Tearsheet: from a sordid background, with a fat drunkard and a prostitute as principals, and a few prose utterances, is created a romantic intensity in comparison with which Milton's Eden pales. Why? Falstaff and Doll may seem very different from a Romeo and Juliet, but not to themselves, at that moment. Shakespeare here allows himself music. He is always recognizing and objectively dramatizing the inward music, the deepest self-hood, the very 'I'-ness, so to speak, of his persons. This is precisely what is meant by love. And, since people do not always know their own self-hood, one of his major themes, from Benedick, Orsino, and Katharina the Shrew through King Lear to

Enobarbus, Leontes, Coriolanus, and Wolsey ('I know myself now'; *Henry VIII*, III. ii. 379), is the gradual recognition by his heroes of their own deepest selves; which is, normally, a kind of love; a kind of eros-music, at once a humility and a royalty. And for a similar reason we too read Shakespeare, to dig deep enough to recognize ourselves. The dignity of human personality is thus central throughout. His people are therefore, unless of the type of Sir Andrew Aguecheek, nearly always courageous, Parolles not excepted: indeed, he is perhaps the bravest.

In this sense Shakespeare is profoundly Christian, though it is important to remember the total acceptance conditioning such integrity. Many passages and many persons, especially Friar Laurence and Cerimon, tone with traditional religion. Moreover, Shakespeare shows properly no conflict of the sexual-romantic and the Christian: Christian sanctities are consistently invoked in the cause of dramatic love, conceived as an enduring emotion. His ladies are allied continually with Christian associations. New Testament references and half-conscious reminiscences often witness a coincidence of the human with the archetypal and the Christian; as when Othello's bearing towards his armed retainers recalls Jesus' dignity in face of arrest; or when Antony's tragedy[1] has its 'last supper' and the desertion of Enobarbus is patterned on that of Judas. Timon and Richard II are impressionistically related to Christ Himself. But I point rather to that even more deeply embedded and instinctive Christianity in the very conception of human personality. In both Christianity and Shakespeare you have a central humility and passivity violently creative, radiating action, a process, as it were, of continual incarnation; and both finally reach, through

---

[1] As has been observed by J. Middleton Murry, in his essay on *Antony and Cleopatra* (*Shakespeare*, 1936; pp. 362–7).

this, the farthest death illuminations of the western world. But Shakespeare is too truly a dramatist and a Renaissance artist, and perhaps also too good a Christian, to place his sole trust in poetry or religious meditation. His studious princes, as in *Measure for Measure* and *The Tempest*, must take up their burdens again; Fortinbras brings his name and army to cure Denmark of its mentally insoluble disease; and the last play of the whole sequence is *Henry VIII*. Perhaps Theseus comes nearest to Shakespeare's ideal of manhood, slight sketch though it be. See how, after the moonlit night of fears and fancies, he enters with the rising sun, to wake the lovers from their dreams.

III

This self-identification with all human positives is not presented uncritically. Mercutio is set beside Romeo, Falstaff's honour-speech beside Hotspur's; Feste is there to criticize Orsino's love, Jaques to criticize Orlando's. Lust is presented as a nightmarish evil as early as *The Rape of Lucrece*; and in fact the second and third parts of *Henry VI* and *Titus Andronicus* have passages of black intensity unequalled again until the great tragedies.[1] Profundities are in Shakespeare's imagery, and often more than that, from the start. Advance is mainly through exploitation and rearrangement of old resources, an ever-deeper penetration of himself. At the turn of the century the darker elements gain force. Disloyalty and ingratitude had for long been emphatic revulsions, to which that supreme giving of himself which Shakespeare's works reflect may have rendered him quiveringly susceptible; and these revulsions are now expanded. His other main negation, apart from death itself, is a blackish lustful evil such as you get in

[1] Our first adequate study of *Titus Andronicus* appears to be Alan Sommers's 'Wilderness of Tigers' (*Essays in Criticism*, x. 3; July 1960).

The Rape of Lucrece and *Macbeth*, the tonings of those two being imaginatively identical. From such disturbances the great tragedies arise.

Two main issues are involved: sex and death. With the first an inward integrity had already made possible an achievement beyond that of Spenser or Marlowe, and similar to, though richer than, Lyly's. Webster's human feeling is not incomparable to Shakespeare's, but with death he, if not his Duchess, fails. Against extremes of ingratitude, marital infidelity, sex-nausea related to jealousy, all evil and death, the Shakespearian trust is now advanced. The very sympathy which sees so deep into the human essence that it creates with equal ease and sureness Juliet and her nurse, cynic Mercutio and romantic Romeo, forces the creation of Iago, Regan, Apemantus, Lady Macbeth. The Shakespearian love is challenged by its own children, like King Lear, and we get a universe in self-conflict.

Hamlet is harshly confronted with infidelity and death. His play turns on the baffling problem of action, thus questioning Shakespeare's most profound sense of human reality. Hamlet's is precisely the dramatist's normal problem: to find an action which can objectify the unrestful and groping intuition. In this Shakespeare's normal success is due to an inward integrity and correct balancing of imaginative material, but here the balance is, for once, gone. Aesthetic positives of feasting and music, kingly dignity, and love, are aligned with Claudius, the murderer; negatives of death and cynicism with Hamlet, the philosopher-hero. *Hamlet* is thus a self-questioning, as is no other play, of the central principle within Shakespeare's creative art. Not only the goodness, but the very dynamic, of life is being questioned. What strong action can be, to a sensitive intelligence, inherently poetic? The situation demands coarse, material revenge, and Hamlet, the poet-hero, is at a loss. But static drama is, for Shakespeare, impossible, and the conflict is resolved by an oscillating action. When in the fourth act natural loveliness aligns itself with Claudius, or at least against Hamlet, we have Shakespeare fighting beside his villain to preserve that cosmic, human, and natural trust which he, as Hamlet, is losing. The result is indeterminate but satisfactory; the crisis is objectified, and afterwards the sense of human force and direction never wavers; the imaginative balance is not again unsteady. But meanwhile *Hamlet* has pointed on to the especially inward conflicts, the spiritualized action, of the great tragedies.

Troilus and Cressida is satirically concerned with both sex and war, though the hero survives madly idealistic and active, showing an impressive romantic force, at the end. Earlier, Ulysses' order-speech sums up the cosmic trust that is felt to be shaking. The material is carefully ordered. *Measure for Measure* analyses the inherent difficulty of practical government to a sensitive mind, while also unfolding a deeply Shakespearian sexual ethic, close alike to Gospel teaching and modern psychology, and bearing directly on my present arguments, since pharisaic rightcousness is shown as superficial and natural instinct treated with sympathy. In *Othello* Renaissance villainy attacks a romantic faith, the opposition of cynicism and love found in Mercutio and Romeo repeated to darker purpose; in *Macbeth* ultimate evil, supernatural, nightmarish, medieval, with strong tonings of folk-superstition, is a rampaging force of murder; in *King Lear* a world of agony, related to a broken love, writhes towards a purgatorial resolution while the world of the Comedies trails behind pathetically in the Fool, just as Hamlet's words on Yorick's songs recall Feste. In *Timon of Athens* loss of love starts a torrent of curses against all false shows of decency and order.

The greater tragedies develop aspects of *The Duchess of Malfi*: a thought which increases our respect for that massively crammed work. But the human contacts are closer and more vivid, usually concerned with excruciating suffering at some sense of blank desertion, the ingratitude-*motif* driving the play now to the borders of sanity. Yet there is no Websterian paralysis of pain. Thought and imagery are carried easily, thrown up by but never clogging the action. Protagonists are never inwardly conquered, are never passive sufferers: they remain kings in a deeper than the obvious sense. Othello's love endures; Macbeth accuses himself before others accuse him, and ends with an honest relation to men, fighting bravely, unrepentant though self-condemned. The force and felt optimism within *King Lear* are generally recognized; and I have written with fervour of *Timon of Athens* as a positive document. The balance of human freedom and outward coercion is carefully maintained, destiny, or chance, urging equally Macbeth to crime and Cleopatra to nobility. The theme of indomitable aspiration running from Marlowe through Milton to Goethe, Byron, and Shelley is here more closely defined in terms of human limitation, and consequently more compressed and explosive. Our sense of victory finally derives from a tough, unburstable, instinctive grip on the human essence and its native invulnerability; barks may be tempest-racked but cannot be lost; the personality, the 'I'-ness of the universe and its creatures, is felt as indivisible; and death cannot enclose the life which contains it. The 'I' cannot properly recognize death, which is known only through the mediation of another: a thought relating to Shakespeare's final plays. Every hideous evil is thus felt to be purified by man's native, though constricted, royalty, every sting of satire subdued to a non-satiric direction in the whole.

The Shakespearian strength arises equally from an inward profundity and a generous sensuousness. Both are as necessary to a universal as to a human marriage; both are needed to grapple with tragedy and death.

The interdependence of deep spiritual understanding and wide sensuous receptivity is intrinsic to poetry, since depths of individual being in the unseen world of human personality are therein to be expressed through a vital and energic language born of sensory perception; and it is too common an error to think that we can explore the Shakespearian profundity without close attention to his surface. Such poetry must be weighty to balance the 'ponderous and substantial' (*Measure for Measure*, III. ii. 298) essences which it weighs; and to match what is organic and natural it must itself have nature-quality and organic, fibrous strength. Poetry, we are told, sees into the 'forms of things unknown' to re-create them in sensory 'shapes', and both art and love show a similar penetration to the 'heart' of their objects (*A Midsummer Night's Dream*, v. i. 12–17; II. ii. 104–5). In Shakespeare's greater plays the process is apparent not only in language but also in action and organization. The unveiling and the re-expressing of psychic depths which characterize all poetic drama is here found in action and symbol on a wide front. The poetry tears away the superficies of human affairs, penetrating essence; re-creates, not copies, from sight of the source. The ship's engine-room is shown us, we hear its clang and hiss. My remarks on Shakespeare's orderly world, or feminine and passive nature, must not be misread. These qualities are—have been all along, but especially are so now—a transparent medium for projecting terrific conflicts. Action was always Shakespeare's strength, a sense of human, or other, energy. In the greater plays violent forces are let loose, often related to those energic sources of life which we call sexual; a stormy and wrenching agony is his theme. Whatever feminine gentleness conditioned his art, a masculine agony of conflict is its material.

This clash of forces, both communal and psychological, he reveals, naked. A veil is lifted in *Julius Caesar* disclosing disorder-portents drizzling blood over Rome, the life-blood of the community exposed; Hamlet is confronted by death's naked terror and his mind flayed by a hideous revelation of sexual unfaith in a mother; in *Macbeth* nature's surface is blasted to show infranatural horrors, weird sisters, ghosts, apparitions, nightmarish things, while a woman's mind sinks shafts into bottomless evil; in *King Lear* a madness-phantasmagoria dances mirage-like, a capering grotesquerie of unreason led by naked Tom. There is a tearing-off of a covering, an exposure. Timon goes naked to his sea-shore tomb, willing that all superficies of orderly life be destroyed; and the resolution of these conflicts comes through the sensuous and burning fascination of hot sun-bred instincts in *Antony and Cleopatra*. Through all, even as the outward is sloughed off, a new structure of inner experience forms, clouds being puffed away to reveal a vaster, numinous, substance of the quality which Nietzsche in his study of tragedy called 'Dionysian'. Analysis reveals significance on significance in this structure.

I have often analysed the logic within Shakespeare's symbolisms: the subtle impressionism, especially the interchange of moonlight and dawn, in *A Midsummer Night's Dream*;[1] the deep unity of *The Merchant of Venice*, pound of flesh, three caskets, and the conflict of Shylock and Portia all contributing to a single, profound statement;[2] the balanced handling of disorder

---

[1] My detailed examination of *A Midsummer Night's Dream* is given in *The Shakespearian Tempest*, III.

[2] See *Principles of Shakespearian Production*, IV.

and central authority in *Julius Caesar*; the baffling opposition in *Hamlet* of an ethical good associated with death against an evil apparently backed by forces of life. The tempest which was used mainly as a symbol of adverse fortune in the Comedies and more subtly, though only imagistically, in the Histories, becomes from *Julius Caesar* onwards violent in effect and meaning, closely in-knitted in the whole. A usual construction is: order and music; thunder of conflict; plaintive or broken music, a backwater of momentary peace following the pattern of the New Testament drama; and then the tragic impact, rounded off by a ceremonial conclusion. Various symbols grow and form from the poetic soil. In *Othello* the handkerchief focalizes and universalizes the action; in *King Lear* the storm is the occasion for a dramatization of both passion and pathos, while a purpose forms on the fringes of consciousness from the tempestuous pain, if only through the wedding of man's agony with cosmic turmoil. In *Macbeth* the miniature conflict of death and life in the three thunderous apparitions, contrasted with the creative harmony symbolized by the procession to music of future kings, is an especially fine example of a revealed and optimistic pattern bursting through, interpreting, and binding the main surface action of nightmarish evil. But there is nothing schematic or mechanical. Symbolism blends with iterative imagery and that with the persons of the play themselves, so that there is scarcely an isolated or isolatable heart to the organism, though the apparitions in *Macbeth*, the handkerchief in *Othello*, the tempest in *King Lear*, might provisionally be called so. For the *King Lear* tempest, in expressing the relation of protagonist to environment, reflects the conflict, that is the action, and therefore the whole play, as does no one person; and the organic heart must sometimes be known rather through these symbols than in the tragic hero. Such symbols are not added to the story-action: they contribute to it, are at once thrown up from the depths by it, are part of it, and urge it on. The play's deepest inwardness expands and encloses it; in *King Lear* the unveiled and psychological almost bursts the apparent universe, almost *is* the objectively natural and cosmic. These symbolisms which we have considered inward must be equally regarded as evidence of an action not so much seen deeply into as widely expanded. A human story is given its full and proper context of society, nature, the universe. The action is shown in its context of the whole of life, and to do so much, in so short a space, demands the shorthand statement of symbolic extravagance. The inward and the outward, as so often in our study of Shakespeare, are found to coincide, while all intermediary appeals of imagery, characterization, historic authenticity and so forth, are contained.

Shakespeare's symbolism is, like his imagery, based on a feeling for nature-forces, life-forces: the child, feasts, music on the one side; ghosts, ill portents, thoughts of disease on the other. The implied metaphysic is optimistic in so far as it regards the created world as good and in the main, certainly in the long run, victorious. Moral law is observed, but only as an aspect of a greater, more universal, whole. The apparent disasters of Macbeth and Antony derive not from any especial condemnation, but simply from understanding of the way things happen, and a deeper ethic matures from a more careful inspection. *Macbeth*, being concerned with evil, is crammed with ghosts and semi-realities, whereas *Antony and Cleopatra*, being concerned with love, has the most realistic surface of the great plays, love tuning, as it were, with creation. But the evil also throws up more life, denying itself, as in the child-apparitions of *Macbeth*. And the worst conflicts are never depressing: they reflect a health and sense of energic being denied to the horror-paralysis and nightmare harmonies of *The Duchess of Malfi*. Lear's 'No, I'll not weep' (*King Lear*, II. iv. 286) is a key passage in the Shakespearian victory. Moreover, spiritual conflict tends to objectify itself into armed opposition and the wound contributes to its own closure. But that wound is itself creative: from it the passionate and naturalistic poetry swells out and the whole action is inspired. The poet's task is easier in *Macbeth* than in *Antony and Cleopatra*, since artistic intensities are often happiest with evil. An inrush of power is shown attending conflict. Only then do Romeo, Macbeth, Lear, and Timon become truly powerful. The agony *is* poetic definition, their suffering felt as of no greater discordance than nature's tempests. The energy and the meaning exist in this very effort of reconciliation, and poetic mastery is often the more evident, indeed easier, the more wild the conflict to be resolved. Finally, we must always remember what the plays are, not only what they say; what they say appearing sometimes merely as dust which obscures the poetry's ultimate direction. Yet also their artistic structures, though only a medium for power, a wire white with electric heat, have their own inevitable, because organic, precisions. There is formal pattern as well as action. In the middle, usually, is our climax, with sense of the swing and leverage of existence; at the end, there is peace. The plays work up to a wild unstudied ritual, of pictorial and sacrificial quality: the star-crossed Romeo and Juliet in the tomb; Hamlet carried off to a dead march, with cannon; the tragic loading of Desdemona's bed; Cordelia limp under the white hairs and burning eyes of Lear; the trailing pikes and dead march of *Coriolanus*; Cleopatra's self-dramatized immolation, guided and guarded by her two girls in their dying loyalty. In close relation are reminders of the community's continuance. The purgatorial conflicts hurl themselves up to these almost formal and ceremonial conclusions, recalling the equally positive, yet equally unforced and naturalistic, beauty in agony of the Crucifixion. The protagonist is happily withdrawn from the front line of a terrific and painful, yet creative, action. A relation to the Christ-tragedy is sometimes suggested, and to a sensitive understanding always embedded, not so much by direct, or even unconscious, influence, but because the same piece of work is being done according to the laws of the same universe: the steady generation from instinctive energy of spiritual power.

We are left with a feeling of both power and peace; of a rhythm, deep as winter or night or sleep necessary to the pulses of existence; of emotional depths which therefore are not finally thwarted; of a thunder which is but a part of some universal music. Shakespeare's naturalistic quality lends itself only provisionally to metaphors from any human art: the structure of verse and symbol certainly creates what we may call a musical-tempestuous design, but it is a breathing organism, one living whole; so that, remembering that a passivity and a psychological harmony were the conditions of the plays' creation, we can say that we find them also to be mysteriously the reward of our reading. Action and inaction, conflict and peace, tempest and music are, in the completed whole, one. And, just as the generated emotion of a Shakespearian speech out-distances its own expression, as each person and event aims not to assert but to submerge itself in the whole, since all and each live entirely on the central creative energy; so some power greater than the play itself, which, as in all greatest art, you feel to be no finished and polished finality but rather a rough approximation and pro-visional expression only, is felt calling each separate

work into being and back at will, like the heave and subsiding of a wave, the ocean mass itself profoundly un-
disturbed. By its very accepted limitations—it is their
especial office—each tragedy throws up the shadowings
of some mysterious otherness, a something behind, which
is also the inmost vitality of its own poetry, rooted like
that in the depths of *personality*; which is, too, felt within
the play's symbolic direction and ritualistic conclusion,
its whole-searching quality. Towards a further inclusion
beyond tragedy the sequence accordingly moves.

IV

Macbeth, *King Lear*, and *Antony and Cleopatra* are toned
respectively as experiences of Hell, Purgatory, and Paradise. In *Antony and Cleopatra* all natural elements inter-
mesh for celebration of a sovereign love. That love,
though backed by impressions of sun and fertility, is,
however, shown in conflict with the social order and
needing death for its proper consummation: 'Husband,
I come' (V. ii. 289). Death is here dynamically conceived
as an entrance into the cosmic harmony, the autonomy
of human instinct creating, through Cleopatra, its own
paradise. The organization and balance of materials are
delicate. Nor is realism slighted. The often harsh phrase-
ology would seem to be labouring to drag back the
aspiring theme, which wins in its despite, a tendency
especially clear in the fine adulation of Cleopatra spoken
by the critical Enobarbus. Shakespeare's dramatization
of the final mystery is established in terms rich in
physical sex and, for once, a barbaric regality; yet also
deep in conception of personality, as when Cleopatra's
dream-lover becomes himself the universe, the strongly
sensuous and authentically spiritual being once again
found to be interdependent. But if we desire a more
directly idealistic treatment of similar penetration
we can turn to *The Phoenix and the Turtle*, a poem

which matches the work of Donne in the delicate refinement of a style recalling Donne's own phrase, in *A Valediction forbidding Mourning*, 'like gold to airy thinness beat'.

The resurrection and reunion plots which logically follow stand alone in our literature.[1] Regarding them as a further exploitation of the mysterious power generated through the great tragedies and *Antony and Cleopatra*, we can say that they dramatize a victory over death. Their nature is, nevertheless, foreshadowed in certain earlier romances, and certainly the Comedies, with their mistakes and discoveries, their untying of tangles and ceremonious conclusions, often contain, as do also the plays of Lyly, hints of a universal. Shakespeare's work develops through a reorganizing and repenetration rather than a change of material. In his last period favourite poetic impressions tend to present themselves as dramatic actualities; as persons, or events, or both. Poetry is itself the solution, its power the revelation.

There is, however, no dissolution of the individual into nature, or a world-soul. Personality must, in the Shakespearian art, remain one certain term of reference. So Hermione is restored as herself, and the restoration is presented as a natural fact; there is no black magic, she is 'warm', Leontes's embrace as 'lawful' as 'eating' (v. iii. 89–105, 109–11). We may observe that the hero does not himself die; it is his experience of another's death that is dramatized. Leontes's repentance and 'faith' (v. iii. 95), Paulina acting as his *conscience*, condition the resurrection. In *Pericles* and *The Winter's Tale* the final discovery of the child either born or lost under conditions of tempestuous conflict reflects nature's creative onwardness as the resurrections of Thaisa and

[1] I say in 'our literature'. The correspondences with the Inca play *Apu-Ollantay*, probably an earlier work, are striking. A translation appears in Sir Clements Markham's *The Incas of Peru*.

Hermione represent the victorious eternity of love. Gods—Diana, Neptune, Apollo, Jupiter—have, variously, significance, especially Jupiter in *Cymbeline*. In *The Winter's Tale*, apart from the resurrection, we have country scenes, golden comedy, and young love set against tragic nausea, bitterness, and death, with final emphasis on creation and peace. *The Tempest* is both an artistic autobiography and a universal pattern of man's relation to the divine, the final identity of the individual and the universal soul being reflected into the very structure of its symbolic action. Prospero's 'cloud-capp'd towers' speech (IV. i. 148–58) magnificently sees creation as ephemeral in a way which does not appear pessimistic, a similar positive being implied to that otherness always felt behind Shakespeare's own poetic impressions, plots, persons, and plays. The language of this last group may be far from smooth; often abstract, elusive, twisted; at the bitter passages reaching an explosive compression even greater than in the Tragedies. The final period of composition marks not so much a changed approach to human existence as a new totality of comprehension within which death is itself annulled, while the inherent Elizabethan pastoralism, and that positive human, and especially feminine, trust, which have vitalized the whole progress, are found the resolving elements of its close.

Prospero's return to Milan is balanced by Shakespeare's writing of *Henry VIII*, which completes the series ending with *Henry V*. The play is massive and epic with three personal tragedies; the usual ingratitude-*motifs*, self-discovery through disaster, and a newly emphatic Christianity. The vision and miracle quality of other late plays recurs in Queen Katharine's vision of the immortal life. *Henry VIII* recalls the early *King John* in balance of a national and royal ascendancy against individual suffering, its last movement cele-

brating both the rise of the king and the birth of Elizabeth. In Cranmer we find humility contrasting with the
more normally Shakespearian pride of the three tragic
persons, and to him Shakespeare entrusts the final
prophecy. Such an acceptance of the contemporary and
the national is not strange. We tend to pass over the
national feeling evident in the show of kings in *Macbeth*, and of which there is even a trace in *King Lear*.
Cymbeline works out a studied union of Britain and
Rome, and indeed things Roman, of central positive
importance to all Elizabethans, are especially so to
Shakespeare, and hence the archetypal significance of
his theme in *Julius Caesar*. Though capable of sharpest
social and militaristic satire, Shakespeare concludes his
lifework in praise of England's destiny.

This last series corresponds to the Tragedies as does
the resurrection to the crucifixion in Christian belief.
It is the inevitable and proper fulfilment of Shakespeare's genius, since his ghosts were from the start
more alive than other dramatists' men. As in Goethe's
Faust, the solution comes through the more feminine
element, as opposed to nationalism and soldiership,
among the Shakespearian values, including a most vital
feeling for the marriage bond and family issues generally, though this leads back to the spiritualized historic
conception of *Henry VIII* with, however, its strong
feminine sympathies. The theme of wronged women is
found from beginning to end of Shakespeare; the
extreme agony induced by suspicion, or proof, of their
unfaith is proportional to the sense of their importance;
and, at the last, they are redeeming forces. That is
why the final act of *Antony and Cleopatra* is of so pivotal
a significance.

Shakespeare's last works are written from a consciousness of the eternal which reflects itself into a new
emphasis on arts of design, such as embroidery, carvings,

and Hermione's living statue; with religious impressions of oracles, chapels, temples, sacrifice, and incense; and, too, an especially sacramental approach to nature, as in the emphasis on the 'fire-robed god' (IV. iii. 29) Apollo and his plot-directing oracle, together with the fertility-festival, in *The Winter's Tale*, and the pagan sun-worship of Guiderius and Arviragus in *Cymbeline*. To withhold the mystical sympathies demanded is to shirk the first duty of interpretation. Eventually the resurrection of Hermione must be considered the most strikingly conceived, and profoundly penetrating, moment in English literature.

Our various conflicts of romantic emotion and critical cynicism, order and disorder, soldierly honour and feminine devotion, life and death, all from a final view dissolve into the opposition, especially strong in the last plays, of the dominating symbols, tempests and music. These apply in turn to conflicts psychological, communal, and cosmic; to the interactivity of dynamic rhythm and formal pattern in the art-form itself; and to the blend of male and female, active and passive, elements in the poetic mind. The Shakespearian poetry grows from an integrity responding directly to the wholeness of creation, all opposing tendencies being allowed to mature in fullest freedom under the final synthesis, which in turn becomes a medium for an almost god-like power. That power is personified in Prospero, to whose 'so potent art' (*The Tempest*, v. i. 50) even graves are obedient. Such an imaginative and holistic medium alone can crash the barriers of human death. So Shakespeare's universe is fundamentally poetical, not philosophical; nor, in our usual, but limited, sense, exactly dramatic. In it we finally meet no negation, but listen rather to a vast breathing, a rhythmic pulse, the surge and sob of a great ocean, which may remind us of Keats's last, and best, sonnet.

The organic indissolubility of Shakespeare's art may be seen from the way his life-work expands the pattern of a single Shakespearian tragedy: from realism, through impassioned imaginative conflict, to mystic intimations, for of these each tragic hero in turn had his share; and finally, in *Henry VIII*, a ritual conclusion. Such is the organic harmony, resembling rather the works of nature than the works of man.

NEVILL COGHILL

(b. 1899)

The Basis of Shakespearian Comedy[1]

I

COMPARED with the comedies of Shakespeare, those of Ben Jonson are no laughing matter. A harsh ethic in them yokes punishment with derision; foibles are persecuted and vices flayed; the very simpletons are savaged for being what they are. The population he chooses for his comedies in part accounts for this: it is a congeries of cits, parvenus, mountebanks, cozeners, dupes, braggarts, bullies, and bitches. No one loves anyone. If we are shown virtue in distress, it is the distress, not the virtue that matters. All this is done with an incredible, stupendous force of style.

In Shakespeare things are different. Princes and dukes, lords and ladies jostle with merchants, weavers, joiners, country sluts, friendly rogues, schoolmasters, and village policemen, hardly one of whom is incapable of a generous impulse; even a bawd may be found nursing a bastard at her own expense.

In all this it is possible to discern the promptings of two opposed temperaments; but, more objectively, we should see the operations of two different theories of comic form: for Shakespeare was not simply following the chances of temperament in designing his comedies, any more than Jonson was; each was following earlier traditions, that evolved during the Middle Ages and at the Renaissance, from the same parent stock of thought which is to be found in the writings of the Latin grammarians of the fourth century, particularly in Evanthius, Diomedes, and Donatus.

[1] *Essays & Studies* III (1950), shortened and revised for this collection.

It must be confessed their observations are sketchy: from their barely co-ordinated jottings I have taken the following for this discussion, omitting nothing that is relevant to the form and content of a comedy.

From *Evanthius*: '. . . As between Tragedy and Comedy, while there are many distinguishing marks, the first is this: in Comedy the characters are men of middle fortune, the dangers they run are neither serious nor pressing, their actions lead to happy conclusions; but in Tragedy things are just the opposite. Then again be it noted that in Tragedy is expressed the idea that life is to be fled from; in Comedy, that it is to be grasped.'

From *Diomedes*: 'Comedy differs from Tragedy in that, in Tragedy, heroes, generals and kings are introduced; in Comedy, humble and private people. In the former, grief, exile and slaughter. In the latter, love-affairs and the abduction of girls (*virginum raptus*). Then in the former there are often and almost invariably sad endings to happy circumstances and a discovery (*agnitio*) of former fortune and family taking an ill turn . . . for sad things are the property of Tragedy. . . . The first comic poets . . . offered plots of the old kind, with less skill than charm . . . in the second age were Aristophanes, Eupolis and Cratinus, who, pursuing the vices of the principal characters, composed very bitter comedies. The third age was that of Menander, Diphilus and Philemon, who palliated all the bitterness (*acerbitatem mitigaverunt*) of Comedy and followed all sorts of plots about agreeable mistakes (*gratis erroribus*).'

From *Donatus*: 'Comedy is a tale containing various elements of the dispositions of town-dwelling and private people, to whom it is made known what is useful in life and what to be avoided.'[1]

Let us rearrange the commonplaces from these rag-bags of analysis into the shapes that evolved from them —the Jonsonian and Shakespearian forms of Comedy, the Satiric and the Romantic. *The Satiric* concerns a middle way of life, town-dwellers, humble and private

[1] *Comicorum Graecorum Fragmenta*, edidit Georgius Kaibel, vol. i, Fasc. Prior, Berlin (1899).

people. It pursues the principal characters with some bitterness for their vices and teaches what is useful and expedient in life and what is to be avoided. *The Romantic* expresses the idea that life is to be grasped. It is the opposite of Tragedy in that the catastrophe solves all confusions and misunderstandings by some happy turn of events. It commonly includes love-making and running off with girls.

The making of this distinction is neither wholly arbitrary nor original; something like it was formulated by Isidore of Seville (*c.* 560–636) in his *Etymologies*. He tells us that Comedies, by word and gesture, sing the doings of private people and portray the loves of courtesans and the rape of virgins (*Etymologies*, XVIII. xlvi). The Archbishop was evidently thinking of such pieces as Terence's *Eunuch* and uses the phrase *stupra virginum*, instead of Diomedes' milder *virginum raptus*: he also says (VIII. vii. 6–7) that comic writers deal with cheerful matters (*rebus laetis*) but are of two kinds, the Old and the New. The Old excel in fun, as entertainers: the New, as Satirists who single out the vices for treatment.

I do not know of any other account or even mention of comic form until the twelfth century. Boethius had defined Tragedy but not Comedy. Unless I am mistaken, the next allusion to it occurs in the *Ars Versificatoria* of Matthieu de Vendôme (*c.* 1150). In true Boethian style he describes a vision of Philosophy, accompanied by Satire and Comedy; he also appears to discriminate between these two: Satire he says is sparing of silence, her brow proclaiming the fear of wrongdoing, with eyes asquint, testifying to the oblique character of her mind; Comedy, in workaday dress, and with humbled head, gives no promise of rejoicing (*nullius festivitatis praetendens delicias*). This appears to imply happy endings unforeseen, for private people in their troubles, and so anticipates Vincent de Beauvais (*c.* 1250) who, in his *Speculum Maius* (vol. ii, bk. iii, p. 53), gives us at last a classic definition:

> *Commedia poesis exordium triste laeto fine commutans.*

Comedy is a kind of poem which transforms a sad beginning into a happy ending. It was, in fact, exactly the opposite of Tragedy, as understood by the Middle Ages, for they were instructed by Boethius on this point.[1] Chaucer, commenting, renders the Boethian view of Tragedy as 'a ditty of prosperity for a while that endeth in wretchedness'.

The simple formula of Vincent de Beauvais is the true basis of Shakespearian Comedy—a tale of trouble that turns to joy. It is not so simple as it looks. The claim is that it not only is the shape of a human comedy, but also of ultimate reality. The story of the Universe is itself to be a Comedy, as defined, for those who deserve it; a *Divine Comedy*. So Dante saw it, and so he named his poem: starting in Hell, it moves upwards into Paradise, through Purgatory.

A prose lecture on this theme is to be found in the *Epistle to Can Grande*, sometimes attributed to Dante himself. It adds a further point, worth noting: '. . . Be it known that the meaning of this work is not single (*simplex*), indeed it can be called *polysemos*, that is of several meanings; for there is the first meaning to be had from the letter; another is to be had from what is signified by the letter. And the first is called the literal (meaning), and the second, the allegorical. . . .'

In these medieval descriptions of comedy we see a selection and an expansion of those hints thrown out by the fourth century that we have considered; what was satiric in them has remained underground, what was romantic has soared upward into divinity; love, men-

[1] Bk. ii, prose 2.

tioned by Diomedes as a theme, has become the centre of all in the Beatific Vision. The more modest genius of Chaucer, however, was content to describe Comedy in purely human terms:

> As whan a man hath been in povre estaat,
> And clymbeth up, and wexeth fortunat,
> And there abydeth in prosperitee,
> Swich thing is gladsom, as it thinketh me.
>
> (*The Knight commenting on the Monk's Tale*)

This was his warm, earthbound but generous way of thinking about it.

The Renaissance view of Comedy was entirely different: suddenly the *Satiric*, after more than a thousand years of hibernation, sprang fully armed out of the ground and possessed the new theorists. For them the proper, the only, concern of Comedy was ridicule; it offered no necessary antithesis to Tragedy, it gave no suggestion, however rudimentary, of containing a narrative line (as did Vincent's definition). Punishment and deterrence were its business; Comedy should be an instrument of social ethics. A few quotations may stand for a host of critics:

George Whetstone, *Dedication to Promos and Cassandra*, 1578.

. . . For by the rewarde of the good the good are encouraged in wel doinge: and with the scowrge of the lewde the lewde are feared from euill attempts. . . .

Sir Philip Sidney, *An Apologie for Poetrie* (*c.* 1583, printed 1593).

. . . Comedy is an imitation of the common errors of our life, which he representeth in the most ridiculous and scornefull sort that may be; so as it is impossible that any beholder can be content to be such a one.

Sir John Harington, *Preface to the Translation of Orlando Furioso*, 1591.

. . . The Comicall, whatsoeuer foolish play-makers make it

(poetry) offend in this kind (i.e. by lewdness) yet being rightly
vsed, it represents them so as to make the vice scorned and
not embraced. . . .

Such, then, were the two theories of Comedy, the
Romantic and the Satirical, of the Middle Ages and the
Renaissance respectively, that twinned out of the late
Latin grammarians to flower in Tudor times. Faced
by a choice in such matters, a writer is wise if he follows
his temperament. Ben Jonson knotted his cat-o'-nine-
tails. Shakespeare reached for his Chaucer.

II

It is true that he did not do so immediately. His first
thoughts in Comedy were for Plautus. Yet anyone
(caring for poetical form) who compares *The Comedy
of Errors* with its source in the *Menaechmi*, will find
significant differences in the shape and content of these
two plays. It is not simply a matter of doubling the
pairs of twins; Shakespeare's play has a new beginning,
a new end and an infusion of tenderness; there is love
in it. In fact he medievalized the story, starting it off
in trouble, ending it in joy. It begins (daringly for a
comedy) with a man led seriously out to execution; it is
Egeon, the father of the Antipholus twins, a major
character: this gambit is not in Plautus. Execution on
Egeon is deferred by the Duke, but he remains (albeit
off-stage) under sentence of death until the last scene.
When, however, he is at last led out once more to
suffer, there emerges from an improbable abbey, a more
improbable abbess, who, most improbably of all, is
discovered to be his long-lost wife, the mother of the
Antipholi, and the means of his deliverance and their
reunion. She also is Shakespeare's invention, and turns
catastrophe to general joy. The scene gathers in the
whole cast and concludes in rejoicing, a model to all
subsequent comedy, with a stage crammed at the end

with happy people. The play-world has been led into delight, and with it the world of the audience.

Although its main business is the fun of mistaken identity, *The Comedy of Errors* is given a touch of delicacy by the language of *amour courtois* (a thing unknown to Plautus) and the invention of a romantic sub-plot—the love-affair between Antipholus of Syracuse and Luciana:

> Teach me deere creature how to thinke and speake:
> Lay open to my earthie grosse conceit:
> Smothred in errors, feeble, shallow, weake,
> The foulded meaning of your words deceit:
> Against my soules pure truth, why labour you,
> To make it wander in an vnknowne field?
> Are you a god? would you create me new?
> Transforme me then, and to your powre Ile yeeld. . . .

Thus could the fantasy of the Middle Ages transform the stolid fun of the world of Roman imagination; it was Shakespeare's earliest comedy;[1] his next, *The Taming of the Shrew*, was another venture with material not mainly romantic.

The Taming of the Shrew has often been read and acted as a wife-humiliating farce in which a brute fortune-hunter carries all, including his wife's spirit, before him. But it is not so at all. True, it is based on the medieval conception of the obedience owed by a wife to her wedded lord, a conception generously and charmingly asserted by Katerina at the end. But it is a total misconception to suppose she has been bludgeoned into defeat. Indeed if either of them has triumphed in the art and practice of happy marriage, it is she.

Why is she a shrew? Shakespeare prepares us perfectly for this aspect of her character. She is a girl of spirit, forced to endure a father who is ready to sell his

[1] I follow the chronology established by E. K. Chambers in *William Shakespeare*, vol. i.

daughters to the highest bidder (as we see in the mar-
riage-market scene, II. i) and who has made a favourite
of her sly little sister. What choice has Katerina but to
show her disdainful temper if she is to keep her self-
respect?

Petruchio is a self-admitted fortune-hunter, but he
is also good-natured, vigorous, candid, humorous, and
likeable. No doubt whatever is left that he admires
Katerina for herself on sight. Though he is loud-
mouthed and swaggering, he is not contemptible; to
Katerina he must have seemed her one hope of escape
from that horrible family, against which she had developed the defensive technique of shrewishness; it is
this which Petruchio is determined to break in her, not
her spirit; and he chooses the method of practical
joking to do so.

At first she does not see the point; her shrew's
armoury is put to its hitherto successful use against his
Hotspur manners; it has no effect whatever, except to
draw his praise of her gentleness. What is still more
surprising, she presently begins to sense in his boisterous behaviour, an element of affection; at first she
resents it as hypocritical:

> And that which spights me more then all these wants,
> He does it vnder name of perfect loue.

It is not until he positively declares that the sun is the
moon that she sees it is all a joke, and how to handle it.
Her victory is found in a sense of fun as extravagant
as his own, and even able to outbid his in fantasy;
when commanded by him to address a totally strange
old gentleman as if he were a beautiful girl, she rises to
the occasion with:

> Yong budding Virgin, faire, and fresh, & sweet . . .

and when Petruchio whirls about once more with

> Why how now *Kate*, I hope thou art not mad,
> This is a man old, wrinckled, faded, withered,
> And not a Maiden, as thou saist he is

she reaches the top of her wit, out-joking her husband with

> Pardon old father my mistaking eies,
> That haue bin so bedazled with the sun. . . .

This line should, of course, be said, as I have heard Dame Peggy Ashcroft, greatest of Katerinas, say it—though typography can barely indicate her sense of its fun, and the glance shot at Petruchio as she said it:

> That have bin so bedazled with the—sun (?)

After that, victory is all the Shrew's, a shrew no longer, for she has no need to be; and like most of those wives that are the natural superiors of their husbands, she allows Petruchio the mastery in public. She has secured what her sister Bianca can never have, a happy marriage, by a solution not far from that imagined by Chaucer for Dorigen in *The Franklin's Tale*:

> Looke who that is moost pacient in love,
> He is at his avantage al above.

Neither of the two plays we have considered falls squarely into the 'Romantic' class of comedy; yet in their troubled beginnings and happy endings and in their infusion of love, or at least of kindliness, they show Shakespeare's attraction to medieval form and content as opposed to the severities of renaissance satire. They are, however, plays of 'middle life'. The kings and princes of his comedies are still to come.

III

As Shakespeare matured in Comedy, he was increasingly taken with the theme of love; he may be said to have come to see it as the core of that kind. As his tragedies end in multiple death, so his comedies end in multiple marriage; and they are all marriages of mutual love, or such as we are encouraged to hope may become so. His lovers, for the most part, love at first sight, like the Lover in the *Roman de la Rose*; and like him they are '*gentil*', for love is essentially an aristocratic experience; that is, an experience only possible to natures capable of refinement, be they high-born or low.[1] In search of this refinement, Shakespeare began to imagine and explore what we have come to call his 'golden world', taking a phrase of his own from *As You Like It*. He found it chiefly peopled with princes and peasants, with Courtesy and Nature in their manners. It was a world of adventure and the countryside, where Jonson's was a world of exposure and the city. The greatest adventure was love; other adventures, and misadventures, were jealousies and ficklenesses, mistaken identities, wrongly reported deaths, separations and reunions, disguises of sex and all the other improbabilities that can be fancied, entangled and at last resolved into whole harmony by some happy turn of events. It is an Eden world, but the apples are still in blossom.

Two Gentlemen of Verona was the first experiment in this kind, not so great a success as the two comedies of 'middle life' we have considered. There was, perhaps, no real model for what he was attempting. Then came *Love's Labour's Lost*, in its exuberance of language creating a new rhetoric for royalty in love, heavily loaded with conceits; it is the work of a young *avant-gardiste*, and full of daring novelties, such as the defying of expectation by bringing Death into the last moments of a farce, and by separating his lovers at the end for a year. He was standing comic form on its head, and he knew it:

[1] See *The Romaunt of the Rose*, in Chaucer's version, lines 2175–84.

Our woing doth not end like an old Play:
Iacke hath not Gill: these Ladies courtesie
Might wel haue made our sport a Comedie.

He did not repeat the experiment, however, and in his next Comedy, *A Midsummer Night's Dream*, he returned to orthodoxy:

Iacke shall haue Iill, nought shall goe ill,
The man shall haue his Mare againe, and all shall bee well.

The definition of Comedy bequeathed to Shakespeare by the Middle Ages has a further aspect, as we have noted already, that was important to his imagination; it indicated a *narrative* structure—of adventures that would lead out of trouble into joy; this again distinguishes his Comedy from Jonson's, in whose work the story is not important; he places his characters in a situation that will display their 'humours', which are like the *data* in a complex structure of argument, leading by their inner logic to some sort of Q.E.D. *Volpone* and *Epicene*, by dint of Jonson's stunning ingenuity, display their various humours in such a way as to form a story, but one can hardly say as much for *The Alchemist*; there is even less story in *Bartholomew Fair*; their powerful virtues must be found in other aspects of their composition. His characters (representing the humours indicated by their names) suffer no changes and offer no enigmas; nor should they, any more than x and y should change their values in an equation.

But Shakespeare's characters have to be changeable, for they are not fashioned to make possible a demonstration in morals, but to be credible in a world of freely imagined actions, where actions have motives other than those that fall neatly under the heading of a 'humour'. Let us consider, for instance, Antonio in *The Merchant of Venice*. One might think him at first to be intended as an embodiment of the humour of melancholy. But his is not the kind of affectation that is created to be ridiculed, like that of Morose in *Epicene*; it is more deeply seated, more secret and more to be compassionated.

Shakespeare has invested Antonio with this deep sadness because every aspect of the story that concerns him is unhappy to the last moment of the play. His is the 'trouble' with which the Comedy begins; he will not say why he is troubled, but the reason (which we learn later) is that he is to lose his lover to a lady of whom he knows nothing, moreover he will have to pay for the wooing. That he loves Bassanio is not only necessary to the story, but clear from Solanio's remark in II. viii,

> I thinke he onely loues the world for him.

To make credible the turn in the plot by which Antonio must show himself willing to offer a pound of his flesh for the convenience of a friend, nothing less than a high homosexual affection, worthy of the *Symposium*, would poetically suffice; it is an affection about which Shakespeare makes Antonio both conscious and shy. When Solanio suggests, as a cause of his melancholy, 'Why then you are in love', he can only answer 'Fie, fie'. Later we hear him say, giving no reason, for the reason is obvious:

> I am a tainted Weather of the flocke,
> Meetest for death. . . .

But it is sadder still that his love does not bring out the best side in Bassanio: that has to be reserved for Portia. Antonio elicits a kind of falsity or bombast from the young man; makes him protest too much:

> You know me well, and herein spend but time
> To winde about my loue with circumstance.

It is another bogus outburst when Bassanio (perfectly

safe himself) tries to encourage Antonio in the Trial scene:

> Good cheere *Anthonio*, What man, corage yet:
> The Iew shall haue my flesh, blood, bones, and all,
> Ere thou shalt lose for me one drop of blood.

At the end of the play Antonio is odd man out. That he recognizes his oddity and rejoices in his friend's happiness is well; but he is left alone, as the others move off to their wedding-beds, to find what consolation he can in the safe return of his argosies. No wonder he is sad; it is the first sounding of a note of melancholy, the first modification of Vincent's formula for comedy.

IV

We have seen that Dante, or his commentator, in the *Epistle to Can Grande*, tells us that a comedy may be '*polysemos*, that is of several meanings', and this seems also true of certain of Shakespeare's comedies. He wrote in an age when allegory was still a living force. *The Faerie Queene* was published within a year of the writing of *The Merchant of Venice*; it was an age that found no difficulty in accepting the *Song of Songs* as a figure for the love of Christ for His Church, and in thinking of human marriage as another allegory of that same reality.

Thinking in allegory is for us an unaccustomed exercise, but it will not be found difficult if we hold fast to the literal meaning and hear other meanings as simultaneous overtones of suggestion. An allegory should be attended to as we attend to a tune with a descant, that is: simultaneously, separately, and together. Each fortifies and enriches the other; they can, of course, be parted and heard one at a time, but that is not how they were designed to be heard. And just as the tune is always the important voice, so the literal meaning in an allegory is in dominance.

It is not always easy to know what the literal meaning is. We may again take *The Merchant of Venice* to serve us as an example relatively easy; others that have proved themselves more difficult of interpretation are *Measure for Measure, The Winter's Tale, Pericles,* and *The Tempest,* most difficult of all.

A director of *The Merchant of Venice* is faced by a seeming problem. It clearly has to do with an enmity between a Jew and a Christian. Is then its theme the racial and religious conflict of character? Should a producer take sides? if so, can he please himself as to which side he takes? The title-page of the second quarto reads:

The Excellent History of The Merchant of Venice.
With the extreme cruelty of Shylocke the Iew towards
the saide Merchant, in cutting a iust pound of his flesh. . . .

This announcement seems to justify an anti-Semitic slant; yet, if a producer attempts one, he finds himself presently faced with moments of dialogue utterly intractable to such interpretation:

> *Shylock.* Shall I bend low, and in a bond-mans key
>   With bated breath, and whispring humblenesse,
>   Say this: Faire sir, you spet on me on Wednesday last;
>   You spurn'd me such a day; another time
>   You cald me dog: and for these curtesies
>   Ile lend you thus much moneyes.
> *Ant.* I am as like to call thee so againe,
>   To spet on thee againe, to spurne thee too.   (F)

Or

Hath not a *Iew* eyes? hath not a *Iew* hands, organs, demen-
tions, senses, affections, passions, fed with the same foode,
hurt with the same weapons, subiect to the same diseases,
healed by the same meanes, warmed and cooled by the same

Winter and Sommer as a Christian is: if you pricke vs doe we not bleede? if you tickle vs, doe we not laugh? if you poison vs doe we not die?

The great speech from which these lines come—and there are others like it—make it impossible to carry through an anti-Semitic presentation of the play; on the other hand to regard Shylock as the wronged hero of an oppressed race falling with final grandeur to a verbal quibble, cannot be reconciled with the last Act, in which the agents of his fall gather by moonlight for their joys in Belmont. Is he to perish and are they to be rewarded?

If then the play will work neither as a Jew-baiter, nor as its opposite, there is nothing to conclude except that either Shakespeare did not know his business, or we have misunderstood it. The latter is the more likely: the title-page of Quarto may have misled us. We must try again, and seek a unifying theme that will include these opposites of race and religion.

There is such a theme and it has a long tradition; its best expression is in *Piers Plowman*. It is the theme of Mercy against Justice. In that poem, Truth, who is God, sent Piers a Pardon for the world. All in two lines it lay:

> Et qui bona egerunt ibunt in vitam eternam
> Qui vero mala in ignem eternum.

'Those who do well shall go into eternal life: but those indeed who do evil, into eternal fire.' In what sense this is a pardon is hard to see, for it states an exactly proportionate requital, an eye for an eye, a tooth for a tooth, as the principle of reward and punishment; this may be justice but where is the pardon? Where is Mercy?

The poem leaves us unsatisfied of an immediate answer, but opens a labyrinth of inquiry that leads to

the story of the Incarnation, the Passion, the Crucifixion, and Descent into Hell. And in Hell, in a great
speech, Christ argues His own payment of man's
debt:

> *Ergo*, soule shal soule quyte . & synne to synne wende,
> And al þat man hath mysdo . I, man, wyl amende.[1]

His payment on Calvary is available to all who acknowledge their debt, says the poet, and render their dues
in confession and obedience; for to do this is to do well,
and therefore to go into eternal life.

Now Christ's right to enter Hell and despoil the
Fiend of his prey in this manner is formally debated
in the poem by the Four Daughters of God, Mercy and
Truth, Righteousness and Peace. Briefly their argument
is this: under the Old Law, God ordained punishment
for sin in Hell, eye for eye and tooth for tooth. But
under the New Law of His ransom paid on Calvary,
He may with perfect justice redeem 'those that he
loved'; and this justice is His mercy. The New Law
does not contradict, but complements the Old. Mercy
and Truth are met together, Righteousness and Peace
have kissed each other.

Almost exactly the same argument is conducted by
the same four daughters of God at the end of *The
Castle of Perseverance*, a morality play of the early
fifteenth century. The protagonist, *Humanum Genus*,
dies in sin and comes up for judgement. Righteousness
and Truth demand his damnation, which the play
would show to be just. Mercy and Peace plead the Incarnation, and *Humanum Genus* is saved.

Now if we allow this Christian tradition of a former
age to show us a pathway into Shakespeare, it will lead

---

[1]   Therefore soul shall pay for soul and sin shall return to sin
And all that man has misdone, I, man, will amend.
Piers Plowman B xviii. 338–9.

us to a theme that can make a unity of *The Merchant of Venice*, and solve our dilemma.

The play can be seen as a presentation of the theme of Justice and Mercy, of the Old Law and the New. This puts an entirely different complexion upon the conflict of Jew and Gentile. The two principles for which, in Shakespeare's play, respectively, they stand, are both inherently right. They are only in conflict because, whereas God is held to be absolutely just as He is absolutely merciful, mortal and finite man can only be relatively so, and must arrive at a compromise. In human affairs either justice must yield a little to mercy, or mercy to justice; the former solution is the triumph of the New Law, and the conflict between Shylock and Portia is an *exemplum* of this triumph. I do not wish to suggest that Portia or Shylock are allegorical figures in the sense that *Wikked-Tunge* or *Bialacoil* are in the *Romaunt of the Rose*, for these are only abstractions; but they are allegorical in the sense that they adumbrate, embody, maintain, or stand for these concepts, while remaining individuals in fullest humanity. Shylock, therefore, should seem a great Old Testament figure, a patriarch perhaps, standing for the Law; and he will be tricked, just as Satan was tricked by the Incarnation, according to the tradition of the Middle Ages. A *Bestiary* of the thirteenth century tells us that no Devil-hunter knew the secret way by which Christ the Lion came down and took His den on earth:

> Migte neure diuel witen,
> þog he be derne hunte,
> hu he dun come,
> Ne wu he dennede him
> in þat defte meiden,
> Marie bi name . . .[1]

---

[1] No fiend was able to know, cunning hunter though he be, how he came down, or how he took his den in that deft Maiden, Mary by name.

And *Piers Plowman* has a like idea:

> . . . the olde lawe graunteth
> That gylours be bigiled . and that is gode resoun.
> *Dentem pro dente, & oculum pro oculo.*[1]

We must not, therefore, think the ruse by which Portia entraps Shylock is some sly part of her character, for it is in the tradition; besides she gives Shylock every chance. Thrice his money is offered him. He is begged to supply a surgeon. But no, it is not in the bond. From the point of view of the medium of theatre, the scene is, of course, constructed on the principle of peripeteia, or sudden reversal of situation, one of the great devices of dramaturgy. At one moment we see Mercy a suppliant to Justice, and at the next, in a flash, Justice is a suppliant to Mercy. The reversal is as instantaneous as it is unexpected to an audience that does not know the story in advance. Portia plants the point firmly:

> Downe, therfore, and beg mercy of the Duke.

And, in a twinkling, mercy shows her quality:

> *Duke.* That thou shalt see the difference of our spirit,
> I pardon thee thy life before thou aske it:
> For halfe thy wealth, it is *Anthonio's,*
> The other halfe comes to the generall state,
> Which humblenesse may driue vnto a fine.

Out of this there comes the second reversal. Shylock, till then pursuing Antonio's life, now has to turn to him for favour; and this is Antonio's response:

> So please my Lord the Duke, and all the Court
> To quit the fine for one halfe of his goods,
> I am content; so he will let me haue
> The other halfe in vse, to render it

---

[1] The Old Law allows that those who use trickery should be tricked themselves; and that is good reasoning. A tooth for a tooth and an eye for an eye.

Vpon his death, vnto the Gentleman
That lately stole his daughter.
Two things prouided more, that for this fauour
He presently become a Christian:
The other, that he doe record a gift
Heere in the Court of all he dies possest
Vnto his sonne *Lorenzo*, and his daughter.

Evidently Antonio recognizes the validity of legal deeds as much as Shylock does, and his opinion on Jessica's relationship with Lorenzo is in agreement with Shakespeare's, namely that the bond between husband and wife overrides the bond between father and daughter. Cordelia and Desdemona would have assented. Nor is it wholly alien to Shylock who is himself a family man. For him to provide for Jessica and Lorenzo is not unnaturally harsh.

It is Antonio's second condition that seems to modern ears so fiercely vindictive. In these days all good humanitarians incline to the view that a man's religion is his own affair, that a religion imposed is a tyranny, and that one religion is as good as another, if sincerely followed.

But the Elizabethans were not humanitarians in this sense. Only in Utopia, where it was one of 'the auncientest lawes among them that no man shall be blamed for reasonynge in the mayntenaunce of his owne religion' (and Utopia was not in Christendom) would such views have seemed acceptable. Whether we dislike it or not, Shylock had no hope, by Elizabethan standards, of entering a Christian eternity of blessedness; he had not been baptized. It would not have been his cruelty that would have excluded him (for cruelty, like other sin, can be repented) but the simple fact that he had no wedding-garment. No man cometh to the Father but by me.

Shylock had spent the play pursuing the mortal life of Antonio (albeit for private motives) in the name of justice. Now, at this reversal, in the name of mercy, Antonio offers him the chance of eternal life, his own best jewel.

It will, of course, be argued that it is painful for Shylock to swallow his pride, abjure his racial faith, and receive baptism. But then Christianity is painful. If we allow our thoughts to pursue Shylock after he left the Court we may well wonder whether his compulsory submission to baptism in the end induced him to take up his cross and follow Christ. But from Antonio's point of view, Shylock has at least been given his chance of eternal joy, and it is he, Antonio, that has given it to him. Mercy has triumphed over justice, even if the way of mercy is a hard way.

Once this aspect of the Trial scene is perceived, the Fifth Act becomes an intelligible extension of the allegory (in the sense defined), for we return to Belmont to find Lorenzo and Jessica in each other's arms. Christian and Jew, New Law and Old, are visibly united in love. And their talk is of music, Shakespeare's recurrent symbol of harmony.

It is not necessary for a single member of a modern audience to grasp this study in justice and mercy by any conscious process during a performance, or even afterwards in meditation. *Seeing one may see and not perceive.* But a producer who wishes to avoid his private prejudices in favour of Shakespeare's meanings, in order that he may achieve the real unity that binds a poetical play, should try to see them and to imagine the technical expedients of production by which that unity will be experienced. If he bases his conception on the resolution of the principles of justice and mercy, he will then, on the natural plane, be left the freer to show Christians and Jews as men and women, equally endowed with such faults and virtues as human beings commonly have.

I now turn to *The Tempest* in which almost all critics have seen adumbrations of mystical meaning. I would first like to seize on what little there is in the way of fact to guide an inquiry that must be mainly subjective. What can we *know* that an Elizabethan audience understood in it?

First, that it is, at the start and at the end, a *Ship-play*. To an Elizabethan audience the stage imaginatively, and as I think to some extent visibly, changed into a ship, both in the first scene and during Prospero's Epilogue. The great bare apron was the main deck, the 'inner stage' the cabin, the gallery above it the forecastle and the second gallery above that the masthead, rigging, or crow's nest. In the cabin were the royal party; above were the Master, the Boatswain, and his men. All this can be seen at once from the text of the dialogue in Act I, scene I. It makes it quite clear that the audience is looking at a stage representing *a ship that is going away from them*. I think it reasonable to suppose that this effect was visibly enhanced by the spreading of sails, ropes, and rigging above in the gallery, all of which at 'We split! We split!' would collapse and disappear, together with the crew. Gonzalo says his last say and also disappears, drawing the curtains behind him, to close upon the King and his party at their prayers.

At the end of the play, when Prospero comes forth from his cell to speak the Epilogue, the sails are hoisted again; up goes the rigging with the mariners in attendance, and the curtains of the inner stage part to show the whole and happy company as a background to Prospero's speech

> Gentle breath of yours, my sailes
> Must fill, or else my proiect failes,
> Which was to please. . . .

If, with whatever scenic additions, the stage at the

start and finish of the play represents a ship going away from the audience, we only now have to ask 'where was it going?' and the answer must be, at the end of the play, '*Home*'. It is a play about going home. Once this simple fact is apprehended it will be seen that all the action leads to it. 'Home' in this case is called *Millaine* and it is associated in the mind of Prospero with the idea of being ready to die:

> Euery third thought shall be my graue.

In between these two ship scenes, we learn that Prospero has been expelled from his natural inheritance (together with his daughter), for having devoted himself too closely to a kind of knowledge that is itself forbidden, that is, to magical knowledge. And he has to abjure it before he can go home with auspicious gales. He has also to reconcile himself with the enemies he has made.

Now if we take such a story on the natural plane of meaning only, it is impossible to account for the deep impression made upon us by the play. Compared with any other play of Shakespeare the sequence of action from scene to scene is tenuously spun. The characters are less sharply observed; villains are merely villainous, comics are merely comic. Prospero himself is not psychologically recognizable in the sense that can be claimed for other male protagonists in Shakespeare. The natural plane of interpretation is insufficient to explain the effect the play produces.

What story then, familiar to Shakespeare and to his audience, does this *Tempest* story of a man and woman exiled from their natural inheritance for the acquisition of a forbidden knowledge resemble? An answer leaps readily to mind; it resembles the story of Adam and Eve, type-story of our troubles. *The Tempest* also contains the story of Prospero and his brother Antonio, that has something of the primal, eldest curse upon it, something near a brother's murder. There is in Genesis, as well as the story of Adam and Eve, the story of Cain and Abel. But in *The Tempest* there is also a turn in both stories by which there may be a repentance and a forgiveness, and a home-coming in harmony. This is the shape of the promise of the New Testament and of the Second Adam. There is the hope of a return to Paradise when we come to die. Trouble will turn to joy.

These simplest and most obvious elements in the Christian story, upon which (but literally and without allegory) the great medieval mystery cycles were built, are, at a distance, mirrored in the story of *The Tempest*, well enough at least to be worth pondering.

There are further suggestions of allegory that an Elizabethan might have grasped more instantly than we can. They believed that man was made of the four elements, the higher, air and fire; the lower, earth and water. It would be no great leap of intuition to see the two first in Ariel, whom Folio calls 'an ayrie spirit' and who tells us he 'flam'd amazement' over the tempest-stricken ship. Caliban, on the other hand, is first addressed as "Thou Earth, thou', and is mistaken by Trinculo for a fish. If it is a fanciful thought, the text suggests it; it is there to be taken. That there is also some picture of the 'Natural Man' in Caliban, whom Folio calls 'a saluage and deformed slaue', is not to be doubted; but when we consider his relation to Ariel, two halves of a pair of servants to Prospero, he corresponds to him very readily in terms of the elements; his behaviour in the play is a long rebellion of grosser things; but he lives to repent and return to control under Prospero's will.

I do not wish to suggest any schematized or formal allegory: rather a kind of allegorical impressionism, dabs of significant colour that Shakespeare placed here and there to excite further ranges of response and yet evade 'this is' and 'this is not'. It is tempting, for instance, to see in Prospero the directing intellect, and in Miranda, the soul he is guarding; their island, shortly to be relinquished for ever, having for its only inhabitants (when they first came to it) the elements that will be left behind at their departure, may seem to stand for his bodily life.

But we must hold fast to the literal story in these symbolisms. Prospero has allowed his studies to take him from his duties as a ruler, and misrule has resulted; his faults have begotten greater faults in others, particularly in his brother; his dedication to the bettering of his mind, he says—

> Awak'd an euill nature, and my trust
> Like a good parent, did beget of him
> A falsehood in its contrarie, as great
> As my trust was. . . .

It takes a tempest to confront them now, across separating seas and the twelve years that had intervened. It is Prospero himself who stirs these deeps, in a propitious hour, to bring back into the foreground of consciousness the guilty creatures that must be faced with their guilt and then forgiven. His power summons these shadows from 'the dark backward and abysm of time'; he has designated Ferdinand for Miranda in advance; their union is to bind the whole reconcilement into harmony. And, at first sight, 'they change eyes'; Prospero has indeed to delay them in their love, for fear the harmony may be too facile; there is a deep wound and it must be healed from below. He sends Ariel to accuse the consciences of his enemies, and the invisible voice reawakens in them the knowledge of their guilt:

> Methought the billowes spoke, and told me of it,
> The windes did sing it to me. . . .

But Prospero has also to make an abjuration; for the last time he uses his 'rough magic' to summon 'Some heauenly Musicke', the harmony in which he can confront and forgive his self-made enemies. The visual image of that reconciliation is the sight of Miranda and Ferdinand at chess.

After that, Stephano and Trinculo can return, chastened, and Caliban comes back to his sober senses to acknowledge his master and be accepted back into the order of things, into grace. Prospero has re-established his control over evil elements, whether or not they are reconciled, and restored degree in the world of the play.[1] Somehow the Old Adam has been mended by the New, through pardon, and a return to Paradise across the waters made possible. A deep kind of trouble ends in a grave kind of joy.

Yet Shakespeare has gone far beyond the formula of Vincent de Beauvais. Even in the 'joyful' ending of *The Merchant of Venice*, Shylock and Antonio are left with their difficult lives to live; and as Shakespeare matured in Comedy, the hint of melancholy, of imperfect harmony, strengthened in almost every conclusion. Someone is left out of the sum of happiness; there is Jaques in *As You Like It* and Feste in *Twelfth Night*, which ends with his sad little song, and a stage empty of all but him; *Measure for Measure* ends in what (I think) we must take for rejoicing, hastily patched up as it may seem; but only after long anxieties; Barnadine and Lucio make their chastened escape from the executioner. It is a play without cheerfulness.

In *The Tempest* there is less stark wickedness, and more entertainment; but there is a pervasive melancholy that strengthens towards the close. Though it is a play of home-coming, it is also one of farewell; the ship sails away from us. Prospero is not only going

[1] I owe this thought to Professor T. P. Dunning, in conversation.

home, but to his long home, with every third thought.
It has often been remarked that it is Shakespeare's
farewell too, when, in another moment of allegorical
impressionism, he seems to take leave of the stage for
ever, 'our revels ended'. The play is indeed '*polysemos*',
as the author of the Epistle to Can Grande would have
said—of many meanings, many allusions.

But the sadness is more than personal in its conclusion; however Prospero may declare his forgiveness,
neither Sebastian nor Antonio have asked for it, nor do
they show any sign of accepting it. There is nothing in
the text that suggests a change of heart. It is for a
director to interpret this as he can. If he sees their
reconcilement as impossible, he must show them sullen
and contemptuous to the end, as if they would be just
as happy to be marooned as to go back with Prospero;
but if not, he may gather them in, with some show of
feeling in the last line of the play, on the colon provided
in Folio:

> . . . My Ariel; chicke
> That is thy charge: Then to the Elements
> Be free, and fare thou well: *please you draw neare.*

I have italicized the cue; it may be made to refer particularly to them. How they respond is for the director
to say. If they go back to Milan as treacherous and un-
reconciled as ever, they will at least be under control
and observation. It is an imperfect world.

And that is the thought that seems to me to be at the
heart of the melancholy of this play, a sense of the
imperfection of things. It is her inexperience, more than
her innocence, that makes Miranda exclaim:

> O wonder!
> How many goodly creatures are there heere?
> How beauteous mankinde is? O braue new world
> That has such people in't.

But the resigned, unillusioned answer of Prospero is more moving even than her exclamation: ' 'Tis new to thee.'

It is the Autumn of the Golden World; the apple-trees have fruited in Eden and the fruit has been tasted. Evil and sorrow have entered it. It is true that the evil has been checked, and is still under control. The next generation will have to see to it; it is to be hoped it may do better. Ferdinand and Miranda are young and fresh and the world is still new to them. But it began a great while ago; and the time will come when, like the insubstantial pageant of their Wedding Masque, it too will fade and leave not a wrack behind.

The Naked Babe and the Cloak of Manliness[1]

THE debate about the proper limits of metaphor has perhaps never been carried on in so spirited a fashion as it has been within the last twenty-five years. The tendency has been to argue for a much wider extension of those limits than critics like Dr. Johnson, say, were willing to allow—one wider even than the Romantic poets were willing to allow. Indeed, some alarm has been expressed of late, in one quarter or another, lest John Donne's characteristic treatment of metaphor be taken as the type and norm, measured against which other poets must, of necessity, come off badly. Yet, on the whole, I think that it must be conceded that the debate on metaphor has been stimulating and illuminating—and not least so with reference to those poets who lie quite outside the tradition of metaphysical wit.

Since the 'new criticism', so called, has tended to centre around the rehabilitation of Donne, and the Donne tradition, the latter point, I believe, needs to be emphasized. Actually, it would be a poor rehabilitation which, if exalting Donne above all his fellow poets, in fact succeeded in leaving him quite as much isolated from the rest of them as he was before. What the new awareness of the importance of metaphor—if it is actually new, and if its character is really that of a freshened awareness—what this new awareness of metaphor results in when applied to poets other than Donne and his followers is therefore a matter of first impor-

[1] *The Well Wrought Urn* (1949).

tance. Shakespeare provides, of course, the supremely interesting case.

But there are some misapprehensions to be avoided at the outset. We tend to associate Donne with the self-conscious and witty figure—his comparison of the souls of the lovers to the two legs of the compass is the obvious example. Shakespeare's extended figures are elaborated in another fashion. They are, we are inclined to feel, spontaneous comparisons struck out in the heat of composition, and not carefully articulated, self-conscious conceits at all. Indeed, for the average reader the connexion between spontaneity and seriously imaginative poetry is so strong that he will probably reject as preposterous any account of Shakespeare's poetry which sees an elaborate pattern in the imagery. He will reject it because to accept it means for him the assumption that the writer was not a fervent poet but a preter-naturally cold and self-conscious monster.

Poems are certainly not made by formula and blue-print. One rightly holds suspect a critical interpreta-tion that implies that they are. Shakespeare, we may be sure, was no such monster of calculation. But neither, for that matter, was Donne. Even in Donne's poetry, the elaborated and logically developed comparisons are outnumbered by the abrupt and succinct comparisons —by what T. S. Eliot has called the 'telescoped con-ceits'. Moreover, the extended comparisons themselves are frequently knit together in the sudden and appar-ently uncalculated fashion of the telescoped images; and if one examines the way in which the famous com-pass comparison is related to the rest of the poem in which it occurs, he may feel that even this elaborately 'logical' figure was probably the result of a happy acci-dent.

The truth of the matter is that we know very little of the various poets' methods of composition, and that what may seem to us the product of deliberate choice may well have been as 'spontaneous' as anything else in the poem. Certainly, the general vigour of metaphor in the Elizabethan period—as testified to by pamphlets, sermons, and plays—should warn us against putting the literature of that period at the mercy of our own personal theories of poetic composition. In any case, we shall probably speculate to better advantage—if speculate we must—on the possible significant interrelations of image with image rather than on the possible amount of pen-biting which the interrelations may have cost the author.

I do not intend, however, to beg the case by over-simplifying the relation between Shakespeare's intricate figures and Donne's. There are most important differences; and, indeed, Shakespeare's very similarities to the witty poets will, for many readers, tell against the thesis proposed here. For those instances in which Shakespeare most obviously resembles the witty poets occur in the earlier plays or in *Venus and Adonis* and *The Rape of Lucrece*; and these we are inclined to dismiss as early experiments—trial pieces from the Shakespearian workshop. We demand, quite properly, instances from the great style of the later plays.

Still, we will do well not to forget the witty examples in the poems and earlier plays. They indicate that Shakespeare is in the beginning not too far removed from Donne, and that, for certain effects at least, he was willing to play with the witty comparison. Dr. Johnson, in teasing the metaphysical poets for their fanciful conceits on the subject of tears, might well have added instances from Shakespeare. One remembers, for example, from *Venus and Adonis*:

> O, how her eyes and tears did lend and borrow!
> Her eyes seen in her tears, tears in her eye;
> Both crystals, where they view'd each other's sorrow. . . .

Or, that more exquisite instance which Shakespeare,

perhaps half-smiling, provided for the King in *Love's Labour's Lost*:

> So sweet a kiss the golden sun gives not
> To those fresh morning drops upon the rose,
> As thy eye-beams, when their fresh rays have smote
> The night of dew that on my cheeks down flows:
> Nor shines the silver moon one half so bright
> Through the transparent bosom of the deep,
> As does thy face through tears of mine give light:
> Thou shin'st in every tear that I do weep,
> No drop but as a coach doth carry thee:
> So ridest thou triumphing in my woe.
> Do but behold the tears that swell in me,
> And they thy glory through my grief will show:
> But do not love thyself—then thou wilt keep
> My tears for glasses, and still make me weep.

But Berowne, we know, at the end of the play, foreswears all such

> Taffeta phrases, silken terms precise,
> Three-piled hyperboles, spruce affectation,
> Figures pedantical . . .

in favour of 'russet yeas and honest kersey noes'. It is sometimes assumed that Shakespeare did the same thing in his later dramas, and certainly the epithet 'taffeta phrases' does not describe the great style of *Macbeth* and *Lear*. Theirs is assuredly of a tougher fabric. But 'russet' and 'honest kersey' do not describe it either. The weaving was not so simple as that.

The weaving was very intricate indeed—if anything, *more* rather than *less* intricate than that of *Venus and Adonis*, though obviously the pattern was fashioned in accordance with other designs, and yielded other kinds of poetry. But in suggesting that there is a real continuity between the imagery of *Venus and Adonis*, say, and that of a play like *Macbeth*, I am glad to be able to avail myself of Coleridge's support. I refer to the remarkable fifteenth chapter of the *Biographia*.

There Coleridge stresses not the beautiful tapestry-work—the purely visual effect—of the images, but quite another quality. He suggests that Shakespeare was prompted by a secret dramatic instinct to realize, in the imagery itself, that 'constant intervention and running comment by tone, look and gesture' ordinarily provided by the actor, and that Shakespeare's imagery becomes under this prompting 'a series and never broken chain . . . always vivid and, because unbroken, often minute . . .'. Coleridge goes on, a few sentences later, to emphasize further 'the perpetual activity of attention required on the part of the reader . . . the rapid flow, the quick change, and the playful nature of the thoughts and images'.

These characteristics, Coleridge hastens to say, are not in themselves enough to make superlative poetry. 'They become proofs of original genius only as far as they are modified by a predominant passion; or by associated thoughts or images awakened by that passion; or when they have the effect of reducing multitude to unity, or succession to an instant; or lastly, when a human and intellectual life is transferred to them from the poet's own spirit.'

Of the intellectual vigour which Shakespeare possessed, Coleridge then proceeds to speak—perhaps extravagantly. But he goes on to say: 'In Shakespeare's *poems*, the creative power and the intellectual energy wrestle as in a war embrace. Each in its excess of strength seems to threaten the extinction of the other.'

I am tempted to gloss Coleridge's comment here, perhaps too heavily, with remarks taken from Chapter XIII where he discusses the distinction between the Imagination and the Fancy—the modifying and creative power, on the one hand, and on the other, that 'mode of Memory' . . . 'blended with, and modified by . . . Choice'. But if in *Venus and Adonis* and *The Rape of Lucrece* the powers grapple 'in a war embrace', Coleridge goes on to pronounce: 'At length, in the *Drama* they were reconciled, and fought each with its shield before the breast of the other.'

It is a noble metaphor. I believe that it is also an accurate one, and that it comprises one of the most brilliant insights ever made into the nature of the dramatic poetry of Shakespeare's mature style. If it is accurate, we shall expect to find, even in the mature poetry, the 'never broken chain' of images, 'always vivid and, because unbroken, often minute', but we shall expect to find the individual images, not mechanically linked together in the mode of Fancy, but organically related, modified by 'a predominant passion', and mutually modifying each other.

T. S. Eliot has remarked that 'The difference between imagination and fancy, in view of [the] poetry of wit, is a very narrow one'. If I have interpreted Coleridge correctly, he is saying that in Shakespeare's greatest work, the distinction lapses altogether—or rather, that one is caught up and merged in the other. As his latest champion, I. A. Richards, observes: 'Coleridge often insisted—and would have insisted still more often had he been a better judge of his reader's capacity for misunderstanding—that Fancy and Imagination are not exclusive of, or inimical to, one another.'

I began by suggesting that our reading of Donne might contribute something to our reading of Shakespeare, though I tried to make plain the fact that I had no design of trying to turn Shakespeare into Donne, or—what I regard as nonsense—of trying to exalt Donne above Shakespeare. I have in mind specifically some such matter as this: that since the *Songs and Sonets* of Donne, no less than *Venus and Adonis*, requires a 'perpetual activity of attention . . . on the part of the reader from the rapid flow, the quick change, and the playful nature of the thoughts and images', the discipline gained from reading Donne may allow us to see more clearly the survival of such qualities in the later style of Shakespeare. And, again, I have in mind some such matter as this: that if a reading of Donne has taught us that the 'rapid flow, the quick change, and the playful nature of the thoughts and images'—qualities which we are all too prone to associate merely with the fancy—can, on occasion, take on imaginative power, we may, thus taught, better appreciate details in Shakespeare which we shall otherwise dismiss as merely fanciful, or, what is more likely, which we shall simply ignore altogether.

With Donne, of course, the chains of imagery, 'always vivid' and 'often minute' are perfectly evident. For many readers they are all too evident. The difficulty is not to prove that they exist, but that, on occasion, they may subserve a more imaginative unity. With Shakespeare, the difficulty may well be to prove that the chains exist at all. In general, we may say, Shakespeare has made it relatively easy for his admirers to choose what they like and neglect what they like. What he gives on one or another level is usually so magnificent that the reader finds it easy to ignore other levels.

Yet there are passages not easy to ignore and on which even critics with the conventional interests have been forced to comment. One of these passages occurs in *Macbeth*, Act I, scene vii, where Macbeth compares the pity for his victim-to-be, Duncan, to

> a naked new-born babe,
> Striding the blast, or heaven's cherubim, hors'd
> Upon the sightless couriers of the air. . . .

The comparison is odd, to say the least. Is the babe

natural or supernatural—an ordinary, helpless baby, who, as newborn, could not, of course, even toddle, much less stride the blast? Or is it some infant Hercules, quite capable of striding the blast, but, since it is powerful and not helpless, hardly the typical pitiable object?

Shakespeare seems bent upon having it both ways—and, if we read on through the passage—bent upon having the best of both worlds; for he proceeds to give us the option: pity is like the babe 'or heaven's cherubim' who quite appropriately, of course, do ride the blast. Yet, even if we waive the question of the legitimacy of the alternative (of which Shakespeare so promptly avails himself), is the cherubim comparison really any more successful than is the babe comparison? Would not one of the great warrior archangels be more appropriate to the scene than the cherub? Does Shakespeare mean for pity or for fear of retribution to be dominant in Macbeth's mind?

Or is it possible that Shakespeare could not make up his own mind? Was he merely writing hastily and loosely, letting the word 'pity' suggest the typically pitiable object, the babe naked in the blast, and then, stirred by the vague notion that some threat to Macbeth should be hinted, using 'heaven's cherubim'—already suggested by 'babe'—to convey the hint? Is the passage vague or precise? Loosely or tightly organized? Comments upon the passage have ranged all the way from one critic's calling it 'pure rant, and intended to be so' to another's laudation: 'Either like a mortal babe, terrible in helplessness; or like heaven's angel-children, mighty in love and compassion. This magnificent passage. . . .'

An even more interesting, and perhaps more disturbing passage in the play is that in which Macbeth describes his discovery of the murder:

> Here lay Duncan,
> His silver skin lac'd with his golden blood;
> And his gash'd stabs, look'd like a breach in nature
> For ruin's wasteful entrance: there, the murderers,
> Steep'd in the colours of their trade, their daggers
> Unmannerly breech'd with gore. . . .

It is amusing to watch the textual critics, particularly those of the eighteenth century, fight a stubborn rear-guard action against the acceptance of 'breech'd'. Warburton emended 'breech'd' to 'reech'd'; Johnson, to 'drench'd'; Seward, to 'hatch'd'. Other critics argued that the *breeches* implied were really the handles of the daggers, and that, accordingly, 'breech'd' actually here meant 'sheathed'. The Variorum page witnesses the desperate character of the defence, but the position has had to be yielded, after all. *The Shakespeare Glossary* defines 'breech'd' as meaning 'covered as with breeches', and thus leaves the poet committed to a reading which must still shock the average reader as much as it shocked that nineteenth-century critic who pronounced upon it as follows: 'A metaphor must not be far-fetched nor dwell upon the details of a disgusting picture, as in these lines. There is little, and that far-fetched, similarity between *gold lace* and *blood*, or between *bloody daggers* and *breech'd legs*. The slightness of the similarity, recalling the greatness of the dissimilarity, disgusts us with the attempted comparison.'

The two passages are not of the utmost importance, I dare say, though the speeches (of which each is a part) are put in Macbeth's mouth and come at moments of great dramatic tension in the play. Yet, in neither case is there any warrant for thinking that Shakespeare was not trying to write as well as he could. Moreover, whether we like it or not, the imagery is fairly typical of Shakespeare's mature style. Either passage ought to raise some qualms among those who retreat to Shakespeare's authority when they seek to urge the claims of 'noble simplicity'. They are hardly simple. Yet it is possible that such passages as these may illustrate another poetic resource, another type of imagery which, even in spite of its apparent violence and complication, Shakespeare could absorb into the total structure of his work.

Shakespeare, I repeat, is not Donne—is a much greater poet than Donne; yet the example of his typical handling of imagery will scarcely render support to the usual attacks on Donne's imagery—for, with regard to the two passages in question, the second one, at any rate, is about as strained as Donne is at his most extreme pitch.

Yet I think that Shakespeare's daggers attired in their bloody breeches can be defended as poetry, and as characteristically Shakespearian poetry. Furthermore, both this passage and that about the newborn babe, it seems to me, are far more than excrescences, mere extravagances of detail: each, it seems to me, contains a central symbol of the play, and symbols which we must understand if we are to understand either the detailed passage or the play as a whole.

If this be true, then more is at stake than the merit of the quoted lines taken as lines. (The lines as constituting mere details of a larger structure could, of course, be omitted in the acting of the play without seriously damaging the total effect of the tragedy—though this argument obviously cuts two ways. Whole scenes, and admittedly fine scenes, might also be omitted—have in fact *been* omitted—without quite destroying the massive structure of the tragedy.) What is at stake is the whole matter of the relation of Shakespeare's imagery to the total structures of the plays themselves.

I should like to use the passages as convenient points of

entry into the larger symbols which dominate the play. They *are* convenient because, even if we judge them to be faulty, they demonstrate how obsessive for Shakespeare the symbols were—they demonstrate how far the conscious (or unconscious) symbolism could take him.

If we see how the passages are related to these symbols, and they to the tragedy as a whole, the main matter is achieved; and having seen this, if we still prefer 'to wish the lines away', that, of course, is our privilege. In the meantime, we may have learned something about Shakespeare's methods—not merely of building metaphors—but of encompassing his larger meanings.

One of the most startling things which has come out of Miss Spurgeon's book on Shakespeare's imagery is her discovery of the 'old clothes' imagery in *Macbeth*. As she points out: 'The idea constantly recurs that Macbeth's new honours sit ill upon him, like a loose and badly fitting garment, belonging to someone else.' And she goes on to quote passage after passage in which the idea is expressed. But, though we are all in Miss Spurgeon's debt for having pointed this out, one has to observe that Miss Spurgeon has hardly explored the full implications of her discovery. Perhaps her interest in classifying and cataloguing the imagery of the plays has obscured for her some of the larger and more important relationships. At any rate, for reasons to be given below, she has realized only a part of the potentialities of her discovery.

Her comment on the clothes imagery reaches its climax with the following paragraphs:

And, at the end, when the tyrant is at bay at Dunsinane, and the English troops are advancing, the Scottish lords still have this image in their minds. Caithness sees him as a man vainly trying to fasten a large garment on him with too small a belt:

> He cannot buckle his distemper'd cause
> Within the belt of rule;

while Angus, in a similar image, vividly sums up the essence of what they all have been thinking ever since Macbeth's accession to power:

> now does he feel his title
> Hang loose about him, like a giant's robe
> Upon a dwarfish thief.

This imaginative picture of a small, ignoble man encumbered and degraded by garments unsuited to him, should be put against the view emphasized by some critics (notably Coleridge and Bradley) of the likeness between Macbeth and Milton's Satan in grandeur and sublimity.

Undoubtedly Macbeth . . . is great, magnificently great. . . . But he could never be put beside, say, Hamlet or Othello, in nobility of nature; and there *is* an aspect in which he is but a poor, vain, cruel, treacherous creature, snatching ruthlessly over the dead bodies of kinsman and friend at place and power he is utterly unfitted to possess. It is worth remembering that it is thus that Shakespeare, with his unshrinking clarity of vision, repeatedly *sees* him.

But this is to make primary what is only one aspect of the old-clothes imagery! And there is no warrant for interpreting the garment imagery as used by Macbeth's enemies, Caithness and Angus, to mean that *Shakespeare* sees Macbeth as a poor and somewhat comic figure.

The crucial point of the comparison, it seems to me, lies not in the smallness of the man and the largeness of the robes, but rather in the fact that—whether the man be large or small—these are not *his* garments; in Macbeth's case they are actually stolen garments. Macbeth is uncomfortable in them because he is continually conscious of the fact that they do not belong to him. There is a further point, and it is one of the utmost importance; the oldest symbol for the hypocrite is that of the man who cloaks his true nature under a disguise. Macbeth loathes playing the part of the hypocrite—

and actually does not play it too well. If we keep this in
mind as we look back at the instances of the garment
images which Miss Spurgeon has collected for us, we
shall see that the pattern of imagery becomes very rich
indeed. Macbeth says in Act I:

> The Thane of Cawdor lives: why do you dress me
> In borrow'd robes?

Macbeth at this point wants no honours that are not
honestly his. Banquo says in Act I:

> New honours come upon him,
> Like our strange garments, cleave not to their mould,
> But with the aid of use.

But Banquo's remark, one must observe, is not cen-
sorious. It is indeed a compliment to say of one that he
wears new honours with some awkwardness. The observation becomes ironical only in terms of what is to
occur later.

Macbeth says in Act I:

> He hath honour'd me of late; and I have bought
> Golden opinions from all sorts of people,
> Which would be worn now in their newest gloss,
> Not cast aside so soon.

Macbeth here is proud of his new clothes: he is happy
to wear what he has truly earned. It is the part of simple
good husbandry not to throw aside these new garments
and replace them with robes stolen from Duncan.

But Macbeth has already been wearing Duncan's
garments in anticipation, as his wife implies in the
metaphor with which she answers him:

> Was the hope drunk,
> Wherein you dress'd yourself?

(The metaphor may seem hopelessly mixed, and a full
and accurate analysis of such mixed metaphors in terms
of the premises of Shakespeare's style waits upon some

critic who will have to consider not only this passage but many more like it in Shakespeare.) For our purposes here, however, one may observe that the psychological line, the line of the basic symbolism, runs on unbroken. A man dressed in a drunken hope is garbed in strange attire indeed—a ridiculous dress which accords thoroughly with the contemptuous picture that Lady Macbeth wishes to evoke. Macbeth's earlier dream of glory has been a drunken fantasy merely, if he flinches from action now.

But the series of garment metaphors which run through the play is paralleled by a series of masking or cloaking images which—if we free ourselves of Miss Spurgeon's rather mechanical scheme of classification —show themselves to be merely variants of the garments which hide none too well his disgraceful self. He is consciously hiding that self throughout the play.

'False face must hide what the false heart doth know', he counsels Lady Macbeth before the murder of Duncan; and later, just before the murder of Banquo, he invokes night to 'Scarf up the eye of pitiful day'.

One of the most powerful of these cloaking images is given to Lady Macbeth in the famous speech in Act I:

> Come, thick night,
> And pall thee in the dunnest smoke of hell,
> That my keen knife see not the wound it makes,
> Nor heaven peep through the blanket of the dark,
> To cry, 'Hold, Hold!'

I suppose that it is natural to conceive the 'keen knife' here as held in her own hand. Lady Macbeth is capable of wielding it. And in this interpretation, the imagery is thoroughly significant. Night is to be doubly black so that not even her knife may see the wound it makes. But I think that there is good warrant for regarding her 'keen knife' as Macbeth himself. She has just, a few lines above, given her analysis of Macbeth's character as one who would 'not play false, / And yet [would] wrongly win'. To bring him to the point of action, she will have to 'chastise [him] with the valour of [her] tongue'. There is good reason, then, for her to invoke night to become blacker still—to pall itself in the 'dunnest smoke of hell'. For night must not only screen the deed from the eye of heaven—conceal it at least until it is too late for heaven to call out to Macbeth 'Hold, Hold!' Lady Macbeth would have night blanket the deed from the hesitant doer. The imagery thus repeats and reinforces the substance of Macbeth's anguished aside uttered in the preceding scene:

> Let not light see my black and deep desires;
> The eye wink at the hand; yet let that be
> Which the eye fears, when it is done, to see.

I do not know whether 'blanket' and 'pall' qualify as garment metaphors in Miss Spurgeon's classification: yet one is the clothing of sleep, and the other, the clothing of death—they are the appropriate garments of night; and they carry on an important aspect of the general clothes imagery. It is not necessary to attempt to give here an exhaustive list of instances of the garment metaphor; but one should say a word about the remarkable passage in II. iii.

Here, after the discovery of Duncan's murder, Banquo says

> And when we have our naked frailties hid,
> That suffer in exposure, let us meet,
> And question this most bloody piece of work—

that is, 'When we have clothed ourselves against the chill morning air, let us meet to discuss this bloody piece of work'. Macbeth answers, as if his subconscious mind were already taking Banquo's innocent phrase, 'naked frailties', in a deeper, ironic sense:

> Let's briefly put on manly readiness. . . .

It is ironic; for the 'manly readiness' which he urges the other lords to put on, is, in his own case, a hypocrite's garment: he can only pretend to be the loyal, grief-stricken liege who is almost unstrung by the horror of Duncan's murder.

But the word 'manly' carries still a further ironic implication: earlier, Macbeth had told Lady Macbeth that he dared

> do all that may become a man;
> Who dares do more is none.

Under the weight of her reproaches of cowardice, however, he *has* dared do more, and has become less than a man, a beast. He has already laid aside, therefore, one kind of 'manly readiness' and has assumed another: he has garbed himself in a sterner composure than that which he counsels to his fellows—the hard and inhuman 'manly readiness' of the resolved murderer.

The clothes imagery, used sometimes with emphasis on one aspect of it, sometimes on another, does pervade the play. And it should be evident that the daggers 'breech'd with gore'—though Miss Spurgeon does not include the passage in her examples of clothes imagery —represent one more variant of this general symbol. Consider the passage once more:

> Here lay Duncan,
> His silver skin lac'd with his golden blood;
> And his gash'd stabs look'd like a breach in nature
> For ruin's wasteful entrance: there, the murderers,
> Steep'd in the colours of their trade, their daggers
> Unmannerly breech'd with gore. . . .

The clothes imagery runs throughout the passage; the body of the king is dressed in the most precious of garments, the blood royal itself; and the daggers too are dressed—in the same garment. The daggers, 'naked' except for their lower parts which are reddened with

blood, are like men in 'unmannerly' dress—men, naked
except for their red breeches, lying beside the red-
handed grooms. The figure, though vivid, is fantastic;
granted. But the basis for the comparison is *not* slight
and adventitious. The metaphor fits the real situation
on the deepest levels. As Macbeth and Lennox burst
into the room, they find the daggers wearing, as Macbeth knows all too well, a horrible masquerade. They
have been carefully 'clothed' to play a part. They are
not honest daggers, honourably naked in readiness to
guard the king, or 'mannerly' clothed in their own
sheaths. Yet the disguise which they wear will enable
Macbeth to assume the robes of Duncan—robes to
which he is no more entitled than are the daggers to
the royal garments which they now wear, grotesquely.

The reader will, of course, make up his own mind
as to the value of the passage. But the metaphor in
question, in the light of the other garment imagery,
cannot be dismissed as merely a strained ingenuity,
irrelevant to the play. And the reader who *does* accept
it as poetry will probably be that reader who knows the
play best, not the reader who knows it slightly and
regards Shakespeare's poetry as a rhetoric more or less
loosely draped over the 'content' of the play.

And now what can be said of pity, the 'naked new-
born babe'? Though Miss Spurgeon does not note it
(since the governing scheme of her book would have
hardly allowed her to see it), there are, by the way, a
great many references to babes in this play—references
which occur on a number of levels. The babe appears
sometimes as a character, such as Macduff's child;
sometimes as a symbol, like the crowned babe and the
bloody babe which are raised by the witches on the
occasion of Macbeth's visit to them; sometimes in a
metaphor, as in the passage under discussion. The
number of such references can hardly be accidental;

and the babe turns out to be, as a matter of fact, perhaps the most powerful symbol in the tragedy.

But to see this fully, it will be necessary to review the motivation of the play. The stimulus to Duncan's murder, as we know, was the prophecy of the Weird Sisters. But Macbeth's subsequent career of bloodshed stems from the same prophecy. Macbeth was to have the crown, but the crown was to pass to Banquo's children. The second part of the prophecy troubles Macbeth from the start. It does not oppress him, however, until the crown has been won. But from this point on, the effect of the prophecy is to hurry Macbeth into action and more action until he is finally precipitated into ruin.

We need not spend much time in speculating on whether Macbeth, had he been content with Duncan's murder, had he tempted fate no further, had he been willing to court the favour of his nobles, might not have died peaceably in bed. We are dealing, not with history, but with a play. Yet, even in history the usurper sometimes succeeds; and he sometimes succeeds on the stage. Shakespeare himself knew of, and wrote plays about, usurpers who successfully maintained possession of the crown. But, in any case, this much is plain: the train of murders into which Macbeth launches aggravates suspicions of his guilt and alienates the nobles.

Yet, a Macbeth who could act once, and then settle down to enjoy the fruits of this one attempt to meddle with the future would, of course, not be Macbeth. For it is not merely his great imagination and his warrior courage in defeat which redeem him for tragedy and place him beside the other great tragic protagonists: rather, it is his attempt to conquer the future, an attempt involving him, like Oedipus, in a desperate struggle with fate itself. It is this which holds our imaginative sympathy, even after he has degenerated into a bloody tyrant and has become the slayer of Macduff's wife and children.

To sum up, there can be no question that Macbeth stands at the height of his power after his murder of Duncan, and that the plan—as outlined by Lady Macbeth—has been relatively successful. The road turns toward disaster only when Macbeth decides to murder Banquo. Why does he make this decision? Shakespeare has pointed up the basic motivation very carefully:

> Then prophet-like,
> They hail'd him father to a line of kings.
> Upon my head they plac'd a fruitless crown,
> And put a barren sceptre in my gripe,
> Thence to be wrench'd with a unlineal hand,
> No son of mine succeeding. If't be so,
> For Banquo's issue have I fil'd my mind;
> For them the gracious Duncan have I murder'd;
> Put rancours in the vessel of my peace
> Only for them; and mine eternal jewel
> Given to the common enemy of man,
> To make them kings, the seed of Banquo kings!

Presumably, Macbeth had entered upon his course from sheer personal ambition. Ironically, it is the more human part of Macbeth—his desire to have more than a limited personal satisfaction, his desire to found a line, his wish to pass something on to later generations—which prompts him to dispose of Banquo. There is, of course, a resentment against Banquo, but that resentment is itself closely related to Macbeth's desire to found a dynasty. Banquo, who has risked nothing, who has remained upright, who has not defiled himself, will have kings for children; Macbeth, none. Again, ironically, the Weird Sisters who have given Macbeth, so he has thought, the priceless gift of knowledge of the future, have given the real future to Banquo.

So Banquo's murder is decided upon, and accomplished. But Banquo's son escapes, and once more, the future has eluded Macbeth. The murder of Banquo thus becomes almost meaningless. This general point may be obvious enough, but we shall do well to note some of the further ways in which Shakespeare has pointed up the significance of Macbeth's war with the future.

When Macbeth, at the beginning of scene vii, Act I, contemplates Duncan's murder, it is the future over which he agonizes:

> If it were done, when 'tis done, then 'twere well
> It were done quickly; if the assassination
> Could trammel up the consequence, and catch
> With his surcease success; that but this blow
> Might be the be-all and the end-all here. . . .

But the continuum of time cannot be partitioned off; the future is implicit in the present. There is no net strong enough to trammel up the consequence—not even in this world.

Lady Macbeth, of course, has fewer qualms. When Macbeth hesitates to repudiate the duties which he owes Duncan—duties which, by some accident of imagery perhaps—I hesitate to press the significance— he has earlier actually called 'children'—Lady Macbeth cries out that she is willing to crush her own child in order to gain the crown:

> I have given suck, and know
> How tender 'tis to love the babe that milks me;
> I would, while it was smiling in my face,
> Have pluck'd my nipple from his boneless gums
> And dash'd the brains out, had I so sworn as you
> Have done to this.

Robert Penn Warren has made the penetrating observation that all of Shakespeare's villains are rationalists. Lady Macbeth is certainly of their company. She knows what she wants; and she is ruthless in her consideration of means. She will always 'catch the nearest way'. This is not to say that she ignores the problem of scruples, or that she is ready to oversimplify psychological complexities. But scruples are to be used to entangle one's enemies. One is not to become tangled in the mesh of scruples himself. Even though she loves her husband and though her ambition for herself is a part of her ambition for him, still she seems willing to consider even Macbeth at times as pure instrument, playing upon his hopes and fears and pride.

Her rationalism is quite sincere. She is apparently thoroughly honest in declaring that

> The sleeping and the dead
> Are but as pictures; 'tis the eye of childhood
> That fears a painted devil. If he do bleed,
> I'll gild the faces of the grooms withal,
> For it must seem their guilt.

For her, there is no moral order: *guilt* is something like *gilt*—one can wash it off or paint it on. Her pun is not frivolous and it is deeply expressive.

Lady Macbeth abjures all pity; she is willing to unsex herself; and her continual taunt to Macbeth, when he falters, is that he is acting like a baby—not like a man. This 'manhood' Macbeth tries to learn. He is a dogged pupil. For that reason he is almost pathetic when the shallow rationalism which his wife urges upon him fails. His tone is almost one of puzzled bewilderment at nature's unfairness in failing to play the game according to the rules—the rules which have applied to other murders:

> the time has been,
> That, when the brains were out, the man would die,
> And there an end; but now they rise again. . . .

Yet, after the harrowing scene, Macbeth can say, with a sort of dogged weariness:

Come, we'll to sleep. My strange and self-abuse
Is the initiate fear that wants hard use:
We are yet but young in deed.

Ironically, Macbeth is still echoing the dominant metaphor of Lady Macbeth's reproach. He has not yet
attained to 'manhood'; that *must* be the explanation.
He has not yet succeeded in hardening himself into
something inhuman.

Tempted by the Weird Sisters and urged on by his
wife, Macbeth is thus caught between the irrational
and the rational. There is a sense, of course, in which
every man is caught between them. Man must try to
predict and plan and control his destiny. That is man's
fate; and the struggle, if he is to realize himself as a
man, cannot be avoided. The question, of course, which
has always interested the tragic dramatist involves the
terms on which the struggle is accepted and the protagonist's attitude toward fate and toward himself.
Macbeth in his general concern for the future is typical
—is Every Man. He becomes the typical tragic protagonist when he yields to pride and *hybris*. The occasion for temptation is offered by the prophecy of the
Weird Sisters. They offer him knowledge which cannot
be arrived at rationally. They offer a key—if only a
partial key—to what is otherwise unpredictable. Lady
Macbeth, on the other hand, by employing a ruthless
clarity of perception, by discounting all emotional
claims, offers him the promise of bringing about the
course of events which he desires.

Now, in the middle of the play, though he has not
lost confidence and though, as he himself says, there
can be no turning back, doubts have begun to arise;
and he returns to the Weird Sisters to secure un-
ambiguous answers to his fears. But, pathetically and
ironically for Macbeth, in returning to the Weird
Sisters, he is really trying to impose rationality on what

sets itself forth plainly as irrational: that is, Macbeth would force a rigid control on a future which, by definition—by the very fact that the Weird Sisters already know it—stands beyond his manipulation.

It is because of his hopes for his own children and his fears of Banquo's that he has returned to the witches for counsel. It is altogether appropriate, therefore, that two of the apparitions by which their counsel is revealed should be babes, the crowned babe and the bloody babe.

For the babe signifies the future which Macbeth would control and cannot control. It is the unpredictable thing itself—as Yeats has put it magnificently, 'The uncontrollable mystery on the bestial floor'. It is the one thing that can justify, even in Macbeth's mind, the murders which he has committed. Earlier in the play, Macbeth had declared that if the deed could 'trammel up the consequence', he would be willing to 'jump the life to come'. But he cannot jump the life to come. In his own terms he is betrayed. For it is idle to speak of jumping the life to come if one yearns to found a line of kings. It is the babe that betrays Macbeth—his own babes, most of all.

The logic of Macbeth's distraught mind, thus, forces him to make war on children, a war which in itself reflects his desperation and is a confession of weakness. Macbeth's ruffians, for example, break into Macduff's castle and kill his wife and children. The scene in which the innocent child prattles with his mother about his absent father, and then is murdered, is typical Shakespearian 'fourth act' pathos. But the pathos is not adventitious; the scene ties into the inner symbolism of the play. For the child, in its helplessness, defies the murderers. Its defiance testifies to the force which threatens Macbeth and which Macbeth cannot destroy.

But we are not, of course, to placard the child as The Future in a rather stiff and mechanical allegory. *Macbeth* is no such allegory. Shakespeare's symbols are richer and more flexible than that. The babe signifies not only the future; it symbolizes all those enlarging purposes which make life meaningful, and it symbolizes, furthermore, all those emotional and—to Lady Macbeth—irrational ties which make man more than a machine—which render him human. It signifies preeminently the pity which Macbeth, under Lady Macbeth's tutelage, would wean himself of as something 'unmanly'. Lady Macbeth's great speeches early in the play become brilliantly ironical when we realize that Shakespeare is using the same symbol for the unpredictable future that he uses for human compassion. Lady Macbeth is willing to go to any length to grasp the future: she would willingly dash out the brains of her own child if it stood in her way to that future. But this is to repudiate the future, for the child is its symbol.

Shakespeare does not, of course, limit himself to the symbolism of the child: he makes use of other symbols of growth and development, notably that of the plant. And this plant symbolism patterns itself to reflect the development of the play. For example, Banquo says to the Weird Sisters, early in the play:

> If you can look into the seeds of time,
> And say which grain will grow and which will not,
> Speak then to me. . . .

A little later, on welcoming Macbeth, Duncan says to him:

> I have begun to plant thee, and will labour
> To make thee full of growing.

After the murder of Duncan, Macbeth falls into the same metaphor when he comes to resolve on Banquo's death. The Weird Sisters, he reflects, had hailed Banquo as

> . . . father to a line of kings.
> Upon my head they placed a fruitless crown,
> And put a barren sceptre in my gripe. . . .

Late in the play, Macbeth sees himself as the winter-stricken tree:

> I have liv'd long enough: my way of life
> Is fall'n into the sear, the yellow leaf. . . .

The plant symbolism, then, supplements the child symbolism. At points it merges with it, as when Macbeth ponders bitterly that he has damned himself

> To make them kings, the seed of Banquo kings!

And, in at least one brilliant example, the plant symbolism unites with the clothes symbolism. It is a crowning irony that one of the Weird Sisters' prophecies on which Macbeth has staked his hopes is fulfilled when Birnam Wood comes to Dunsinane. For, in a sense, Macbeth is here hoist on his own petard. Macbeth, who has invoked night to 'Scarf up the tender eye of pitiful day', and who has, again and again, used the 'false face' to 'hide what the false heart doth know', here has the trick turned against him. But the garment which cloaks the avengers is the living green of nature itself, and nature seems, to the startled eyes of his sentinels, to be rising up against him.

But it is the babe, the child, that dominates the symbolism. Most fittingly, the last of the prophecies in which Macbeth has placed his confidence, concerns the child: and Macbeth comes to know the final worst when Macduff declares to him that he was not 'born of woman' but was from his 'mother's womb / Untimely ripp'd'. The babe here has defied even the thing which one feels may reasonably be predicted of him—his time of birth. With Macduff's pronouncement, the unpredictable has broken through the last shred of the net of calculation. The future cannot be trammelled up. The naked babe confronts Macbeth to pronounce his doom.

The passage with which we began this essay, then, is an integral part of a larger context, and of a very rich context:

> And pity, like a naked new-born babe,
> Striding the blast, or heaven's cherubim, hors'd
> Upon the sightless couriers of the air,
> Shall blow the horrid deed in every eye,
> That tears shall drown the wind.

Pity is like the naked babe, the most sensitive and helpless thing; yet, almost as soon as the comparison is announced, the symbol of weakness begins to turn into a symbol of strength; for the babe, though new-born, is pictured as 'Striding the blast' like an elemental force—like 'heaven's cherubim, hors'd / Upon the sightless couriers of the air.' We can give an answer to the question put earlier: is Pity like the human and helpless babe, or powerful as the angel that rides the winds? It is both; and it is strong because of its very weakness. The paradox is inherent in the situation itself; and it is the paradox that will destroy the over-brittle rationalism on which Macbeth founds his career.

For what will it avail Macbeth to cover the deed with the blanket of the dark if the elemental forces that ride the winds will blow the horrid deed in every eye? And what will it avail Macbeth to clothe himself in 'manliness'—to become bloody, bold, and resolute—if he is to find himself again and again, viewing his bloody work through the 'eye of childhood / That fears a painted devil'? Certainly, the final and climactic appearance of the babe symbol merges all the contradictory elements of the symbol. For, with Macduff's statement about his birth, the naked babe rises before Macbeth as not only the future that eludes calculation but as avenging angel as well.

The clothed daggers and the naked babe—mechanism and life—instrument and end—death and birth—that which should be left bare and clean and that which should be clothed and warmed—these are facets of two of the great symbols which run throughout the play. They are not the only symbols, to be sure; they are not the most obvious symbols: darkness and blood appear more often. But with a flexibility which must amaze the reader, the image of the garment and the image of the babe are so used as to encompass an astonishingly large area of the total situation. And between them— the naked babe, essential humanity, humanity stripped down to the naked thing itself, and yet as various as the future—and the various garbs which humanity assumes, the robes of honour, the hypocrite's disguise, the in- human 'manliness' with which Macbeth endeavours to cover up his essential humanity—between them, they furnish Shakespeare with his most subtle and ironically telling instruments.

L. C. KNIGHTS

(b. 1906)

King Lear[1]

IF, at the end of *King Lear*, we feel that the King's angry and resounding question, 'Who is it that can tell me who I am?' has indeed been answered, that is because Shakespeare has submitted himself to a process equivalent in the emotional and imaginative sphere to the famous Cartesian intellectual doubt. Some of the most fundamental questions concerning the nature of man are posed in a way that precludes all ready-made answers, that, in fact, so emphasizes the difficulty of the questions as to make any kind of answer seem all but impossible. Only thus could the urgent perplexities of the earlier plays be brought into full consciousness and confronted at the deepest level of significance. For these reasons *King Lear* has the three characteristics of the very greatest works of art: it is timeless and universal; it has a crucial place in its author's inner biography; and it marks a moment of great importance in the changing consciousness of the civilization to which it belongs. In the preceding chapters I have indicated some of the converging pressures that compelled Shakespeare to the writing of *King Lear*. In this chapter I shall be mainly concerned with the play's essential significance as I see it. But before passing from the one to the other, and as a convenient way of bringing to focus this intrinsic significance, I should like briefly to consider the play in its third aspect, as indicating a stage in the emergence of the modern European consciousness. To do this we must first turn

[1] *Some Shakespearean Themes* (1960). The footnotes are here abbreviated.

from the question of 'human nature' to that of the wider 'Nature' within which human life has its setting. In our own 'philosophies of life', as in the play, the two questions prove in the long run to be inseparable.

I

In an essay on 'Nature', published in the posthumous *Three Essays on Religion* but written in the eighteen-fifties, John Stuart Mill attempted to clear up some of the confusion that had gathered about that ambiguous word. The question he was mainly concerned with was whether Nature, in the sense of that which 'takes place without the agency, or without the voluntary and intentional agency, of man', could offer a standard of human conduct. Should we deliberately, as the phrase goes, 'follow Nature'? His answer was an emphatic No. Man's progress is a continual triumph over nature; and although we may feel awe in the presence of 'the greater natural phenomena . . . a hurricane; a mountain precipice; the desert; the ocean, either agitated or at rest; the solar system . . .', we must not confuse 'the astonishment, rising into awe' caused by the vastness of these things with the admiration due to moral excellence, or fondly imagine that their attributes are such as we ought to emulate.

For how stands the fact? That next to the greatness of these cosmic forces, the quality which most forcibly strikes every one who does not avert his eyes from it, is their perfect and absolute recklessness . . . In sober truth, nearly all the things which men are hanged or imprisoned for doing to one another, are nature's everyday performances. Killing, the most criminal act recognized by human laws, Nature does once to every being that lives; and in a large proportion of cases, after protracted tortures such as only the greatest monsters whom we read of ever purposely inflicted on their living fellow-creatures. If, by an arbitrary reservation, we refuse to account anything murder but what abridges a certain term supposed to be allotted to human life, Nature also does this to all but a small percentage of lives, and does it in all the modes, violent or insidious, in which the worst human beings take the lives of one another. Nature impales men, breaks them as if on the wheel, casts them to be devoured by wild beasts, burns them to death, crushes them with stones like the first Christian martyrs, starves them with hunger, freezes them with cold, poisons them by the quick or slow venom of her exhalations, and has hundreds of other hideous deaths in reserve, such as the ingenious cruelty of a Nabis or a Domitian never surpassed. All this, Nature does with the most supercilious disregard both of mercy and of justice, emptying her shafts upon the best and noblest indifferently with the meanest and the worst; upon those who are engaged in the highest and worthiest enterprises, and often as the direct consequence of the noblest acts; and it might almost be imagined as a punishment for them. She mows down those on whose existence hangs the well-being of a whole people, perhaps the prospects of the human race for generations to come, with as little compunction as those whose death is a relief to themselves, or a blessing to those under their noxious influence. Such are Nature's dealings with life.

It will be agreed that this passage sounds a familiar nineteenth-century note[1]—and that it could not possibly have been written in the sixteenth century. It certainly was not that the facts that Mill instances—famine, pestilence, and so on—were not known, but that no one in the Middle Ages or in the sixteenth century could have written of Nature in that tone and with those implications. It was taken for granted that Nature was often cruel (there had, after all, been a Fall from Paradise), but the whole disposition of things, independent of man's will, served a providential plan. Nature, in this sense, though subject to disorder, was essentially ordered, and it was ordered for the good of man. George Herbert's poem, 'Providence', shows a world

[1] Hardy, of course, comes to mind; and we may turn also to Leopardi's 'La Ginestra' (1836).

where everything is ordered and all things serve a
purpose.

> Thy cupboard serves the world: the meat is set,
> Where all may reach: no beast but knows his feed.
> Birds teach us hawking; fishes have their net:
> The great prey on the less, they on some weed.
>
> Nothing ingendred doth prevent his meat:
> Flies have their table spread, ere they appeare.
> Some creatures have in winter what to eat;
> Others do sleep, and envie not their cheer.
>
> How finely dost thou times and seasons spin,
> And make a twist checker'd with night and day!
> Which as it lengthens windes us in,
> As bouls go on, but turning all the way.
>
> Each creature hath a wisdome for his good.
> The pigeons feed their tender off-spring, crying,
> When they are callow; but withdraw their food
> When they are fledge, that need may teach them flying.
>
> Bees work for man; and yet they never bruise
> Their masters flower, but leave it, having done,
> As fair as ever, and as fit for use;
> So both the flower doth stay, and hony run.
>
> Sheep eat the grasse, and dung the ground for more:
> Trees after bearing drop their leaves for soil:
> Springs vent their streams, and by expense get store:
> Clouds cool by heat, and baths by cooling boil.

We may not always be able to recognize that order, but
as Herbert says in the same poem, 'If we could heare
Thy skill and art, what musick would it be!'

Within this natural order man had a unique place.
There was no question of his 'following Nature' in the
vague nineteenth-century sense that was to annoy Mill,
but only of realizing the potentialities of his own nature.
His nature was corrupted by the Fall, but was capable
of receiving Grace. It was 'natural' for him to sin, but

his essential nature was fulfilled in doing what he ought
to do: so that in another and more important sense
'natural' as applied to man tended to suggest a standard
to be achieved—that which was right and proper for
man. Thus Hooker speaks of 'our . . . intent of discovering the natural way, whereby rules have been
found out concerning that goodness wherewith the Will
of man ought to be moved in human actions; as everything naturally and necessarily doth desire the utmost
good and greatest perfection whereof Nature hath made
it capable, even so man'.[1]

Thus the word 'natural' as applied to man had a
peculiar resonance; it was a kind of short-hand that
could be used effectively even when the complex philosophical implications were not immediately present.
There is a fine passage in Ben Jonson's *The Staple of
News* (1626) that illustrates this.

> They covet things
> Superfluous still, when it were much more honour
> They could want necessary: what need hath nature
> Of silver dishes, or gold chamber-pots?
> Of perfumed napkins, or a numerous family
> To see her eat? poor, and wise, she requires
> Meat only; hunger is not ambitious:
> Say, that you were the emperor of pleasures,
> The great dictator of fashions, for all Europe,
> And had the pomp of all the courts, and kingdoms,
> Laid forth unto the shew, to make yourself
> Gazed and admired at; you must go to bed,
> And take your natural rest: then all this vanisheth.
> Your bravery was but shown; 'twas not possest:
> While it did boast itself, it was then perishing. (III. ii)

Here, and in similar passages, 'nature' has partly a
biological reference: it means what is necessary to
maintain man's natural constitution; and at the same
time it refers to what is customary and sanctioned by

[1] *Of the Laws of Ecclesiastical Polity*, book i, chap. viii, sect. 1.

tradition in a certain kind of community. But behind it—adding depth and volume—is the structure of theological and philosophical belief to which I have referred.

A firm conviction of what is distinctively 'natural' or proper for man does not of course necessarily depend on a belief in the providential ordering of non-human Nature, just as relativism in morals does not necessarily follow from a belief in Nature's indifference, as Mill's essay shows. But in the age of Shakespeare the partial erosion of the established assumptions about Nature does seem to have had a share in the undermining of the older conception of human nature and the traditional sanctions of morality.[1] By the beginning of the seventeenth century to some minds Nature was ceasing to appear as a divinely ordained order and was beginning to appear as an amoral collection of forces. Now if man himself is *only* part of Nature as thus conceived, then 'natural impulse' (or so it may be argued) cannot be questioned; and natural impulse inevitably means the more powerful drives—sexual appetite, the desire for dominance, and so on. In *Les Libertins en France au XVIIe Siècle*: F. T. Perrens tells us that the most serious charge brought by the Jesuit Father Garassus against the free-thinkers was that they 'recognize no other sovereign power but Nature, maintaining that she has done nothing that is not wise, that therefore man must follow her, and even if one wished to resist her it would not be possible'. It is a convenient doctrine; and although it is certainly not true that all the free-thinkers were dissolute, it is likely that the dissolute were glad of the doctrine, in the manner of Don John and his associates in Shadwell's play *The Libertine*:

---

[1] Other causes were, of course, at work as well. For example, the discovery of new lands, where institutions and forms of behaviour were radically different from those of western Europe, suggested that the 'natural' was only the customary. Montaigne's essay 'Of the Cannibals' is well known.

Hermit. Lay by your devilish Philosophy, and change the
dangerous and destructive course of your lewd lives.

Don Antonio. Change our natures; go bid a Blackamoor be
white, we follow our Constitutions, which we did not give
ourselves.

Don Lopez. What we are, we are by Nature, our reason tells
us we must follow that.

Don John. Our Constitutions tell us one thing, and yours
another; and which must we obey? If we be bad, 'tis
Nature's fault, that made us so.   (Act III)

That, of course, comes from the Restoration period
(1675), though Shadwell was following traditional
material. More than half a century previously Tourneur, in *The Atheist's Tragedy* (1611, or earlier), had
exhibited similar muddled philosophizing in conversations between the Atheist, D'Amville, and his instrument Borachio.

> *D'Amville.* Borachio, thou art read
>   In nature and her large philosophy.
>   Observ'st thou not the very self-same course
>   Of revolution, both in man and beast?
> *Borachio.* The same, for birth, growth, state, decay and
>   death;
>   Only a man's beholding to his nature
>   For the better composition of the two.
> *D'Amville.* But where the favour of his nature is
>   Not full and free, you see a man becomes
>   A fool, as little-knowing as a beast.
> *Borachio.* That shows there's nothing in a man above
>   His nature; if there were, considering 'tis
>   His being's excellency, 'twould not yield
>   To nature's weakness.
> *D'Amville.* Then, if Death cast up
>   Our total sum of joy and happiness,
>   Let me have all my senses feasted in
>   The abundant fulness of delight at once,
>   And, with a sweet insensible increase
>   Of pleasing surfeit, melt into my dust.   (I. i)

In the end D'Amville is caught in his own toils, and is forced to confess,

> There was the strength of natural understanding.
> But Nature is a fool,

but his course of action throughout the play has been rationalized in the belief

> That Nature, since herself decay doth hate,
> Should favour those that strengthen their estate.

We cannot say how widespread were the sentiments here attributed to the Atheist, but it seems likely that Tourneur was reflecting a good deal of contemporary discussion, some of it no doubt at a higher level of disinterestedness than that displayed by Borachio and pointing forward to the more painful searching of an Ivan Karamazov ('If there is no God, everything is permitted'). To say that Shakespeare felt it as deeply significant is not to attribute to him a greater prophetic power than belongs to a supreme—and supremely intelligent—artist. If the 'libertine' assumption—man is a natural force in a world of natural forces—is incorporated in *King Lear*, that is because it appeared to envisage nothing but the bare facts of existence; and for Shakespeare's present purpose, as we have seen, it was necessary to get at the bare facts. The positives that emerge from the play are indeed fundamentally Christian values, but they are reached by an act of profound individual exploration: the play does not take them for granted; it takes nothing for granted but Nature and natural energies and passions.

II

The fact that *King Lear* was written so soon after *Othello* (1604) is a reminder of how misleading the phrase 'Shakespearian Tragedy' can be. Each play is 'a new beginning', a fresh 'raid on the inarticulate', for although there is development there is no repetition. Even from the narrowly technical point of view there are marked differences of manner and approach between the tragedies, corresponding to equally marked differences of intention. Thus *Othello*, although a poetic drama, of which the success is determined by specifically poetic effects of language and symbolism, comes closer than any of the other tragedies to what is commonly understood by 'revelation of character', and its focus is on individual and, we might say, domestic qualities. *Lear*, on the other hand, is a universal allegory (though the word 'allegory' does justice to neither the depth nor the movement within the experience it presents), and its dramatic technique is determined by the need to present certain permanent aspects of the human situation, with a maximum of imaginative realization and a minimum regard for the conventions of naturalism.[1] In the scenes on the heath, for example, we do not merely listen to exchanges between persons whom, in the course of the play, we have got to know; we are caught up in a great and almost impersonal poem in which we hear certain *voices* which echo and counterpoint each other; all that they say is part of the tormented consciousness of Lear; and the consciousness of Lear is part of the consciousness of human kind. There is the same density of effect throughout. One character echoes another: the blinding of Gloucester parallels the cruelty done to Lear; Gloucester loses his eyes, and Lear's mind is darkened; Gloucester learns to 'see better' (as Kent had bidden Lear) in his blindness, and Lear reaches his final insights, the recognition of his supreme need, through madness. But there is not

[1] See Theodore Spencer, *Shakespeare and the Nature of Man*, pp. 135–52—pages to which I am considerably indebted.

only this mutual reinforcement *within* the play: there is constantly the felt presence of a range of experience far wider than could be attributed to any of the persons regarded simply as persons. This is achieved partly by the use of simple but effective symbols—the bare heath, the hovel, the nakedness of Poor Tom ('unaccommodated man'), the 'cliff' from which Gloucester thinks to cast himself down; partly by the use made of certain organizing ideas such as the Elizabethan conception of a necessary interrelation between man (the 'little world of man'), the social body, and the cosmos; but above all by the poetry. The poetry of *Lear* is not only vivid, close packed, and wide ranging, involving in the immediate action a world of experience, it has a peculiar resonance that should leave us in no doubt of Shakespeare's intention. It is what we hear when the blind Gloucester declares:

> I have no way, and therefore want no eyes;
> I stumbled when I saw,　　　(IV. i. 18–19)

or when Lear, crossed by Goneril, exclaims, 'Who is it that can tell me who I am?' and the Fool replies, 'Lear's shadow' (I. iv. 238–9).

III

Lear, at the opening of the play, is the embodiment of perverse self-will. Surrounded by obsequious flattery ('They told me I was everything'), he knows neither himself nor the nature of things. It is his human self-will that is stressed, and we need not fuss very much about the apparent absurdity of his public test of his daughters' affections in the division of the kingdom. It is a dramatically heightened example of something not uncommon—the attempt to manipulate affection which can only be freely given.

Which of you shall we say doth love us most?
That we our largest bounty may extend
Where nature doth with merit challenge.[1] (I. i. 51–53)

To a demand of this kind the only honest reply is Cordelia's 'Nothing'. Now one result of perverse demands is a distorted view of the actual, and one way of discovering that your own lanthorn gives no light is, as Swift put it, by running your head into a post—something that is unquestionably there. Because Lear is perverse he is deceived by appearances; and because he allows himself to be deceived by appearances he sets in motion a sequence of events that finally brings him face to face with an actuality that can be neither denied nor disguised.

The subsequent action of the play is designed not only to force the hidden conflict in Lear into consciousness, and, with the fullest possible knowledge of the relevant facts, to compel a choice, but to force each one of us to confront directly the question put by Lear as Everyman, 'Who is it that can tell me who I am?' One answer to that question is embodied in the group of characters who are most directly opposed to Lear. Edmund, Goneril, and Regan take their stand on the unrestrained self-seeking of natural impulse. The two daughters, by their actions, by what they say, and by the imagery of beasts of prey so consistently associated with them,[2] represent a ferocious animality. Their indifference to all claims but those of their own egotism is made explicit by Edmund, who brings into the play conceptions of Nature and human nature, radically

[1] Lear's habit of arithmetical computation of degrees of affection—Coleridge's 'debtor and creditor principles of virtue'—is amusingly illustrated in Act II, scene iv, when, after he has been rebuffed by Regan, he turns to Goneril:
I'll go with thee:
Thy fifty yet doth double five-and-twenty,
And thou art twice her love

[2] See A. C. Bradley, *Shakespearean Tragedy*, pp. 266–8.

opposed to the traditional conceptions, that were beginning to emerge in the consciousness of the age. For Edmund, man is merely a part of the morally indifferent world of nature, and his business is simply to assert himself with all the force and cunning at his command: 'Thou, Nature, art my goddess' (I. ii. 1); 'All with me's meet that I can fashion fit' (I. ii. 191). It is into the world of indifferent natural forces, so glibly invoked by Edmund, that Lear is precipitated by a perversity of self-will that clung to the forms of human affection whilst denying the reality.

We can now see how the play at the personal or psychological level is able to bring to a focus far wider issues. Lear goes mad because he is a mind in conflict; because his conscious view of himself, to which he clings with the whole force of his personality, is irreconcilably opposed to what are in fact his basic attitudes. ' "Ay" and "no" too was no good divinity' (IV. vi. 101), and from the start there is 'division' in his 'kingdom'. His talk is of love and paternal care, but both his action in casting off Cordelia and—those infallible signs of what a man truly is—his assumptions as they appear in moments of emotional stress, together with his whole tone and manner, reveal a ferocious egotism. Early in the play the contrast is more than once starkly enforced.

> Here I disclaim all my paternal care,
> Propinquity and property of blood,
> And as a stranger to my heart and me
> Hold thee from this for ever. The barbarous Scythian,
> Or he that makes his generation messes
> To gorge his appetite, shall to my bosom
> Be as well neighbour'd, pitied, and reliev'd,
> As thou my sometime daughter. (I. i. 113–20)

> Yea, is it come to this?
> Let it be so: I have another daughter,

Who, I am sure, is kind and comfortable:
When she shall hear this of thee, with her nails
She'll flay thy wolvish visage.

(I. iv. 313–17)

In each of these passages the implications of the opening lines collide sharply with what follows. Whatever
Lear thinks of himself, one side of his nature is already
committed—even before he is thrust into it—to the
world that Edmund, Goneril, and Regan take for
granted, a world where everything that might conceivably be regarded as mere sentimental illusion or the
product of wishful thinking is absent, where neither
'humane statute', custom nor religion checks the free
play of brute natural force. If Lear is ever, as Kent bids
him, to 'see better', this is the world he must see and
feel in its full impact.

The storm scenes, and the scenes immediately following, represent a twofold process of discovery—of the
'nature' without and within. No summary can attempt
to do them justice, and perhaps the best way of indicating what goes on in them is to revert to what has been
said of Shakespeare's superb and daring technique.
The effect is analogous to that of a symphony in which
themes are given out, developed, varied, and combined.
And since one of the characters goes mad, one is an
assumed madman, and one is a Fool, there is a freedom
without precedent in the history of the drama—a freedom only limited by the controlling purpose of the
play—to press into service all that is relevant to the full
development of the main themes.

The storm itself is vividly presented in all its power
to harm; but this is far from being the only way in
which the action of Nature is brought home to us. Part
of the dramatic function of Edgar is to reinforce the
message of the storm. Disguised as one of the lowest
creatures to be found in rural England in the sixteenth

century (and therefore, for the purpose of the play, becoming one), a wandering madman and beggar,

> the basest and most poorest shape
> That ever penury, in contempt of man,
> Brought near to beast,

he brings with him continual reminders of rural life at its most exposed and precarious—'the winds and persecution of the sky', 'low farms, Poor pelting villages, sheep-cotes and mills' (II. iii). When Lear with Kent and the Fool surprises him in the hovel, he at once strikes the note of the familiar indifference of Nature—familiar, that is, to those who live close to nature, though not to those who, like Edmund, invoke an abstraction that suits their bent. His talk is of cold and fire, of whirlpool, whirlwind and quagmire, of natural calamity and disease. Nothing he says but has this far-reaching yet precise suggestiveness.

> Poor Tom; that eats the swimming frog, the toad, the tadpole, the wall-newt, and the water; that in the fury of his heart, when the foul fiend rages, eats cow-dung for sallets; swallows the old rat and the ditch-dog; drinks the green mantle of the standing pool . . . (III. iv. 132–7)

This is more than a mad fantasy of an extremity of deprivation. The effect is as though the evolutionary process had been reversed to show where man as mere earth-bred creature belongs. One recalls Timon's invocation of the earth:

> Common mother, thou,
> Whose womb unmeasurable, and infinite breast,
> Teems, and feeds all; whose self-same mettle,
> Whereof thy proud child, arrogant man, is puff'd,
> Engenders the black toad and adder blue,
> The gilded newt and eyeless venom'd worm,
> With all the abhorred births below crisp heaven
> Whereon Hyperion's quickening fire doth shine . . .
>
> (*Timon of Athens*, IV. iii. 176–83)

Man may indeed pride himself on the achievements of civilization, riding 'proud of heart . . . on a bay trotting-horse over four-inch'd bridges' (III. iv. 56–57), but the structure is frail; it is Tom's world that endures. 'You talk of Nature', Shakespeare seems to say, 'well, take a good look at her.' 'Still through the hawthorn blows the cold wind.'

This then is the Nature 'outside'. What of human nature, the nature within? Here too the direct revelation of the action is extended and reinforced—almost overwhelmingly so—by the poetry of allusion. A long catalogue of sins—ranging from the adulteration of beer to usury, slander, perjury, and murder—could be collected from the exchanges of Lear, Edgar, and the Fool, and as they accumulate they give a sorry enough picture of man in his meanness. But the recurring themes are lust and cruelty. Lust and cruelty are demonstrated in the action of the play; they are harped on in Edgar's 'mad' talk; they are the horrible realities that Lear discovers beneath appearances. In the great speech beginning,

> Thou rascal beadle, hold thy bloody hand!
> Why dost thou lash that whore? Strip thine own back . . .
>
> (IV. vi. 162 ff.)

lust and sadism are—with superb insight—identified. The world of appearances is based on artificial and unreal distinctions—'Robes and furr'd gowns hide all'. Strip them off and you find what Lear found in the storm.

> Is man no more than this? Consider him well. Thou ow'st the worm no silk, the beast no hide, the sheep no wool, the cat no perfume. Ha! here's three on's are sophisticated; thou art the thing itself; unaccommodated man is no more but such a poor, bare, forked animal as thou art. Off, off, you lendings! Come, unbutton here. (III. iv. 105–12)

The 'thou' of that speech, the 'thing itself', is—we have just heard—'one that slept in the contriving of lust, and wak'd to do it . . . false of heart, light of ear, bloody of hand; hog in sloth, fox in stealth, wolf in greediness, dog in madness, lion in prey' (III. iv. 90–95). This, we may say, is the Edmund philosophy, though presented with a violence of realization quite foreign to the Edmund of the play. 'Lechery?' says Lear in his madness when finally broken by the storm, 'the world of nature is completely lustful. Let us admit it. Anything else is mere pretence.' 'To't, Luxury, pell-mell! For I lack soldiers' (IV. vi. 119–20).

IV

Lear's expression of revulsion and disgust, when, 'a ruin'd piece of nature', he confronts the blind Gloucester, is, I suppose, one of the profoundest expressions of pessimism in all literature. If it is not the final word in the play, it is certainly not because Shakespeare has shrunk from any of the issues. Pessimism is sometimes regarded as a tough and realistic attitude. Shakespeare's *total* view of human life in this play has a toughness and actuality that make most pessimism look like sentimentality. It is because the play has brought us to this vision of horror—seen without disguise or palliation— that the way is open for the final insights. In the successive stripping away of the layers of appearance, what remains to discover is the most fundamental reality of all. In the play it takes the form of the love and forgiveness of Cordelia. But that love has to be earned in the way in which all things most worth having are earned— by the full admission of a need, the achievement of honesty and humility, the painful shedding of all that is recognized as incompatible with the highest good, by, in short, making oneself able to receive whatever it may be. Now if there is one truth that the play brings home with superb force it is that neither man's reason nor his powers of perception function in isolation from the rest of his personality: *quantum sumus, scimus.*[1] *How* Lear feels, in short, is as important as *what* he feels, for the final 'seeing' is inseparable from what he has come to be. For us, as readers or spectators, Lear's vision of life can only be apprehended in close conjunction with the attitudes with which he confronts experience.

There is, of course, no straight line of progress: there are developments, eddies, and recessions, as the tumultuous feelings whirl into sight now one, now another aspect of what lies below the surface. Although horror and rejection form the substance of Lear's last great outbursts, other feelings and other attitudes have, during the storm itself, broken through the hard crust of his will. In order to take the full force of the play's climax we must make an encircling movement, bringing into our consciousness more than can be described in objective terms of what Lear sees and suffers.

Lear's dominant attitude is obviously self-will; his sentences fall naturally into the imperative mood, his commands are threats, and his threats are curses. When crossed by Goneril he invokes Nature—Edmund's goddess—to enforce 'the untented woundings of a father's curse' (I. iv. 284 ff.); the 'Heavens' are bidden to take his part (II. iv. 163 ff., 191 ff.): and when Goneril and Regan jointly demonstrate how much power he has in fact given away his threats are vague but enormous.

> I will do such things,
> What they are, yet I know not, but they shall be
> The terrors of the earth.   (II. iv. 282–4)

In all this, as Shakespeare takes care to tell us through

[1] This is a truth that Coleridge insists on throughout his work. See, for example, *Aids to Reflection*, Aphorism xxiii (footnote), and *Biographia Literaria* (ed. Shawcross), vol. ii, p. 216.

the Fool, there is something conspicuously infantile—
the craving not only for immediate gratification of his
desires but for complete endorsement of the self, just
as it is, the assumption of a power ludicrously beyond
the possibility of performance, the resort to tantrums
and tears of rage when that power proves inadequate.
In these ways Lear proves his kinship with the common
run of mankind long before he is prepared to admit it
at a different level. Above all there is an immense
capacity for self-pity. When the storm breaks self-pity
joins itself incongruously to Lear's self-identification
with its rage. He thinks still in terms of getting back
something for what one has given: the elements are
not so bad as his daughters, for they don't, like his
daughters, *owe* him anything.

> I tax you not, you elements, with unkindness;
> I never gave you kingdom, call'd you children,
> You owe me no subscription: then let fall
> Your horrible pleasure; here I stand, your slave,
> A poor, infirm, weak, and despis'd old man . . .
>
> (III. ii. 16–20)

But this, like almost everything one can say about the
poetry of the play, is an over-simplification. In Lear's
next invocation there is very great complexity of feeling.

> Let the great gods,
> That keep this dreadful pudder o'er our heads,
> Find out their enemies now. Tremble, thou wretch,
> That hast within thee undivulged crimes,
> Unwhipp'd of Justice; hide thee, thou bloody hand,
> Thou perjur'd, and thou simular of virtue
> That art incestuous; caitiff, to pieces shake,
> That under covert and convenient seeming
> Hast practis'd on man's life; close pent-up guilts,
> Rive your concealing continents, and cry
> These dreadful summoners grace. I am a man
> More sinn'd against than sinning.   (III. ii. 49–60)

The concern with 'undivulged crimes', with the evil that lies below the surface, is characteristic of Lear, and is developed later. Here it serves to distinguish between men, who can be deceived, and 'the great Gods', who cannot. But the implication is that the consistory of the gods, immeasurably more powerful than its earthly counterpart (for its mere summoners are thunderbolts), is yet like it in the exaction of merely retributive penalties. 'Unwhipp'd of justice' is indeed one of those revealing phrases that, simply by what it takes for granted, sums up a fundamental attitude. Lear will not question the validity of earthly justice, with its fallible ministers, nor will he question the possibility of a more than human justice that, though severe, has no merely punitive intention, until he has identified himself with the sinners. At this point it is clear that he dissociates himself from those whom the gods are required to punish, and there is even a note of grim satisfaction as he thinks of the guilty quaking. As the words gather momentum, culminating in the explosive energy of

> close pent-up guilts,
> Rive your concealing continents. . . .

it seems indeed that Lear is half-referring to himself, but that thought is not allowed to reach full consciousness—'*I* am a man More sinn'd against than sinning'. When Kent brings him to the hovel he is still torn between the desire for vengeance—'I will punish home'—and self-pity,

> O Regan Goneril!
> Your old kind father, whose frank heart gave all. . . .

But 'that way madness lies' (III. iv. 16–21); the sore and angry spot in his consciousness is precisely there, for whatever his hand gave, his heart had not been as he insists on thinking of it.

It is this warring of contradictory impulses that the storm, a vividly evoked instance of elemental conflict, serves to define. It is also through the storm—the storm in the first place, and then through all the associated images of Nature's cruelty—that reality breaks into a mind wilfully closed against it. The question of 'true need' has already been given some prominence (II. iv. 266–73); posed in this setting only the truth will serve.

> How dost, my boy? Art cold?
> I am cold myself. Where is this straw, my fellow?
> The art of our necessities is strange,
> And can make vile things precious. Come, your hovel.
>
> (III. ii. 68–71)

In a play of stark contrasts subtler shifts of tone may go unregarded, and it is worth recalling here that earlier question in which Lear's self-revelation came to a head—'Which of you shall we say doth love us most?' Then the question was asked in a tone that implied the expectation of a gratifying answer: the leisurely and expansive rhythm evokes the movement of settling with complacence into prepared comfort. Now the broken rhythm marks the confrontation of what is new and disturbing. Then the demand was for exclusive possession, for that 'all' which Cordelia could not pretend to give. Now what is in question is need that must be recognized as common to all. In the scene before the hovel, Lear's desire to share these 'vile things' with the Fool ('In boy; go first') is, then, shown as part of a dawning feeling for a wider human relationship. We have already heard,

> Poor Fool and knave, I have one part of my heart
> That's sorry yet for thee.   (III. ii. 72–73)

Now comes the famous prayer on behalf of 'houseless poverty'.

Poor naked wretches, whereso'er you are,
That bide the pelting of this pitiless storm,
How shall your houseless heads and unfed sides,
Your loop'd and window'd raggedness, defend you
From seasons such as these? O! I have ta'en
Too little care of this. Take physic, Pomp;
Expose thyself to feel what wretches feel,
That thou mayst shake the superflux to them,
And show the Heavens more just.
(III. iv. 28–36)

This is pity, not self-pity; and condemnation of others momentarily gives way to self-condemnation: 'O! *I* have ta'en too little care of this.' It is also, we may say, a genuine prayer, and as such it is answered: it is *after* this that Lear endures the physic of his vision of un-accommodated man.

The nature of that vision—which includes the suffering of the poor and outcast, the indifference of Nature and all the disreputable impulses that find a home in the heart of man—we have already taken some account of. From now on the question put to Lear, which is indeed the question posed by the whole play, is how to cope with the world so revealed, with the self so revealed. It can, of course, be said that Lear does not cope at all, since from the entrance of Poor Tom (with whom he promptly identifies himself—'Didst thou give all to thy daughters?') he is mad. What that means, however, is that, no longer subjected to inter-ference from the self hitherto offered to the world as Lear and which has proved so woefully inadequate under stress, he is free to express attitudes previously concealed from himself, though, as we have seen, rather more than glimpsed by the audience. In this region where honesty is as it were compelled—mental and material trappings alike discarded ('Off, off, you lendings!')—impulses issue with the uninhibited frank-ness of the symbolic actions of dreams. At the centre of

the whirlpool lies the obsession with guilt and punishment. What constitutes the torture—Lear's 'wheel of
fire'—is that each successive attitude, bearing the stamp
of its utter inadequacy, can only breed recoil and a fresh
plunge into madness. Denial of involvement ('they
cannot touch me for coining'—IV. vi. 83) bears a confession of guilt. Fantasies of aggression promptly transform themselves into situations where Lear himself is
the victim. Most significant of all is the extended
attempt to 'have the law on' the offenders. But the
mock trial of Goneril and Regan (III. vi. 20–56) is not
only an obliquely ironic comment on human justice
that will be made more explicit later, it offers a direct
rebuff to Lear's habitual appeal to a merely legalistic
code.

> And here's another, whose warp'd looks proclaim
> What store her heart is made on. Stop her there!
> Arms, arms, sword, fire! Corruption in the place!
> False justicer, why hast thou let her 'scape?

'Corruption in the place' indeed! Lear's fantasy spins
right when, bringing the trial to an end in mad confusion, it tells him that he cannot get at human realities
in that way.

If none of the familiar postures of the self will serve,
for the correlative of each attitude is illusion, what is
there to which Lear's mind can hold? Nothing, it seems,
except the recognition of his own share in a depravity
felt as universal. At two points indeed the recognition
of his own utter failure is not in fact accompanied by
the more general reference, and these are, I think,
significantly distinguished. In the first instance (IV. iii.
43 ff.) we are told about the 'shame'—the 'sovereign'
and 'burning' shame—that accompanies the realization
of his 'unkindness' to the daughter he had rejected. In
the second, where self-accusation takes on a curiously

impersonal tone, Lear himself tells how false was the flattery that he had encouraged and accepted—'They flattered me like a dog. . . . When the rain came to wet me once and the wind to make me chatter, when the thunder would not peace at my bidding, there I found 'em, there I smelt 'em out' (IV. vi. 97 ff.). But although each of these passages represents a foothold in reality, although it is immediately after the first of them that Cordelia reappears, seeking her father, the nadir of Lear's vision is still to come.

V

In the two great tirades addressed to the blind Glouces-ter (IV. vi. 110 ff., and 151 ff.) Lear brings to a head all he has discovered concerning Appetite and Autho-rity. The discovery is that appetite is well nigh universal and that authority is a sham. For the man who knows this, who knows too how little he can dissociate himself from what he denounces, aggression and self-assertion are alike irrelevant: all that is left is a 'patience' hardly distinguishable from despair.

> Thou must be patient; we came crying hither:
> Thou know'st the first time that we smell the air
> We wawl and cry. I will preach to thee: mark . . .
> When we are born, we cry that we are come
> To this great stage of fools.
> (IV. vi. 180–5)

There is no immediate way of deciding how we should take these lines. It is important that we should know since it is virtually on this note (after a momentary return to a futile fantasy of revenge) that Lear gives way completely, sleeps, and is carried to Cordelia. The question is whether what we have here is a weary sub-sidence into the only wisdom that is ultimately possible, or whether, although representing an extreme point of weariness and denial, it masks the possibility of some genuine resilience of the spirit. In order to determine this we must recall the familiar truth that dramatic statements exist in a context, and that their meaning is in relation to—often in tension with—that context. Lear is indeed the central consciousness of the play, but nothing, so far, has put us under any compulsion to accept him as solely qualified as an interpreter of the action. At this point then we must briefly recall the part played by Gloucester, the Fool, Kent, and some others.

Both Gloucester and the Fool powerfully affect our sense of the central experience embodied in Lear, but they belong to two quite different aspects of Shakespeare's wide-embracing dramatic technique. The Gloucester sub-plot is plainly 'a device of intensification',[1] and the progress of Gloucester himself is something like a simplified projection of the Lear experience on to a 'morality' plane: in the bewildering world of the play it helps to give us our bearings. It is commonly recognized that just as Lear finds 'reason in madness' (IV. vi. 177) so Gloucester learns to 'see' in his blindness, and there is no need to rehearse the many parallels of situation, the verbal echoes and cross-references. All that concerns us here can be plainly stated. Gloucester, at the beginning of the play, is sufficiently characterized by his coarse man-of-the-world conversation; he is as blind as Lear to the truth of things, credulous and, one would have said, ineffective. Caught up in the struggle of good and evil his decision to help Lear is deliberate and heroic—'If I die for it, as no less is threatened me, the King, my old master, must be reliev'd' (III. iii. 18–20)—and his blinding is a kind of martyrdom. It is a martyrdom, however, from which any consolatory vision is completely absent, and his subsequent progress, always so close to despair, is deliberately deprived of any obvious 'nobility' matching his conduct—as in

[1] J. I. M. Stewart, *Character and Motive in Shakespeare*, p. 22.

the grotesque comedy of his attempted suicide.[1] But
it is Shakespeare's refusal to romanticize Gloucester
that so guarantees the validity of the qualities with
which he is endowed. Gloucester learns to suffer, to
feel, and in feeling to see; and under Edgar's guidance
he comes as near as he may to thoughts that are not
only 'patient' but 'free'. At that point in the play which,
it may be recalled, this consideration of Gloucester is
intended to bear on, he has yet to undergo further
vicissitudes of feeling—the 'ill thoughts' with which
Edgar taxes him (v. ii. 9)—before, reconciled to the
son who has saved him from 'despair', his heart bursts
'smilingly', ' 'twixt . . . joy and grief' (v. iii. 188–99).
But we have been left in no doubt of what he contributes to the play. The Gloucester who listens to Lear's
tirades is someone quite other than his earlier self,
someone incredibly—miraculously, the play suggests[2]—
better. And the change in him, defined and emphasized
by the touching simplicity of the verse he speaks, is
something that our imagination completely endorses.

The nature of Gloucester's experience is clearly
presented, without ambiguity. The Fool, on the other
hand, speaks to (and out of) a quite different order of
apprehension: his function is to disturb with glimpses
of confounding truths that elude rational formulation.
At times he seems like something only partly recognized
in the depths of Lear's own personality that will not be
kept down ('Take heed, sirrah; the whip'), but because
he is only licensed, not enfranchised—not, we may say,
integrated with the conscious self, which yet has a vein
of tenderness towards him—the truth he tells is disguised, paradoxical, sometimes grotesque. He *looks
towards* Cordelia, pining when she is banished and

[1] See G. Wilson Knight, *The Wheel of Fire*, pp. 186–8.
[2] Thy life's a miracle (IV. vi. 55)
    Think that the clearest Gods, who make them honours
    Of men's impossibilities, have preserved thee. (IV. vi. 73–74)

slipping out of the play before her reappearance; at the
end there is some confusion in Lear's mind between
the two (v. iii. 305). Miss Welsford, in the penetrating
account she gives of him in her book, *The Fool*, places
him firmly in the tradition of 'the sage-fool who sees
the truth' ('his role', she adds, 'has even more *intellectual*
than emotional significance'). The truths he tells are
of various kinds. He can formulate the tenets of worldly
wisdom with a clarity that worldly wisdom often prefers
to blur. He defines the predatory self-seeking of Goneril
and Regan, and has a variety of pithy phrases both for
the outward form of Lear's mistaken choice and its
hidden causes and results. In relation to these last
indeed he shows an uncanny insight, pointing directly
to Lear's infantile craving 'to make his daughters his
mothers' (I. iv. 179–81), and hinting at that element of
dissociated sexuality that plays into so many human
disorders—something that will later rise to the surface
of Lear's mind with obsessive force. The world picture
he creates is of small creatures in a world too big—and,
in its human aspects, too bad—to be anything but
bewildering. His sharply realistic, commonplace instances—like Tom's mad talk, though with a different
tone—insist on the alien aspect of Nature and on all
that detracts from man's sense of his own dignity—
corns, chilblains, lice, and the mere pricking of sexual
desire. The Fool's meaning, however, lies not merely in
what he says but in the way he says it—those riddling
snatches which partly reflect the moral confusion of
the world, but whose main function is to cast doubt
on such certainties as the world (including the audience)
thinks it possesses. Not only, therefore, is he an agent
of clarification, prompting Lear towards the recognition of bitter truths: it is he, as Miss Welsford insists, who forces the question, What is wisdom? and
what is folly? It is through him, therefore, that we

come to see more clearly the sharp distinction between those whose wisdom is purely for themselves and those foolish ones—Kent, Gloucester, Cordelia, and the Fool himself—who recklessly take their stand on loyalties and sympathies that are quite outside the scope of any prudential calculus. Like Gloucester, though in a very different way, the Fool is directed towards an affirmation.

Both the Fool and Gloucester stand in a peculiarly close relation to Lear, but whereas the Fool is inseparable from him, Gloucester also connects with a wider world—a world existing independently of Lear's own consciousness (the alternation of scenes throughout Act III has great dramatic force and significance). Now that world has so far been dominated by those active promoters of their own fortunes, Goneril, Regan, Edmund, and Cornwall, but Shakespeare has also included in it quite other types of representative humanity. Kent, who follows Lear without coming close to him like the Fool or sharing something of the inner nature of his experience like Gloucester, has an especially significant role. Even in a play that is far from naturalistic we are bound to reflect that a king who could inspire the dogged devotion of such a man must be remarkable for something else besides perversity: his mere presence helps to check such inclination as we might harbour to regard Lear as foolish and wilful in such wildly improbable ways that we can safely dissociate ourselves. And his headstrong loyalty is a reminder of certain permanent possibilities of human nature. Moreover, fellow-feeling, loyalty, even sacrifice are not confined to the more conspicuous figures. It is a mere serving-man who gives his life in a vain attempt to save Gloucester; another fetches 'flax and whites of eggs To apply to his bleeding face', and, with a fellow, is allowed to act as final chorus to that

monstrous scene (III. vii. 71–106); and there is the Old
Man, tenant of the Gloucesters 'these fourscore years',
who leads Gloucester to Poor Tom, then goes to fetch
for 'the naked fellow' 'the best 'parel' that he has—
'Come on't what will' (IV. i. 10–50). These also play
their part on Lear's 'great stage'.

Even apart from the central movement of Lear's own
consciousness, therefore, the development of the play
as a whole towards the last great outburst of his pessimism is very far indeed from a simple descent through
deepening horrors that would justify an unqualified
endorsement of his rejection of the world. There is
indeed a full and passionate confrontation of 'the
worst', including Edgar's recognition that there is no
term that can be set to suffering (IV. i. 24). But not only
does the play compel our recognition of positive values
and emerging insights, the same ruthless honesty that
has stripped Lear of every rag of illusion is directed
also to the brutal 'realism' of his opponents. It is indeed
in the fourth act that the mutual treachery of competing egotisms begins to reveal itself (IV. ii, IV. v,
IV. vi. 258 ff.), and the logic of events underlines the
penetrating explicitness of Albany's judgement of
Goneril:

> O Goneril!
> You are not worth the dust which the rude wind
> Blows in your face . . .
> That nature, which contemns its origin,
> Cannot be border'd certain in itself;
> She that herself will sliver and disbranch
> From her material sap, perforce must wither
> And come to deadly use . . .
> If that the heavens do not their visible spirits
> Send quickly down to tame these vilde offences,
> It will come,
> Humanity must perforce prey on itself,
> Like monsters of the deep.   (IV. ii. 30 ff.)

When, therefore, Lear 'preaches' to Gloucester on the vanity of human life, there is, as so often in Shakespeare, a clash between the personal or immediate meaning of the words and their full dramatic meaning.

> . . . we came crying hither:
> Thou know'st the first time that we smell the air
> We wawl and cry . . .
> When we are born, we cry that we are come
> To this great stage of fools.

The force and bitterness of 'this great stage of fools' takes this far beyond the accepted commonplaces on the new-born infant's tears: for Lear, at this point, life is a meaningless comedy of pain. But no more than Macbeth's 'Life is a tale told by an idiot' can this be regarded simply as a summarizing comment emerging from the play as a whole. To be sure the accumulated meaning of the play puts sufficient weight behind the bitterness, but the whole relevant context forbids a simple response. The context, of course, is not something 'out there' that can be demonstrated in terms of the understanding, it is all that our minds and imaginations, awakened and directed by Shakespeare's art, hold ready to receive and interpret the immediate situation. And what our imaginations now hold is not only a sense of Lear's folly and suffering, of the folly, suffering, cruelty, and injustice to be found in the world at large, but a heightened recognition of all that, even in the face of these, the whole personality endorses as clear insight and genuinely human feeling. And behind the widening circle of reference within the play itself there is a context even more extensive. This indeed is slippery ground for interpretation, but it is at least relevant to recall that in other plays of roughly the same period—notably perhaps in *Timon of Athens*, so close to *Lear* in its probing of certain moods of revulsion—Shakespeare was concerned with the way in which the world of the individual is in part created by the non-rational structure of attitudes and feelings that are inseparable from perception. Only an inhibiting fear of life could prevent us from taking the full force of Lear's great indictment: only a refusal to meet honestly—so far as we may—*all* that Shakespeare sets in relation to it could make us blind to the irony—yes, even in this moment of keenest suffering—that plays about it.

What then are the reflections that, with a reversal of the usual effect of dramatic irony, qualify our recognition of all that is valid in Lear's bitterness? Surely they include such thoughts as that the image Lear finds for the world is partly at least a projection of his own folly; that not all the inhabitants of Lear's world are fools in the sense immediately intended here; that folly is a word whose meaning changes according to the standpoint of the speaker, and that in the pain of madness Lear had at least learnt more about human nature than he knew before. With this we bring into focus the three times repeated reference to the birth-cry. Whatever the physiological reasons, the baby's cry at smelling the air (and nothing can deprive that phrase of its disturbing wholesomeness) is commonly taken as a cry of fright and protest—'Helpless, naked, piping loud'. As such it is analogous to the protest, the frightened movement towards headlong regression, of the adult who is called upon to undergo a radical transformation of consciousness. In the subtle and complex interplay of recognitions that surrounds our sympathy with Lear's agony this thought also has its place.

VI

It is through such varied probings, questionings, rejections, recognitions, that a direction is established and a

way prepared. Cordelia, though rarely appearing in the
play, is very much a positive presence. Her tenderness
is rooted in the same strength that enabled her to reject
Lear's misconceived demands. Her love is of a kind
that, confronted with a real demand, does not bargain
or make conditions; it is freely given, and it represents
an absolute of human experience that can stand against
the full shock of disillusion. When Lear, dressed in 'fresh
garments' and to the accompaniment of music (the
symbolism is important) is brought into her presence,
there follows one of the most tender and moving scenes
in the whole of Shakespeare. But it is much more than
moving. Since each line engages us to the whole extent
of our powers the briefest reminders set vibrating all
the chords of the past experience. It is even whilst we
respond to the swift sure play of feeling—with a sense
as of the actual bodily presence of the protagonists—
that we are made to live again the central scenes.

> *Cordelia.* O my dear father! Restoration hang
>   Thy medicine on my lips, and let this kiss
>   Repair those violent harms that my two sisters
>   Have in thy reverence made!
> *Kent.*   Kind and dear Princess!
> *Cordelia.* Had you not been their father, these white flakes
>   Did challenge pity of them. Was this a face
>   To be oppos'd against the warring winds?
>   To stand against the deep dread-bolted thunder?
>   In the most terrible and nimble stroke
>   Of quick, cross lightning? to watch—poor *perdu!*—
>   With this thin helm? Mine enemy's dog,
>   Though he had bit me, should have stood that night
>   Against my fire. And wast thou fain, poor father,
>   To hovel thee with swine and rogues forlorn,
>   In short and musty straw? Alack, alack!
>   'Tis wonder that thy life and wits at once
>   Had not concluded all. . . .
>   (IV. vii. 26–42)

Hence as recognition dawns in Lear, as consciousness

first renews his suffering, then admits it has no terms
for a world not known before, we are aware that this
still moment is surrounded by nothing less than the
whole action of the play; and if questions that have been
asked now await their answer, the painful knowledge
that has been won will reject anything that swerves a
hair's breadth from absolute integrity.

Cordelia.　　　　He wakes; speak to him.

Doctor. Madam, do you; 'tis fittest.

Cordelia. How does my royal Lord? How fares your Majesty?

Lear. You do me wrong to take me out o' th' grave;
　　Thou art a soul in bliss; but I am bound
　　Upon a wheel of fire, that mine own tears
　　Do scald like molten lead.

Cordelia.　　　　Sir, do you know me?

Lear. You are a spirit, I know; where did you die?

Cordelia. Still, still, far wide.

Doctor. He's scarce awake; let him alone awhile.

Lear. Where have I been? Where am I? Fair daylight?
　　I am mightily abus'd. I should e'en die with pity
　　To see another thus. I know not what to say.
　　I will not swear these are my hands: let's see;
　　I feel this pin prick. Would I were assur'd
　　Of my condition!

Cordelia.　　　　O! look upon me, Sir,
　　And hold your hand in benediction o'er me.
　　No, Sir, you must not kneel.

Lear.　　　　Pray, do not mock me:
　　I am a very foolish fond old man,
　　Fourscore and upward, not an hour more or less;
　　And, to deal plainly,
　　I fear I am not in my perfect mind.
　　Methinks I should know you and know this man;
　　Yet I am doubtful: for I am mainly ignorant
　　What place this is, and all the skill I have
　　Remembers not these garments; nor I know not
　　Where I did lodge last night. Do not laugh at me;
　　For, as I am a man, I think this lady
　　To be my child Cordelia.

Cordelia.   And so I am, I am.
Lear. Be your tears wet? Yes, faith. I pray, weep not;
  If you have poison for me, I will drink it.
  I know you do not love me; for your sisters
  Have, as I do remember, done me wrong:
  You have some cause, they have not.
Cordelia.   No cause, no cause.
Lear. Am I in France?
Kent. In your own kingdom, Sir.   (IV. vii. 42–76)

It is in the light of everything that has gone before that
we recognize this as a moment of truth.

King Lear, however, is more than a purgatorial
experience culminating in reconciliation: what it does
in fact culminate in we know, and the play's irony, its
power to disturb, is sustained. Does this mean, then,
that *King Lear* is 'a sublime question, to which no
answer is supplied by the play'?[1] I do not think so.
What it does mean is that questioning, disturbance, the
absence of demonstrable answers, form an essential
part of a meaning that lies not in a detachable moral
but in the activity and wholeness of the imagination.
To the extent, therefore, that *King Lear* does make a
positive affirmation (and I think it does) it is one which
takes up into itself the questioning: it is an affirmation
'in spite of'.[2]

In the last act, by the definite withdrawal of Albany
from the forces opposed to Lear, the killing of Edmund
by Edgar in single combat, and the mutual treachery of
Goneril and Regan, the way is apparently cleared for an
ending far different from that represented by the stark
stage-direction: 'Enter Lear, with Cordelia dead in his
arms.' The scene of Lear's final anguish is so painful
that criticism hesitates to fumble with it: where no one
can remain unaffected the critic's business is to supply
something other than his own emotions. What may be

[1] D. G. James, *The Romantic Comedy*, p. 121.
[2] See Paul Tillich, *The Courage to Be*, especially pp. 152–3, 159 ff.

said, however, is that there are at least two reasons
why no other ending would have been imaginatively
right, and for a proper understanding they are of the
greatest importance. We do not only look at a masterpiece, we enter into it and live with it. Our suffering,
then, and our acceptance of suffering, not simply our
sympathy with what we see on the stage, form an
intrinsic part of what the play is; for as with Lear and
Gloucester our capacity to see is dependent upon our
capacity to feel. Now what our seeing has been directed
towards is nothing less than *what man is*. The imaginative discovery that is the play's essence has thus involved
the sharpest possible juxtaposition of rival conceptions
of 'Nature'. In the Edmund–Goneril–Regan group the
philosophy of natural impulse and egotism has been
revealed as self-consuming, its claim to represent
strength as a self-bred delusion. What Lear touches in
Cordelia, on the other hand, is, we are made to feel,
the reality, and the values revealed so surely there are
established in the face of the worst that can be known
of man or Nature. To keep nothing in reserve, to slur
over no possible cruelty or misfortune, was the only way
of ensuring that the positive values discovered and
established in the play should keep their triumphant
hold on our imagination, should assert that uncon-
ditional rightness which, in any full and responsive
reading of *King Lear*, we are bound to attribute to them.

Perhaps a final question remains. It has been argued
here that at the centre of the action is the complete
endorsement of a particular quality of being. We may
call it love so long as we remember that it is not simply
an emotion, and that, although deeply personal, it has
also the impersonality that comes from a self-forgetful
concentration—momentary or enduring—upon the true
being of 'the other': it is perhaps this kind of im-

personality—not a negation of personal consciousness but its heightening and fulfilment—that is most insisted on in Edgar's strange phrase, 'Ripeness is all' (v. ii. 11). In this sense—so the play reveals—love is that without which life is a meaningless chaos of competing egotisms; it is the condition of intellectual clarity, the energizing centre from which personality may grow unhampered by the need for self-assertion or evasive subterfuge; it is the sole ground of a genuinely self-affirming life and energy. But—it may still be asked—how does this apply to Lear when he prattles to Cordelia about gilded butterflies, or when, thinking his dead daughter is alive, his heart breaks at last? For answer, we must consider once more the play's marvellous technique, the particular way in which it enlivens and controls our sympathies and perceptions. King Lear is indeed, for most of the play, 'the centre of consciousness': what he sees we are forced to see. But the question, ultimately, is not what Lear sees but what Shakespeare sees, and what we, as audience, are prompted to see with him. At the end, however poignantly we may feel—Lear's suffering is one of the permanent possibilities, and we know it—we are still concerned with nothing less than the inclusive vision of the whole; and it is that which justifies us in asserting that the mind, the imagination, so revealed is directed towards affirmation *in spite of everything*. Other readings of the play are possible, and have been made. But those who think that it is 'pessimistic', that it is no more than a deeply moving contemplation of man's helplessness, should consider a remarkable and obvious fact: that the tragedies written after *King Lear* everywhere proclaim an intellectual and imaginative energy that, in the firmness of its grasp, the assurance of its sense of life, shows no sign of perplexity, fear, or strain. For what takes place in *King Lear* we can find no other word than renewal.

J. I. M. STEWART

(b. 1906)

Shakespeare's Men and Their Morals[1]

I

As the industrious years go by, it becomes increasingly
difficult not only to add to the criticism of Shakespeare,
but even to report adequately upon a single aspect of it.
Today, we find a greater variety of opinions about
Shakespeare, and a larger body of controversy about
his work, than any previous age has known. I shall try,
if very briefly, to place this unrest in Shakespeare
studies (as one conservative commentator has dis-
approvingly called it) by relating it to two central works
in the history of Shakespeare criticism: Dr. Johnson's
Preface to his edition of the plays, published in 1765,
and A. C. Bradley's *Shakespearean Tragedy*, published
in 1904.

It was Johnson's grand contention—as it had been
Dryden's, indeed, immediately before him—that Shakespeare gives us Nature: Shakespeare's world is our
world in concentration. The heroes of other playwrights
are often only phantoms, but Shakespeare's heroes are
men. Shakespeare discerns truly and depicts faithfully.
His book is thus a map of life, an epitome of human
experience. It is true that the plays are not planned
moral fables, contrived to edify and instruct, as is
Johnson's own tragedy, *Irene*, or as is Johnson's novel,
Rasselas. Nevertheless, Shakespeare affords knowledge
immensely valuable to us as moral beings. And he does
this all the way through. Even 'the character of Polonius
is serious and useful, and the gravediggers themselves

[1] *More talking of Shakespeare*, a symposium of Stratford lectures (1959).

may be heard with applause'. It is important to notice that Johnson sees no great difficulty in the fact that these intensely real people of Shakespeare's are involved in some rather unreal fables. Shakespeare's stories are merely the vehicles on which the characters and their moral life are brought to us. It is from the characters, copiously diversified and justly pursued as they are, that our delight and instruction derive. We need not much labour, then, to rationalize the stories. Again it is important to notice Johnson's strong sense of these so natural characters as yet being fictions. The plays are not *records* of human transactions. They are 'faithful miniatures' of human transactions. They make us free of Nature only by themselves yielding to the rules of Art.

A good many things happen between Johnson and Bradley. First, the characters march out of the plays, led by Falstaff in Maurice Morgann's famous essay. Presently they are being discussed as if they were historical personages, and on this basis a swelling flood of commentary continues throughout the nineteenth century. I think myself that Shakespeare criticism has been enriched in consequence. But the dangers are obvious. There is an invitation to irrelevant reverie, as upon, say, the girlhood of Shakespeare's heroines. We may also come to feel that with a play, as with an historical action, crucial facts are likely to have perished tantalizingly from the record, so that they are recoverable only by ingenious inference. It is incumbent upon us, we may be brought to feel, to reconstruct the truth on the basis of such fragmentary evidence as the play has preserved for us. How many oddities has this persuasion produced!

A second development, unknown to Johnson and associated with the romantic critics (notably Coleridge), has been towards the dogma that Shakespeare never nods, that his judgement is always equal to his genius, and that the several elements in his plays are with a quite exceptional perfection always fused into an artistic unity. This conviction has been reinforced, I imagine, by the rise to the position of a major literary form of realistic and psychological prose fiction. The effect is to make us feel something mildly shocking in any proposal to be merely light-hearted about Shakespeare's plots and situations.

These, then, were the developing trends before Bradley. Correspondingly, we must notice certain aspects of Shakespeare that were no longer much attended to. Any marked feeling for Shakespeare as an Elizabethan, as a man developing and writing within a certain intellectual atmosphere, had died out. So had any strong sense of him as working for a particular theatre and within particular theatrical conventions. Criticism concerned itself, very confidently, with absolute and not with historical judgements.

Bradley came to crown this situation. He brought to it first his genius (for the writer of the best book on Shakespeare must, I think, be allowed that) and secondly a great interest in the philosophy of tragedy. For Bradley, as for Johnson, Shakespeare's heroes are men. But now they are men realized for us, in the two-hours traffic of the stage, in the richest and most delicate psychological detail. They are men moving through actions at once perfectly realistic and supremely poetic —actions subtly contrived in their every implication and affiliation. But, although they belong to works owning the highest degree of artistic unity, they yet have a life that, mysteriously, extends far beyond the limits of their play. Shakespeare's characters have, as it were, a larger personal history which can be reached from the springboard of the play. And they have, too, this as their final greatness: they embody (triumphantly and—we must say—by a mysterious anachronism) a theory of tragedy to the shaping of which Aristotle, Coleridge, and Hegel have all contributed the finest essence of their thought.

Perhaps he is a little too good to be true, this serene and timeless Shakespeare, with Aristotle and Hegel in one pocket, the Oxford of 1904 in the other, and the sacred coal ever at his lips. But only perhaps—for who can tell? Is there anything, then, *demonstrably* wrong with Bradley?

Many people now say, Yes. The plays and characters Bradley offers us are his own creation quite as much as Shakespeare's. Really attend to Shakespeare's plain text, disregard the mass of anachronistic subtlety that has long been projected upon it, and you will find no elaborately developed psychological studies and not many genuine human predicaments. You will find— Robert Bridges announced in 1907 in an essay called *The Influence of the Audience on Shakespeare's Drama*— grossly inconsistent characters being bumped and jockeyed through a variety of sensational incidents by a great poet who was constrained by the barbarity of his audience to work in terms of the crudest melodrama. In 1919 Professor Levin Schücking developed this theme in a book shortly afterwards translated as *Character Problems in Shakespeare's Plays*.[1] Schücking maintained that Shakespeare's dramaturgy is essentially popular and primitive. Shakespeare simply moves from scene to scene seeking immediate theatrical effect. Cleopatra is a harlot at the beginning of her play because plays about harlots were a good draw, and is somebody quite different at the end because her creator became belatedly conscious that he must make some contact with the Cleopatra of Plutarch whose story he is following.

But more important than Schücking was Professor Elmer Edgar Stoll, a trenchant, pertinacious, and

[1] Harrap, 1922.

learned American critic who, in a sense, stands Bridges's contention on its head. The psychological incoherence and the ruthless pursuit of a hodge-podge of emotions which Bridges sees as destroying Shakespeare's art Stoll declares to be, in drama, a splendid artistic strength. For, essentially, we go to the theatre to be thrilled—and to be thrilled by 'another world, not a copy of this'. 'Life', Stoll says, 'must be . . . piled on life, or we have visited the theatre in vain.' Shakespeare, knowing this, chiefly seeks a kind of 'emotional effect, with which psychology or even simple narrative coherence often considerably interferes'.[1]

You see, then, what a confusion of voices the appraisal of Shakespeare's characters can evoke. Take, for example, Othello. For Bradley, Othello is a marvellous study in depth of an extremely noble and at the same time wholly convincing individual. His conflict with Iago—again a complex and perfectly credible figure—fulfils the strictest laws of tragic causality in that the hero's very nobility is his undoing. He is *too* trustful; 'his trust, where he trusts, is absolute'; and so he is helpless before deception. His fate is plausible, convincing, deeply moving, and consonant with a just and elevating philosophical reading of life. Bridges will have nothing of all this. 'The whole thing is impossible', he cries. There is nothing elevating about it. Shakespeare's aim was merely to scarify a particularly thick-skinned audience. And for Professor Stoll, too, Othello is an impossible figure. Bradley's crucial contention ('his trust, where he trusts, is absolute') is mere cob-web—since, if trustfulness is the key to the character, then surely Othello should trust his wife and friend at least as fully as he trusts a stranger. 'What is to be made of this heap of contradictions?' Stoll exclaims, when he has analysed the hero—and answers, in effect: 'In

[1] Stoll, *Art and Artifice in Shakespeare* (Cambridge, 1933).

terms of actual human psychology, nothing; in terms of the emotional artifice that constitutes a good play, a great deal.'

Now, what we may call the negative or destructive side of Stoll's historical realism was much more effective than the obscure aesthetic of sensation that it throws out as a sort of life-line to Shakespeare's reputation. It is almost possible to say that our faith in Shakespeare's characters was shaken; we were at a loss for a reply to the onslaught; and we turned our attention to other things. Textual research very fascinating to keen minds, re-creatings of the Elizabethan 'climate of opinion', studies (very valuable indeed, the best of them) in Shakespeare's poetic, explorations of a possible symbolical content, conscious or unconscious, in the plays: there are all these approaches and many more available to the inquirer who hesitates before this perplexed matter of the characters. But ought we not to face up to the problem? 'Shakespeare's heroes are men.' Is it true, or was Dr. Johnson wrong?

I suspect that we are apt to be a little intimidated, some of us, by the erudition of these 'realists'. We have not read nearly so many plays as they have, and those that we have read we don't seem to remember nearly so well or be anything like so sure about. Indisputable, too, is their claim to know whatever can be discovered about the Elizabethan theatre and audience, about conventional types and roles and situations, about the views of learned and simple Elizabethans regarding the state, and the solar system, and the human soul; about ghosts and witches and devils and angels. And yet I am not quite confident that all this valuable information is really at the heart of the matter. When I ask myself why I have some confidence in Dr. Johnson and am reluctant to scrap him I find that it is because he is known to have been intensely interested not only in Shakespeare's men but in real men as well. Johnson, so to speak, tackled the problem from both ends. And, in the field we have been considering, I should have more confidence in the judgement of one who sat for months on end in what we should now call a police court, just because men interested him, than I should have in one who sat ever so much longer in a carrel in a library, with any distracting view of his fellow mortals ingeniously cut off by worm-eaten oak or by steel shutters. Again, I should listen to a wise man who had worked long in actual theatres for actual audiences more attentively than I should to a man, equally wise, whose frequentation had been all of the ghost of the Globe. I am interested, then, in what men of the theatre think about our problem—and in what is thought about it, too, by certain comparative new-comers to the game, the depth psychologists.

Is it not significant that the late Harley Granville-Barker, a scholar who was at the same time an experienced Shakespearian actor and a brilliant Shakespearian producer, entirely rejected the notion of Shakespeare's primitivism, sensationalism, psychological incoherence and the like; and that he should have given us in his great series of *Prefaces* character-studies almost in the direct line of Bradley, only informed and (we may say) pruned by a closer knowledge of the stage? And is it not significant, too, that Freud vindicated Shakespeare, whose works he had abundantly studied, as a psychologist of genius? As long ago as 1923 a conservative but acute commentator on the cockpit of Shakespeare criticism, the late Professor C. H. Herford, remarked that modern psychology, by its disclosure of such phenomena as those of dual and multiple personality, might unexpectedly illuminate the vexed problem of apparent inconsistency in Shakespeare.

In point of fact, modern psychology has been rather

more ambitious than that. Dr. Johnson, you remember, set little store by Shakespeare's stories; it seemed to him of small consequence whether these were probable or unlikely. Freud and his followers have contended that, where the stories are unlikely, they are unlikely much after the fashion of dreams, and for the same reason.

A tragedy is essentially a symbolical representation of wishes and conflicts urgent in us all, but of which a psychic censorship forbids the direct and undisguised expression. Hence the power of tragedy, when imaginatively received either in the theatre or in reading. It affords tremendous relief. It is just the cathartic or purging instrument that Aristotle long ago declared it to be. Hence too all those irrational and puzzling elements evident in tragedy when *not* imaginatively received. For Shakespeare's stories and his people often follow the logic of myth and the unconscious rather than the logic of waking life. This means that they are, in one sense, less 'realistic' than Bradley was inclined to suppose them. But the psychological critics are inclined to maintain, at the same time, that Shakespeare's major characters, taken simply as very actual men and women, become far more explicable in terms of what is now known about the mechanisms and motives of the human mind. Thus when older critics have maintained that the credulity of Othello, the malignity of Iago, the sudden senseless jealousy of Leontes, the equally sudden depravity of Angelo are implausible and theatrical, these newer critics would say: 'No, men are like that, although you find it more comfortable to believe that they are not. People come into our consulting-rooms who are capable of behaving just like Othello, or Iago or Leontes or Angelo. And we can explain how they come to behave as they do.'

I confess to finding all this of great interest. At the same time I am sure that we should be a little chary of

feeling, 'Ah—light at last!' Mr. T. S. Eliot has somewhere made fun of criticism that comes forward as
'revealing for the first time the gospel of some dead
sage, which no one has understood before; which
owing to the backward and confused state of men's
minds has lain unknown to this very moment'. And if
we trace out the fascinating history of 'Hamlet' criticism
(as an American scholar, Dr. Paul Conklin, has begun
to do)[1] we shall quickly come upon the chastening fact
that Shakespeare's Prince of Denmark is a veritable
chameleon, who has taken on, century by century and
generation by generation, the very form and pressure
of the age. What was Hamlet to the Elizabethan audience? A malcontent, Dr. Conklin assures us; a bitterly
eloquent and princely avenger on the verge of a lunacy
from which the players would sometimes extract a good
laugh; but withal a formidable young man and one
much admired for his mouth-filling flood of iambic
pentameter. Later, when England fell under the influence of Scotsmen and went soft, this young tough
went soft too—and softer in the study than on the
stage. In the age of Sterne and Mackenzie, Hamlet
becomes a man of sentiment, a man of feeling; Goethe
finds him closely related to his own Werther; Coleridge
announces that Hamlet is in fact Coleridge—an extremely impressive person of vast intellectual powers
embarrassed by an unfortunate weakness of will. Prose
fiction takes on a new complexity in its presentation of
character: just such a complexity is discovered in the
Prince. Scholars distil subtle theories of tragedy out of
philosophies old and new: Hamlet turns out to be the
hero who fits perfectly. Other scholars fall to studying
the Elizabethan drama at large: Hamlet loses his
uniqueness and becomes less a character than a role, a

[1] *A History of Hamlet Criticism, 1601–1821* (King's Crown Press, New
York, 1947).

series of stage dodges. The text of Shakespeare is studied with a new minuteness: it is discovered (as by Dr. Richard Flatter in a most ingenious book)[1] that the text gives tiny indications which must revolutionize our conceptions of Hamlet's disposition. And finally—finally for the present—comes Dr. Ernest Jones, with his deeply interesting psycho-analytic study, *Hamlet and Oedipus*.[2]

What is the lesson of this? The lesson is surely not that all critical interpretation of Shakespeare's characters is ephemeral modish nonsense. We merely learn that we ought not to let one theory, one reading, sweep away all the others. These people of Shakespeare's really are extraordinarily like life, and life is susceptible of many interpretations which do not necessarily invalidate each other. The danger point comes when we persuade ourselves that the characters are *only* this or that: only artifice, only allegory, only theology, only advice to Elizabethan statesmen, only concealed pointers to Sir Francis Bacon or the Earl of Derby, and so on. And there is perhaps one other danger; that of forgetting that all these inquiries are for the satisfaction of the intellect, since Shakespeare has already satisfied the imagination. When our imagination is kindled we do not think to 'interpret' the characters. We know that the characters are interpreting us.

II

So much for the debate on Shakespeare's men; let me now say something about their morals—and about *his* morals, too. And, this time, let our first critic be a lady. It was in 1775 that Mrs. Elizabeth Griffith[3] determined upon 'placing his Ethic merits in a more conspicuous

---

[1] *Shakespeare's Producing Hand: A Study of his marks of expression to be found in the First Folio* (Heinemann, 1948).
[2] Gollancz, 1949.   [3] *The Morality of Shakespeare's Drama Illustrated.*

point of view'—and became thereby (I am afraid) one of a good many writers to contrive mainly absurdity in the consideration of this difficult topic. It would appear that Mrs. Griffith proposed (in addition to giving numerous excerpts of an edifying cast from the plays) to offer compendious remarks on the moral intention animating each play in turn. She begins with *The Tempest*—which teaches (she says):

that the ways, the justice, and the goodness of Providence, are so frequently manifested toward mankind, even in this life, that it should ever encourage an honest and a guiltless mind to form hopes, in the most forlorn situations; and ought also to warn the wicked never to rest assured in the false confidence of wealth or power, against the natural abhorrence of vice, both in God and man.

That is very well, no doubt—but the next play in the Folio is *A Midsummer Night's Dream*. Poor Mrs. Griffith is already stumped. 'I shall not trouble my readers', she says, 'with the Fable of this piece, as I can see no general moral that can be deducted from the argument.' Then comes *The Two Gentlemen of Verona*. 'The Fable', she says, 'of this play has no more moral in it, than the former.' *Measure for Measure* follows and the poor lady becomes desperate: 'I cannot see what moral can be extracted from this Piece.' And with the fifth play, *The Comedy of Errors*, she gives up: 'I shall take no further notice of the want of a moral fable in the rest of these plays.' It is true, indeed, that Mrs. Griffith does not altogether quit the field. In *As You Like It*, for instance, she triumphantly finds 'a very proper hint given . . . to women, not to deviate from the prescribed rules and decorums of their sex'. But on the whole she must be said to discover (what Dr. Johnson could already have told her) that Shakespeare 'is so much more careful to please than to instruct, that he seems to write without any moral purpose'.

Johnson backs up this stricture of Shakespeare by declaring that 'he makes no just distribution of good or evil', thereby ranging himself with those who require of the dramatist the administration of poetical justice. And the conception of poetical justice, indeed, was for a very long time the focal point round which most debate on Shakespeare's morality turned. Eugenius in Dryden's *Essay of Dramatic Poesy* had censured the ancient dramatists for not taking care to punish the wicked; and Dryden's contemporary Thomas Rymer[1] (who seems actually to have coined the phrase *poetical justice*) transferred the censure to Shakespeare. John Dennis[2] argued with great ingenuity for poetical justice. Real people, he said, must face Judgement in a hereafter. But characters in a play have no hereafter; their sole creator is the dramatist; and therefore the dramatist must, so to speak, play deity to them, and reward or punish them while they are yet on the stage and before they escape into nothingness. Dennis in this was partly actuated by his hatred of Addison, in whose *Cato* a virtuous hero is allowed to perish in a just cause. Addison's counter-arguments in *The Spectator* must at first seem very sensible: *good and evil happen alike to all men on this side of the grave*; and poetical justice must entirely vitiate the drama as a mirror of life. Yet Johnson, although working the mirror-of-life idea hard, was unconvinced by Addison, and at least hankered after poetical justice. He could not bear poetry not to vindicate a moral governance of the world; he believed that at the end of plays the evidence should (as it were) be fudged in order to chasten vice and encourage virtue. The dramatist can't go on to show the Last Judgement in operation. He is therefore obliged (if he is to suggest the final and just balance of things) to anticipate, and to show felicity

---

[1] *The Tragedies of the Last Age* (1678).
[2] *The Genius and Writings of Shakespeare* (1712).

under the figure of prosperity achieved here below. On this ground Johnson preferred Tate's 'happy-ending' *Lear* to Shakespeare's.

The later history of the 'poetical justice' doctrine is more full of curiosity than instruction. Subscribing to it must necessarily lead, in Shakespeare criticism, to one of two conclusions. Either the major tragedies of Shakespeare are extremely faulty performances in which the principle is for the most part flatly contradicted (and this is what Dennis boldly concludes); or the tragedies present a succession of persons only speciously virtuous, who meet a merited doom, intelligible to us if we will only sufficiently reflect. Since the secure establishing of Shakespeare's reputation in the later eighteenth century it is only this second supposition that has appeared tenable. Or if this has not been held tenable it has yet frequently been held possible to argue for that (as it were) modified or attenuated form of poetical justice represented by the Aristotelian *hamartia*—the notion that there is *some* relationship or correspondence between conduct and character on the one hand and earthly destiny on the other. Critics consequently find themselves labouring to create for each victim some *hamartia* or other. Thus Rymer would jeeringly find in Desdemona this tragic flaw: that she was careless about her linen—that the play is the tragedy of a handkerchief. Others with more seriousness have averred that Cordelia was blameworthy in failing of a little harmless and tactful prevarication. Even King Duncan has been held gravely at fault in imperilling not only his own life but that of his chamber grooms by rashly disregarding that *hoarser croak* whereby the sagacious raven would have apprised him of the inadvisability of entering Macbeth's castle.

It is apparent to us nowadays (whether rightly or wrongly) that all this represents a false cast in the interpretation of Shakespeare. Yet when Dr. Johnson puts the thing at its most general, and declares 'it is always a writer's duty to make the world better', we are conscious of a proposition which, at least, must be treated more warily. Has Shakespeare any aim to instruct? Poets in his time were certainly *taught* that they had a duty to do so. Even if he had no didactic intention, did he yet take for granted any religious or ethical system, within the affirmations of which he un-questioningly worked? Answering this is very difficult, for the simple and obvious reason that all in Shakespeare is expressed in dramatic or personative form. Thus much has been written of recent years about Shake-speare's adherence to medieval notions of order and degree. A speech by Ulysses in *Troilus and Cressida* (I. iii. 75 ff.), another by the Archbishop of Canterbury in *Henry V* (I. ii. 183 ff.), a third by Menenius in *Corio-lanus* (I. i. 101 ff.) are constantly cited as vindicating this. Yet we may well ask, as Professor Harbage does in *As They Liked It*,[1] perhaps the best book on our subject yet published, if anything of all this is designed as doctrinal. 'It cannot be ignored that each of the three speeches is delivered by an unscrupulous politician meeting an immediate problem—advocating a practical programme of somewhat debatable merit.' Moreover, Professor Harbage shows, this is only one instance of a pervasive ambiguousness in Shakespeare's dealing with ethical issues. It may almost be said to be the rule that when his characters come hard up against a moral problem proper—a moral dilemma or hard choice—the dramatist finds means to let them off. The issue is suspended, dissolved, or dodged; some theatricality, some trick of distraction is brought in. Even in *Measure for Measure*, the play most commonly cited in argu-ments here, the dramatist is thoroughly evasive in the

[1] The Macmillan Company, New York, 1947.

end. Then again, a somewhat similar phenomenon confronts us in the study of Shakespearian character. Swinburne[1] describes Brutus as the 'very noblest figure of a typical and ideal republican in all the literature of the world'. But when we look hard at Brutus we see something more complicated and less edifying. Morally, indeed, it is surely the prime characteristic of Shakespeare's major characters that they keep us guessing all the time. Are they, perhaps, constructed to that end? Here, once more, is Professor Harbage:

> Claudius, Gertrude, and Hamlet require constant evaluation on our part. We have to keep weighing them on our scales. Always in Shakespeare we perceive that the good might be better and the bad might be worse, and we are excited by our perceptions. The virtuous seem to need our counsel, and the vicious seem capable of understanding our censure. We are linked to the former by sensations of solicitude, and to the latter by moments of sympathy and understanding. We are constantly *involved*.

In all this, Shakespeare's characters are at an opposite remove from, say, Corneille's. They never give the impression of being moral athletes—a sort of ethical Brains Trust knowing all the answers and existing in order to give an exhibition of them. They are not, in fact, the creations of a moralist. They are not even the creations of an artist who is obliged to pretend at all hard to be a moralist. Rather they are the elements in an entertainment of which the stuff and substance is, indeed, the moral nature of man, but the end of which is not moralistic. Shakespeare, in short, sees it as the business of the poet to exhibit, not to pronounce upon, moral behaviour. In one sense he is dealing with morals all the time. There is scarcely a speech, scarcely even a song in all his plays untouched by ethical sentiment. He deals with morals always; but as a moralist, never.

[1] Algernon Charles Swinburne, *A Study of Shakespeare* (1880).

He renders us more aware of ourselves as creatures of good and evil; but he seems to do this rather because such awareness is pleasurable than because it conduces to salvation. He does not work out moral problems for us; yet he leaves us, as moral beings, more alert than he found us. This may itself be a moral act, and laudable. But certainly if (as Johnson would have the artist do) Shakespeare 'makes the world better' it is by exercising our moral interests and perceptions rather than by any deliberate proposal to alter them, to expound patterns of behaviour, or to bend fiction to the support of principle and precept.

It comes down then (I think) to this. Shakespeare is not ambitious to instruct us. He tells us, indeed, in that Epilogue to *The Tempest* which is conceivably his artistic testament, that *his project was to please*. He pleases us as moral beings—in virtue of our being creatures of good and evil, interested in good and evil. But the interest in good and evil for which he caters is the common man's, not the professional's: Shakespeare does not write as a casuist or for casuists. He writes as one good-hearted for the good-hearted. He has perhaps more insight into how human beings do behave than curiosity about how they *ought* to behave.

But to all this it must be added that the plays create for themselves, and exist in, a real and distinguishable moral climate. It is unmistakable! The Victorians were fond of assuring us that Shakespeare, morally, was as sound as a bell; and there can be no doubt that the Victorians were right. Study Shakespeare's silences and avoidances; study the things he dropped as he worked from his sources. The conclusion to which we are bound to come is that he was a thoroughly wholesome person. Some of his plays must strike us as holding shadows dark enough. But the air is clean, the soil sweet, and the plenty (as with Chaucer) distinguishably God's.

W. H. AUDEN

(b. 1907)

Music in Shakespeare[1]

ITS DRAMATIC USE IN HIS PLAYS

PROFESSOR WILSON KNIGHT and others have
pointed out the important part played in Shakespeare's
poetry by images related to music, showing, for instance, how music occupies the place in the cluster of
good symbols which is held in the bad cluster by the
symbol of the Storm.

His fondness for musical images does not, of course,
necessarily indicate that Shakespeare was himself musical—some very good poets have been musically tone
deaf. Any poet of the period who used a musical imagery
would have attached the same associations to it, for
they were part of the current Renaissance theory of the
nature of music and its effects.

Anyone at the time, if asked 'What is music?' would
have given the answer stated by Lorenzo to Jessica in
the last scene of *The Merchant of Venice*. Mr. James
Hutton in an admirable article in the *English Miscellany*
on 'Some English Poems in praise of Music' has traced
the history of this theory from Pythagoras to Ficino
and shown the origin of most of Lorenzo's images. The
theory may be summarized thus:

1. Music is unique among the arts for it is the only
   art practised in Heaven and by the unfallen creatures. Conversely, one of the most obvious characteristics of Hell is its discordant din.
2. Human reason is able to infer that this heavenly

[1] *Encounter* (December 1957).

music exists, because it can recognize mathematical proportions. But the human ear cannot hear it, either since man's Fall or simply because the ear is a bodily organ subject to change and death. What Campanella calls the *molino vivo* of the self drowns out the celestial sounds. In certain exceptional states of ecstasy, however, certain individuals have heard it.

3. Man-made music, though inferior to the music which cannot be heard, is a good, for in its mortal way it recalls or imitates the Divine order. In consequence, it has great powers. It can tame irrational and savage beasts, it can cure lunatics, it can relieve sorrow. A dislike of music is a sign of a perverse will that defiantly refuses to submit to the general harmony.

4. Not all music, however, is good. There is a bad kind of music, which corrupts and weakens. 'The Devil rides a fiddlestick.' Good is commonly associated with old music, bad with new.

Nobody today, I imagine, holds such a theory, i.e. nobody now thinks that the aesthetics of music have anything to do with the science of acoustics. What theory of painting, one wonders, would have developed if Pythagoras had owned a spectroscope, and learned that colour relations can also be expressed in mathematical proportions?

Indeed, for us there is something comic about Milton's lines

> the fair music that all creatures made
> To their great Lord, whose love their motion swayed
> in perfect Diapason

with its suggestion that, in the music of Paradise, the only musical interval is the octave.

But if he has never heard of the theory, there are

many things in Shakespeare which the playgoer will miss. For example, the dramatic effect of the recognition scene in *Pericles*.

Pericles. But what music?
Helicanus.   My lord, I hear none.
Pericles. None! The music of the spheres! List, my Marina!
Lysimachus. It is not good to cross him; give him way.
Pericles. Rarest sounds! Do ye not hear?
Helicanus.   My Lord, I hear.

(Act V, scene i)

or even such a simple little joke as this from *Othello*:

Clown. If you have any music that may not be heard, to't again: but, as they say, to hear music the general does not greatly care.
1st Mus. We have none such, sir.

(Act III, scene i)

Music is not only an art with its own laws and values; it is also a social fact. Composing, performing, listening to music are things which human beings do under certain circumstances just as they fight and make love. Moreover, in the Elizabethan age, music was regarded as an important social fact. A knowledge of music, an ability to read a madrigal part were expected of an educated person, and the extraordinary output of airs and madrigals between 1588 and 1620 testify to both the quantity and quality of the music-making that must have gone on. When Bottom says 'I have a reasonable good ear in music: let's have the tongs and the bones', it is not so much an expression of taste as a revelation of class, like dropping one's aitches; and when Benedict says 'Well, a horn for my money when all's done', he is being deliberately *épatant*.

Whether he cared for music itself or not, any dramatist of the period could hardly have failed to notice the part played by music in human life, to observe, for instance, that the kind of music a person likes or dislikes, the kind of way in which he listens to it, the sort of occasion on which he wants to hear or make it, are revealing about his character.

A dramatist of a later age might notice the same facts, but it would be difficult for him to make dramatic use of them, unless he were to write a play specifically about musicians.

But the dramatic conventions of the Elizabethan stage permitted and encouraged the introduction of songs and instrumental music into the spoken drama. Audiences liked to hear them, and the dramatist was expected to provide them. The average playgoer, no doubt, simply wanted a pretty song as part of the entertainment, and did not bother about its dramatic relevance to the play as a whole. But a dramatist who took his art seriously had to say, either 'musical numbers in a spoken play are irrelevant episodes and I refuse to put them in just to please the public', or 'I must conceive my play in such a manner that musical numbers, vocal or instrumental, can occur in it, not as episodes, but as essential elements in its structure'.

If Shakespeare took this second line, it should be possible, on examining the occasions where he makes use of music, to find answers to the following questions:

1. Why is this piece of music placed just where it is and not somewhere else?

2. In the case of a song, why are the mood and the words of this song what they are? Why this song instead of another?

3. Why is it this character who sings and not another? Does the song reveal something about this character which could not be revealed so well in any other way?

4. What effect does this music have upon those who

listen to it? Is it possible to say that, had the music been omitted, the behaviour of the characters or the feelings of the audience would be different from what they are?

II

When we now speak of music as an art, we mean that the elements of tone and rhythm are used to create a structure of sounds which are to be listened to for their own sake. If it be asked what such music is 'about', I do not think it too controversial to say that it presents a virtual image of our experience of living as temporal, with its double aspect of recurrence and becoming. To 'get' such an image, the listener must for the time being banish from his mind all immediate desires and practical concerns and only think what he hears.

But rhythm and tone can also be used to achieve non-musical ends. For example, any form of physical movement, whether in work or play, which involves accurate repetition, is made easier by sounded rhythmical beats, and the psychological effect of singing, whether in unison or in harmony, in a group, is one of reducing the sense of diversity and strengthening the sense of unity, so that on all occasions where such a unity of feeling is desired or desirable, music has an important function.

> If the true concord of well-tuned sounds
> By unions married do offend thine ear,
> They do but sweetly chide thee, who confounds
> In singleness the parts that thou shouldst bear.
> Mark how one string, sweet husband to another,
> Strikes each in each by mutual ordering;
> Resembling sire and child and happy mother,
> Who all in one, one pleasing note do sing:
> Whose speechless song, being many, seeming one,
> Sings this to thee, 'Thou single wilt prove none.'
> (Sonnet VIII)

The oddest example of music with an extra-musical

purpose is the lullaby. The immediate effect of the rocking rhythm and the melody is to fix the baby's attention upon an ordered pattern, so that it forgets the distractions of arbitrary noises, but its final intention is to make the baby fall asleep, that is to say, to hear nothing at all.

Sounds, instrumental or vocal, which are used for social purposes, may of course have a musical value as well, but this is usually secondary to their function. If one takes, say, a sea-shanty out of its proper context, and listens to it on the gramophone as one might listen to a *lied* by Schubert, one is very soon bored. The beauty of sound which it may have been felt to possess when accompanied by the sensation of muscular movement and visual images of sea and sky cannot survive without them.

The great peculiarity of music as an art is that the sounds which comprise its medium can be produced in two ways, by playing on specially constructed instruments and by using the human vocal chords in a special way. Men use their vocal chords for speech, that is, to communicate with each other, but also, under certain conditions, a man may feel, as we say, 'like singing'. This impulse has little, if anything, to do with communication or with other people. Under the pressure of a certain mood, a man may feel the need to express that mood to himself, by using his vocal chords in an exceptional way. If he should sing some actual song he has learnt, he chooses it for its general fitness to his mood, not for its unique qualities.

None of the other arts seem suited to this immediate self-expression. A few poets may compose verses in their bath—I have never heard of anyone trying to paint in his bath—but almost everyone, at some time or other, has sung in his bath.

In no other art can one see so clearly a distinction,

even a rivalry, between the desire for pattern and the desire for personal utterance, as is disclosed by the difference between instrumental and vocal music. I think I can see an analogous distinction in painting, though it may sound rather far-fetched. To me, vocal music plays the part in music that the human nude plays in painting. In both there is an essential erotic element which is always in danger of being corrupted for sexual ends, but need not be, and without this element of the erotic which the human voice and the nude have contributed, both arts would be a little lifeless.

In music it is from instruments that rhythmical and tonal precision and musical structure are mostly derived, so that, without them, the voice would have remained tied to impromptu and personal expression. Singers, unchastened by the orchestral discipline, would soon lose interest in singing and wish only to show off their voices. On the other hand, the music of a dumb race who had invented instruments would be precise but dull, for the players would not know what it means to strive after expression, to make their instruments 'sing'. The kind of effect they would make is the kind we condemn in a pianist when we say: 'He just plays the notes.'

Lastly, because we do not have the voluntary control over our ears that we have over our eyes, and because musical sounds do not denote meanings like words or represent objects like lines and colours, it is far harder to know what a person means, harder even for himself to know, when he says: 'I like this piece of music', than when he says: 'I like this book or this picture.' At one extreme, there is the professional musician, who not only thinks clearly and completely what he hears, but also recognizes the means by which the composer causes him so to think. This does not mean that he can judge music any better than one without his technical knowledge, who has trained himself to listen and is familiar with music of all kinds. His technical knowledge is an added pleasure, perhaps, but it is not a musical experience. At the other extreme is the student who keeps the radio playing while he studies, because he finds that a background of sound makes it easier for him to concentrate on his work. In his case the music is serving the contradictory function of preventing him from listening to anything, either to itself or to the noises in the street.

Between these two extremes, there is a way of listening which has been well described by Suzanne Langer.

There is a twilight zone of musical enjoyment when tonal appreciation is woven into day-dreaming. To the entirely uninitiated hearer it may be an aid in finding expressive forms at all, to extemporise an accompanying romance and let the music express feelings accounted for by its scenes. But to the competent it is a pitfall, because it obscures the full vital import of the music, noting only what comes handy for a purpose, and noting only what expresses attitudes and emotions the listener was familiar with before. It bars everything new and really interesting in a world, since what does not fit the *petit roman* is passed over, and what does fit is the dreamer's own. Above all it leads attention, not only to the music, but away from it—via the music to something else that is essentially an indulgence. One may spend a whole evening in this sort of dream and carry nothing away from it, no musical insight, no new feeling, and actually nothing heard.

(*Feeling and Form*, chap. x)

It is this kind of listening, surely, which is implied by the Duke in *Twelfth Night*, 'If music be the food of love, play on', and by Cleopatra, 'Give me some music—music, moody food / Of us that trade in love', and which provoked that great music-lover, Bernard Shaw, to the remark, 'Music is the brandy of the damned.'

III

Shakespeare uses instrumental music for two purposes: on socially appropriate occasions, to represent the voice of this world, of the collective rejoicing as in a dance or mourning as in a dead march; and unexpectedly as an auditory image of a supernatural or magical world. In the second case the music generally carries the stage direction 'Solemn'.

It may be directly the voice of Heaven, the music of the spheres heard by Pericles, the music under the earth heard by Antony's soldiers, the music which accompanies Queen Katherine's vision, or it may be commanded, either by spirits of the intermediate world like Oberon or Ariel, or by wise men like Prospero and the physicians in *King Lear* and *Pericles*, to exert a magical influence on human beings. When doctors order music, it is, of course, made by human musicians, and to the healthy it may even sound 'rough and woeful', but in the ears of the patient, mad Lear or unconscious Thaisa, it seems a platonic imitation of the unheard celestial music and has a curative effect.

'Solemn' music is generally played off-stage. It comes, that is, from an invisible source which makes it impossible for those on-stage to express a *voluntary* reaction to it. Either they cannot hear it or it has effects upon them which they cannot control. Thus, in Act II, scene i of *The Tempest*, it is an indication of their villainy, the lack of music in their souls, that Antonio and Sebastian are not affected by the sleeping-spell music when Alonso and the others are, an indication which is forthwith confirmed when they use the opportunity so created to plan Alonso's murder.

On some occasions, e.g. in the vision of Posthumus (*Cymbeline*, Act V, scene iv), Shakespeare has lines spoken against an instrumental musical background.

The effect of this is to depersonalize the speaker, for the sound of the music blots out the individual timbre of his voice. What he says to music seems not *his* statement but a message, a statement that has to be made.

Antony and Cleopatra (Act IV, scene iii) is a good example of the dramatic skill with which Shakespeare places a supernatural musical announcement. In the first scene of the act we have had a glimpse of the cold, calculating Octavius refusing Antony's old-fashioned challenge to personal combat and deciding to give battle next day. To Octavius chivalry is one aspect of a childish lack of self-control and 'Poor Antony' is his contemptuous comment on his opponent. Whereupon we are shown Antony talking to his friends in a wrought-up state of self-dramatization and self-pity:

> Give me thy hand,
> Thou hast been rightly honest; so hast thou;
> Thou—and thou—and thou; you have serv'd me well. . . .
> Perchance to-morrow
> You'll serve another master. I look on you
> As one that takes his leave. Mine honest friends,
> I turn you not away; but like a master
> Married to your good service, stay till death:
> Tend me to-night two hours, I ask no more,
> And the gods yield you for 't.

We already know that Enobarbus, who is present, has decided to desert Antony. Now follows the scene with the common soldiers in which supernatural music announces that

> The god Hercules whom Antony lov'd
> Now leaves him.

The effect of this is to make us see the human characters, Octavius, Antony, Cleopatra, Enobarbus, as agents of powers greater than they. Their personalities and actions, moral or immoral, carry out the purposes of these powers but cannot change them. Octavius's self-confidence and Antony's sense of doom are justified though they do not know why.

But in the ensuing five scenes it appears as if they were both mistaken, for it is Antony who wins the battle. Neither Octavius nor Antony have heard the music, but we, the audience, have, and our knowledge that Antony must lose in the end gives a pathos to his temporary triumph which would be lacking if the invisible music were cut.

Of the instances of mundane or carnal instrumental music in the plays, the most interesting are those in which it is, as it were, the wrong kind of magic. Those who like it and call for it use it to strengthen their illusions about themselves.

So Timon uses it when he gives his great banquet. Music stands for the imaginary world Timon is trying to live in, where everybody loves everybody and he stands at the centre as the source of this universal love.

> *Timon.* Music, make their welcome!
> *First Lord.* You see, my lord, how ample y'are beloved.
> (*Timon of Athens*, Act I, scene ii)

One of his guests is the professional sneerer, Apemantus, whose conceit is that he is the only one who sees the world as it really is, as the absolutely unmusical place where nobody loves anybody but himself. 'Nay,' says Timon to him, 'an you begin to rail on society once, I am sworn not to give regard to you. Farewell, and come with better music.'

But Timon is never to hear music again after this scene.

Neither Timon nor Apemantus have music in their souls, but, while Apemantus is shamelessly proud of this, Timon wants desperately to believe that he has music in his soul, and the discovery that he has not, destroys him.

To Falstaff, music, like sack, is an aid to sustaining the illusion of living in an Eden of childlike innocence where nothing serious can happen. Unlike Timon, who does not love others as much as he likes to think, Falstaff himself really is loving. His chief illusion is that Prince Hal loves him as much as he loves Prince Hal, and that Prince Hal is an innocent child like himself.

Shakespeare reserves the use of a musical background for the scene between Falstaff, Doll, Poins, and Hal (*Henry IV, Part II*, Act II, scene iv). While the music lasts, Time will stand still for Falstaff. He will not grow older, he will not have to pay his debts, Prince Hal will remain his dream-son and boon companion. But the music is interrupted by the realities of historical time with the arrival of Peto. Hal feels ashamed.

> By heaven, Poins, I feel me much to blame
> So idly to profane the present time. . . .
> Give me my sword and cloak. Falstaff, good-night!

Falstaff only feels disappointed:

> Now comes in the sweetest morsel of the night, and we must hence, and leave it unpick'd.

In Prince Hal's life this moment is the turning point; from now on he will become the responsible ruler. Falstaff will not change because he is incapable of change but, at this moment, though he is unaware of it, the most important thing in his life, his friendship with Hal, ceases with the words, 'Good-night'. When they meet again, the first words Falstaff will hear are—'I know thee not, old man.'

Since music, the virtual image of time, takes actual time to perform, listening to music can be a waste of time, especially for those, like kings, whose primary concern should be with the unheard music of justice.

Ha! Ha! keep time! How sour sweet music is
When time is broke and no proportion kept!
So is it in the music of men's lives.
And here have I the daintiness of ear
To check time broke in a disordered string;
But, for the concord of my state and time,
Had not an ear to hear my true time broke.

(*Richard II*, Act V, scene v)

IV

We find two types of song in Shakespeare's plays, the called-for song and the impromptu song.

A called-for song is one which is sung by one character at the request of another who wishes to hear some music and, while it lasts, all action and speech are halted. Nobody is asked to sing unless it is believed that he can sing well and, little as we may know about the music which was actually used in contemporary performances of Shakespeare's plays, we may safely assume from the contemporary songs which we do possess that they must have made demands which only a good voice and a good musician could satisfy.

On the stage, this means that the character so asked ceases to be himself and becomes a performer; the audience are not interested in him, but in the quality of his singing. We are thinking, of course, of songs introduced into a play written in verse or prose which is spoken, not of arias in an opera, where the dramatic medium is itself song, and we forget that the singers are performers as we forget that the actor speaking blank verse is an actor.

An Elizabethan theatrical company, giving plays in which such songs occurred, would therefore have to hire at least one person as a singer rather than as an actor. If they had not been needed to sing, the dramatic action in *Much Ado*, *As You Like It*, and *Twelfth Night* could have got along quite well without Balthazar, Amiens, and the Clown.

Yet, minor character though the singer may be, he has a character which is peculiar to those who practise his mystery, and, when he gets a chance, Shakespeare draws our attention to it. He notices the mock or polite modesty of the singer, certain of his talents.

Don Pedro. Come, Balthazar, we'll hear that song again.
Balthazar. O good my lord, tax not so bad a voice
    To slander music any more than once.
Don Pedro. It is the witness still of excellency
    To put a strange face on his own perfection.

> *(Much Ado About Nothing*, Act II, scene iii)

He marks the annoyance of the professional who must sing for others' pleasure whether he feels like it or not.

Jaques. More, I prithee, more.
Amiens. My voice is ragged: I know I cannot please you.
Jaques. I do not desire you to please me: I do desire you to
    sing . . . will you sing?
Amiens. More at your request than to please myself.

> *(As You Like It*, Act II, scene v)

And in the scene between Peter and the musicians in *Romeo and Juliet*, he contrasts the lives and motives of ill-paid musicians and their rich patrons. The musicians have been hired by the Capulets to play at Juliet's marriage to Paris. Their lives mean nothing to the Capulets: they are things that make music. The lives of the Capulets mean nothing to the musicians: they are things that pay money. The musicians arrive only to learn that Juliet is believed to be dead and that the wedding is off. Juliet means nothing to them, but her death means a lot: they will not get paid. Whether either the Capulets or the musicians actually like music is left in doubt. Music is something you have to have at weddings: music is something you have to make if that is your job. With a felicitous irony Shakespeare introduces a quotation from Richard Edwardes's poem, *In Commendation of Musick*:

Peter. When griping grief the heart doth wound
  And doleful dumps the mind oppress
  Then music with her silver sound—
  Why 'silver sound'? Why 'music with her silver sound'?
  What say you, Simon Catling?
1st Mus. Marry, sir, because silver hath a sweet sound.
Peter. Pretty! What say you, Hugh Rebeck?
2nd Mus. I say, 'silver sound', because musicians sound for
  silver.
                                    (*Romeo and Juliet*, Act IV, scene v)

The powers the poet attributes to music are exaggerated. It cannot remove the grief of losing a daughter or the pangs of an empty belly.

Since action must cease while a called-for song is heard, such a song, if it is not to be an irrelevant interlude, must be placed at a point where the characters have both a motive for wanting one and the leisure to hear it. Consequently we find few called-for songs in the tragedies, where the steady advance of the hero to his doom must not be interrupted, or in the historical plays in which the characters are men of action with no leisure.

Further, it is rare that a character listens to a song for its own sake, since when someone listens to music properly, he forgets himself and others which, on the stage, means that he forgets all about the play. Indeed, I can only think of one case where it seems certain that a character listens to a song as a song should be listened to, instead of as a stimulus to a *petit roman* of his own, and that is in *Henry VIII*, Act III, scene i, when Katherine listens to *Orpheus with his lute*. The Queen knows that the King wants to divorce her and that pressure will be brought upon her to acquiesce. But she believes that it is her religious duty to refuse, whatever the consequences. For the moment there is nothing she can do but wait. And her circumstances are too serious and painful to allow her to pass the time day-dreaming:

> Take thy lute, wench; my soul grows sad with troubles;
> Sing and disperse them, if thou canst: leave working.

The words of the song which follows are not about any human feelings, pleasant or unpleasant, which might have some bearing on her situation. The song, like Edwardes's poem, is an *encomium musicae*. Music cannot, of course, cure grief, as the song claims, but in so far that she is able to attend to it and nothing else, she can forget her situation while the music lasts.

An interesting contrast to this is provided by a scene which at first seems very similar, Act IV, scene i of *Measure for Measure*. Here, too, we have an unhappy woman listening to a song. But Mariana, unlike Katherine, is not trying to forget her unhappiness; she is indulging it. Being the deserted lady has become a role. The words of the song, *Take, O take those lips away*, mirror her situation exactly, and her apology to the Duke when he surprises her, gives her away.

> I cry you mercy, sir; and well could wish
> You had not found me here so musical:
> Let me excuse me, and believe me so—
> My mirth it much displeas'd, but pleas'd my woe.

In his reply, the Duke, as is fitting in this, the most puritanical of Shakespeare's plays, states the puritanical case against the heard music of this world:

> 'Tis good; though music oft hath such a charm
> To make bad good, and good provoke to harm.

Were the Duke to extend this reply, one can be sure that he would speak of the unheard music of Justice.

On two occasions, Shakespeare shows us music being used with conscious evil intent. In *The Two Gentlemen of Verona*, Proteus, who has been false to his friend, has forsworn his vows to his girl and is cheating Thurio, serenades Sylvia while his forsaken Julia listens. On his side, there is no question here of self-deception through music. Proteus knows exactly what he is doing. Through music which is itself beautiful and good, he hopes to do evil, to seduce Sylvia.

Proteus is a weak character, not a wicked one. He is ashamed of what he is doing, and just as he knows the difference between good and evil in conduct, he knows the difference between music well and badly played.

Host. How do you, man? the music likes you not?

Julia. You mistake; the musician likes me not.

Host. Why, my pretty youth?

Julia. He plays false father.

Host. How? Out of tune on the strings?

Julia. Not so; but yet so false that he grieves my very heart-strings. . . .

Host. I perceive you delight not in music.

Julia. Not a whit, when it jars so.

Host. Hark, what a fine change is in the music!

Julia. Ay, that change is the spite.

Host. You would have them always play but one thing?

Julia. I would always have one play but one thing.

(*Two Gentlemen of Verona*, Act IV, scene ii)

The second occasion is in *Cymbeline*, when Cloten serenades Imogen. Cloten is a lost soul without conscience or shame. He is shown, therefore, as someone who does not know one note from another. He has been told that music acts on women as an erotic stimulus, and wishes for the most erotic music that money can buy:

First a very excellent, good, conceited thing; after, a wonderful sweet air, with admirable rich words to it, and then let her consider.

For, except as an erotic stimulus, music is, for him, worthless:

> If this penetrate, I will consider your music the better; if it do not, it is a vice in her ears which horse-hairs and calves' guts, nor the voice of the unpaved eunuch to boot, can never amend.   (*Cymbeline*, Act II, scene iii)

[Section V is omitted]

VI

So much for the called-for song. Let us now consider the impromptu. The impromptu singer stops speaking and breaks into song, not because anyone else has asked him to sing or is listening, but to relieve his feelings in a way that speech cannot do, or to help him in some action. An impromptu song is not art but a form of personal behaviour. It reveals, as the called-for song cannot, something about the singer. On the stage, therefore, it is generally desirable that a character who breaks into impromptu song should not have a good voice. No producer, for example, would seek to engage Madame Callas for the part of Ophelia, because the beauty of her voice would distract the audience's attention from the real dramatic point which is that Ophelia's songs are to the highest degree *not* called-for. We are meant to be horrified both by what she sings and by the fact that she sings at all. The other characters are affected but not in the way that people are affected by music. The King is terrified, Laertes so outraged that he becomes willing to use dirty means to avenge his sister.

Generally, of course, the revelation made by an impromptu song is comic or pathetic rather than shocking. Thus the Gravedigger's song in *Hamlet* is first a work-song, which helps to make the operation of digging go more smoothly, and, secondly, an expression of the *galgenhumor* which suits his particular mystery.

Singing is one of Autolycus's occupations, so he may be allowed a good voice, but *When daffodils begin to peer* is an impromptu song. He sings as he walks, because it makes walking more rhythmical and less tiring, and he sings to keep up his spirits. His is a tough life, with hunger and the gallows never very far away, and he needs all the courage he can muster.

One of the commonest and most deplorable effects of alcohol is its encouragement of the impromptu singer. It is not the least tribute one could pay to Shakespeare when one says that he manages to extract interest from this most trivial and boring of phenomena.

When Silence gets drunk in Shallow's orchard, the maximum pathos is got out of the scene. We know Silence to be an old, timid, sad, poor, nice man, and we cannot believe that, even when he was young, he was ever a gay dog yet, when he is drunk, it is of women, wine, and chivalry that he sings. Further, the drunker he gets, the feebler becomes his memory. The first time he sings, he manages to recall six lines, by the fifth time, he can only remember one:

And Robin Hood, Scarlet, and John.

We are shown, not only the effect of alcohol on the imagination of a timid man, but also its effect on the brain of an old one.

Just as the called-for song can be used with conscious ill-intent, so the impromptu song can be feigned to counterfeit good fellowship.

The characters assembled on Pompey's galley at Misenum, who sing *Come, thou monarch of the Vine*, are anything but pathetic; they are the lords of the world. The occasion is a feast to celebrate a reconciliation, but not one of them trusts the others an inch, and all would betray each other without scruple if it seemed to their advantage.

Pompey has indeed refused Menas's suggestion to murder his guests, but wishes that Menas had done it without telling him. The fact that Lepidus gets stinking and boasts of his power, reveals his inferiority to the others, and it is pretty clear that the Machiavellian Octavius is not quite as tight as he pretends.

Again, when Iago incites Cassio to drink, and starts singing

> And let the can clink it

we know him to be cold sober, for one cannot imagine any mood of Iago's which he would express by singing. What he sings is pseudo-impromptu. He pretends to be expressing his mood, to be Cassio's buddy, but a buddy is something we know he could never be to anyone.

VII

Ariel's songs in *The Tempest* cannot be classified as either called-for or impromptu, and this is one reason why the part is so hard to cast. A producer casting Balthazar needs a good professional singer; for Stephano, a comedian who can make as raucous and unmusical a noise as possible. Neither is too difficult to find. But for Ariel he needs not only a boy with an unbroken voice, but also one with a voice far above the standard required for the two pages who are to sing *It was a lover and his lass*.

For Ariel is neither a singer, that is to say, a human being whose vocal gifts provide him with a social function, nor a non-musical person who in certain moods feels like singing. Ariel *is* song; when he is truly himself, he sings. The effect when he speaks is similar to that of *recitativo secco* in opera, which we listen to because we have to understand the action, though our real interest in the characters is only aroused when they start to sing. Yet Ariel is not an alien visitor from the world of opera who has wandered into a spoken drama by mistake. He cannot express any human feelings because he has none. The kind of voice he requires is exactly the kind that opera does not want, a voice which is as lacking in the personal and the erotic and as like an instrument as possible.

If Ariel's voice is peculiar, so is the effect that his songs have on others. Ferdinand listens to him in a very different way from that in which the Duke listens to *Come away, come away, death*, or Mariana to *Take, O take those lips away*. The effect on them was not to change them but to confirm the mood they were already in. The effect on Ferdinand of *Come unto these yellow sands* and *Full fathom five*, is more like the effect of instrumental music on Thaisa: direct, positive, magical.

Suppose Ariel, disguised as a musician, had approached Ferdinand as he sat on a bank, 'weeping against the king, my father's wrack', and offered to sing for him; Ferdinand would probably have replied— 'Go away, this is no time for music'; he might possibly have asked for something beautiful and sad; he certainly would not have asked for *Come unto these yellow sands*.

As it is, the song comes to him as an utter surprise, and its effect is not to feed or please his grief, not to encourage him to sit brooding, but to allay his passion, so that he gets to his feet and follows the music. The song opens his present to expectation at a moment when he is in danger of closing it to all but recollection.

The second song is, formally, a dirge, and, since it refers to his father, seems more relevant to Ferdinand's situation than the first. But it has nothing to do with any emotions which a son might feel at his father's grave. As Ferdinand says: 'this is no mortal business.' It is a magic spell, the effect of which is, not to lessen his feeling of loss, but to change his attitude towards his grief from one of rebellion—'How could this bereavement happen to me?'—to one of awe and reverent acceptance. As long as a man refuses to accept whatever he suffers as given, without pretending he can understand why, the past from which it came into being is an obsession which makes him deny any value to the present. Thanks to the music, Ferdinand is able to accept the past, symbolized by his father, as past, and at once there stands before him his future, Miranda.

The Tempest is full of music of all kinds, yet it is not one of the plays in which, in a symbolic sense, harmony and concord finally triumph over dissonant disorder. The three romantic comedies which precede it, *Pericles*, *Cymbeline*, and *The Winter's Tale*, and which deal with similar themes, injustice, plots, separation, all end in a blaze of joy—the wrongers repent, the wronged forgive, the earthly music is a true reflection of the heavenly. *The Tempest* ends much more sourly. The only wrongdoer who expresses genuine repentance is Alonso; and what a world of difference there is between Cymbeline's 'Pardon's the word to all', and Prospero's

> For you, most wicked sir, whom to call brother
> Would even infect my mouth, I do forgive
> Thy rankest fault—all of them; and require
> My dukedom of thee, which perforce I know
> Thou must restore.

Justice has triumphed over injustice, not because it is more harmonious, but because it commands superior force; one might even say because it is louder.

The wedding masque is peculiar and disturbing. Ferdinand and Miranda, who seem as virginal and innocent as any fairy-story lovers, are first treated to a moral lecture on the danger of anticipating their marriage vows, and the theme of the masque itself is a plot by Venus to get them to do so. The masque is not allowed to finish, but is broken off suddenly by Prospero, who mutters of another plot, 'that foul conspiracy of the beast Caliban and his confederates against my life'. As an entertainment for a wedding couple, the masque can scarcely be said to have been a success.

Prospero is more like the Duke in *Measure for Measure* than any other Shakespearian character. The victory of Justice which he brings about seems rather a duty than a source of joy to himself.

> I'll bring you to your ship and so to Naples
> Where I have hope to see the nuptials
> Of these our dear-beloved solemnis'd
> And thence retire me to my Milan, where
> Every third thought shall be my grave.

The tone is not that of a man who, putting behind him the vanities of mundane music, would meditate like Queen Katherine 'upon that celestial harmony I go to', but rather of one who longs for a place where silence shall be all.

KENNETH MUIR

(b. 1907)

Pericles[1]

WHETHER we accept Mr. Philip Edwards's view that the difference between the first two acts of the play and the remainder is due to the differing skill of two reporters, or assume that Shakespeare based his play on the work of another dramatist, making few alterations in the opening acts and completely rewriting the last three, we may agree that the text given in the Quarto is a bad one, and almost certainly reported. But the two theories have different editorial implications. Those who believe that Wilkins's novel[2] is based on an earlier play which Shakespeare revised should be less ready to accept readings from the novel into the text of the last three acts of the play than those who regard Wilkins's novel as a kind of rival report. On the other hand, those who think that Wilkins was reporting Shakespeare's play ought to have the courage of their convictions and print the Lysimachus–Marina dialogue almost as given in the novel. In any case we may assume that the text of the play is so poor that it is only a garbled version of what Shakespeare actually wrote. Whole lines and parts of lines have been omitted by reporters or compositors, and others have been so corrupted that not even the most confident textual critic can hope to restore them: On the other hand, there are speeches, and even whole scenes, where little emendation is required, and which appear to be so accurate that Hardin Craig could believe that they must have been printed from Shakespeare's foul papers.

[1] *Shakespeare as Collaborator* (1960); the second of two chapters on *Pericles*.
[2] *The Painfull Aduentures of Pericles.*]

Although, as I have argued, Shakespeare was probably using an old play as his main source, it was his usual custom to consult more than one source.[1] Wilkins made extensive use of Twine's version of the Apollonius story in *The Painfull Aduentures of Pericles*, and it is not unlikely that Shakespeare made use of it too. It was readily accessible in the 1607 reprint, but it is impossible to prove that Shakespeare consulted it. He would certainly have referred to Gower's *Confessio Amantis*. It is probable that Shakespeare himself was responsible for the renaming of the main characters; and, as I have suggested elsewhere,[2] he may have taken Marina from the story of the Mexican girl who became interpreter to Cortes and who was baptized under that name. She had been born the daughter of a chief, and on her father's death she had been sold to some Indians by her own mother, so as to ensure the succession of her son by her second husband. Years later, while acting as interpreter to Cortes in the province in which she was born, she was seen and recognized by her mother and half-brother, who were terrified that she would take vengeance on them. But Marina, either moved by their tears or taking her newly acquired religion seriously, forgave them and made them presents. This story of a princess, who was sold into slavery by her mother and stepfather and who forgave her mother and the son for whom the crime had been committed when she had them in her power, would have appealed to Shakespeare while he was writing the plays of the last period. The story resembles the plot of *The Tempest* in one respect, and the plot of *Pericles* in others. Unfortunately the full story is not known to have been published in Shakespeare's lifetime. The brief version given by Francisco Lopez de Gomara (whose *Historie*

[1] Cf. K. Muir, *Shakespeare's Sources* (1957), *passim*.
[2] *English Studies*, xxxix (1958), 74–75.

of the Conquest of the Weast India, now called new Spayne appeared in translation in 1578) lacks the touch of maternal treachery and the sequel of filial forgiveness. The stealing of the child, her name, and her gift of the tongues would be somewhat tenuous links with *Pericles*; but Shakespeare may have come across a published version of the story nearer to the one outlined above, and have been reminded of the Mexican Marina when he read of Dionyza's treatment of Apollonius's daughter, of the seizure of the girl by pirates, and of her escape from the brothel by means of her various accomplishments, as Marina earned a Spanish husband by her gift of the tongues. The name Marina, moreover, would strike Shakespeare as appropriate for one who was born at sea.

Ben Jonson referred to *Pericles*, in a moment of pique, as 'a mouldy tale'—a hit, presumably, not merely at the antiquity of the Apollonius story, but at its *naïveté*. It consists of a series of events linked together only by the fact that they illustrate the operations of fortune in the life of the hero. There is no integral connexion between Apollonius's wooing of the daughter of Antiochus and the later episodes of his marriage, the loss of his wife and daughter, and his final reunion with them. Apollonius happens to meet his bride when he leaves Tyre for fear of the wrath of Antiochus. Even if Shakespeare had dramatized only the second part of the story—the separation of his hero from his wife and daughter and his ultimate reunion with them— he would not have been able to imbue it with the kind of significance to be found in *Cymbeline* or *The Winter's Tale*. Posthumus loses his wife, and Leontes his wife and children, through their own fault; and they earn the restoration of their lost ones by their penitence. The misfortunes which befall Pericles can hardly be said to be due to his own sins, though it has been suggested that he was paying for his inability to recognize until too late the evil hidden beneath the fair exterior of Antiochus's daughter. It is possible, however, that an attempt by Shakespeare to impose significance on his material has been blurred by the corruption of the text.[1] In Act II, scene iv Simonides informs Thaisa's suitors that she will not marry for at least twelve months:

> One twelve moons more she'll wear Diana's livery.
> This by the eye of Cynthia hath she vow'd,
> And on her virgin honour will not break it.

We are not told definitely whether Simonides is speaking the truth. His words immediately after the departure of the suitors—'So, they are well despatch'd'—suggest, perhaps, that he has invented the vow to rid himself of the suitors so as to leave the field free for the favoured Pericles. Whether the vow was an invention or not, it is worth noting that Diana is mentioned several times in the Shakespearian parts of the play and once, as Lucina, in the first scene. (Lucina, incidentally, was Twine's name for Thaisa.) Pericles prays to Lucina during his wife's labour—

> Divinest patroness, and midwife gentle
> To those that cry by night—

and his prayer is rejected. When Thaisa is restored to life, her first words are addressed to the same goddess— 'O dear Diana!' Assuming that she will never see Pericles again—why is not explained—she decides to put on a vestal livery and serve as priestess in the temple of Diana at Ephesus. Gower, as chorus, speaks of Diana as Marina's mistress. Pericles vows 'by bright Diana' to leave his hair 'unscissored'. Marina, appropriately, prays to Diana in the brothel; and in the last act

[1] Cf. *N.Q.* (1948), p. 362.

Diana appears to Pericles in a vision, telling him to visit her temple at Ephesus. He promises to obey 'Celestial Dian, goddess argentine'. The last scene takes place in the temple. In his address to the goddess, Pericles describes his child as wearing yet Diana's 'silver livery'; and, after his wife has been restored to him, he declares:

> Pure Dian, bless thee for thy vision! I
> Will offer night-oblations to thee.

It looks as though Shakespeare intended Thaisa's time in the temple to be a means of expiating the sin of taking the name of the goddess in vain, and that his intentions have been partially hidden by the corrupt text.[1] But the trials which Pericles and his family undergo are also a means of testing them; and their final reunion is in accordance with Jupiter's pronouncement in *Cymbeline*—

> Whom best I love I cross; to make my gift
> The more delay'd, delighted—

an echo, no doubt, of the scriptural 'Whom the Lord loveth, He chasteneth'.

It has often been observed that in the plays of the final period the characters are much less complex, less realistic, than they had been in the great tragedies and comedies of Shakespeare's middle period. They are not merely simplified: they tend to be puppets, unable to control their own destinies. Although Hamlet speaks of the 'divinity that shapes our ends', Malvolio declares that 'all is fortune', Kent exclaims that 'it is the stars that govern our condition', Edmund acknowledges that 'the wheel has come full circle', Macbeth comes to think that life is 'a tale told by an idiot', and Othello asks despairingly 'Who can control his fate?', we recognize in all those plays that fate works through character.

---

[1] To judge from the Wilkins novel, Shakespeare did not find the broken vow motivation in the source-play.

In *Cymbeline* and *The Winter's Tale*, although human evil and weakness are equally apparent, these do not produce their logical results, since the action of the play appears to be controlled by the gods.[1] Mr. T. S. Eliot has suggested that Shakespeare in his last plays makes us feel not so much that his characters are creatures like ourselves, as that we are creatures like his characters, 'taking part like them in no common action of which we are for the most part unaware'. The characters are 'the work of a writer who has finally seen through the dramatic action of men into a spiritual action which transcends it'. A similar idea is expressed in the well-known lines in *Murder in the Cathedral*:

> Neither does the actor suffer
> Nor the patient act. But both are fixed
> In an eternal action, an eternal patience
> To which all must consent that it may be willed
> And which all must suffer that they may will it
> That the pattern may subsist, for the pattern is the action
> And the suffering, that the wheel may turn and still
> Be forever still.

But although Shakespeare might see some such pattern in the story of Apollonius—the converting of the wheel of fortune into the wheel of Providence—the difficulty remained of imposing a strictly dramatic unity on such an episodic story. Shakespeare had read Sidney's amusing account of a dramatic treatment of this kind of material:

You shall have *Asia* of the one side, and *Affricke* of the other, and so manie other under Kingdomes, that the Player when he comes in, must ever begin with telling where he is, or else the tale will not be conceived. Now you shall have three Ladies walke to gather flowers, and then we must beleeve the stage to be a garden. By and by we heare newes of

[1] The following paragraphs are based on a lecture given at Wayne State University, Detroit, to be published in a volume entitled *Last Periods*.

shipwreck in the same place, then we are to blame if we accept it not for a Rock. Upon the back of that, comes out a hidious monster with fire and smoke, and then the miserable beholders are bound to take it for a Cave: while in the meane time two Armies flie in, represented with foure swords & bucklers, and then what hard hart wil not receive it for a pitched field. Now of time, they are much more liberall. For ordinarie it is, that two yoong Princes fall in love, after many traverses she is got with child, delivered of a faire boy: he is lost, groweth a man, falleth in love, and is readie to get an other childe, and all this in two houres space: which howe absurd it is in sence, even sence may imagine: and Arte hath taught, and all aunctient examples justified. . . . But they will say, how then shall we set foorth a storie, which contains both many places and many times?

Sidney answers that a tragedy is not tied to the laws of history, that events can be reported by a *Nuntius*, and that

if they will represent an Historie, they must not (as *Horace* saith) beginne *ab ovo*, but they must come to the principall poynte of that one action which they will represent.

In the choruses of *Henry V* Shakespeare seems to be apologizing for not taking Sidney's advice; and Father Time, in *The Winter's Tale*, asks the audience to impute it not a crime that he disobeys the unity of time and slides over sixteen years. In *Pericles* Shakespeare uses the device of Ancient Gower, whether borrowed from an earlier play or suggested to Shakespeare by his reading of *Confessio Amantis*. Although the Gower choruses would not satisfy a modern student of Middle English, they do suggest, with remarkable skill, the general atmosphere of Gower's garrulous masterpiece. His rudimentary art, with its monotonous octosyllabic lines, its neutral diction, its rare imagery, and its pervasive moralizing, appealed to the simple curiosity of its readers. They asked, 'What happened next?' The causal relationship between one incident and the next and the psychology of the characters were equally unimportant. Incident followed after incident, with a running commentary designed to point the appropriate morals. Shakespeare has caught the manner to perfection, even though he cannot refrain from an occasional touch of better poetry. He doubtless recalled Chaucer's epithet for Gower—'moral'—when he penned the last lines of the play:

> In Antiochus and his daughter you have heard
> Of monstrous lust the due and just reward:
> In Pericles, his queen, and daughter, seen,
> Although assail'd with fortune fierce and keen,
> Virtue preserv'd from fell destruction's blast,
> Led on by heaven, and crown'd with joy at last.
> In Helicanus may you well descry
> A figure of truth, of faith, of loyalty;
> In reverend Cerimon there well appears
> The worth that learned charity aye wears. . . .

The *naïveté* of Gower's chorus provides a suitable framework for the play. Shakespeare was asking his audience to listen to the story in an unsophisticated frame of mind, forgetting for the time being the kind of intelligent response they would make to *King Lear* or *Twelfth Night*, and adopting rather the simpler and relaxed attitude suitable to a play like *Mucedorus* or *The Rare Triumphs of Love and Fortune*. It is said that the tale of Apollonius is still told by professional storytellers in the villages and round camp-fires in the Lebanon. A good thing, we are told, is the better for being ancient:

> Et bonum quo antiquius, eo melius.

It was presumably because he wished to suggest the unsophisticated way in which the story should be received that the producer of *Pericles* at the Memorial Theatre, Stratford upon Avon, in 1958, hit upon the

ingenious idea of turning a Middle English poet,
Gower, into a Negro boatswain, and provided him with
an audience on the stage of simple-minded seamen who
followed the story with open-eyed wonder. But it should,
of course, be borne in mind that when a sophisticated
audience is asked to respond in an unsophisticated way
it does so with some ambivalence. When Mr. Eliot, for
example, introduces into *Murder in the Cathedral* verse
apparently imitated from *Everyman*, the effect on an
audience is complex. It does not react in a purely unsophisticated way, but with a mixture of simplicity and
sophistication.

When all allowances have been made for textual
corruption, it is apparent that both character and incident in *Pericles* have been deliberately simplified. The
characters are either very good or very evil. The
daughter of Antiochus in the first act, though sur-
passingly beautiful,

> clothed like a bride
> For the embracements even of Jove himself,

is entirely evil. The mouldering remains of her former
suitors which tell Pericles

> with speechless tongues and semblance pale,
> That without covering, save yon field of stars,
> Here they stand martyrs, slain in Cupid's wars;
> And with dead cheeks advise thee to desist
> From going on death's net,

inform the audience that they are watching a romantic
and unrealistic play, set in a remote and unreal world.
It is a world where murderers carry out their orders
with the minimum of fuss, as when Antiochus orders
the assassination of Pericles:

> Thaliard, behold here's poison and here's gold;
> We hate the Prince of Tyre, and thou must kill him.
> It fits thee not to ask the reason why,
> Because we bid it. Say, is it done?

Thaliard replies laconically: 'My lord, 'tis done.' Even in the Shakespearian part of the play, where 'Leonine, a murderer' is endowed with some scruples, these are felt to be a tribute to Marina's beauty and goodness rather than a means of humanizing Leonine:

> I will do't; but yet she is a goodly creature.

The scene between Cleon and Dionyza is almost a parody of scenes between Albany and Goneril or between Macbeth and his wife. Dionyza, like the hypocritical and devilish Queen in *Cymbeline*, has no redeeming characteristics: she is a picturesque and melodramatic villain.

On the other side of the moral fence, the good people are perfectly good—Helicanus is a perfect counsellor, Marina is a paragon, Cerimon is a type of aristocratic learning, benevolence, and wisdom. Only with Lysimachus is there any doubt. He has to be fundamentally decent to enable him to marry Marina; but he has to be something of a rake to enable him to be a prospective client in the brothel. Most of Shakespeare's audience would not have worried about this; and they would cheerfully assume that he had been converted, as even Boult is converted, by Marina's purity. But Shakespeare himself seems to have had a twinge of uneasiness on the matter, and he throws in a hint at the end of the brothel-scene that Lysimachus, like Duke Vincentio in *Measure for Measure* or a modern social scientist, was making a study of the red-light district for reputable motives:

> Had I brought hither a corrupted mind
> Thy speech had altered it . . .
> For me, be you thoughten
> That I came with no ill intent; for to me
> The very doors and windows savour vilely.

These lines are difficult to reconcile with the way Lysi-

machus is greeted by the Bawd as an old customer, and
we have to assume either that Lysimachus is white-
washing himself to Marina or that Shakespeare belatedly
realized that Lysimachus as he had depicted him was
not a suitable husband for her.[1]

There are no lines in the first two acts which are certainly Shakespeare's, though there are a number which
could be his. It is a thrilling moment in the theatre
when at the beginning of Act III the voice of Shakespeare is heard, indubitable and potent, with a tempest
at sea to match the storm in *King Lear*:

> Thou god of this great vast, rebuke these surges,
> Which wash both heaven and hell; and thou that hast
> Upon the winds command, bind them in brass,
> Having call'd them from the deep! O, still
> Thy deaf'ning dreadful thunders; gently quench
> Thy nimble sulphurous flashes!—O, how, Lychorida,
> How does my queen?—Thou stormest venomously:
> Wilt thou spit all thyself? The seaman's whistle
> Is as a whisper in the ears of death,
> Unheard.

The whole scene is palpably Shakespearian, and this is
evident in spite of the misprints, the mislineations, and
one obvious omission in the Quarto. On the whole, the
reporter has done his work surprisingly well, better
than one could expect from existing methods of short-
hand.[2] A later speech in the same scene exhibits both

[1] The verse in Lysimachus's speech is so bad that we may suppose that
the text is corrupt. In Wilkins's novel, as we have seen, Lysimachus says
'and for my parte, who hither came but to haue payd the price, a peece of
gold for your virginitie'. Possibly this more nearly represents the correct
text—it is, it will be noticed, in verse—but it is surely more likely that
Shakespeare altered his source at this point with the object of presenting
Marina a more presentable husband.

[2] In the above speech the Quarto prints *The god* for *Thou god*, *then
storme* for *Thou stormest*, and *Unheard* is attached not to *whisper* but to the
word *Lichorida* which follows. These errors might well be due to the compositor rather than to the reporter. Although we have no good text with
which to compare that of the *Pericles* quarto, it would appear to be far more
accurate in this scene than (say) the bad quarto of *Hamlet*.

the colloquial ease and the magical phrasing of Shake-speare's last period:

> A terrible childbed hast thou had, my dear;
> No light, no fire. Th'unfriendly elements
> Forgot thee utterly; nor have I time
> To give thee hallow'd to thy grave, but straight
> Must cast thee scarcely coffin'd, in the ooze;
> Where, for a monument upon thy bones,
> And aye-remaining lamps the belching whale
> And humming water must o'erwhelm thy corpse,
> Lying with simple shells.

This is not the first storm in the play, and the recurrence of tempest imagery even in the early acts made Wilson Knight suspect that Shakespeare was revising an early play of his own. At the beginning of Act II Pericles had been wrecked on the shore of Pentapolis, the sole survivor; and his speech may derive any Shakespearian quality it may be thought to possess from the acquaintance of its author with Shakespeare's earlier plays:

> Yet cease your ire, you angry stars of heaven!
> Wind, rain and thunder, remember earthly man
> Is but a substance that must yield to you;
> And I, as fits my nature, do obey you.
> Alas, the sea hath cast me on the rocks,
> Wash'd me from shore to shore, and left me breath
> Nothing to think on but ensuing death.

The opening lines of this speech are reasonably effective; but the last three are a sad anti-climax, whether due to the inefficiency of the reporter or to the uncertain mastery of the author. In itself the speech can hardly be regarded as a proof that Shakespeare was himself the author of the original *Pericles*. Some account of a storm was demanded by the story at this point in the play, and any author would have had to provide it.

The scene in which Thaisa is restored, though reported less accurately than the scene in Marina's birth, is equally authentic in its conception. Cerimon, of whom Pericles later remarks—

> The Gods can have no mortal officer
> More like a god than you—

is a character of wisdom and nobility, who seems to embody the essential spirit of the plays of Shakespeare's last period. In some ways he resembles Prospero, though he lacks the touch of asperity and disillusionment of that character. He speaks in verse which is worlds away from the crudity of that used in the first two acts of the play:

> I held it ever,
> Virtue and cunning were endowments greater
> Than nobleness and riches: careless heirs
> May the two latter darken and expend,
> But immortality attends the former,
> Making a man a god. 'Tis known, I ever
> Have studied physic, through which secret art,
> By turning o'er authorities, I have,
> Together with my practice, made familiar
> To me and to my aid the blest infusions
> That dwell in vegetives, in metals, stones;
> And I can speak of the disturbances
> That nature works, and of her cures; which doth give me
> A more content in course of true delight
> Than to be thirsty after tottering honour,
> Or tie my treasure up in silken bags,
> To please the fool and death.

This self-portrait prepares the way for the 'resurrection' of Thaisa, which is accompanied by music, as Lear's had been and as Hermione's was to be. Thaisa bequeaths to death her dumbness, and Cerimon uses the jewel imagery which is taken up and developed in the last act of the play:

> Behold,
> Her eyelids, cases to those heavenly jewels
> Which Pericles hath lost, begin to part
> Their fringes of bright gold; the diamonds
> Of a most praised water do appear,
> To make the world twice rich.

So Cerimon, in the last scene, tells Pericles:

> I op'd the coffin,
> Found there rich jewels;

and Pericles is reminded of Thaisa when he sees his daughter in the ship:

> Her eyes as jewel-like
> And cased as richly.

This imagery is appropriate to a play which is concerned with the finding of that which was lost, and we may suspect that it was suggested, like the pearl and the chrysolite in *Othello*, by the Gospel parable of the pearl of great price.

The first of the Marina scenes (IV. i) contains a flower passage comparable to similar ones in *The Winter's Tale*, *Cymbeline*, and *The Two Noble Kinsmen*, a superb example of tempest imagery—

> Ay me! poor maid,
> Born in a tempest, when my mother died,
> This world to me is like a lasting storm,
> Whirring me from my friends—

and one or two passages which well suggest Marina's crystalline innocence; but there are other passages of stumbling verse which appear to be corrupt. The feebleness of the following lines and the awkward internal rhyme are presumably the ruins of a genuine Shakespearian speech:

> My father, as nurse says, did never fear,
> But cried 'Good seamen' to the sailors, galling

His kingly hands hauling ropes,
And clasping to the mast, endured a sea
That almost burst the deck.

The prose of the brothel scenes is sometimes masterly (e.g. in IV. ii) but, as we have seen, the verse of Act IV, scene vi is fragmentary, and less sustained than the verse-fossils contained in Wilkins's novel. It is not till the first scene of Act V, in which Pericles is reunited to his daughter, that Shakespeare's imagination seems to be again working at full pressure, unless the weakness of the Marina–Lysimachus scene is due to the failure of the reporters rather than to that of the poet.

In the restoration scene,[1] tempest imagery is again used, but now no longer expressing hatred and discord—

Lest this great sea of joys rushing upon me
O'erbear the shores of my mortality,
And drown me with their sweetness.

Once again, as in *King Lear*, the restoration is accompanied by music, first by Marina's lost song, and then by the music of the spheres; it is followed by Pericles's demand for fresh garments and by the appearance of Diana in a vision—the first theophany in Shakespeare's works.[2]

The quality of the scene may be illustrated by a single image.[3] In *Twelfth Night* Viola speaks of the love-sick maid who

sat like Patience on a monument,
Smiling at grief.

[1] The reader may be referred to the chapter in Derek Traversi's *Shakespeare's Last Period* and to the masterly analysis by G. Wilson Knight in *The Crown of Life*.

[2] The appearance of Hymen in *As You Like It* is in a masque performed by human actors.

[3] This paragraph is based on a passage in my article 'The Future of Shakespeare' (*Penguin New Writing* 28).

A similar image is used in this scene in *Pericles* with even greater dramatic force. The hero, meeting his daughter after many years of suffering, sees in her face the signs of her suffering and of ordeals bravely borne. He then uses the following image:

> Yet thou dost look
> Like Patience, gazing on King's graves, and smiling
> Extremity out of act.

This wonderful image suggests all that Marina has undergone and all that Pericles himself has endured. It suggests that Marina is a king's daughter; it suggests her courage and patience in adversity—pursued by a murderer, captured by pirates, and sold to a brothel. Pericles is to be reborn; Thaisa is to be restored to him from the sea; and the whole family is to be reunited in an earthly resurrection. This is the situation in the play, and the image is exquisitely appropriate to it. The theme of the play is the restoration of the lost and the conquest of death by love—in so far as the theme of one of Shakespeare's plays can be expressed in abstract terms. This theme, this particular scene, its antecedents and its sequel, and the face of the girl imagined by the poet called up the inevitable image which is not merely a symbolic description of Marina but also helps to create the vision of the play.

Journeys that end in lovers' meeting, scenes in which brother and sister, husband and wife, or parents and children meet again after long separation, when each believed the other dead, were frequent episodes in Elizabethan fiction—and in the Greek Romances on which they were sometimes based—and they have always been effective on the stage, whether in Greek tragedy or Latin comedy. Two of Euripides' most effective scenes are the meeting of Iphigenia and Orestes in Tauris and the restoration of Alcestis to her husband. Even the reunion of Egeon and his wife in *The Comedy of Errors* is a moving scene in a play which is largely farcical; the silent reunion of Isabella and Claudio is a little-recognized master-stroke in *Measure for Measure*; and the meeting of Viola and Sebastian in *Twelfth Night* is a touching climax to that play. The meeting of Pericles and Marina surpasses all these. Its effectiveness, and the effectiveness of the whole play, is due partly to Shakespeare's creation of a kind of myth which he could set up against the changes and chances of this mortal life. He is calling in a new world to redress the balance of the old, a new world in which the designs of evil men are frustrated and in which everything comes right in the end—the beautiful queen is not really dead, the beautiful princess is saved from murder and rape and the contamination of the brothel, and the hero, after more trials and tribulations than are normally the lot of man, is rewarded with unforeseen and unimagined happiness. Shakespeare is aware that his story is too good to be true, but such fables are a criticism of life as it is, and (as some think) a statement of faith. In a pagan setting he creates what is virtually an immortality myth.

The misfortunes that befall Pericles are undeserved, and the restoration to him of his wife and child is due to the inscrutable workings of Providence. In the plays which followed Shakespeare set out to eliminate accident, and to infuse the restoration theme with ethical meaning. This could be done only by replacing the workings of an arbitrary providence by the operations of sin and forgiveness. Leontes's jealousy causes the death of Mamillius, and apparently of Hermione also, the loss of Perdita, and estrangement from Polixenes. But the two kings are reconciled through the marriage of their children; and when Leontes by his penitence has earned forgiveness, Hermione is restored to him.

In *Pericles* Shakespeare had dealt at length with the finding of the lost daughter and only cursorily with the reunion of husband and wife. In *The Winter's Tale* the emphasis is reversed. The father–daughter recognition takes place off stage, and Shakespeare concentrates on the reunion of Leontes and Hermione— because Leontes has sinned chiefly against her and needs her forgiveness before the play can end in reconciliation. In *Cymbeline* Imogen forgives Posthumus for his attempted murder, and their reconciliation does not require a marriage of children to cement it. In *The Tempest* Shakespeare concentrates on the act of forgiveness itself. In *The Winter's Tale* and *Cymbeline* the hero is the sinner; in *The Tempest* the hero is sinned against, and the betrayal had taken place sixteen years before. By this means Shakespeare eliminated the break of sixteen years which occurs in both *Pericles* and *The Winter's Tale*. The advantages are not all on one side; and the French critic who remarked that Shakespeare finally succeeded in obeying the unity of time by eliminating action altogether was not without some justification. The looser structure of *The Winter's Tale* is necessary to the particular effects at which Shakespeare was aiming; and the yet looser structure of *Pericles* is the only way by which the story of Apollonius could be put on the stage.

In recent years there has been a revival of interest in the play, heralded by T. S. Eliot's exquisite *Marina* and by Wilson Knight's eloquent reassessment in *The Crown of Life*, and exemplified by productions at the Old Vic and Birmingham and by two at Stratford. One Stratford production omitted the first act, and the liberties taken in the other seemed to indicate a lack of confidence in the play's ability to appeal to a modern audience. But at Birmingham the audience was captivated throughout the performance; and this was yet another indication that Shakespeare knew better than his critics, and better even than modish producers, that he had hit on precisely the right form for the material he was dramatizing, and that we have no right to deplore the taste of the groundlings who were enthusiastic when the play was first performed.

HELEN GARDNER

(b. 1908)

The Noble Moor[1]

AMONG the tragedies of Shakespeare *Othello* is supreme
in one quality: beauty. Much of its poetry, in imagery,
perfection of phrase, and steadiness of rhythm, soaring
yet firm, enchants the sensuous imagination. This kind
of beauty *Othello* shares with *Romeo and Juliet* and
Antony and Cleopatra; it is a corollary of the theme
which it shares with them. But *Othello* is also remarkable for another kind of beauty. Except for one trivial
scene with the clown, all is immediately relevant to the
central issue; no scene requires critical justification.
The play has a rare intellectual beauty, satisfying the
desire of the imagination for order and harmony
between the parts and the whole. Finally, the play has
intense moral beauty. It makes an immediate appeal to
the moral imagination, in its presentation in the figure
of Desdemona of a love which does not alter 'when it
alteration finds', but 'bears it out even to the edge of
doom'. These three kinds of beauty are interdependent,
since all arise from the nature of the hero. Othello's
vision of the world expresses itself in what Mr. Wilson
Knight has called the 'Othello music'; the 'compulsive
course' of his nature dominates the action, driving it
straight on to its conclusion; Othello arouses in Desdemona unshakeable love. I am unable, therefore, to
accept some recent attempts to find meaning in a play,
which has to more than one critic seemed to lack meaning, in its progressive revelation of the inadequacy of

[1] British Academy Shakespeare lecture (1955).

the hero's nobility. Such an interpretation disregards
the play's most distinctive quality. It contradicts that
immediate and overwhelming first impression to which
it is a prime rule of literary criticism that all further
analysis must conform.

A variety of critics in this century, while recognizing
its poignancy, human veracity, and dramatic brilliance,
have agreed in being unwilling to praise *Othello* without
some reservations. Bradley found in it 'a certain limitation, a partial suppression of that element in Shakespeare's mind which unites him with the mystical poets
and with the great musicians and philosophers'. Granville-Barker said of Othello that he 'goes ignorantly to
his doom'. 'The mere sight of such beauty and nobility
and happiness, all wickedly destroyed, must be a
harrowing one. Yet the pity and terror of it come short
of serving for the purgation of our souls, since Othello's
own soul stays unpurged. . . . It is a tragedy without
meaning, and that is the ultimate horror of it.' Bradley's
complaint that *Othello* is unphilosophic, and Granville-
Barker's, that it is 'without meaning', echo faintly the
most famous of all attacks upon *Othello*. The absurd
morals which Rymer found in it were a witty way of
declaring it had no meaning, since Rymer equated
meaning with general moral truth. The absence of
general moral truth he made clear by his preposterously
particular axioms. When Granville-Barker adds, 'It
does not so much purge us as fill us with horror and
anger. . . . Incongruity is the keynote of the tragedy',
we are hearing a polite version of Rymer's summary
judgement: 'The tragical part is plainly none other
than a Bloody Farce, without salt or savour.' And Mr.
T. S. Eliot, whose comments on Othello's last speech[1]

---

[1] See 'Shakespeare and the Stoicism of Seneca', a lecture delivered in
1927, reprinted in *Selected Essays* (1932). Mr. Eliot was making a general
comment on Elizabethan tragic heroes and took this speech as an extreme

gave the hint for subsequent discussions of the hero as a study in self-dramatization, self-idealization, and self-deception, remarked in a note to his essay on *Hamlet* that he had never seen 'a cogent refutation of Thomas Rymer's objections to *Othello*', thus implying that he found some cogency in Rymer's attack.

There are various reasons why *Othello* should seem more remote from us than the other tragedies. A feature of Shakespearian studies in the last twenty years has been the interest in the Histories and the comparative neglect of the Comedies. The social and political ideas of the Elizabethans: the Tudor conception of history as the realm of providential judgements, the ideas of natural order, the chain of being, and 'degree, priority and place', obviously relevant to the Histories, have also some relevance to *Hamlet*, *King Lear*, and *Macbeth*. They throw some light there, though perhaps rather 'a dim religious one', and on the periphery rather than on the centre. They cast no light upon *Othello*, whose affinities are with the Comedies. We must shut up the *Book of Homilies* and *The Mirror for Magistrates* and open the love poets for a change.

Then, again, the revival of interest in allegory, and indeed of the ability to read allegory, is one of the critical achievements of this century. This has naturally influenced the interpretation of Shakespeare's plays. Whether or not allegorical and symbolical interpretations hold in other plays, they are defeated in *Othello* by the striking human individuality of the characters. What Shelley rather intemperately called 'the rigidly-defined and ever-repeated idealisms of a distorted superstition' are not to be found in a play which abounds in 'living impersonations of the truth of human

example. His comment touches, I think, all tragic heroes, and not merely Elizabethan ones. It raises the whole question of how the characters in a poetic drama present themselves, of the self-consciousness of the tragic hero by which he creates himself in our imagination.

passions'. It is perhaps not wholly improper to see Cordelia as Truth. But Desdemona's truth is the devotion of her whole heart to the husband of her choice, and is quite consistent humanly, but not allegorically, with her marked tendency to economize with truth. And how can one attempt to allegorize a heroine whose companion is Emilia? The attempt to treat plays as if they were poems cannot succeed with a work which so signally exemplifies Ezra Pound's distinction: 'The medium of drama is not words, but persons moving about on a stage using words.'

It has been suggested that the frequent references to Heaven and Hell, angels and devils make a theological interpretation necessary. On the contrary, their very frequency deprives them of any imaginative potency. They are a part of the play's vivid realism, setting it firmly in the contemporary world. Because Macbeth so explicitly excludes 'the life to come', we may, I think, legitimately see in his tragedy a representation of 'judgement here', analogous to what men have thought the state of the lost to be, and say that *Macbeth* makes imaginatively apprehensible the idea of damnation. In the pagan world of *King Lear*, the sudden Christian phrase 'Thou art a soul in bliss' is like the opening of a window on to another landscape. For a moment analogy is suggested, and works upon the imagination. But Heaven and Hell are bandied about too lightly in *Othello* for the words to have any but a flat ring. The only great and moving lines which look beyond the grave are Othello's

O ill-starr'd wench!
Pale as thy smock! When we shall meet at compt,
This look of thine will hurl my soul from heaven,
And fiends will snatch at it.

Damnation and salvation are outside the field of reference of a play in which the Last Day is so conceived, as the confrontation of two human beings.[1] When Othello exclaims

> I look down towards his feet; but that's a fable.
> If that thou be'st a devil, I cannot kill thee.

and Iago tauntingly replies: 'I bleed, sir; but not kill'd', the point is too explicit to be suggestive. 'Devil' is a cliché in this play, a tired metaphor for 'very bad', as 'angel' is for 'very good'. Theological conceptions help us as little as do social and political ones.

But the fundamental reason, I think, for *Othello*'s appearing of limited interest to many critics today is our distaste for the heroic, which has found little expression in our literature in this century, with the splendid exception of the poetry of Yeats. In *Othello* the heroic, as distinct from the exemplary and the typical: what calls out admiration and sympathy in contrast to what is to be imitated or avoided, the extraordinary in contrast to the representative, directly challenges the imagination. There are various ways in which, in discussing *Hamlet*, *King Lear*, and *Macbeth*, we can evade the challenge of the heroic. In *Othello* we cannot.

Othello is like a hero of the ancient world in that he is not a man like us, but a man recognized as extraordinary. He seems born to do great deeds and live in legend. He has the obvious heroic qualities of courage and strength, and no actor can attempt the role who is not physically impressive. He has the heroic capacity for passion. But the thing which most sets him apart is his solitariness. He is a stranger, a man of alien race, without ties of nature or natural duties. His value is

[1] It is a little curious that members of a generation which has been so harsh to Bradley for inquiring about Lady Macbeth's children, and has rebuked Ellen Terry for speculating on how Sir Toby will get on with Maria as a wife, should pronounce so confidently on the eternal destiny of fictitious characters.

not in what the world thinks of him, although the world rates him highly, and does not derive in any way from his station. It is inherent. He is, in a sense, a 'self-made man', the product of a certain kind of life which he has chosen to lead. In this he is in sharp contrast to the tragic hero who immediately precedes him. Hamlet is son and prince. He is in the universal situation of man born in time, creature of circumstances and duties which he has not chosen. The human relation which arises from choice is the least important in the play, or rather it is important in its failure. Hamlet the son, Ophelia the daughter, are not free to love. The possibility of freedom is the very thing which is in question in *Hamlet*. The infected will, the dubieties of moral choice, the confusions of speculation are different aspects of our sense of bondage. The gate of death is barred in *Hamlet*; man, who has not chosen to be born, cannot choose to die. The choice of death is forbidden by religion in the first soliloquy; later it is seen as a choice made impossible by our ignorance of what we choose in choosing death, so that the puzzled will cannot be absolute for life or death. At the close the hero finds death at another's hand, and not by choice.

To this vision of man bound *Othello* presents a vision of man free. The past, whose claim upon the present is at the heart of *Hamlet*, is in *Othello* a country which the hero has passed through and left behind, the scene of his 'travels' history'. The ancestors of royal siege, the father and mother, between whom the hand-kerchief passed and from whom it came to him, have no claim upon him. His status in Venice is contractual. The Senate are his 'very noble and approv'd good masters' because he and they have chosen it should be so. His loyalties are not the tangle of inherited loyalties, but the few and simple loyalties of choice. His duties are not the duties of his station, but the duties of his profession. Othello is free as intensely as Hamlet is unfree, and the relation which fails to establish itself in *Hamlet* is the one relation which counts here, the free relation of love. It is presented in its most extreme, that is in heroic, form, as a relation between individuals, owing nothing to, and indeed triumphing over, circumstances and natural inclination. The universality of the play lies here, in its presentation of man as freely choosing and expressing choice by acts: Desdemona crossing the Senate floor to take her place beside her husband, Othello slaying her and slaying himself, Emilia crying out the truth at the cost of her life. *Othello* is particularly concerned with that deep, instinctive level where we feel ourselves to be free, with the religious aspect of our nature, in its most general sense. (This is why a theological interpretation seems so improper.) Othello's nobility lies in his capacity to worship: to feel wonder and give service.

Wonder is the note of Othello's greatest poetry, felt in the concreteness of its imagery and the firmness of its rhythms. Wonder sharpens our vision of things, so that we see them, not blurred by sentiment, or distorted by reflection, but in their own beautiful particularity. The services which he has done he speaks of at his first appearance as in his dying speech. He has taken service with the state of Venice. When it calls upon him on his marriage night he accepts, not merely without hesitation, but with alacrity: ' 'Tis well I am found by you.' This is the 'serious and great business' of his life, his 'occupation', source of his disciplined dignity and self-control. He is dedicated to the soldier's life of obedience and responsibility. The 'hardness' of his life gives to his sense of his own worth an impersonal dignity and grandeur. It is grounded in his sense of the worth of the life and the causes he has chosen. It is consistent with humility. This appears in the serious simplicity with which he lays before the Senate the story of his wooing, and later asks their permission, as a favour, to take his wife with him; for he is their servant and will not demand what in their need they could hardly refuse. It appears more movingly in his acknowledgement of his own 'weak merits' as a husband; and finally, most poignantly, in his image of himself as supremely fortunate, through no merit of his own stumbling upon a pearl. It is fitting that the word 'cause' should come to his lips at the crisis of his life. He has always acted for a cause. Othello is often spoken of as a man of action, in tones which imply some condescension. He is primarily a man of faith, whose faith has witnessed to itself in his deeds.

The love between Othello and Desdemona is a great venture of faith. He is free; she achieves her freedom, and at a great cost. Shakespeare, in creating the figure of her wronged father, who dies of grief at her revolt, sharpened and heightened, as everywhere, the story in the source. Her disobedience and deception of him perhaps cross her mind at Othello's ominous 'Think on thy sins.' If so, she puts the thought aside with 'They are loves I bear you.' She can no more confess herself wrong than John Donne, writing to his father-in-law: 'I knew that to have given any intimacion of it had been to impossibilitate the whole matter.' Heroic decision is seen in its rigour in the gentle Desdemona as well as in her husband.

That love as the union of free souls, freely discovering each in the other, is a mystery, inexplicable in terms of nature and society, is the assumption underlying the endless riddles, quibbles, paradoxes, and conceits of love poets, who in this age busied themselves with 'Metaphysical Ideas and Scholastical Quiddities' to explain, or more frequently to make more baffling, the mystery of how 'we two being one are it'.[1] The famous double time, which has so vexed critics, though it does not trouble spectators, is in accord with this conception of love as beyond nature. That lovers' time is not the time of the seasons is a commonplace. Shakespeare laughs at it in his comedies and Donne rings endless changes on the theme. *Othello* is like an illustration to the lecture which Donne read his mistress on Love's Philosophy, comparing the growth of their love to the course of the sun, the morning shadows wearing away until 'to brave clearnesse all things are reduc'd'. But the point of the lecture was that the analogy breaks down. There is no parallel between the shadows of afternoon and evening and the shadows which fall on love:

> The morning shadowes weare away,
> But these grow longer all the day,
> But oh, loves day is short, if love decay.
>
> Love is a growing, or full constant light;
> And his first minute, after noone, is night.[2]

If love cannot perform the miracle of Joshua and make the sun stand still in the heavens, it will not suffer a slow decline. It is not in the nature of things: it has no afternoon. *Othello* is a drama of passion and runs to the time of passion; it is also a drama of love which, failing to sustain its height of noon, falls at once to night. To borrow Mr. Edwin Muir's distinction, the long time belongs to the Story, the short belongs to the Fable. *Othello* is also a drama of marriage. As the hero is more than a Homeric doer of great deeds, he is more than a lover; he is a husband. Desdemona is not only

[1] Donne, 'The Canonization':
> The Phœnix riddle hath more wit
> By us, we two being one, are it.
> So, to one neutrall thing both sexes fit.

[2] Donne, 'A Lecture upon the Shadow'.

the 'cunning'st pattern of excelling nature' and the girl who 'saw Othello's visage in his mind'; she is his 'true and loyal wife'. Her soul and fortunes are 'consecrated' to him. The play is not only concerned with passion and love, but with what Montaigne and other experienced observers have thought incompatibles: love and constancy.[1]

My subject being the Noble Moor, I cannot spend as long as I should wish upon his Ancient. There is an assumption current today that Iago expresses in some way a complementary view of life to Othello's. His power over Othello is said to derive from the fact that 'into what he speaks are projected the half-truths that Othello's romantic vision ignored, but of which his mind held secret knowledge'. I am quoting Miss Maud Bodkin, since she has been much quoted by later writers. She also speaks of the reader 'experiencing the romantic values represented in the hero, and recognizing, in a manner secretly, the complementary truths projected into the figure of Iago'.[2] Professor Empson has put this view more breezily:

The thinking behind the 'melodrama' is not at all crude, at any rate if you give Iago his due. It is only because a rather unreal standard has been set up that the blow-the-gaff man can take on this extraordinary power. It is not merely out of their latent 'cynicism' that the listeners are meant to feel a

---

[1] 'It is against the nature of love, not to be violent, and against the condition of violence to be constant' (Essays, iii. 5). Cf. Iago's 'It was a violent commencement in her, and thou shalt see an answerable sequestration.'

[2] Archetypal Patterns in Poetry (1934), pp. 223 and 333. When Miss Bodkin writes that as psychological critics we must note that the plot is built 'not merely on falsehoods . . . but also on partial truths of human nature that the romantic vision ignores' and cites as examples of such 'truths' that 'a woman, "a super-subtle Venetian", suddenly wedding one in whom she sees the image of her ideal warrior, is liable to experience moments of revulsion' and that 'a woman's love may be won, but not held, by "bragging and telling her fantastical lies" ', the irrelevance of psychological criticism, which generalizes and abstracts, where drama particularizes, is obvious. Whatever truth there may be in these two generalizations the plot is built on their untruth in this case.

certain sting of truth in Iago's claim to honesty, even in the broadest sense of being somehow truer than Othello to the facts of life.[1]

I cannot resist adapting some Johnsonian expressions and saying this is 'sad stuff': 'the man is a liar and there's an end on't.' What Iago injects into Othello's mind, the poison with which he charges him, is either false deductions from isolated facts—she deceived her father—and from dubious generalizations—Venetian women deceive their husbands—or flat lies. Whatever from our more melancholy experiences we choose to call the facts of life, in this play there is one fact which matters, upon which the plot is built and by which all generalizations are tested:

> Moor, she was chaste; she lov'd thee, cruel Moor.

The notion that by striking a mean between the 'high-mindedness' of Othello and the 'low view' of Iago we shall arrive at a balanced view, one that is not 'crude', could only have arisen in an age which prefers to the heroic that strange idol of the abstracting intelligence, the normal, and for the 'beautiful idealisms of moral excellence' places before us the equally unattainable but far more dispiriting goal of 'adaptation to life'. But, in any case, the sum will not work out, for Iago has not a point of view at all. He is no realist. In any sense which matters he is incapable of speaking truth, because he is incapable of disinterestedness. He can express a high view or a low view to taste. The world and other people exist for him only to be used. His definition of growing up is an interesting one. Maturity to him is knowing how to 'distinguish betwixt a benefit and an injury'. His famous 'gain'd knowledge' is all generalizations, information docketed and filed. He is monstrous because, faced with the manifold richness

[1] *The Structure of Complex Words* (1951), p. 248.

of experience, his only reaction is calculation and the desire to manipulate. If we try to find in him a view of life, we find in the end only an intolerable levity, a power of being 'all things to all men' in a very un-apostolic sense, and an incessant activity. Iago is the man of action in this play, incapable of contemplation and wholly insusceptible to the holiness of fact. He has, in one sense, plenty of motives. His immediate motives for embarking on the whole scheme are finan-cial, the need to keep Roderigo sweet, and his desire for the lieutenancy. His general motive is detestation of superiority in itself and as recognized by others; he is past master of the sneer. Coleridge has been much criticized for speaking of his 'motiveless malignity' and yet the note of glee in Iago confirms Coleridge's moral insight. Ultimately, whatever its proximate motives, malice is motiveless; that is the secret of its power and its horror, why it can go unsuspected and why its revelation always shocks. It is, I fear, its own reward.

Iago's power is at the beginning of the action, where he appears as a free agent of mischief, creating his plot out of whatever comes to hand; after the middle of the third act he becomes the slave of the passion which he has aroused, which is the source of whatever grandeur he has in our imagination. Othello's agony turns the 'eternal villain', the 'busy and insinuating rogue', the 'cogging cozening slave' of the first acts into the 'Spartan dog, more fell than anguish, hunger, or the sea' of the close. The crisis of the action comes when Othello returns 'on the rack', determined that he will not 'make a life of jealousy', and demands that Iago furnish him with proof. Iago's life is from now on at stake. Like Desdemona's it hangs upon the hand-kerchief. He must go forward, to everyone's ruin and his own.

Iago ruins Othello by insinuating into his mind the

question, 'How do you know?' The tragic experience with which this play is concerned is loss of faith, and Iago is the instrument to bring Othello to this crisis of his being. His task is made possible by his being an old and trusted companion, while husband and wife are virtually strangers, bound only by passion and faith; and by the fact that great joy bewilders, leaving the heart apt to doubt the reality of its joy. The strange and extraordinary, the heroic, what is beyond nature, can be made to seem the unnatural, what is against nature. This is one of Iago's tricks. But the collapse of Othello's faith before Iago's hints, refusals, retreats, reluctant avowals, though plausible and circumstantiated, is not, I believe, ultimately explicable; nor do I believe we make it so by searching for some psychological weakness in the hero which caused his faith to fail, and whose discovery will protect us from tragic experience by substituting for its pleasures the easier gratifications of moral and intellectual superiority to the sufferer. There is only one answer to Iago's insinuations, the answer Othello made to Brabantio's warning: 'My life upon her faith.' It is one thing to retort so to open enmity; more difficult to reply so to the seemingly well-meant warnings of a friend. That Othello does not or cannot reply so to Iago, and instead of making the venture of faith, challenges him to prove his wife false, is his tragic error.

Tragic suffering is suffering which a nature, by reason of its virtues, is capable of experiencing to the full, but is incapable of tolerating, and in which the excellencies of a nature are in conflict with each other. The man of conscience suffers the torment of confusion of conscience, the man of loving heart the torment of love spurned and of invasion by the passion of hatred. The one finds himself 'marshalled to knavery', the other driven to bitter curses. The man of moral imagination and human feeling will suffer the extremity of moral despair and human isolation. The man of faith is most able to experience what loss of faith is: but he is also unable to endure existence in a world where faith is dead. Othello has known 'ecstasy', which doth 'unperplex'. The loss of that leaves him 'perplexed in the extreme' and conscious of sex and sex only as 'what did move'.[1] He has seen Desdemona as his 'soul's joy'. It is intolerable to be aware in her of only what 'the sense aches at'.

Until the end is reached drama looks always ahead. If Shakespeare has, in fact, presented his hero and his love as flawed, then he has done it so subtly that I do not see how any spectator can have been aware of it. As soon as his agony is upon him we look forward to its resolution, not backwards to find some imperfection in his nature to account for his error. What matters to the tragic dramatist is wherefore, not why: not what causes suffering, but what comes of it. We distract ourselves, and to no purpose, by asking insoluble questions such as: Why 'seems it so particular' to Hamlet? Why does so small a fault in Cordelia seem so ugly to Lear? Why does a prophecy of 'things that do sound so fair' arouse in Macbeth not a glorious image of himself as a king, but a 'horrid image' of himself as a murderer? *Macbeth* is not a psychological study of ambition, or, if it is, it is a singularly unilluminating one. It is about murder. *Othello* is not a study in pride, egoism, or self-deception: its subject is sexual jealousy, loss of faith in a form which involves the whole personality at the profound point where body meets spirit.

[1] Donne, 'The Extasie':

> This Extasie doth unperplex
> (We said) and tell us what we love,
> We see by this, it was not sexe,
> We see, we saw not what did move.

The solution which Othello cannot accept is Iago's: 'Put up with it.' This is as impossible as that Hamlet should, like Claudius, behave as if the past were done with and only the present mattered. Or that Lear should accept Goneril and Regan's view of the proper meekness of the old and, in Freud's words, should 'renounce love, choose death, and make friends with the necessity of dying'. Or that Macbeth should attempt a tedious returning. The heroic core of tragedy is in this refusal of the hero to accommodate himself: it is why he can always be treated as a moral warning. Let Hamlet remember that 'Vengeance is the Lord's', allow the world to go its own way and mind the business of his own soul. Let Lear recognize that it is a law of life that the young should thrust out the old, and moderate his demands for love. Let Macbeth accept the human condition that life is a 'fitful fever', the future always uncertain, and there is no possibility of being 'safely thus'. Let Othello remember that perfection is not to be looked for, that though two may at times feel one, at other times they will feel very much two. Desdemona is beautiful, whether she is true or not.

But to Othello loyalty is the very principle of his moral being. He cannot say tenderly with a modern poet

> Lay your sleeping head, my love,
> Human on my faithless arm;

and accepting that

> Certainty, fidelity
> On the stroke of midnight pass
> Like vibrations of a bell,

enjoy her as

> Mortal, guilty, but to me
> The entirely beautiful.[1]

[1] W. H. Auden, *Look Stranger* (1936), p. 43.

Nor, since, far from being one who lives to himself alone, his nature goes out to seek value beyond itself, can he steel his senses against her beauty. He has not the invulnerability of the proud, and cannot armour himself with the thought of his own self-sufficient virtue, arguing that 'the Honour of a true heroique spirit dependeth not upon the carriage or behaviour of a woman', and remembering that 'the Gallantest men in the world were all Cuckolds' and 'made no stirre about it'.[1]

Tragic responsibility can only be savoured within a fixed field of moral reference. Mercy killings, honour slayings, and innocent adulteries are not the stuff of tragedy. But tragic responsibility is not the same as moral guilt. It shows itself in Hamlet's acceptance of the imperative to stay at his post, although this involves many deaths and his own commission of acts which outrage the very conscience which impels him; in Lear's flinging out into the storm to take upon himself the role of universal sufferer and universal judge; and in Macbeth's perseverance in 'knowing the deed'. It shows itself in Othello's destruction of an idol, his decision to regain his freedom by destroying what he must desire, but cannot honour. That baser passions are mingled with this imperative to sacrifice, that in the final moment Othello kills his wife in rage, only means

[1] 'The more discretion a man hath, the lesse shall hee bee troubled with these franticke fits: and seeing, as a certaine noble Gentleman sayth, the Honour of a true heroique spirit dependeth not upon the carriage or behaviour of a woman, I see no reason why the better sort should take this false playing of their Wives so much at the heart as they doe, especially, when it is their Destinie, and not Desert, to be so used. *Montaigne*, that brave French Barron, being of this minde; for saith he, the Gallantest men in the world, as *Lucullus, Cæsar, Anthony, Cato*, and such like Worthies, were all Cuckolds; yea, and (which was more) knew it, although they made no stirre about it: neither was there in all that time, but one Gull, and Coxcombe, and that was *Lepidus*, that dyed with the anguish thereof.' Marginal note by Robert Toft in his translation of Benedetto Varchi: *The Blazon of Jealousie* (1615), p. 29. The reference is to Montaigne, *Essays*, iii. 5.

that in presenting man as 'an animal that worships', Shakespeare, keeping to 'the truth of human passions' presents both terms. But, in its mixture of primitive animality and agonizing renunciation, the murder of Desdemona has upon it the stamp of the heroic. It has what Yeats saw in the Easter Rising, which neither his moral nor his political judgement approved, and one of whose leaders he had disliked and despised: a 'terrible beauty', contrasting with the 'casual comedy' of daily life.

The act is heroic because Othello acts from inner necessity. Although the thought of social dishonour plays a part in his agony, it has no place in this final scene. He kills her because he cannot 'digest the poison of her flesh';[1] and also to save her from herself, to restore meaning to her beauty. The act is also heroic in its absoluteness, disinterestedness, and finality. Othello does not look beyond it. It must be done. The tragic hero usurps the functions of the gods and attempts to remake the world. This *hubris*, which arouses awe and terror, appears in an extreme form in Othello's assumption of the role of a god who chastises where he loves, and of a priest who must present a perfect victim. He tries to confess her, so that in her last moment she may be true, and suffering the death of the body as expiation may escape the death of the soul. Her persistence in what he believes to be a lie and her tears at the news of Cassio's death turn the priest into the murderer. The heroic is rooted in reality here: the godlike is mingled with the brutal, which Aristotle saw as its true opposite, and Desdemona, love's martyr, dies like

---

[1] Cf. Adriana in *The Comedy of Errors*, II. ii. 144–8:
> I am possess'd with an adulterate blot;
> My blood is mingled with the crime of lust:
> For if we two be one and thou play false,
> I do digest the poison of thy flesh,
> Being strumpeted by thy contagion.

a frightened child, pleading for 'but half an hour' more of life.

'I am glad I have ended my revisal of this dreadful scene. It is not to be endured', said Johnson. And yet, this terrible act has wonderful tragic rightness. Only by it can the tragic situation be finally resolved, and in tragedy it is the peace of finality which we look for. Living, Desdemona can never prove her innocence. There is nothing she can do to 'win her lord again'. She could, of course, save herself, and in so doing save her husband from crime, dishonour, and death. She could leave this terrifying monster and ask for the protection of her own countrymen, the messengers of Venice. This sensible solution never crosses her mind. She remains with the man her 'love approves', and since

> There is a comfort in the strength of love,

for all her bewilderment and distress she falls asleep, to wake to find her faith rewarded by death. But in death she does 'win her lord again'.

Emilia's silence while her mistress lived is fully explicable in terms of her character. She shares with her husband the generalizing trick and is well used to domestic scenes. The jealous, she knows,

> are not ever jealous for the cause,
> But jealous for they are jealous.

If it was not the handkerchief it would be something else. Why disobey her husband and risk his fury? It would not do any good. This is what men are like. But Desdemona dead sweeps away all such generalities and all caution. At this sight, Emilia though 'the world is a huge thing' finds that there is a thing she will not do for it. By her heroic disregard for death she gives the only 'proof' there can be of Desdemona's innocence:

the testimony of faith. For falseness can be proved, innocence can only be believed. Faith, not evidence, begets faith.

The revival of faith in Othello which rings through his last speech overrides that sense of his own guilt which we have been told he ought to be dwelling on. His own worth he sees in the services he has rendered. It is right that he should be conscious of what has given his life value when he is about to take it, as he was conscious of her beauty when about to sacrifice that. His error he cannot explain. He sees it in an image which asserts her infinite value and his supreme good fortune, which in ignorance he did not realize, accepting and translating into his own characteristic mode of thought Emilia's characteristic 'O gull! O dolt! As ignorant as dirt!' The tears he weeps now are not 'cruel tears', but good tears, natural and healing. He communicates this by an image drawn from his life of adventure. Perhaps the Arabian trees come to his mind because in that land of marvels 'the Phoenix builds her spicy nest'. Then, as he nerves himself to end everything, there flashes across his mind an image from his past which seems to epitomize his whole life and will 'report him and his cause aright'; an act of suicidal daring, inspired by his chosen loyalty to Venice. With the same swiftness he does justice on himself, traducer and murderer of his Venetian wife. As, at their reunion, after the tempest, his joy stopped his speech, so now his grief and worship express themselves finally in an act, the same act: he dies 'upon a kiss'.

No circumstances point away from this close. No living Fortinbras or Malcolm, no dead Goneril and Regan allow us to speak of a purged realm or of the justice of the heavens. There is nothing but the 'tragic loading of this bed' and the comment of the generous Cassio: 'For he was great of heart.' Yet in this terrible end there is so solemn a sense of completeness that it might well be called the most beautiful end in Shakespearian tragedy.

Each of Shakespeare's great tragedies has its own design. The ground plan of the tragedy of *Othello* is that of a tragedy of fortune, the fall of a great man from a visible height of happiness to utter loss. This is not at all the shape the story has in the source; but this is how Shakespeare saw Cinthio's powerful but sordid story of a garrison intrigue. He spent his first two acts in presenting wonder great as content, and content that is absolute, delaying the opening of his tragic conflict until his third act. The design of the tragedy of fortune has a very different effect from the design of what may be called the tragedy of dilemma, in which, as in *Hamlet*, the hero is presented to us in circumstances not of his own making, confronted with another's crime; or from the design of the tragedy of error, where the hero's initial act releases evil forces and brings enormous suffering, or from that of the tragedy of crime and retribution. We never see Hamlet prosperous. Lear's rash and cruel act opens the action. Macbeth is no sooner before us than he is in temptation, 'rapt' in inner struggle. In plays with these designs, the conclusions have something of the nature of solutions: the end answers the beginning.

In its simplest form the tragedy of fortune cannot be rationalized. It takes man out of the realm of natural causality, the steady course which birth holds on to death, showing him as the victim of the illogical, what can neither be avoided nor foreseen. To achieve its effect it glorifies human life, displaying the capacity of the human heart for joy and leaving on the mind an ineffaceable impression of splendour, thus contradicting the only moral which can be drawn from it: *Vanitas vanitatum. Othello* has this in common with the tragedy of fortune that the end in no way blots out from the imagination the glory of the beginning. But the end here does not merely by its darkness throw up into relief the brightness that was. On the contrary, beginning and end chime against each other. In both the value of life and love is affirmed.

But *Othello* is also pre-eminently the tragedy of a deed. The 'deed of horror', *to deinon*, which in *Hamlet* lies behind the direct action, in *Macbeth* inaugurates it, and in *King Lear* is diffused through many acts of cruelty during the middle action, is, in *Othello*, the consummation of the action. Crime and catastrophe virtually coincide. Here again the shape of the play is quite different from the shape of the story in the source. The murder of Desdemona is not an act for which Heaven will in the end provide vengeance; it is a means of immediate revelation.

Fortune has been said to be the mistress of comedy, as opposed to Destiny, the mistress of tragedy. The vision of life which Shakespeare embodied in *Othello* cannot be analysed in terms of either destiny or fortune, and this is, I think, why more than one critic has complained that the play, although thrilling, lacks 'meaning'. The hero is a great individual, with all the qualities of a tragic hero, who expresses the strength of his nature in a terrible deed. But he finds the value of his life not within himself but without himself. He is the most obviously heroic of the tragic heroes, but he is unlike the great-hearted man of Aristotle, who is 'unable to make his life revolve round another' and is not 'given to admiration'. His nobility lies in his capacity to recognize value and give loyalty. The rhythm of pure tragedy is of a single life fulfilling itself and coming to an end in death. The rhythm of pure comedy is of relationships dissolved and reformed. The truth of tragedy is that each of us is finally alone. The truth of comedy is that man's final end is union with others, that he is 'in unitie defective'.

When, at the close of the *Symposium*, Socrates defended the wild paradox that 'the same person is able to compose both tragedy and comedy and that the foundations of the tragic and comic arts were essentially the same', his audience, who were so unfortunate as to live two thousand years before he was proved to be right, 'rather convicted than convinced went to sleep'. The foundation of Shakespeare's comedy and tragedy is the conception of man as finding his fulfilment in love, and therefore as not self-sufficient, but dependent upon others. In none of Shakespeare's great tragedies is the rhythm of fate felt in its purity, with the exception of *Macbeth*, whose hero rejects chance and chooses solitude. Over *Macbeth*, which is oracular, the future, the tense of destiny, lowers. Both 'fate' and 'fortune' are spoken of in *Othello*. In *King Lear* the word 'fate' does not occur, and its shockingly capricious end has poetic not dramatic logic. The presence of comedy 'universal, ideal and sublime' in *King Lear* made Shelley award it the palm over the masterpieces of the ancient world, the *Agamemnon* and the *Oedipus Rex*. For Shelley, though he does not make the connexion, believed that the 'great secret of morals is love'.

In *Othello* the two rhythms are so finely poised against each other that if we listen to either without the other we impoverish the whole. Othello is the tragic hero, fulfilling his destiny, who comes to the limit, 'the very sea-mark of his utmost sail', expressing his whole nature in a tragic act. He is the comic hero, discovering at the close a truth he knew at the beginning, and so he appears, dazed and blundering beneath the scourge of Emilia's tongue, remote for the time from our sympathy. Should the course of his life be described as a pilgrimage to a goal, or is it a straying from a centre which he finds again in death? Such straying is of the essence of life, whose law is change. Failures and recoveries of faith are the rhythm of the heart, whose movement is here objectified and magnified for our contemplation. If the old saying is true 'Qui non zelat non amat', then the greater love is, the greater jealousy will be. Perfect love casts out fear; but beneath the moon, mistress of change, only in death can

> Beauty, truth, and rarity,
> Grace in all simplicity,

be safe from mistaking, and constancy find its true image. The close of *Othello* should leave us at peace, for

> Death is now the phoenix' nest;
> And the turtle's loyal breast
> To eternity doth rest.

The significance of *Othello* is not to be found in the hero's nobility alone, in his capacity to know ecstasy, in his vision of the world, and in the terrible act to which he is driven by his anguish at the loss of that vision. It lies also in the fact that the vision was true. I cannot agree to find lacking in meaning this most beautiful play which seems to have arisen out of the same mood as made Keats declare: 'I am certain of nothing but of the holiness of the Heart's affections and the truth of Imagination.'

M. C. BRADBROOK

(b. 1909)

The Fashioning of a Courtier[1]

SHAKESPEARE'S 'sugred sonets' were as popular as *Romeo and Juliet* in the mouths of young gallants. Though unpublished till 1609, without clue to the order of their disposition or their relation to Shakespeare's personal life, the relation to his other work would seem to place them in the early and middle nineties. This is also where they would naturally belong in the history of sonnet-writing as a whole, and where, in spite of Dr. Hotson, I would place them. They tell a story too obscure, too odd, and too closely linked with recurrent themes in the plays to make it likely that they were either a coronet for his Mistress Philosophy or a bait for some other man to fish with. Such theories belong to an age which could not accept Dante's Beatrice as a real woman, and which saw everything which was not spontaneous as impersonal.

The range of the sonnets is startling. Petrarchists and anti-Petrarchists who wove their flowery sequences through the eighties were generally consistent in their tone, imagery, and style. On the whole the sonneteers were more gentlemanly than fiery:[2] the conventions were well established, and translation was allowed a broad interpretation. The character and exploits of Cupid, the warfare in which the lady ambushed, attacked, slaughtered, or enslaved her unresisting victim: his own melancholy, wasting, sleeplessness, and

---

[1] *Shakespeare and Elizabethan Poetry* (1951). The footnotes are here abbreviated.

[2] See L. C. John, *The Elizabethan Sonnet Sequences* (New York, 1938).

pangs of absence are the regular themes. The praise of
the lady is no less conventional. Demetrius at the first
sight of Helena after he has been anointed with the
love philtre, runs through his stock-in-trade of compliment:

> O Helen, goddesse, nymph, perfect divine,
> To what, my love, shall I compare thine eyne?
> Cristall is muddy. O how ripe, in showe,
> Thy lippes, those kissing cherries, tempting growe!
> That pure coniealed white, high *Taurus*' snow
> Fand with the Easterne winde, turns to a crowe
> When thou holdst up thy hand. O let me kisse
> This Princesse of pure white, this seale of blisse.
>
> (III. ii. 137–44)

Florizel, some fifteen years later, is still talking of the
fann'd snow, though he allows Perdita's hand only to
equal and not to surpass its whiteness (*Winter's Tale*,
IV. iii. 374–7).

The Petrarchan lover was a despairing lover: perhaps when the lady was won, sonnets became unnecessary. Yet Spenser's charming banter

> See how the Tyrannesse doth joy to see
> The huge massacres that her eyes do make
>
> (*Amoretti*, x)

or

> Sweet Warrior! when shall I have peace with you?
>
> (Ibid. lvii)

has more weight when seen as the product of one of the
English Garrison, living in what had been a stronghold
of the dispossessed Fitzgeralds, and consequently liable
to reprisals of the kind that eventually cost him his all.
Sidney too, in his military metaphors, writes as a professional soldier,[1] and often with an ironic twist.

---

[1] The fashion is continued to the present day in such ballads as 'There's
no A.M.O. about Love'.

Nor were Elizabethan ideas of decorum always equivalent to what the word might now imply. Spenser's *Amoretti* xlvi is in a good medieval tradition; it is as broad as the most notorious of Shakespeare's sonnets, or the broadest of Mercutio's jests, and like Mercutio, witty enough to justify its impropriety.

Sidney approaches nearest to Shakespeare in the range of his mood, in his logical and closely articulated form, in the natural tenderness and humour which plays over the surface of his conventional despair, and in his easy blend of the conventional and the personal, the formal simile and the colloquial phrase, giving an impression both of sincerity and control. Stella has at last been undeniably identified with Penelope Devereux,[1] a woman of whose charm and beauty there are other testimonies than Sidney's. Yet a series of laments for Sidney under his name of Astrophel could be dedicated to his widow, Frances Walsingham—though not indeed before she had become the wife of Stella's brother, the Earl of Essex. The tangled relationships of Elizabeth's court circle could today be equalled only in some small remote country village. How much of the love-making was genuine and how much was fashion will never be known, for the whole object of the system was to conceal that very fact; and even the ladies of *Love's Labour's Lost* miscalculated completely. In addressing a friend and not a mistress Shakespeare deprived himself at once of a good deal of the sonneteer's stock-in-trade; the promise that he will 'eternize' the virtues which he celebrates is of course a commonplace,[2] and some of the conceits, particularly in the first eighteen sonnets, the most formal and distant of the group, are of the traditional kind.

[1] See Ruth Hughey, *The Library*, xv (1935).
[2] See L. C. John, op. cit., and Sir Sidney Lee, *Elizabethan Sonnets*, 1904, i. lv.

The one convention which provided Shakespeare with the means of making something new, something that went beyond the convention itself, was that in which the lover described the exchange of hearts between his lady and himself. Sidney had used this conceit in the song from *Arcadia*:

> My true love hath my heart and I have his.

The eye and the heart were both invoked in songs of this kind ('Send back my long strayed eyes to me'), and debates between the eye and the heart on their mutual responsibility for the singer's plight went back to medieval poems of the Courts of Love.[1] But the interchange of hearts is used as symbol for that 'marriage of true minds' which makes the natural self-centred life of any individual reverse itself, establishing the centre of all hopes, needs, desires, plans, pleasures, and pain in the beloved. Throughout the Sonnets this theme appears, playfully, painfully, triumphantly and bitterly.

> In our two loves there is but one respect,
> Though in our lives a separable spight   (xxxvi)
>
> Oh how thy worth with manners may I singe,
> When thou art all the better part of me?   (xxxix)
>
> All mine was thine, before thou hadst this more   (xl)
>
>   my friend and I are one,
> Sweete flattery, then she loves but me alone.   (xlii)
>
> I in thy abundance am suffic'd,
> And by a part of all thy glory live.   (xxxvii)
>
> Being your slave what should I doe but tend,
> Upon the houres, and times of your desire?   (lvii)
>
> Oh let me suffer (being at your beck)
> Th' imprison'd absence of your libertie   (lviii)

[1] See L. C. John, op. cit., pp. 92–102.

Sinne of selfe-love possesseth al mine eie . . .
Tis thee (my selfe) that for my selfe I praise, (lxii)

I love you so
That I in your sweet thoughts would be forgot
If thinking on me then should make you woe. (lxxi)

When thou shalt be disposde to set me light,
And place my merrit in the eie of skorne,
Upon thy side, against my selfe Ile fight (lxxxviii)

For thee, against my selfe Ile vow debate,
For I must nere love him whom thou dost hate (lxxxix)

But doe thy worst to steale thyself away,
For tearme of life thou art assured mine . . .
Thou canst not vex me with inconstant minde,
Since that my life on thy revolt doth lie (xcii)

yet like prayers divine,
I must each day say ore the very same,
Counting no old thing old, thou mine, I thine,
Even when as first I hallowed thy faire name. (cviii)

In the Dark Lady's sonnets, the friend is called 'my
next selfe' (cxxxiii) and 'that other mine' (cxxxiv). Such
complete devotion can almost invite the charge of
'idolatry' which Shakespeare rebuts in Sonnet cv; yet
it also justifies the uncommonly plain speaking which
is so unusual a feature of his sonnets:

You to your beautious blessings adde a curse,
Being fond on praise, which makes your praises worse
(lxxxiv)

the reproaches of Sonnets xciii–xcvi—matched by the
self-reproaches of cxvii–cxx—and the agonized defiance of:

Then hate when thou wilt, if ever, now,
Now while the world is bent my deeds to crosse. (xc)

Instead of the comparatively simple relationship of

other sonneteers—where all subtlety dwells in the art of the chase, the lady's powers of coquetry and the balance between pose and feelings, courtship and passion—Shakespeare presents a dramatic and flexible situation. It has neither the distance of Spenser's respectful worship of his 'Angel', nor the Platonic calm of the Phoenix and the Turtle, 'two distincts, division none', of Sidney's *Eighth Song* or Lord Herbert of Cherbury's *Ecstacie*. But it springs from the convention of the exchange of hearts, set out in an early Sonnet:

> all that beauty that doth cover thee,
> Is but the seemely rayment of my heart,
> Which in thy brest doth live, as thine in me,
> How can I then be elder then thou art?
> O therefore love, be of thy selfe so wary,
> As I not for my selfe, but for thee will,
> Bearing thy heart which I will keepe so chary
> As tender nurse her babe from faring ill,
> > Presume not on thy heart when mine is slaine,
> > Thou gav'st me thine not to give backe againe.   (xxii)

If this be compared with Sidney's song, it will be seen already how far personal feeling has informed the argument. Shakespeare developed his sensibility in the sonnets, far beyond anything which he achieved in the drama of the nineties; but the sonnets must have helped in the very rapid growth of the years 1594–6, to which Chambers assigns *Two Gentlemen of Verona*, *Love's Labour's Lost*, *Romeo and Juliet*, *Richard II*, *Midsummer Night's Dream*, and *The Merchant of Venice*. The year 1594 saw also the publication of *The Rape of Lucrece*, and the foundation of the Lord Chamberlain's Company, the great and stable fellowship which replaced the shifting groups of earlier days, providing Shakespeare with his true dramatic environment. He now was thirty years of age, old enough to write about youth with an understanding mind. His subject in general

was the world of the court, or as Spenser said, the fashioning of a gentleman. He had learnt enough of courtly
manners to be able to laugh at them, and at the same
time to admire. He could disclaim the conventional poetry
of praise (Sonnet cxxx) and then write a sonnet to his
mistress's eyes (never, it must be admitted, to her eye-
brow) in a manner which borrows quite shamelessly
from Sidney's praise of the black eyes of Stella (Sonnet
cxxxii: compare *Astrophel and Stella*, vii). Both ladies'
eyes are in mourning for the cruelties they have inflicted
upon their lovers. Detached enough for mockery, sympathetic enough to absorb the manners to which he held
up a mirror, Shakespeare achieved, through the depiction of a world, the eventual delineation of persons.

[Section II, a discussion of *The Two Gentlemen of
Verona*, is omitted]

III

In *A Midsummer Night's Dream* Shakespeare did not
rely either on old stories or old plays. There may be
faint traces of Chaucer,[1] but the whole thing is virtually
his own. Three contrasted worlds—the lovers', the
rustics', and the fairies'—have each their own idiom and
their own codes, but in the woods of Athens, as in the
Forest of Arden, divided worlds meet and intermingle.
This simple trick of contrasted plot and subplot has
in it the germ of all Shakespeare's later construction—
it shows the artist's eye that could pick out an old
chronicle play, crude but serviceable, and a story
from the most elegant fiction of the day, put them
together and make *King Lear*. His mind full of images
of the countryside, and Ovid's *Metamorphoses* (for he
had not long since written *Venus and Adonis*, where the
two combined), the distressed lovers who were parted

[1] See F. Sidgwick, *Sources and Analogues of A Midsummer Night's
Dream* for the connexions with *The Knight's Tale*.

by their family, and a picture of Queen Mab (for he had also not long since written *Romeo and Juliet*) Shakespeare combined them, perhaps for a wedding masque, and wrote *A Midsummer Night's Dream*.

The lovers of the Athenian Court are drawn in a spirit of parody perfectly in keeping with an occasion which would mark the triumphant end of a real courtship. They are, moreover, contrasted with the heroic loves of Theseus and Hippolita.

The opening scene, daylight and Athens, maintains a formal style which sets the death penalty hanging over Hermia and the treachery of Helena in their proper perspective. The bouts of wit between Hermia and Lysander or Hermia and Helena are on professedly serious subjects, but their manner is that of Valentine's exchanges with Thurio:

Hermia. I frowne upon him, yet he loues me still
Helena. O that your frownes would teach my smiles such skil . . .
Hermia. The more I hate, the more he followes mee
Helena. The more I loue, the more he hateth mee
Hermia. His folly, *Helena*, is no fault of mine.
Helena. None but your beauty; would that fault were mine.
(I. i. 194–201)

Yet here and there, within the scene, there is heard an impersonal note of description, depicting love in terms of the natural world, which brings into the rhetorical stiffness of the dramatic exchanges such lively contrasts as that of the holy maids 'chanting faint hymnes to the cold fruitless Moone', and the sound of Hermia's voice:

> More tuneable then Larke, to shepherdes eare,
> When wheat is greene, when hauthorne buddes appeare.
(I. i. 184–5)

So after Egeus's speech—quite in the tone of Old Capulet—on Lysander's wicked use of love tokens, songs at the window by moonlight, and other means 'of strong prevailment in unhardened youth' there is a more powerful echo of the loves of *Romeo and Juliet*.

> If there were a sympathy in choice,
> Warre, death or sicknesse did lay siege to it,
> Making it momentany, as a sound:
> Swift as a shadow short as any dreame,
> Briefe as the lightning in the collied night,
> That (in a spleene) unfolds both heauen and earth,
> And ere a man hath power to say, behold,
> The iawes of darknesse do devour it up,
> So quicke bright thinges come to confusion.
>
> (I. i. 141–9)

Yet, taken in a different key, this confusion of darkness, swift brevity of love, and dangerous portents of the collied night are to be the lot of the quartet of lovers in their woodland wanderings. The enchantments of the night were a topic of the hour: Nashe had recently written a not altogether serious pamphlet on them, in a tone of rustic credulity.

The nocturnal was itself a recognized species at a later date, with 'the mistakes of a night' providing the opportunity for broad farce. The *Two Angry Women of Abingdon* is the best-known example where the wrangling of the good wives and the runaway antics of Moll and Frank weave a homespun version of some of Shakespeare's scenes. Shakespeare's only models were the fairy plays of Greene and Peele, *James IV*, *Friar Bacon*, and *The Old Wives' Tale*, all charming, innocent, and completely shapeless, depending upon the inconsequence of the folk tale and the 'shows' with which the early stage abounded. *A Midsummer Night's Dream* combines in the most paradoxical way the natural and to Elizabethan eyes pastoral and humble beauty of the woodland and its fairies with the highly sophisticated pattern of the lovers' quarrel and the straight burlesque provided by the loves of Pyramus and Thisbe. Seen from the courtly point of view, the play has many elements of the masque, as Miss Welsford pointed out: '*A Midsummer Night's Dream* is a dance, a movement of bodies. The plot is a pattern, a figure, rather than a series of events occasioned by human characters and passions, and this pattern, especially in the moonlight parts of the play, is the pattern of a dance.'[1] The enchantments of Puck are a deft parody of the normal operation of fancy, which is

> engenderd in the eyes,
> With gazing fed,

and little more reasonable than his magic. Theseus describes the lover's power of metamorphosis:

> Louers and madmen haue such seething braines,
> Such shaping phantasies, that apprehend more
> Then coole reason euer comprehends . . .
> Sees *Helen's* beauty in a browe of *Egipt*.

> (v. i. 4–11)

This is a theme which was to be more subtly and fully explored in later plays, but the jests of Puck are not much beyond the ordinary scope of Cupid.

Bottom and his friends are drawn, as Mr. Sidgwick observed, 'from observation', but also from the stage clowns who have already been allowed to mock Valentine and Proteus. Their mimic play apes the flight from Athens, though of course the parallel is not visible either to them or to their highly condescending auditory: it is part of the 'mirror' technique of the play-within-the-play, where Bottom so laboriously makes everyone comfortable with explanations of the difference between life and art, and where the fun puts both players and audience together inside the jest of professional actors pretending to be mechanicals trying to be amateur actors before an unreal audience. There is a

[1] E. Welsford, *The Court Masque* (Cambridge, 1927), p. 331.

special pleasure in this play within the play from the actors' point of view, and the hilarious bit of business which is preserved by a contemporary reference, 'Like Thisbe in the play h'as almost killed himself with the scabbard',[1] shows that it was played with gusto.

The mechanicals are out of their element when they get into the wood but the heroical Bottom is ready to adapt himself to any situation. His transformation may recall the tricks of witches, who sometimes loved and were loved by transformed animals: it may recall the *Golden Asse*: it may be mockery of the legend of Circe which held a tragical implication for Elizabethans: but it is primarily a comic Metamorphosis, a simple and splendid opportunity for the low comedian to bring off a telling stage hit. When Falstaff is transformed into a horned beast under the magic oak of Windsor Forest, the fairies might plead their most moral intentions, as they pinch him black and blue:

Fie on sinneful Phantasie: Fie on Lust and Luxurie:
Lust is but a bloody fire, kindled with unchaste desire.

but the fairies of Athens have no such highmindedness.

Oberon, Titania, and Puck, though they were figures of folk-lore, are completely transformed in Shakespeare's imagination. (Greene's Oberon is a wizard who acts as Presenter to *James IV*.) It was he who devised the tiny fairy of modern fantasy, and his charming inventions were seized upon by his contemporaries almost at once. Drayton's *Nimphidia*, Herrick's *Oberon's Palace*, *Oberon's Feast*, and *Oberon's Chapel*, and the fairies of the Jacobean masques, derive from Shakespeare.[2] In all his supernatural creations, he seems to have created completely new species of

---

[1] E. Sharpham, *The Fleire* (1607).
[2] e.g. the charming little 'nation of faies' in Ben Jonson's *Oberon the Fairy Prince* (1611) were acted by little girls, with the young Prince Charles in their midst.

creatures, and these of all his characters were most eagerly copied by his contemporaries and immediate successors. The Witches in *Macbeth* were not the first attempt to present a serious treatment of the evil supernatural on the Elizabethan stage, but they set a fashion for witch plays; the spirits of *The Tempest* again set a fashion: Caliban is the prototype of the Witch's Son, a popular stage figure in Caroline drama, and Ariel made a deep impression on the Restoration stage. Throughout the seventeenth century Shakespeare's spirits and fairies served and inspired other playwrights and poets of all kinds.

The fairies are spirits of the woods and the flowers—their names betray them. The description of their life is a description of the woodland itself, its freckled cowslips, its wild thyme, oxlips, and nodding violets, its luscious woodbine. Titania woos Bottom in the accents of Drayton's Phoebe wooing his Endimion, even promising to transform him to a spirit, 'purged from earthly grossness'.

Her little fairies who attend on him and offer him their courtesies are exquisitely set off by his earthly if laboured politeness. The contrast is even bolder than that which put the description of Queen Mab into the mouth of the gracelessly broadspoken Mercutio: and perhaps in this clumsy response to the queenly proffer of love, the author of *Venus and Adonis* is providing a 'squandering glance' at his own earlier and somewhat fleshly idyll. Some light parody of *Romeo and Juliet* is also discernible. The fairies are born of that same minute observation which depicted the hunting of poor Wat, dew-bedabbled and scratched with briars, the snail:

> whose tender hornes being hit,
> Shrinks backward in his shellie cave with paine,

and from the chidden hounds of Adonis's hunt come the hounds of Theseus.

The whole anthropomorphic world of the Ovidian romance, the world of Lodge's *Scilla* and of Drayton's *Endimion and Phoebe*, is embodied in the magnificent speech of Titania which places the fairies in control of the whole natural scene, and evokes so richly and powerfully Nature's waste fertility, all to disorder wandering. This speech may be reminiscent of Vergil in his pastoral poetry;[1] Titania's later appeal to Bottom recalls the Eclogues quite directly.

> tibi lilia plenis
> ecce ferunt Nymphae calathis, tibi candida Nais,
> pallentis violas et summa papavera carpens,
> narcissum et florem iungit bene olentis anethi;
> tum casia atque aliis intexens suavibus herbis
> mollia luteola pingit vaccinia calta.
> ipse ego cana legam tenera lanugine mala
> castaneasque nuces, mea quas Amaryllis amabat.
>
> (*Eclogue* II. 45)

In their recriminations over Theseus and Hippolita, Titania and her Oberon seem to be deputizing for the ancient gods, for Juno and Jove himself, so that their final appearance to bless and hallow the marriage bed is not unfitting for a king's bridal. They are masquers like the Masquers of Prospero's Vision, but the Masque is that of the whole flowery natural world—*Natura naturans*—blossoming, ripening, decaying and renewing. In spite of the fact that the picture in Titania's first speech is one of disorder, the effect is not destructive, or horrifying, or at all akin to the tragic speeches of *Richard II*, for example, which is of the same date as the *Dream*. If Titania's speech be compared with the gardeners' scene, it becomes clear that the natural beauties of the Queen's territory are not being used as symbols, or reflections in another mode, of the fairy

---

[1] There is possibly some recollection of the Sixth Eclogue, I feel, though it is not a case of parallel passages.

quarrel, as she asserts they are; but rather that in the fairies themselves, as in those later 'elues of hils, brooks, standing lakes and groves' which Prospero invokes,[1] the very quality of the too-much-loved earth has been given a local habitation and a name. Here if anywhere is the 'cause' and germ of the play:

> Neuer since the middle Summers spring
> Met we on hil, in dale, forest, or mead,
> By paued fountain or by rushie brooke
> Or in the beached margent of the sea,
> To dance our ringlets to the whistling winde. . . .
> The Spring, the Sommer
> The childing Autumn, angry Winter change
> Their wonted Liueries, and the mazed worlde
> By their increase, now knowes not which is which. . . .
>
> (II. i. 52 ff.)

The voice of Venus Genetrix is the same in Vergil's Sicily, or Shakespeare's England; the particular country-side, heavily wooded, with rushy streams, broad water meadows, and rich undulating pasture, is that of War-wick. As a faint light beside the full splendour of Shakespeare's play may be set Nashe's *Summers Last Will and Testament*, with its figures of Winter and Back-Winter, its song of

> Spring the sweet spring is the years pleasant king

alternating with the grim picture of the plague-stricken city from which the entertainers have fled to the safety of Croydon. But compared with Shakespeare, this is an artless piece of revelry. His first completely individual comedy was to remain, *sui generis*, a 'species' of which only one specimen was found in nature.

---

[1] The connexion between these two speeches has been noted by G. H. W. Rylands, in *A Companion to Shakespeare Studies* (Cambridge, 1934), p. 93. Prospero's speech is, of course, based on Ovid.

CLIFFORD LEECH

(b. 1909)

The Unity of 2 Henry IV[1]

IT should perhaps be made clear that this is not a contribution to the debate on Shakespeare's original planning of the Prince Henry plays. It has been argued by Dover Wilson in *The Fortunes of Falstaff* and in his New Cambridge edition, and by E. M. W. Tillyard in *Shakespeare's History Plays*, that the two parts of *Henry IV* constitute one long play, envisaged at least in its main outlines from the very beginning of Part I. M. A. Shaaber, on the other hand, has put a case for regarding Part II as a sequel, outside Shakespeare's original plan, brought into being through the remarkable success of Part I.[2] Whichever of these views is correct, it is possible for Part II to have its own characteristic mood and structure, its separate dramatic impact, and my concern will be to demonstrate that this is indeed the case. The only assumption I shall make, which I think will be readily granted to me, is that Part II was written after Part I.

In writing the series of eight plays which give an outline of English history from the reign of Richard II to the accession of Henry VII, Shakespeare can hardly at the beginning have seen the scheme as a whole. If he had, it would be odd to start with the troubles of Henry VI. The mention of Prince Henry near the end

[1] *Shakespeare Survey 6* (1953): based on a paper read at Stratford in 1951.

[2] 'The Unity of *Henry IV*', *Joseph Quincy Adams Memorial Studies*, 1948, pp. 217–27. Since this article was written, H. Edward Cain has supported Shaaber's case in 'Further Light on the Relation of *1* and *2 Henry IV*', *Shakespeare Quarterly*, iii (Jan. 1952), 21–38.

of *Richard II* suggests it was then that Shakespeare began to think of plays in which he would be the central figure, plays which would close the gap between Bolingbroke's usurpation and the funeral of Henry V. But clearly the plays in the sequence already written had been markedly different from one another in structure and atmosphere. This was partly, of course, because Shakespeare's grasp of play-making and dramatic language was rapidly becoming more secure, but partly too it was because the action of each play had demanded a specific handling. There are recognizable distinctions in material and manner between the three *Henry VI* plays, and when Shakespeare continued the story with *Richard III* he employed a new massiveness and formality of structure in his presentation of a strong man who abused his sovereign power in the wanton exercise of his own will: Richard of Gloucester, the Samson in the devil's cause who brought down the temple upon himself, demanded a play in which all his followers and adversaries were reduced almost to a choric function, until Henry of Richmond came, as a god from over sea, to confront him. The play of *Richard II*, because Shakespeare saw the King as a man too conceited for scruple, complacent in his royalty, and yet with an exquisite taste in suffering, had necessarily a quieter tone, a more human presentation of the usurper, an elegiac note because this play marked the beginning of England's trouble. So, later on, with *Henry V*, the glorious interlude which had its centre in Agincourt was to be punctuated only with marks of exclamation, those chorus-passages directed at keeping the mind alight: the only conflict was that of arms, and for once it is not the sickness of the commonwealth that we are asked to consider, but the success of a foreign campaign. In describing these plays, I have of course simplified their effects. There are quieter, elegiac moments even in the grim ritual of *Richard III*; national glory is for a little, when Gaunt dies, the theme of *Richard II*; and there are passages in *Henry V* which demonstrate that the strife and intrigue of the previous reign are by no means done. Yet there is a dominant tone in each drama. Similarly, each of the two parts of *Henry IV* makes its characteristic and distinct impression on us.

When Shakespeare began to write of the youth of Prince Henry, he had indeed a subject that called for lightness of heart. Here was a young man, having his fun, yet not compromising himself so far that he could not later shine in council and on the field of battle. The civil troubles of his usurping father could not be shirked, but at least these troubles were manageable and might even afford some apprenticeship for the growing Prince. Coleridge has described *Romeo and Juliet* as a play given unity of feeling by the youth and springtime that permeate every character and moment: even its old men, he says, have 'an eagerness, a hastiness, a precipitancy—the effect of spring'.[1] That might almost be our judgement too of *1 Henry IV*. There is a graver note in the portraits of the King and old Northumberland, but the dominant feeling is young, excited, good-hearted. The Prince must not forget his future, must not think exclusively in terms of personal glory, as Hotspur does, must not think only of the moment's pleasure, as Falstaff does: but he can and should value these things, while recognizing their subordination to the obligations and opportunities that will come to him with the golden round. When seeing Part I, we may prefer the company of either Hotspur or Falstaff to that of the Prince, but we are not out of sympathy with him, and esteem him when he shows respect for Hotspur and liking for Falstaff. At the end of Part I, he has overcome Hotspur in single combat, an incident

[1] *Coleridge's Shakespearean Criticism* (ed. Raysor, 1930), ii. 265.

not found in Holinshed: he has revealed himself as the good and honourable fighter needed for the play of Agincourt.

In arguing that Part II was an 'unpremeditated addition', which need not concern us here, R. A. Law[1] has emphasized the morality characteristics of that Part, the placing of Prince Henry between the personified representations of order (in the Lord Chief Justice) and disorder (in Falstaff). This account of the play's structure has been elaborated by Tillyard, though of course he disagrees with Law on the play's origin. It does indeed now seem beyond question that the Prince, no longer on the field of battle, is exhibited as slowly abandoning his old associations with disorder and becoming ultimately at one with its opposite. Not that we have a 'conversion', as in the old moralities, but rather a manifestation of a hitherto concealed adherence. This part of the play's substance becomes most noticeable towards its end, when Falstaff is ready to steal any man's horses because his 'dear boy' is on the throne, and Doll and the Hostess are taken to prison for being concerned in a man's death. To demonstrate this second phase in Hal's apprenticeship is the overt intention of this Part, as we may say that the overt intention of *Macbeth* is to demonstrate the ills that come upon a man and his country when he murders his King and steals the crown. But just as we may think that there is a secondary intention to *Macbeth*, to hint at a protest against the very frame of things, so in this Second Part of *Henry IV* we may feel that the dramatist, in giving us the preparation for Agincourt, hints also at a state of dubiety concerning basic assumptions in the great historical scheme. He shows us the new King adhering to political order, yet makes us half-doubt

---

[1] 'Structural Unity in the Two Parts of *Henry the Fourth*', *Studies in Philology*, xxiv (1927), 223–42.

whether that order is worth its price, whether in fact it is of the deepest importance to men. And with this element of doubt, the poet's awareness of mutability grows more intense.

Whether Part II was a new play or a continuation of one already begun, the battle of Shrewsbury had marked the end of a phase. Shakespeare, returning to his subject, and to a more sober aspect of that subject (for law has not the manifest attractiveness of chivalrous encounter), was bound to approach his task with less light-heartedness, with a cooler and more objective view. Just as Marlowe in *Tamburlaine* appears to see his hero with less enthusiasm in Part II than in Part I, recognizing his excess as such and not keeping him immune from ridicule, so here Shakespeare weighs his characters more carefully and questions even the accuracy of his balance.

This note in the play is, I think, struck in the Induction itself. Clearly Shakespeare needed an introductory speech here, both to remind his auditors of what had happened at Shrewsbury and to make plain the irony of the false news brought to Northumberland in the first scene of the play. But he is not content with a simple Prologue. His speaker is a quasi-morality figure, and no pleasant one. Rumour expresses scorn for the credulity of men, and even—though irrelevantly—for their love of slander. The scorn is brought home when Rumour calls the audience he addresses 'my household'. In tone this Induction is similar to the Prologue to *Troilus and Cressida*: there too the speaker was in a costume appropriate to the mood of the play— 'A Prologue arm'd . . . suited in like conditions as our argument'—and there too the tone was not gentle.

In the play we at once meet Northumberland, who has not gained much of our affection in either of the two earlier plays in which he appeared. Here he is the first of a series of old and sick men that we are to encounter. Falstaff and Justice Shallow, King Henry IV and the Lord Chief Justice, are all burdened with their years, and the only one in full command of his wits and his body is the character given no personal name and conceived almost as a morality-presentment of the Justice which he executes. Dover Wilson has drawn our attention to the way in which our attitude to Falstaff is made to change in the course of this Second Part,[1] though in concentrating on the figures of Prince Hal and the Knight he does not perhaps fully relate this change to the new atmosphere in the drama as a whole. When we first meet Falstaff in I. ii, his talk is at once of his diseases, and he reverts to this at the end of the scene when, like Ancient Pistol in *Henry V*, he asserts his readiness to 'turn diseases to commodity'. There is, of course, plenty of gaiety in this talk of disease, as there is in the scene with Doll at the Boar's Head: we delight in the comedy of it, but the frailty of ageing flesh is grotesque as well as amusing. Before we see 'Saturn and Venus in conjunction', we are told by the Drawers of how Falstaff was once 'anger'd . . . to the heart' when the Prince jested rudely on his age. The comedy here and in Gloucestershire has a sharper savour because we are never allowed to forget the evidence of decay. Justice Shallow, wrapping his thin frame in a fanciful tapestry of wild youth, is comedy of the rarest sort, but 'Jesu, the days that we have seen!' is a line with a barb in it for us all. And the King, in his different way, belongs with these men. When we first meet him in Act III, he is longing for the sleep denied him; he cannot rid himself of guilt, ever more and more pathetically he talks of the crusade he will never make; and when he is dying he asks to be carried to the chamber called Jerusalem, so that the prophecy may

[1] *The Fortunes of Falstaff* (1943), pp. 93–98.

be fulfilled and he may derive consolation from submitting to what has been decreed.

Along with the Falstaff scenes and the scenes at court, we have other parts of this play where a rebellion is launched and destroyed. This enterprise is contrasted sharply with the rebellion in Part I. There is no Hotspur to give dash and gaiety to it. His father is once more 'crafty-sick', and the leadership of the revolt is in the grave hands of the Archbishop of York. He is not presented as a man scheming for advancement but as one who gives a measure of sanctification to the rebels' cause. Yet when they come together for the planning of their campaign, their language is hesitant, cautious, argumentative, as if they would talk themselves out of a situation from which there is no escape. At the end of I. i there is little hope in Northumberland's voice as he bids

> Get posts and letters, and make friends with speed:
> Never so few, and never yet more need.

And Hastings's concluding cry in I. iii—'We are time's subjects, and time bids, be gone'—has a fatalistic ring. It is no surprise to us when Northumberland's defection is shown, and it seems appropriate that these rebels, so given to sober talk, should be vanquished by a verbal trick before a blow is exchanged. In Holinshed it is not Prince John of Lancaster but the Earl of Westmoreland who dupes the rebels: Shakespeare uses Westmoreland as an ambassador of Prince John, but gives to the King's son all the doubtful credit of the action. The change can, I think, only be explained by the assumption that Shakespeare wanted to bring this line of conduct more closely home to the royal house. Because Prince John is the King's son and Hal's brother, the stain of the exploit falls partly on them. Perhaps some will claim that such conduct was justified in the cause of law and order, that an Elizabethan would simply admire the skill of it Yet is it possible not to find irony in John's concluding speech in the scene of Gaultree Forest?

> I promised you redress of these same grievances
> Whereof you did complain; which, by mine honour,
> I will perform with a most Christian care.
>
> (IV. ii. 113–15)

In the mouth of the astute Prince John the word 'Christian' has an effect gross and palpable. When he proceeds to claim 'God, and not we, hath safely fought to-day', we seem to recognize blasphemy. If this is not plain enough, one can turn to the next scene, where Falstaff demands from Prince John recompense for taking Sir John Colevile prisoner: he will otherwise, he says, see to his own glorification in ballad and picture: if that does not come to pass, he tells Prince John to 'believe not the word of the noble'. A few lines before we have seen the value of a noble's word in Gaultree Forest, and there is therefore strong irony in Falstaff thus exhorting Prince John. Nor should we overlook Shakespeare's reminder that Prince John's adroit handling of the situation is but a momentary trick. Hastings has told him that, if this revolt is put down, others will rise against the House of Lancaster:

> And though we here fall down,
> We have supplies to second our attempt:
> If they miscarry, theirs shall second them;
> And so success of mischief shall be born,
> And heir from heir shall hold this quarrel up,
> Whiles England shall have generation.
>
> (IV. ii. 44–49)

To that John replies:

> You are too shallow, Hastings, much too shallow,
> To sound the bottom of the after-times.

It is Hastings who is right: John is too vain to see the total situation.

I have said that Shakespeare's substitution of Prince John for Westmoreland in the Gaultree affair brings the taint of it nearer to the King and Hal. When the play ends, and the new King has banished his old followers, the stage is empty except for Prince John and the Lord Chief Justice. Before mentioning the talk of French wars, Prince John spares a moment to praise his brother: 'I like this fair proceeding of the king's', he says. It is surely not enviable to be praised by such men as Prince John. It is like Flamineo in *The White Devil* praising Brachiano's hypocritical display of grief for Isabella's death. Praise like that is a burden for a man to carry. We need not dispute that it was necessary to banish Falstaff if England was to be for a time secure and Agincourt won. But we are made to realize that there is a heavy price to pay for political success. Indeed, we are reminded of it in the succeeding play, when, during the battle itself, Fluellen refers to the rejection of the fat knight whose name he has forgotten.

In Shakespearian drama there is often a condition of tension between the play's overt meaning and its deeper implications. The gaiety of *Twelfth Night* is enriched by the thread of sadness that runs through it, but we cannot say that the baiting of Malvolio is in easy accord with the play's surface texture. In *Macbeth* the enfolding of the tragic idea within a morality pattern leaves us with a feeling of suspended judgement in which we resent Malcolm's concluding reference to 'this dead butcher, and his fiend-like queen'. So in this Second Part of *Henry IV* the deeper, more disturbing implications impinge directly on the main action of the drama, and then, as in *Macbeth*, the writer appears to strain for the re-establishment of the original framework. We get this feeling in the harshness of the words that Henry V uses to Falstaff, for we have come to wonder a little whether there is ultimately much to choose between Falstaff and Prince John, and indeed we greatly prefer Falstaff's company. And the same feeling emerges, I think, in the often praised scene where Hal is reconciled to his father. Justifying his taking of the crown when he believed his father dead, he says:

> I spake unto this crown as having sense
> And thus upbraided it: 'The care on thee depending,
> Hath fed upon the body of my father;
> Therefore, thou best of gold art worst of gold.
> Other, less fine in carat, is more precious,
> Preserving life in medicine potable:
> But thou, most fine, most honour'd, most renown'd,
> Hast eat thy bearer up.' Thus, my most royal liege,
> Accusing it, I put it on my head,
> To try with it, as with an enemy
> That had before my face murder'd my father,
> The quarrel of a true inheritor.
>
> (IV. v. 158–69)

The elaborateness of the imagery is notable: the burden of the crown is a devouring monster, its gold is contrasted to *aurum potabile*, it is a murderer with whom the dead man's son must wage a blood-feud. In this scene and in the new King's rejection of Falstaff, the note of sternness and sobriety is heavily, almost clumsily, pressed down, in an attempt to silence the basic questions that so often in the play demand to be put. And perhaps, when he had done, Shakespeare realized that this close was altogether too ponderous for a play that had taken us to the Boar's Head and into Gloucestershire, and altogether too assured for a play persistently though not obtrusively concerned with change and ineradicable frailty. So he gave us the dancer's epilogue, in tripping prose, with its casual half-promise that Falstaff would come again in the next play: the banishment was to be merely from the King,

and not from us. Later he was to change his mind
again, perhaps because he realized that Sir John was
no longer a figure of delight: around him had grown a
small forest of disturbing thoughts, which might well
choke the brief glory of Agincourt. *Henry V* was not
the climax of a series, but rather an interlude, a holiday-
play, in which for a while disaster was kept remote.
Its epilogue does make plain that by this time Shakespeare had come to see his eight-play sequence as a
whole, and within that sequence the Agincourt play
must be predominantly sun-lit. He had to avoid, not
too much gaiety with Falstaff, but too little. It is all
the more remarkable that the questioning mood of
2 Henry IV does show itself here and there in the
succeeding play—with the intrigues of Canterbury and
Ely; the frank presentation of many unchivalrous
details of the war, from Bardolph's stealing of a 'pax' to
the King's twice-given order that every man shall kill
his prisoners; the repeated reminder that a war-maker
must have a just cause. But these things on the whole are
kept in their place, and an audience for *Henry V* is not
much disturbed in its dream of glory. In *2 Henry IV*,
on the other hand, an audience is rarely at its ease.

In Law's paper on *Henry IV*, to which I have already
acknowledged a debt, the darker side of Part II is in
no way brought out. But Law does draw attention to
the comic echoing of serious things in the play:
Henry IV's sick memories of his early life are immediately followed, he points out, by Justice Shallow's
maunderings on his deeds in the same period; Davy's
petition to Shallow that 'a knave should have some
countenance at his friend's request' reminds us of
Prince Hal's vigorous intercession for Bardolph with
the Lord Chief Justice. There are a number of other
ironic echoes in the play. At the end of the Boar's
Head scene, when 'a dozen captains' come to summon

Falstaff to court, the Knight rises to the occasion, putting his rest from him:

Pay the musicians, sirrah. Farewell Hostess; farewell Doll. You see, my good wenches, how men of merit are sought after: the undeserver may sleep, when the man of action is called on.
(II. iv. 403–6)

It is immediately after this that Henry IV has his famous utterance on the sleeplessness of kings. We are the less inclined to contemplate the ills of greatness with awe, because Falstaff has taken them to himself already. We have noted the way in which Falstaff's 'believe not the word of the noble' comes immediately after the scene in Gaultree Forest, but in III. ii there is an echo at Falstaff's expense. In Part I he has this exchange with the Prince when the battle of Shrewsbury is about to begin:

Fal. I would 'twere bed-time, Hal, and all well.
Prince. Why, thou owest God a death.
Fal. 'Tis not due yet; I would be loath to pay him before his day.
(v. i. 125–9)

Then there follows the 'catechism' on 'Honour'. In Part II the despised Feeble has a moment of splendour when, unlike Bullcalf and Mouldy, he does not attempt to escape from impressment:

By my troth, I care not; a man can die but once: we owe God a death: I'll ne'er bear a base mind: an't be my destiny, so; an't be not, so: no man is too good to serve's prince: and let it go which way it will, he that dies this year is quit for the next. (III. ii. 250–5)

There is, of course, an absurdity in these words of bravery poured from so weak a vessel, yet they demand respect. Bardolph's reply, 'Well said; thou'rt a good fellow', cannot be wholly ironic, and the impressiveness of the effect is only mitigated, not destroyed, when Feeble comes out again with his 'Faith, I'll bear no base mind'. The interplay of feelings in this Second Part is so complex that our sympathy resides securely nowhere. Falstaff can be used to direct our feelings, as he does with Prince John, and often through the play we prefer his gross and witty animality to the politic management of the Lancastrians. But just as the dramatist makes no attempt to disguise his age and sickness or even a churlish arrogance in him, so here he is put down by Feeble's curious, inverted echo of his own words in the First Part. I am, of course, not suggesting that Shakespeare could expect an audience to note the echo: for us, however, it seems to indicate a trend of feeling in the writer's mind.

The remarkable degree of objectivity in the presentation of the characters reminds us of certain later plays of Shakespeare, those that we call the 'dark comedies'. It is not merely through our latter-day squeamishness, I believe, that we are made uneasy by the presentation of the Duke and Isabella in *Measure for Measure*; and in *Troilus and Cressida* Shakespeare's own Prologue warns us that the expectation of armed strife is 'tickling skittish spirits, On one and other side'. And *2 Henry IV* is close to these plays also in the peculiarly acrid flavour of certain generalized utterances. On his first appearance in the play, the King sees the process of time in geological change and in the pattern of a human life, and there is no comfort in the vision, only a desire to have done:

> O God! that one might read the book of fate,
> And see the revolution of the times
> Make mountains level, and the continent,
> Weary of solid firmness, melt itself
> Into the sea! and, other times, to see
> The beachy girdle of the ocean

Too wide for Neptune's hips; how chances mock
And changes fill the cup of alteration
With divers liquors! O, if this were seen,
The happiest youth, viewing his progress through,
What perils past, what crosses to ensue,
Would shut the book, and sit him down and die.

(III. i. 45–56)

And when he is himself dying and he believes that his son has greedily seized the crown in advance of his right, he speaks of the human greed for gold, a theme no Elizabethan could long avoid, and how each generation is impatient for possession:

See, sons, what things you are!
How quickly nature falls into revolt
When gold becomes her object!
For this the foolish over-careful fathers
Have broke their sleep with thoughts, their brains with care,
Their bones with industry;
For this they have engrossed and piled up
The canker'd heaps of strange-achieved gold;
For this they have been thoughtful to invest
Their sons with arts and martial exercises:
When, like the bee, culling from every flower
The virtuous sweets,
Our thighs pack'd with wax, our mouths with honey,
We bring it to the hive, and, like the bees,
Are murdered for our pains. This bitter taste
Yield his engrossments to the ending father.

(IV. v. 65–80)

This is not far from what the Duke has to say to the condemned Claudio in *Measure for Measure*. Though he wears a friar's habit, he gives no religious consolation, but bids him see the vanity of existence, the impossibility of any sure possession, the cold impatience of an heir:

Friend hast thou none;
For thine own bowels, which do call thee sire,

The mere effusion of thy proper loins,
Do curse the gout, serpigo, and the rheum,
For ending thee no sooner.

(III. i. 28–32)

It seems probable that *2 Henry IV* was written some three years before *Troilus*, some six before *Measure for Measure*, yet here Shakespeare anticipates that objectivity of manner, fused with a suggestion of deep and personal concern, which is characteristic of these two later plays. The sequence of the histories depends on the cardinal assumption that order in a commonwealth is a prime good: it is not altogether surprising that, as his task came towards its conclusion, and with the additional effort required in writing a second play on a young king's apprenticeship, Shakespeare should have reached a condition of dubiety, should have felt less secure in his assumptions. The 'dark comedies' come during the tragic period, and in their way give evidence of a similar slackening of grasp. The basic assumption made by the tragic writer is that a personal goodness, inexplicable and apparently futile, can nevertheless be realized. But, unless the writer has the sense of a direct revelation, this assumption can be maintained only by strong effort: in the 'dark comedies' the mind is not kept tragically taut.

So far from demonstrating 'the unity of *2 Henry IV*', it may appear that I have shown only a clash of feelings within the play, an overt morality intention, a preoccupation with the effects of time, and a latent scepticism. That I would acknowledge, while maintaining that such a contradiction persists in all the major plays of the Elizabethan and Jacobean years. The tragic figures of the time are of great stature, compelling our awe, but we are not spared realization that they can be petty and grotesque and villainous as well. They are made to seem free agents in their choice of good or evil, yet simultaneously we are made certain, from the beginning of the play, that destruction will be theirs. So, in the best comedy, the gay march from wooing to wedding, from pretence to its merry discomfiture, is counterpointed with a low murmur of regret. Elizabethan dramas are rich in implication because they have emotional, but not logical, coherence. We travel two roads, or more, at once. We arrive at no destination. But, home again once more, we feel that—if we could but speak effectively of such things—we should have travellers' tales to tell.

But it has been apparent, I think, that *2 Henry IV* differs from Part I in its dominant tone. Of course, there are sharp incidental things in the earlier play, but they do not weigh heavily on the spectator's mind. Falstaff abuses the press in both Parts, but his activities in this direction are shown at closer quarters in Part II. And there is broad merriment in the later play, but it is worked into a pattern where good humour is not the main theme. Towards the end of Part II there is, indeed, a strong measure of simplification. From the Prince's last interview with his father to the rejection of Falstaff, Shakespeare strives to make the morality-element all-pervading, until we have the curious spectacle of Henry V urging repentance on his old companions: banishment was, of course, required, but he is an odd preacher to men whom kingship did not call to the disciplined life. And, as we have seen, the prose epilogue pretends that, after all, merriment is the prime concern of this play and the one to come. But, until Henry IV's death-scene, the delicate balance between the two layers of meaning is skilfully maintained.

When one is interpreting a Shakespeare play, one is always in danger of being reminded that Shakespeare was an Elizabethan, that his assumptions and standards of judgement were therefore different from ours.

Tillyard has commented thus on Prince Hal's treatment of Francis in Part I:

> The subhuman element in the population must have been considerable in Shakespeare's day; that it should be treated almost like beasts was taken for granted.[1]

But is not this to overlook the fact that Shakespeare can make us resent the ill-treatment of any human being, and respect the most insignificant of creatures, a Feeble or a servant of the Duke of Cornwall? In *Measure for Measure* he reminds us even that an insect shares with us the experience of death and corporal suffering. He was an Elizabethan certainly: he made assumptions about kingship and 'degree' and incest and adultery that perhaps we may not make. But he was also a human being with a remarkable degree of sensitivity: it is indeed for that reason that he can move us so much. If he merely had skill in 'putting over' characteristic Tudor ideas, we could leave him to the social and political historians. Because his reaction to suffering, his esteem for good faith, his love of human society, his sense of mutability and loss, his obscure notion of human grandeur, his ultimate uncertainty of value, are not basically different from ours—though more deeply felt and incomparably expressed—he belongs supremely to literature. We do him, I think, scant justice if we assume that he could write complacently of Prince John of Lancaster, and could have no doubts about Prince Hal.

[1] *Shakespeare's History Plays* (1944), p. 277.

REPRINTED LITHOGRAPHICALLY IN GREAT BRITAIN
AT THE UNIVERSITY PRESS, OXFORD
BY VIVIAN RIDLER
PRINTER TO THE UNIVERSITY